OXFORD HISTORY OF THE BRITISH EMPIRE
COMPANION SERIES

THE OXFORD HISTORY OF THE BRITISH EMPIRE

Volume I. *The Origins of Empire*
EDITED BY Nicholas Canny

Volume II. *The Eighteenth Century*
EDITED BY P. J. Marshall

Volume III. *The Nineteenth Century*
EDITED BY Andrew Porter

Volume IV. *The Twentieth Century*
EDITED BY Judith M. Brown and Wm. Roger Louis

Volume V. *Historiography*
EDITED BY Robin W. Winks

THE OXFORD HISTORY OF THE BRITISH EMPIRE

COMPANION SERIES

Wm. Roger Louis, CBE, D.Litt., FBA

*Kerr Professor of English History and Culture, University of Texas, Austin
and Honorary Fellow of St Antony's College, Oxford*

EDITOR-IN-CHIEF

∽

Missions and Empire

∽

Norman Etherington

Professor and Chair of History, University of Western Australia

EDITOR

OXFORD

UNIVERSITY PRESS

OXFORD
UNIVERSITY PRESS

Great Clarendon Street, Oxford OX2 6DP
Oxford University Press is a department of the University of Oxford.
It furthers the University's objective of excellence in research, scholarship,
and education by publishing worldwide in

Oxford New York

Auckland Cape Town Dar es Salaam Hong Kong Karachi
Kuala Lumpur Madrid Melbourne Mexico City Nairobi
New Delhi Shanghai Taipei Toronto

With offices in

Argentina Austria Brazil Chile Czech Republic France Greece
Guatemala Hungary Italy Japan Poland Portugal Singapore
South Korea Switzerland Thailand Turkey Ukraine Vietnam

Oxford is a registered trade mark of Oxford University Press
in the UK and in certain countries

Published in the United States
by Oxford University Press Inc., New York

© Oxford University Press 2005

The moral rights of the author have been asserted
Database right Oxford University Press (maker)

First published 2005

All rights reserved. No part of this publication may be reproduced,
stored in a retrieval system, or transmitted, in any form or by any means,
without the prior permission in writing of Oxford University Press,
or as expressly permitted by law, or under terms agreed with the appropriate
reprographics rights organization. Enquiries concerning reproduction
outside the scope of the above should be sent to the Rights Department,
Oxford University Press, at the address above

You must not circulate this book in any other binding or cover
and you must impose the same condition on any acquirer

British Library Cataloguing in Publication Data

Data available

Library of Congress Cataloging in Publication Data

Data available

Typeset by SPI Publisher Services, Pondicherry, India
Printed in Great Britain
on acid-free paper by
Biddles Ltd, King's Lynn, Norfolk

1 3 5 7 9 10 8 6 4 2

ISBN 0-19-925347-1

FOREWORD

The purpose of the five volumes of the *Oxford History of the British Empire* was to provide a comprehensive survey of the Empire from its beginning to end, to explore the meaning of British imperialism for the ruled as well as the rulers, and to study the significance of the British Empire as a theme in world history. The volumes in the Companion Series carry forward this purpose. They pursue themes that could not be covered adequately in the main series while incorporating recent research and providing fresh interpretations of significant topics.

Wm. Roger Louis

PREFACE

The planning for this volume began in 2001 with the recruitment of a core of contributors, some of whom attended a planning symposium by the beach in Perth, Western Australia, in February 2002, with support from the Academy of the Social Sciences in Australia and the Institute of Advanced Studies at the University of Western Australia. By the end of that year a full complement of authors had accepted the challenge of their commission, which required each of them to write a chapter exploring a single theme connected to the overarching subject of Christian missions and the British Empire. The originality of the project lay principally in the thematic approach, which required each of the authors to write beyond the area of their own regional specialization. Some of the themes are hardy perennials, while others have only recently attracted scholarly attention.

Initial findings were presented and compared at a second symposium held at the Missions House of the Basel Missionary Society with generous sponsorship from the Centre for African Studies at the University of Basel and Oxford University Press. The authors were given leeway to write up to 10,000 words in their first drafts, a limit that all exceeded by a considerable margin. After a round of mutual criticism and encouragement, they were required to condense their chapters to 8,000 words. From this process of cross-fertilization and distillation emerged a book more than usually imbued with a shared purpose. On the other hand, no attempt has been made to force a single theoretical framework or vision on the contributors. The contributions range from traditional empirical investigations to work on the pioneering edge of post-colonial and transnational theory. The authors include committed Christians as well as agnostics and atheists. Their evaluations of the results of three centuries of missionary enterprise range from the sanguine to the sceptical. All share the convictions, however, that the British Empire would have been very different in the absence of missions, that the agenda for future research is lengthy, and that the religious convictions of peoples around the world who accepted Christianity in all its myriad forms must be taken as seriously as the faith of the European Middle Ages or the American Puritans.

The editor wishes to thank all the contributors for putting up with my demands, all the sponsors of the project, and the editorial staff of Oxford University Press. Special thanks go to Professor W. Roger Louis, general editor of the *Oxford History of the British Empire*, who first recognized the need for this volume, to Emeritus Professor Terence Ranger of St Antony's College, Oxford, who made valuable suggestions in the early stages of the project, and to Alaine Low, who commented extensively on the penultimate draft.

Norman Etherington

Perth, Western Australia

CONTENTS

List of Abbreviations	x
List of Contributors	xi
1. Introduction *Norman Etherington*	1
2. Prelude: The Christianizing of British America *Eliga H. Gould*	19
3. An Overview, 1700–1914 *Andrew Porter*	40
4. Humanitarians and White Settlers in the Nineteenth Century *Alan Lester*	64
5. Where the Missionary Frontier Ran Ahead of Empire *John Barker*	86
6. Christian Missions and the Raj *Robert Eric Frykenberg*	107
7. New Christians as Evangelists *Peggy Brock*	132
8. 'Trained to Tell the Truth': Missionaries, Converts, and Narration *Gareth Griffiths*	153
9. Women and Cultural Exchanges *Patricia Grimshaw and Peter Sherlock*	173
10. Language *Paul Landau*	194
11. New Religious Movements *Robert Edgar*	216
12. Anthropology *Patrick Harries*	238
13. Education and Medicine *Norman Etherington*	261
14. Decolonization *David Maxwell*	285
Index	000

ABBREVIATIONS

AFM	Apostolic Faith Mission
AIM	African Inland Mission
AME	African Methodist Episcopal Church
BMS	Baptist Missionary Society
CIM	China Inland Mission
CMI	*Church Missionary Intelligencer*
CMS	Church Missionary Society
CSM	Church of Scotland Mission
CWM	Council for World Mission Archives, Library of the School of Oriental and African Studies, University of London
EIC	East India Company (Great Britain)
IRM	*International Review of Missions*
LMS	London Missionary Society
MMS	Methodist Missionary Society Archives, School of Oriental and African Studies, University of London
NENZC	*Nelson Examiner and New Zealand Chronicle*
OHBE	*Oxford History of the British Empire*
OHBECS	Oxford History of the British Empire Companion Series
PEMS	Paris Evangelical Mission Society
PP	*Parliamentary Papers*
SPCK	Society for the Promoting of Christian Knowledge
SPG	Society for the Propagation of the Gospel in Foreign Parts
TNA	Tamil Nadu Archives
UMCA	Universities' Mission to Central Africa
WMMS	Wesleyan Methodist Missionary Society

LIST OF CONTRIBUTORS

JOHN BARKER (Ph.D., University of British Columbia) is Associate Professor of Anthropology at the University of British Columbia. His publications include 'Between Heaven and Earth: Missionaries, Environmentalists and the Maisin', in Victoria Lockwood, ed., *Globalization and Culture Change in the Pacific Islands*, and *At Home with the Bella Coola Indians: T. F. McIlwraith's Field Letters*, co-edited with D. Cole.

PEGGY BROCK (Ph.D., University of Adelaide) is Associate Professor of History at Edith Cowan University. Her books include *Outback Ghettos: A History of Aboriginal Institutionalisation and Survival*, *Yura and Udnyu: A History of the Adnyamathanha of the North Flinders Ranges*, and (with D. Kartinyeri) *Poonindie: The Rise and Destruction of an Aboriginal Community*.

ROBERT EDGAR (Ph.D., University of California at Los Angeles) is Professor of African Studies at Howard University. His books include *Because they Chose the Plan of God: The Story of the Bullhoek Massacre*, *An African American in South Africa: The Travel Notes of Ralph J. Bunche*, and (with Hilary Sapire) *African Apocalypse: The Story of Nontetha Nkwenkwe, a Twentieth-Century South African Prophet*.

NORMAN ETHERINGTON (Ph.D., Yale University) is Professor of History at the University of Western Australia and a Fellow of the Academy of the Social Sciences in Australia. His books include *Preachers, Peasants and Politics in Southeast Africa*, *Theories of Imperialism: War, Conquest and Capital, Rider Haggard*, and *The Great Treks: The Transformation of Southern Africa, 1815–1854*.

ROBERT E. FRYKENBERG (Ph.D., London University) is Emeritus Professor of History at the University of Wisconsin. He is the author of *Guntur District, 1788–1848: A History of Local Influence and Central Authority in South India* and *History and Belief: The Foundations of Historical Understanding*. His edited books include *Land Control and Central Authority in Indian History* and *Christians and Missionaries in India: Cross-cultural Communication since 1500*.

ELIGA H. GOULD (Ph.D., Johns Hopkins University) is Associate Professor of History at the University of New Hampshire, where he teaches early American, British, and Atlantic history. He is the author of *The Persistence of Empire: British*

xii   LIST OF CONTRIBUTORS

Political Culture in the Age of the American Revolution and *America and the Atlantic World, 1670–1815.*

GARETH GRIFFITHS (Ph.D., University of Wales) is Professor of English at the State University of New York, Albany. His books include *A Double Exile: African and West Indian Writing between Two Cultures* and the co-edited books *The Empire Writes Back*, *The Post-colonial Studies Reader*, and *Key Concepts in Post-colonial Studies.*

PATRICIA GRIMSHAW (Ph.D., University of Melbourne) is the Max Crawford Professor of History at the University of Melbourne and a Fellow of the Academy of the Social Sciences in Australia. She is the author of *Women's Suffrage in New Zealand* and *Paths of Duty: American Missionary Women in Nineteenth Century Hawaii*, and co-author of *Creating a Nation.*

PATRICK HARRIES (Ph.D., London University) is Professor of African History and Director of the Centre for African Studies at the University of Basel and Visiting Professor at the University of Cape Town. He is the author of *Work, Culture and Identity: Migrant Workers in Mozambique and South Africa, c.1860–1910.*

PAUL LANDAU (Ph.D., University of Wisconsin) is Associate Professor of History at the University of Maryland, College Park. He is the author of *The Realm of the Word: Language, Gender and Christianity in a Southern African Kingdom* and co-editor of *Images and Empires: Visuality in Colonial and Postcolonial Africa.*

ALAN LESTER (Ph.D., London University) is Senior Lecturer in Human Geography at the University of Sussex. His books include *Imperial Networks: Creating Identities in Nineteenth Century South Africa and Britain*, *Colonial Discourse and the Colonization of Queen Adelaide Province, South Africa*, and *From Colonisation to Democracy: A New Historical Geography of South Africa.*

DAVID MAXWELL (D.Phil., Oxford University) is Senior Lecturer in International History at Keele University and long-time editor of the *Journal of Religion in Africa*. He is the author of *Christians and Chiefs in Zimbabwe: A Social History of the Hwesa People c.1870s–1990s* and co-edited *Christianity and the African Imagination: Essays in Honour of Adrian Hastings.*

ANDREW PORTER (Ph.D., Cambridge University) is Rhodes Professor of Imperial History at King's College London. His books include *Origins of the South African War*, *Victorian Shipping, Business, and Imperial Policy*, *European*

Imperialism, 1860–1914, and *Religion versus Empire? British Protestant Missionaries and Overseas Expansion, 1700–1914*.

PETER SHERLOCK (D.Phil., Oxford University) is an Australia Research Council Postdoctoral Fellow at the University of Melbourne. His publications include articles in the *New Dictionary of National Biography* and the journals *Gender and History* and *Lilith: A Feminist History Journal*.

1

Introduction

NORMAN ETHERINGTON

The explosive expansion of Christianity in Africa and Asia during the last two centuries constitutes one of the most remarkable cultural transformations in the history of mankind. Because it coincided with the spread of European economic and political hegemony, it tends to be taken for granted as a reflex of imperialism. However, the precise connections between religion and Empire have yet to be fully delineated by historians. This book aims to make a contribution to the very small shelf of literature devoted to exploring those connections in a vast library of scholarship on the history of the Christian religion. Much work remains to be done.

Unfinished Business

Christian missions are also unfinished business for the *Oxford History of the British Empire*. Christian missions and missionaries are remarkable for their absence in the first five volumes. Only once do they occupy a whole chapter (volume V, *Historiography*, chapter 19). For the rest, extended discussion of the missionary role in Imperial history occurs only in Andrew Porter's chapters on religion and trusteeship in volume III and Nicholas Owen's chapter on critics of empire in volume IV. Missionaries briefly step onto centre stage in chapters on West Africa, the Pacific Islands, and the West Indies, but otherwise receive brief generic references (e.g. 'British missionaries as well as British businessmen required protection' (IV, p. 42); 'the most visible group among the British in China was one that many Consuls tended to regard as a nuisance: the missionaries' (III, p. 158)). The marginal status of missions in volumes I to V contrasts markedly with the iconic importance accorded to the missionary in popular literature on Empire. J. A. Hobson memorably summarized the supposed sequence of imperial progress: 'first the missionary, then the Consul, and at last the invading army'.[1] The same aphorism appears in many guises without attribution: 'first the missionary, then the trader, then the gunboat'; 'first comes the Missionary, then comes the Resident, lastly comes the Regiment'.[2] A variation conveying much the same assumption about the relationship between evangelization and imperial expansion has often been quoted by spokesmen for anti-colonial nationalisms: 'First they had the Bible and we had the land; now we have the Bible and they have the land.' One reason that historians distrust such easy generalizations is that rarely, if ever, do they accord with the record of British colonization. Plantation owners in the West Indies and officials of the East India Company put up stubborn resistance to missionaries seeking admission to lands already under imperial control. Colonial administrators barred Christian missionaries from parts of Nigeria and Sudan. Elsewhere missionaries worked for decades in lands that never came under imperial control. They pointedly resisted colonization schemes for New Zealand, South Africa, Malawi, and other regions.

The whole relationship between Christian missions and the Empire is problematic. For historians of religion, missions in the era of European imperialism constitute only a small chapter in a 2,000-year-old narrative of the expansion of Christianity—a story that is much more than a British or even a European enterprise. Christianity originated in Palestine and spread through the Middle East and North Africa before it reached Scandinavia and eastern Europe. The religion flourished in Tunisia, Ethiopia, Sudan, and south India before there was a British Empire. And despite predictions that 'the white man's religion' would decline when the hand of imperial protection was removed, evangelization prospered as never before. The number of professing Christians in countries formerly under the British flag has multiplied many times since decolonization. Today significant numbers of African, East Asian, and South Asian Christian missionaries are at work in Europe and North America. Confounding the prediction that Islam would outrun Christianity in twentieth-century Africa, the Christian population of the continent grew from some 9 million in 1900 to 117 million in 1970 and 335 million in 2000—a transition that has been called 'one of the most extraordinary phenomena of human history'.[3] Andrew Walls points out that 'in the

---

[1] *Imperialism: A Study* (London, 1938), p. 204.

[2] Frederick S. Downs, *History of Christianity in India*, V/5, *Northeast India in the Nineteenth and Twentieth Centuries* (Bangalore, 1992), p. 30.

[3] D. B. Barrett and T. M. Johnson, 'Annual Statistical Table on Global Mission: 2000', *International Bulletin of Missionary Research*, XXIV (2000), pp. 24–5.

course of the twentieth century, Christianity has become a mainly non-Western religion'.[4]

Just as the history of the British Empire can be written without much attention to missions, the history of missions can be written without much attention to the Empire. The index of a book entitled *Christian Mission in the Twentieth Century* contains five references to imperialism, two references to Britain, and none to colonialism; in contrast, communism and communists get eleven references, along with thirteen to the United States.[5] This underlines the important point that the story of missions in the Empire is not simply the story of British missions. Many British missionaries worked outside the Empire, and many of the missions that worked inside the Empire were not British. Continental European and North American missionaries predominated in parts of many British colonies. Nor were the British ever in the vanguard of missionary work. Catholic missions accompanied the expansion of Spain and Portugal in the early modern period; in the eighteenth century European Pietists launched missions to the most distant corners of the globe long before missionary societies began sprouting in Britain in the last decade of the eighteenth century and the first two decades of the nineteenth century. And when British societies did appear, most of their first agents were drawn from other countries. From its foundation to 1830 forty-nine of the Church Missionary Society's agents came from continental Europe.[6] In the twentieth century American missionaries far outdistanced Protestant British counterparts, and Roman Catholic missions enjoyed a resurgence that eventually eclipsed the celebrated achievements of the sixteenth and seventeenth centuries. All things considered, the trajectories of missions and Empire hardly bear comparison. The expansion of Christianity pre-dated the British Empire by a very long time and entered a period of explosive growth after most of the imperial enterprise had been wound up. By the same token, a map of worldwide missionary activity—even British missionary activity—does not resemble the map of formal Empire in any era.

These plain facts largely explain why missions so seldom figure in the *Oxford History of the British Empire*. Why then call missions unfinished business? One reason is that, although missions and the official Empire

---

[4] B. Stanley, ed., *Christian Missions and the Enlightenment* (London, 2001), p. 22.
[5] Timothy Yates, *Christian Mission in the Twentieth Century* (Cambridge, 1994).
[6] Stanley, ed., *Christian Missions*, p. 35.

were quite different operations, they play related parts in a larger drama—the spread of modernization, globalization, and Western cultural hegemony.

Another reason is that, when they are considered on a micro level, they often appear to enact or mimic the operations of political and economic imperialism at the macro level. Clifton Crais sees the mission station as 'a colonialist institution *par excellence*' that 'communicated many of the essential ingredients of British rule and the capitalist world economy'.[7] Scholars outside the world of religious and historical studies were recently introduced to this view of missions by a massive and influential study of London Missionary Society work among the Tswana people of southern Africa: *Of Revelation and Revolution* by the anthropologists Jean and John Comaroff.[8] While historians generally welcomed the Comaroffs' work with lukewarm enthusiasm, anthropologists, literary scholars, and post-colonial theorists hailed the book as a revelation.[9] Leon de Kock probably correctly identified the reason for these divergent responses by pointing to historians' valorization of archival texts over ritual and performance. The Comaroffs view the London Missionary Society's stations as 'performing civilization, in the hope of educating the Tswana to adopt Western cultural practices through the power of display'.[10] In many cases a strong case can be made for the mission station as a microcosm or trope of Empire. Like the explorer, the missionary arrived in regions barely touched by Western influences, preaching the superiority of Western religion, technology, and cultural practices. After a period of resistance, people began to adopt the new ways. Perversely, missionaries resisted the attempts of their converts to assume an equal social and clerical status in the Church until, in an act of spiritual decolonization, mission churches broke free from foreign control. Without denying that

---

[7] Clifton C. Crais, *White Supremacy and Black Resistance in Pre-industrial South Africa: The Making of the Colonial Order in the Eastern Cape, 1770–1865* (Cambridge, 1992), p. 104.

[8] Jean Comaroff and John Comaroff, *Of Revelation and Revolution*, I, *Christianity, Colonialism and Consciousness in South Africa* (Chicago, 1991); II, *The Dialectics of Modernity on a South African Frontier* (Chicago, 1997). From the historian's point of view, the Comaroffs' work is in some ways a throwback to an earlier era. Steven Kaplan in 1982 expressed relief that 'the opposing figures of the missionary–hero and the missionary–imperialist have begun to vanish from the scholarly literature'; 'Ezana's Conversion Reconsidered', *Journal of Religion in Africa*, XIII (1982), p. 101. While the Comaroffs cannot be accused of resuscitating missionary heroes, they have breathed new life into the almost lifeless corpse of the missionary-as-imperialist.

[9] The parameters of the debate are set out in Elizabeth Elbourne, 'Word Made Flesh: Christianity, Modernity and Cultural Colonialism in the Work of Jean and John Comaroff', *American Historical Review*, CVIII (2003), pp. 435–59.

[10] Elbourne, 'Word Made Flesh', p. 453.

just such a sequence of events occurred in many mission fields, one of the aims of this volume is to show why a simple analogy with formal imperialism is misleading and to demonstrate the complexity of the evolving relationship between missions and the Empire.

Plan and Scope of This Volume

The failure of the geographical empire of faith to fit any map of British colonies, mandates, and protectorates posed an obvious difficulty for me as editor of this volume. Casting the geographical net too wide would locate the book among histories of the expansion of Christianity and risk losing sight of Empire altogether. Setting the bounds too narrowly, for example at the boundaries of formal Empire, would omit important chapters in the story, such as David Livingstone's journeys of discovery and the struggle between French Catholics and British Protestants for state support in Tahiti, Madagascar, and New Caledonia. The ultimate decision was made to concentrate attention on all regions that at one time or another belonged to, or might well have become part of, the formal Empire. As a result Christian missions to South Asia fall within the purview of the volume, while the greater part of China—the great hope of European and North American evangelists from 1860 to 1950—is omitted. Within this broad rubric the margins have been deliberately left fuzzy.

A related question was whether the volume itself should be organized by geographical region, with one chapter on the South Pacific, another on India, a third on North America, and so on. The benefits of a regional organization were considerable. Most historians ground their expertise in a single country or region, so it would be easier to attract collaborators. On the other hand, it seemed equally apparent that a regional approach would involve a good deal of duplication. The most important themes to have emerged from recent work on the history of missions and Empire would have to be repeated for each region—the role of indigenous evangelists, language, gender, the creation of ethnicity, and tensions between missions and government. Similar problems would have arisen from a chronological framework. In the end a desire to emphasize the emerging themes won out over geography and chronology. This placed additional burdens on the individual authors. While concentrating on what they know best, each of them had to stretch to encompass a wider world. That said, regional and chronological biases creep in as a matter of course. The book needed a starting point, which

Chapter 2, by Eliga Gould, establishes in the seventeenth and eighteenth centuries. For most of this period the Asian and African territorial Empire was very small; most religious work outside the British Isles took place in North America and the West Indies so there is a definite tilt in the direction of a particular time and place. Explaining how the work of mission changed from supplying the religious needs of new colonies in the eighteenth century to plans for 'the conversion of the world in this generation' in the early twentieth century requires a close look at the emergence of evangelical Christianity in the eighteenth century and the organization of mission societies in the nineteenth century. With the United States lost to the Empire in the American Revolution, this story centres on developments in the British Isles and Europe, thus giving Andrew Porter's delineation of trends in British missions in Chapter 3 both a regional and a chronological focus.

It was commonplace for nineteenth-century missionaries to point to the growth of the British Empire as specifically intended by Divine Providence as an instrument for the conversion of the world to Christianity, just as promoters of Empire spoke of missions as partners in the work of spreading commerce and civilization. For all the talk of partnership the relationship between missionaries and other agents of empire was never easy. Keith Hancock's great *Survey of Commonwealth Affairs* (1937–42) conceptualized the expansion of Empire as a series of overlapping frontiers: the traders' frontier, the settlers' frontier, the missionaries' frontier, and the officials' frontier. Hancock could see better than most the way that missionaries were practically forced to assume the role of moral guardians. They were seldom popular with officials and traders and generally in conflict with white settlers. In South Africa the missionary frontier collided spectacularly with the settlers' frontier: on one side 'the ideals of humane individuals working for the protection of the weak' and, on the other, 'the will of a racial group which has found its unity in the determination to survive, to possess, and to dominate.'[11] Although the worlds of missionaries, officials, traders, and settlers were not as separate as Hancock's schema would seem to imply—many former missionaries and children of missionaries became settlers and occupied important positions in colonial bureaucracies—there were many spectacular collisions between missionaries and government. Chapter 4, by Alan Lester, examines the success of missions and mission-linked

---

[11] W. K. Hancock, *Survey of Commonwealth Affairs*, II 2, *Problems of Economic Policy 1918–1939* (Oxford, 1942), p. 10.

philanthropic societies in imperial politics following the abolition of slavery and the gradual decline from that high point of influence.

The most important late twentieth-century scholarly insight into the growth of Christianity in the British Empire was that European missionaries accomplished very little in the way of conversion.[12] The greatest difficulty faced by those who have tried to argue that Christian missions were a form of cultural imperialism has been the overwhelming evidence that the agents of conversion were local people, not foreign missionaries. None of them were coerced into believing and very few were paid. For example, during the entire nineteenth century in the Travancore state of southern India the London Missionary Society employed a total of fifty European missionaries, compared to many times that number of so-called 'native agents'. In 1900 there were 882 of these agents—pastors, readers, schoolmasters, etc.[13] In addition to these formal operatives, Christian beliefs were spread by ordinary people, whose numbers grew as colonial development increased mobility. Unfortunately their experience remains largely undocumented in the mountains of paper generated by European and American missions. Indeed, the balance of documentation is usually inversely proportionate to the actual numbers. A very recent biographical dictionary of Christian missions lists 2,400 individuals, only 258 of whom are 'non-western persons' from Asia, Africa, and the Pacific Islands.[14] Voices of white missionaries predominate in mission publications and archives for understandable, if regrettable, reasons. As voluntary societies, mission organizations faced constant pressures to raise money. Individual missionaries had to justify their lonely underpaid existences by writing regular reports. Pressures of fund-raising and accountability generated streams of written reports aimed at pricking the consciences of contributors, celebrating conversions, and explaining failures. Missionary martyrs and heroes like Bishop Patteson and David Livingstone provided riveting reading for pious audiences at home. Descriptions of the 'hardhearted, sinful, slothful heathen' helped European missionaries account for their slow progress in winning converts. As Natasha Erlank observes, historians who only study printed texts run the risks of underestimating the

---

[12] Richard Gray, *Black Christians and White Missionaries* (New Haven, 1990), pp. 80–1.

[13] Dick Kooiman, 'Mass Movement, Famine and Epidemic: A Study in Interrelationship', *Modern Asian Studies*, XXV (1991), p. 286.

[14] Gerald H. Anderson, ed., *Biographical Dictionary of Christian Missions* (Cambridge, 1999), pp. vii, 808–10.

complexity and particularity of the individual missionary experience and missing the voice of the indigenous evangelist altogether.[15]

The phenomenon of local people carrying Christianity far ahead of advancing imperial frontiers first appeared in the southern Pacific in the nineteenth century, which explains the regional and chronological weighting of Chapter 5, by John Barker. The areas that proved most resistant to Christian evangelizing whether by European or by indigenous agents were regions dominated by well-entrenched universalizing creeds and sacred written texts. Outside the Empire this was best demonstrated in China and Japan. Within the formal Empire, resistance was stiffest in South Asia, where the appearance of missionaries produced a backlash of religious revitalization among Hindus, Buddhists, and Muslims. Where such competing religions were deeply rooted among large populations, as in Burma, Ceylon, and the sub-Saharan Sudanic regions, imperial authority did little to advance the cause of Christian missions. In fact, as Robert Frykenberg points out in Chapter 6, the British Raj assumed the role of protector of Hindu religious establishments. That did not mean, however, that Christianity made no headway. As in other areas of the Empire, people marginalized by social class and geography proved to be exceptionally susceptible to the power of the new religion. Local lay evangelists opened the way for overseas missionaries to establish schools, printing presses, and hospitals.

One of the greatest drawbacks to the study of the people most responsible for the spread of Christianity is the relative paucity of texts in their own words that describe their motivations and attitudes to political and economic change. Chapter 7, by Peggy Brock, tries to redress the balance by closely examining some of the rare texts, published and unpublished, produced by 'new Christians' who engaged in formal and informal missionary work. In Chapter 8 a literary scholar, Gareth Griffiths, tries to penetrate the stylized formal recounting of conversion in published texts in an effort to hear individual indigenous voices.

Many aspects of the imperial experience would have been very different in the absence of the missionary movement. Outside the colonies of white settlement European women played a minor role in the imperial enterprise. Very few gained official posts, and almost none worked in the military services, trade, or commerce. For a long time fears of disease deterred British

---

[15] '"Civilizing the African": The Scottish Mission to the Xhosa, 1821–64', in Stanley, ed., *Christian Missions and the Enlightenment*, p. 151.

officials from taking their wives to the tropics. In contrast, women were omnipresent in Christian missions. After some early experiments in sending unmarried men resulted in sexual scandals, most Protestant missionary societies insisted on employing only married men. This produced the extraordinary spectacle of would-be missionaries on whirlwind speaking tours in a frantic search for suitable partners before they were due to sail for their foreign posting. Training institutions like Mount Holyoke College in Massachusetts sprang up for the specific purpose of educating appropriate missionary wives.[16] Once in the field, missionaries and their wives were expected to act as exemplars of monogamous, pious, Christian family life. By the middle of the nineteenth century single women began to find employment as teachers in mission schools. Though the Catholic Church had no place for married priests, female religious orders put women to work in schools and orphanages throughout the Empire. While every chapter in this volume touches on questions of gender in one way or another, Chapter 9, by Patricia Grimshaw and Peter Sherlock, is entirely devoted to the subject of women as agents and converts of missions.

A frequent complaint of white settlers and traders in many places was that missionaries gave their converts too much book-learning, making them unfit for menial labour. Most missions refused to give ground on the issue because, especially for Protestants, the chief accomplishment of the Reformation had been to put the Bible in the hands of ordinary people. Because the ability to read and interpret Scripture was central to the faith, teaching converts to read the Bible was a top priority. Several consequences flowed from this commitment. The West African theologian Lamin Sanneh has emphasized the centrality of translation to the Christian religion.[17] Key concepts of the faith had to be conveyed in many different languages to a multitude of cultures; otherwise Christianity would never have spread beyond Palestine. Missionaries of all denominations, Catholic as well as Protestant, expected their clergy to have a working knowledge of Hebrew, Greek, and Latin when they set about translating the Bible into other languages. In Chapter 10, on missions and language, Paul Landau explores some of the momentous consequences of the translation exercise. While utilitarian theorists argued strenuously for English as the language of education in British colonies, missionaries were unwilling to put

---

[16] Dana Robert, 'Mount Holyoke Women and the Dutch Reformed Missionary Movement, 1874–1904', *Missionalia*, XXI (1993), p. 107.

[17] Lamin O. Sanneh, *Translating the Message: The Missionary Impact on Culture* (Maryknoll, NY, 1990).

the educational cart before the evangelistic horse. It would be easier to get their sacred texts into the hands of their converts by translating them into indigenous languages. Once in possession of sound translations, local evangelists could communicate 'the good news' in the familiar dialects of their fellow countrymen. Making Bibles in new languages required the compilation of vocabularies and translations on a truly heroic scale. Had there been no missions in the Empire, who knows how many languages might have become extinct? Martin Luther is generally credited with standardizing the German language through his translation of the Bible. By the nineteenth century language had become central to German concepts of national identity. Language proved equally important to the emergence of new identities among colonized peoples.

Shakespeare's Caliban complained to Prospero that 'You taught me language; and my profit on't is, I know how to curse'. Missionaries could hardly have anticipated all the ways that their translations would be employed, especially in opposition to themselves and imperial rule. Literate converts founded newspapers and used them to communicate commercial and political information. Some were surprised to learn while reading the Old Testament in their own language that King Solomon the wise had numerous wives and concubines, while missionaries insisted on monogamy. Applying their own interpretative powers to the book of Revelation and prophetic books of the Bible, some concluded that Christ would shortly return in Glory to strike down wicked rulers. As Christianity took on a local character, new heresies opposed mission orthodoxies, and indigenous prophets denounced the oppression of settlers and imperial authorities. Chapter 11, by Robert Edgar, demonstrates some of the many ways in which Christianity could be turned against ecclesiastical and secular authority by independent-minded preachers. While some missionaries denounced these innovations as heresies or 'a return to paganism', others attempted to understand the cultural lenses through which non-European societies viewed the world. Translation necessarily involved understanding other cultures. It is therefore not surprising, as Patrick Harries demonstrates in Chapter 12, that missionaries were often in the vanguard of what became known as the discipline of anthropology—sometimes called the scholarly handmaiden of Empire. Missionaries included voluminous ethnographic detail in their reports of Pacific Island and African societies. Henry Callaway collected Zulu nursery tales and legends, which were eagerly seized as precious raw material by armchair anthropologists in late Victorian England. Susan Bayly recounts in volume III of the *Oxford History of the British Empire* how missionary attempts to refute the errors of Hinduism through translations of Indian sacred texts had the ironic consequence of making those very texts more available than ever before to South Asian people.[18] Those same translations made fundamental contributions to European theories of language, race, and culture. When Edwin Smith, the Methodist missionary and future President of the Royal Anthropological Society, became a fellow of the Royal Anthropological Institute in 1900, he was one of eleven clergy on the membership list.[19] Only gradually did a rupture develop between missions and 'professional' anthropology.

The Empire may have been indifferent to the linguistic and anthropological work of the missions, but it could hardly have done without their assistance in the fields of education and medicine, subjects taken up in Chapter 13 by Norman Etherington. Lord Hailey's *African Survey* of 1938 remarked that until very recently 'nine-tenths of the education in Africa was in the hands of missionary bodies'.[20] The same was largely true for most other parts of the tropical Empire and for indigenous people trapped within white settler societies. The predominance of mission schools distinguished the British on the one hand from the French Empire, where a strong anticlerical tradition permeated the Third Republic, and the Portuguese Empire on the other hand, where a Papal Concordat of 1940 gave Catholic missions a virtual monopoly of education. Missions founded schools for their evangelical purposes: to train local people as ministers and missionaries; to spread literacy so the Bible could be read; and to form the minds of children when adults proved indifferent or hostile to the Christian message. As the example of missions to independent island societies of the South Pacific and the 'tribal' regions of India demonstrate, missions would have built schools without government assistance. However, when imperial grants became available, cash-strapped missionaries grabbed them. Unlike the United States, whose founding charter insisted on the separation of Church and State, the British constitution enshrined their union. Public education in the British Isles had developed in the first instance through the provision of grants-in-aid to church schools, so it seemed natural to apply the same

---

[18] Andrew Porter, ed., *OHBE* III, *The Nineteenth Century* (Oxford, 1999), pp. 460–4.

[19] W. John Young, *The Quiet Wise Spirit: Edwin W. Smith, 1876–1957 and Africa* (Peterborough, 2002), p. 75.

[20] Lord Hailey, *An African Survey: A Study of Problems Arising in Africa South of the Sahara* (Oxford, 1938), pp. 1208–9.

system in the colonies. However welcome the funding, missions soon found that assistance bred dependence and a large measure of government regulation. Throughout the Empire, but especially in the colonies of white settlement, there was relentless government hostility to 'literary education' and a demand for 'practical' vocational training. Since race-conscious white settlers had no desire to create competitors for skilled jobs, the cry for practical education was in truth a demand that the missions train people for menial jobs and domestic service. While the missions could not cave in to such demands without betraying their converts, neither could they ignore the threat that government funds might be suddenly withdrawn. The tension remained constant, sometimes surviving decolonization. Some of the worst abuses of mission education occurred in boarding schools. Begun as a means for removing children from the 'baneful influence of heathenism', they were endorsed as 'the most effective method of training' by the Advisory Committee on Education in the Colonies in 1925.[21] However, when linked to government funding, they could be turned to less worthy uses, as in Australia, where racist policies aimed to remove children of mixed descent from their Aboriginal mothers. The so-called 'stolen children' were picked up by police and dropped at mission boarding schools; in most cases they never saw their mothers again.

Government assistance to medical missions was less controversial. Unlike schools, medical work was an optional extra for most mission societies, who accepted sickness, death, and miraculous cures as part of the Providential ordering of the cosmos. Medical missions were mainly supported as a holy imitation of Christ the healer and as bait for their preaching. Before the Second World War, British governments did not regard the provision of medical services as a necessary service to their tropical subjects. Aside from mission hospitals, medical services concentrated on maintaining the health of white functionaries and certain classes of native employees, especially mineworkers. When government and mission medical services did begin to converge in the post-war period, decolonization was already under way, a process that is the subject of Chapter 14, by David Maxwell. It first appeared that missions might disappear along with imperial authority. Leaders of independence movements who had been less than impressed with mission support for their cause not only cut government funding but nationalized mission schools and other facilities. After the period covered by this volume,

---

[21] Lord Hailey, *An African Survey, revised 1956* (Oxford, 1957), p. 1168.

local clergy, who were by now mostly leaders of independent national churches, called for a 'Moratorium on Mission' in the 1970s. It soon became evident, however, that the end of Empire did not mean the end of Christianity or even the foreign missionary presence. African clergy who broke their links with mission societies during the colonial era made it plain that their quarrel was not with Christianity but with patterns of authority that denied them an equal place in mission councils. In the post-independence period, congregations continued to swell, particularly among the Pentecostal churches, which paid little attention to politics. American fundamentalist Protestant missionaries arrived in large numbers, preaching uncompromising born-again Christianity—to the consternation of liberal churchmen who had bent over backwards to avoid offending cultural sensitivities. Eventually, sheer financial necessity caused many newly independent nations to reconsider their early opposition to mission schools. Non-governmental organizations, many of which had historic ties to Christianity, carried on many of the welfare functions previously performed by missions—including human rights advocacy that echoed the old humanitarian crusades of Exeter Hall.

Placing Missions and Empire in a Global Historical Context

Theologians like to base missions on biblical texts, especially the so-called 'Great Commission' given by the risen Christ to his disciples (Mark 16: 5): 'Go ye into all the world, and preach the gospel to every creature.' That command is given an eschatological dimension in Matthew 24: 14, when Jesus on the Mount of Olives prophesies about the end of the world and the Last Judgement: 'this gospel of the kingdom shall be preached in all the world for a witness unto all nations; and then shall the end come'. It is also commonplace to cite St Paul as the exemplar of evangelization, a man who virtually invented the notion of conversion, and whose method was to preach in one place until a new church was formed, leaving the recent converts to govern and sustain themselves.[22] Scripture notwithstanding, Christian missions have varied markedly from century to century. The missions depicted in this volume differed in many respects from those prominent in earlier times.

---

[22] Andrew Walls, 'Converts or Proselytes? The Crisis over Conversion in the Early Church', *International Bulletin of Missionary Research*, XVIII (2004), pp. 2–6.

The schism in Western Christianity provoked by the Protestant Reformation ensured that Britain played no part in the sixteenth-century efflorescence of Catholic missions. Although some features of the Spanish and Portuguese missionary experience prefigured later Protestant missions—the encounter with other cultures, the struggle to attract converts, and tensions with state-sanctioned land seizures and forced labour—there were also very significant differences. The Portuguese and Spanish Empires took for granted that Christendom should be coterminous with the boundaries of Christian kingdoms, so Christianity was a state-sponsored enterprise. When the Pope made his celebrated division of the world between those powers in 1498, he also granted them the right of Padroado, which made religion a Crown monopoly. Not only did this give monarchs the sole right to appoint bishops and other ecclesiastical authorities, it also enabled them to employ coercion in converting infidels and heathen to their religion at home and abroad. Portuguese expansion brought the Inquisition to India in 1560.[23] No mission ever enjoyed such advantages under the British Crown, even though the monarch was the constitutional head of the Church of England. Although long barred from holding public offices, Catholics and Dissenters were free to practise their religion. Little or nothing of the special status enjoyed at home by the established churches of England, Ireland, and Scotland was extended to overseas colonies. Deliberate policy opposed the multiplication of state-supported Anglican bishops in the colonies.[24]

The word 'mission' held different meanings for different churches at different periods. The Society for the Propagation of the Gospel in Foreign Parts and the Society for the Promoting of Christian Knowledge were founded in the eighteenth century principally for the purpose of supplying the needs of British Christians in North America—not for the conversion of native peoples. The Roman Catholic Church long continued to regard the clergy it sent to Protestant Britain and those sent from Ireland to serve the needs of Irish in other parts of the Empire as missionaries. The Wesleyan Methodist Missionary Society similarly referred to the evangelists it sent to Ireland as missionaries. In the twentieth century Pentecostals, Adventists, Mormons, and Jehovah's Witnesses mounted missions aimed at converting the already Christian populations of the settlement colonies to membership of their sects. Attempts to recall the English urban working class to practising

---

[23] Kranti K. Farias, *The Christian Impact in South Kanara* (Mumbai, 1999), p. 31.

[24] A. Porter, 'Religion, Missionary Enthusiasm, and Empire', *OHBE* III, pp. 223–31.

Christianity were called Home Missions. However, when most British people in the nineteenth and twentieth centuries spoke of missions, they meant enterprises devoted to conversion of people who were not Christian: Muslims, Jews, Hindus, Confucians, Buddhists, and people of no recognized faith—the heathen.

The launch of missions to Pacific Islands by the London Missionary Society in the 1790s marked the first occasion in modern British history when ministers of religion went to work in alien societies on terms set by other people.[25] Far from enjoying royal patronage, missionaries had to struggle for the right to preach in territories held by the East India Company before an act of Parliament specifically sanctioned them in 1813. Missions' primary reliance on private funding helps explain the often tense relations between imperial officials and missionaries. Britain's policy of religious toleration and the voluntary character of missionary enterprise prevented any single denomination from predominating in the Empire. In this volume the most striking feature of missions is *diversity*. Not only did a variety of approaches to missions coexist at any one point, the missionary enterprise as a whole went through remarkable changes over time. Missions at the dawn of the nineteenth century differed markedly from missions at the turn of the twentieth century. When British societies sponsoring missions to non-Christian lands began to proliferate in the 1790s, they faced indifference if not outright opposition from entrenched powers in Church and State. The vocal championing of liberty of thought by dissenting denominations made them suspect in a nation at war with the French Revolution. Apart from some continental Europeans working for British missionary societies, most of the home-grown agents were drawn from the lower ranks of society: stonemasons, carpenters, and printers with little formal education. The English class system put most European missionaries at the bottom of the totem pole of prestige in British colonies. Until well into the nineteenth century the Church of England had no procedures for appointing bishops outside British territory and distrusted mission organizations without an ecclesiastical hierarchy. The Calvinist theology of the established Church of Scotland had difficulty coming to terms with projects for converting the heathen in a world where God had already predestined some for salvation and others for damnation. The General Assembly of the Church of Scotland in 1796

---

[25] Andrew Walls, 'The Eighteenth-Century Protestant Missionary Awakening', in Stanley, ed., *Christian Missions and the Enlightenment*, pp. 27–8.

declared the preaching of the Gospel 'among barbarians and heathen natives to be highly preposterous in so far as it anticipates, nay even reverses, the order of Nature'.[26] Many of the agents of the new missionary societies in Europe and America held radical theological views based on their readings of the book of Revelation. Unlike the philosophers of the Enlightenment, they did not look forward to endless vistas of secular progress. The political upheavals and wars raging around them seemed to presage the last days of sinful humanity and the imminent return of Christ. Almost all early nineteenth-century missionaries condemned non-Christian societies as sinks of iniquity. As Bishop Heber's popular missionary hymn put it, European evangelists were venturing into beautiful but godless lands, 'where every prospect pleases, and only man is vile'. This attitude gradually disappeared in many denominations. Even before the Victorian age concluded, some missionaries were preaching that European Christianity could be enriched by contact with other cultures. According to 'fulfilment theology', God had granted special insights to Hindus, Africans, and other peoples that would give new dimensions to European worship, just as their acceptance of Christ would fulfil their progress towards salvation.[27]

Many unsuccessful attempts have been made to specify a single factor that can explain the explosion of Christian missions in the period 1780–1900. One is the idea that millennial expectations excited the flurry of activity. Some historians stress the effects of pre-millennialism and post-millennialism.[28] Pre-millennialists believed that the world was living through a dark thousand-year reign of Satan, after which Christ would return to reign on earth during a golden age lasting a further thousand years prior to the Last Judgement. Post-millennialists believed that the golden age had already dawned but that Christ would not be returning until it had run its course. Particular missions can be cited as examples of each persuasion. The German Pastor Louis Harms founded a mission in his little village of Hermannsburg, near Hanover, that sent missionaries to the heart of Africa and Australia. Believing that the reign of Satan had already begun, Harms was looking for isolated refuges where pure Christianity might survive the darkness. Operations of the London Missionary Society, on the other hand, expressed an optimistic faith in progress linked to post-millennial expectations that the

[26] Arthur Mayhew, *Christianity and the Government of India* (London, 1929), p. 28.
[27] Martin Maw, *Visions of India: Fulfilment Theology, the Aryan Race Theory, and the Work of British Protestant Missionaries in Victorian India* (Frankfurt, 1990).
[28] Yates, *Christian Mission*, p. 9.

golden age had arrived. Millenarians who ignored the thousand-year periods mentioned in the book of Revelation sometimes argued that missions could accelerate the Second Coming by simply fulfilling Christ's prophecy that the end would come when the gospel had been preached to all the world—regardless of whether anyone believed it. The British philanthropist Robert Arthington funded missions because he 'believed it was only necessary for the evangelist to pass through all these tracts of country (as yet untouched by the Truth) distributing Gospels, and preaching the Word, in order that Christ might come and restore all things'.[29] The trouble with millenarianism of any variety as a catch-all explanation for modern missions is that some mission theorists never mentioned the millennium and missions continued to flourish even after millennialism was a spent force in Europe (though it still flourishes in many parts of the Third World). (pp. 47–56) Post-millennial beliefs so closely resemble secular doctrines of progress springing from the European Enlightenment that the difference hardly seems to matter. However, attempts to explain the new era of missions by reference to Enlightenment alone run up against many examples of evangelical organizations that deliberately set their face against the French Revolution and all its works. Eugène de Mazenod founded the Oblates of Mary Immaculate in Marseille to defend the restored Catholic monarchical order against the forces of godless atheism. Catholic missions in general evidenced the strength of Ultramontane forces in the Church. In place of the Padroado arrangements, which put missionary orders in the hands of Spanish and Portuguese monarchs, there was now direct control by the Pope through the *propaganda fide*.[30]

Not only is it difficult to point to any one cause of missionary enthusiasm, but different causes predominated at different times. Nationalism, barely evident in the late eighteenth-century missionary movement, had become a driving force one hundred years later. At the international missionary conference of 1900 in New York's Carnegie Hall, delegates spontaneously burst into the American patriotic hymn 'My Country 'tis of Thee' following an

---

[29] Downs, *History of Christianity in India*, V/5, *Northeast India*, p. 83; Brian Stanley, *History of the Baptist Missionary Society, 1792–1992* (Edinburgh, 1992), p. 381. Seventh-Day Adventists only became active in foreign missions when their prophet Ellen White 'began to stress the idea that believers could hasten Christ's coming by mission activity'; Dennis Steely, 'Unfinished: The Seventh-Day Adventist Mission in the South Pacific, Excluding Papua New Guinea, 1886–1986', Ph.D., thesis (Auckland, 1989), p. 53.

[30] Edmund M. Hogan, *The Irish Missionary Movement: A Historical Survey, 1830–1980* (Dublin, 1990), pp. 55–6.

address by President McKinley.[31] Struggling Trappist missionaries in South Africa were suddenly overwhelmed with offers of funding in the 1880s as German nationalism invigorated Bavarian Catholics. The revival of Spanish and Portuguese nationalism resulted in massive support for Catholic missions in African colonies that had previously been neglected backwaters. However, every advance for nationalism was balanced by a step forward for an international ecumenical movement. Today's World Council of Churches can trace its pedigree directly back to the World Missionary Conference at Edinburgh in 1910. King George V congratulated the gathering for 'its bearing upon the cementing of international friendship, the cause of peace, and the well-being of mankind', while William Jennings Bryan, who had been a candidate for the presidency of the United States in 1896, made several addresses.[32] By the end of the twentieth century such fervent messages of support from monarchs and politicians were practically unknown in the West, even as Pentecostal evangelists permeated the globe with messages supremely indifferent to national borders. It seems likely that future scholars, like the authors of this volume, will shy away from mono-causal explanations of the modern missionary movement.

[31] Yates, *Christian Mission*, p. 12.
[32] *World Missionary Conference, 1910: The History and Records of the Conference, together with Addresses Delivered at the Evening Meetings* (London, 1910), p. 141.

2
Prelude: The Christianizing of British America

ELIGA H. GOULD

Although the history of Britain's overseas missions properly begins in the American colonies, one can read extensively in the history of early American religion without encountering either missions or missionaries. While acknowledging the pre-revolutionary dynamism of the Anglican Society for the Propagation of the Gospel in Foreign Parts (SPG) and the Anglican-dominated Society for Promoting Christian Knowledge (SPCK), early American historians place far more emphasis on the efforts of revivalists like Whitefield and his fellow evangelicals, depicting the Church of England's missions as of secondary importance. As we are often told, the growth of Protestant Christianity in British America—especially those parts that became the United States—was a voluntaristic, market-driven phenomenon, a decentralized (and decentralizing) project fundamentally different from the clerically dominated initiatives that we associate with missionary movements in subsequent phases of Britain's expansion.[1]

One consequence of this inattention to missions has been to encourage an 'exceptionalist' interpretation of early American Protestantism, and to dissociate the Christianizing of British America from the spread of Christianity in Britain and the other parts of the British Empire. In several respects, this tendency is misleading. Not only was British America the crucible of what Andrew Porter has called an 'Atlantic system' of international missionary endeavour, both for the Church of England and for its dissenting competitors,[2] but the Christianizing of British America was itself the product of an evangelical culture far more similar to its missionary counterparts than is sometimes realized. Indeed, if we accept the essential 'ambiguity of the term

---

[1] See Boyd Stanley Schlenther, 'Religious Faith and Commercial Empire', in P. J. Marshall, ed., *OHBE* II, *The Eighteenth Century* (Oxford, 1998), pp. 128–50.

[2] Andrew Porter, 'Church History, History of Christianity, Religious History: Some Reflections on British Missionary Enterprise since the Late Eighteenth Century', *Church History*, LXXI (2002), pp. 568–75.

"mission"'' for the entire sweep of British imperial history—as Norman Etherington has urged—it becomes evident that the religious history of which Whitefield and his fellow evangelicals are a central part is but one chapter in a larger story of British missions and missionary enterprise.[3]

American Indians

As in the nineteenth century, Protestant missions to indigenous peoples featured prominently in the rhetoric of Britain's early modern expansion. In the well-known formulation of John Winthrop's 1630 sermon on board the *Arbella*, New England envisioned itself 'as a Citty upon a hill', a biblical commonwealth whose Christian example would reform the world.[4] Although Winthrop was thinking chiefly of Archbishop Laud's England, many writers directed their proselytizing energy towards the Indians. 'The people of America crye out unto us ... to come and helpe them,' wrote the younger Richard Hakluyt in 1584.[5] In his instructions to the Virginia Company, James VI and I enjoined settlers bound for the new colony to 'well entreate' the Indians 'whereby they may be the sooner drawne to the true knowledge of God, and the Obedience of us'.[6] A hundred years later the SPG's charter included native conversion among the society's main objectives, and during the eighteenth century Protestants on both sides of the Atlantic regarded 'Christianizing the Indians' both as a sacred duty and as a necessary expedient for checking the power of Catholic France.[7]

If Britons everywhere affirmed the desirability of spreading the Christian gospel in Indian country, the reality was often different. Outside southern New England, where Puritans established a series of 'praying Indian' towns during the seventeenth century, Anglo-American missionaries encountered frequently insurmountable obstacles, including native resistance, Jesuit competition, and the insistence of both Anglicans and Dissenters that

---

[3] Norman Etherington, 'Missions and Empire', in Robin W. Winks, ed., *OHBE* V, *Historiography* (Oxford, 1999), p. 303.

[4] Winthrop, 'A Modell of Christian Charity' (1630), cited in Jerome Reich, *Colonial America*, 3rd edn. (Englewood Cliffs, NJ, 1994), p. 78.

[5] Cited in James Axtell, *The Invasion Within: The Contest of Culturer in Colonial North America* (New York, 1985), p. 133.

[6] Edmund S. Morgan, *American Slavery—American Freedom: The Ordeal of Colonial Virginia* (New York, 1975), p. 46.

[7] Schlenther, 'Religious Faith and Commercial Empire', p. 131; Axtell, *Invasion Within*, pp. 242–67.

Indians be 'reduced' to civilization before they could be converted to Christianity. During the 1740s David Brainerd achieved temporary success through his Indian mission in New Jersey, but early death ensured that his efforts did not outlive him. More typical was Moor's Charity School for Indians in Lebanon, Connecticut. Founded by Eleazar Wheelock in 1754, the Congregational school counted among its graduates Sampson Occum and Joseph Brandt. However, Wheelock regarded the venture as a failure; when the school moved to New Hampshire as Dartmouth College in 1769, it largely abandoned its original emphasis on Indian education. Even the Moravians who followed Count Nicholas von Zinzendorf to eastern Pennsylvania achieved only partial success. Despite winning several hundred converts during the 1740s and 1750s, they found that most Indians rejected their message. As Jeremy Belknap reported to the Scottish SPCK following his 1796 mission to the Oneidas, the Indian who adopted English ways and creeds found himself (or herself) living in two incompatible worlds: 'He is neither white man nor an Indian; as he had no character with us, he has none with them.'[8]

Although Indian missions rarely conformed to their benefactors' expectations, Christianity still had far-reaching implications for native culture. In the eighteenth-century European contests for influence on North America's 'middle ground', religious affiliation was often the basis for military and diplomatic cooperation—a fact nicely illustrated by Joseph Brandt's tripartite character as Mohawk sachem, Anglican missionary, and British officer.[9] Even when Indians resisted formal Christianization, they incorporated elements of Christian worship into their own practices and beliefs. As a group of Moravians reported of a mission to the Indian village of Goschgoschuenk on the Allegheny River, several prophets who preached against them 'claimed to have been to heaven, and one said he had seen the Christian God'.[10] According to both Protestants and rival Catholic orders, the Indian penchant for selective borrowing was a principal reason for the unusual success of the Jesuits, who sought converts not through the outright suppression of Indian culture but by accepting, at least provisionally, some analogies between native beliefs and Christian doctrine. In Nova Scotia and New Brunswick such efforts helped create an indigenous Mi'kmaq Catholicism that included

---

[8] Axtell, *Invasion Within*, pp. 131–78, 204–17, 275.
[9] Richard White, *The Middle Ground* (Cambridge, 1991).
[10] Eric Hinderaker, *Elusive Empires* (Cambridge, 1997), p. 65.

catechisms written in native hieroglyphs, feasts of patron saints with significance for local culture, and special formulas for baptizing infants, all of which survived Britain's annexation of the region in 1713 and are still practised today.[11]

Despite the persistence of native religion (or perhaps because of it), the resources that British and colonial missionaries devoted to indigenous conversion were relatively meagre compared to what they expended along the Atlantic seaboard. Although this was especially true of dissenting churches and denominations, whose decentralized structure provided few salaried positions other than service as a parish minister, even the Anglican SPG, which sent more than 600 missionaries to America during the eighteenth century, showed a 'limited return' for its efforts in Indian country.[12] In response to episcopal queries during the mid-1720s, southern Anglicans were virtually unanimous that Indians rejected Christianity. At the Mohawk Castle in central New York, one hapless priest wrote that Indians who attended his chapel went away 'laughing'; others tried to disrupt services by beating drums; and those who did convert—mainly women—led lives that were too debauched (in English eyes) to admit to communion.[13] If SPG missionaries were the 'good soldiers of Jesus Christ', as White Kennett told the Society's London sponsors in 1706, both they and their dissenting rivals achieved their greatest triumphs east of the Appalachians.[14]

Settler Indifference

In the settled colonies Protestant missionaries and evangelical ministers confronted a population that, though nominally Christian, seemed at times to be no more thoroughly churched than the Indians to the west. Colonial church adherence rates—defined somewhat loosely as a 'regular or steady attachment to institutional Christianity'—varied widely at mid-century, from two-thirds of eligible adults (men and women) in rural New England to less than 15 per cent in New York City. Despite pockets of religiosity, the general pattern was indifference, with the overall figure for the thirteen colonies that became the United States falling short of the 25 to

---

[11] Axtell, *Invasion Within*, p. 277.
[12] Schlenther, 'Religious Faith and Commercial Empire', p. 131.
[13] Patricia U. Bonomi, *Under the Cope of Heaven: Religion, Society, and Politics in Colonial America* (Oxford, 1986), pp. 120–1.
[14] *An Account of the Society for Propagating the Gospel in Foreign Parts* (London, 1706), p. 8.

30 per cent that obtained on the eve of the Civil War, and well below 'the 60 percent of adults who belonged to churches in America in the 1960s'.[15] In the West Indies planter absenteeism probably intensified such patterns, making the settlers' indifference still more pronounced. Even Patricia Bonomi, who has argued for higher rates of adherence, accepts that figures at the end of the eighteenth century were higher than those at its beginning and that the 'era presents itself as one of rising vitality in religious life, an era not of decline but the reverse—of proliferation and growth'.[16]

In part, low adherence rates reflected the relative scarcity of institutional assets like church buildings, religious books, and qualified ministers. In Virginia, where the Church of England was legally established, there were fifty parishes in 1680, only thirty-five of which had churches or priests.[17] Elsewhere, churches and clergy were in even shorter supply; only Congregational New England and Anglican Barbados possessed the infrastructure necessary to meet the spiritual needs of most Protestant inhabitants.[18] Many localities experienced similar shortages of religious literature. Until the first American edition appeared during the Revolution, even Bibles had to be imported from Europe.[19] To rectify the situation, Thomas Bray, the Anglican commissary for Maryland, helped found the SPCK (1698) to distribute Bibles and religious tracts to British Atlantic territories. Bray also helped launch the SPG (1701), complaining that 'the *English Colonies* . . . [had] been in a manner abandoned to *Atheism*; or, what is much at one, to *Quakerism*, for want of a clergy settled among them'.[20] According to Hugh Jones, Anglican ministers in Virginia, most of whom were British or Irish natives, found their situation 'very odd . . . being different to what they have been heretofore accustomed to'.[21] Dissenting clergy who had been educated in Britain or Europe invariably agreed.

Some contrasts drawn between the colonies and Britain were more apparent than real. In their institutional poverty, the American colonies resembled other outlying regions of the British Atlantic, especially Britain's Gaelic

[15] Jon Butler, *Awash in a Sea of Faith: Christianizing the American People* (Cambridge, Mass., 1990), pp. 4, 191–3, 283.
[16] Bonomi, *Under the Cope of Heaven*, p. 6.
[17] Butler, *Awash in a Sea of Faith*, pp. 99–101.
[18] Schlenther, 'Religious Faith and Commercial Empire', p. 129.
[19] Paul C. Gutjahr, *An American Bible* (Stanford, Calif., 1999).
[20] Quoted in John Frederick Woolverton, *Colonial Anglicanism in North America* (Detroit, 1984), p. 88.
[21] Quoted in Bonomi, *Under the Cope of Heaven*, p. 54.

hinterland. Speaking of missions to Native Americans in the 1650s, Roger Williams remarked, 'we have Indians at home [England], Indians in Cornewall, Indians in Wales, Indians in Ireland'.[22] According to an archdiocesan report from 1743, nearly a third of Yorkshire's Anglican parishes lacked ministers.[23] Not surprisingly, decentralized religious movements that flourished in America often experienced similar success in Britain and Ireland. During the second half of the eighteenth century, Methodist cells meeting in private homes, often under the leadership of devout women, took root wherever established churches were absent or under-represented: northern New England, Virginia's Piedmont, the sugar plantations of the West Indies, rural Wales, and Yorkshire's manufacturing districts. Yet if the problems that beset the colonies differed from those of the metropolis 'in degree rather than in kind', the differences still mattered.[24] Even Anglicans in Britain could draw on institutional resources unavailable to their colonial brethren: ancient schools and universities, large ecclesiastical and charitable endowments, and—in some colonies—legal establishment. (The Church was established in two-thirds of the colonies.)

Compounding these institutional weaknesses was the indifference of colonists who did belong to churches. In Congregational New England such 'horse-shed' Christians accepted the teachings of the Church and attended services with some regularity, but substantial numbers refrained from taking communion, with men in particular postponing full membership until they were in their thirties or forties. In response, many churches adopted the compromise known as the Half-Way Covenant of 1662, which permitted the children of church members who had not yet 'owned the covenant' to become 'half-way' members.[25] One result was to diminish the political and ecclesiastical influence of the seventeenth-century Puritan 'saints', bringing New England's religious culture more closely into line with that of moderate Calvinists elsewhere in the British Atlantic.[26] Another was to feminize the region's churches. Because women continued to become full members just before or after marriage, nearly every Congregational

---

[22] Quoted in Carla Gardina Pestana, 'Religion', in David Armitage and Michael J. Braddick, eds., *The British Atlantic World, 1500–1800* (New York, 2002), p. 76.

[23] Butler, *Awash in a Sea of Faith*, p. 35.

[24] Pestana, 'Religion', pp. 75–7.

[25] David D. Hall, *Worlds of Wonder, Days of Judgment: Popular Religious Belief in Early New England* (Cambridge, Mass., 1989), pp. 15–17, 117–65.

[26] See Richard Sher, *Church and University in the Scottish Enlightenment* (Princeton, 1985).

church in New England had membership rolls with a female majority by the early eighteenth century.[27]

Still another challenge to Christian authority was popular belief in the occult. Although the massive literature on New England's seventeenth-century witch trials provides good reason to treat reports of popular occultism with scepticism, the ubiquity of statutes against witchcraft and other dark arts is a reminder that British Americans inhabited a world of imagined wonders.[28] Colonial records are full of people like the Pennsylvania German Simon Graf, who 'dealt in witchcraft and the exorcism of devils'; the Boston publisher Nathaniel Ames, who used astrological predictions of the future to boost sales of his almanac; and the Newport, Rhode Island, woman whom Ezra Stiles claimed sold urine cakes for divining.[29] Although British colonists believed themselves immune to Indian and African black magic, they were also keenly aware of the 'superstitions' prevalent among non-Europeans living in their midst.[30] The Indian raids that beset New England after 1676 probably heightened colonists' fears of Satanism, contributing to the witchcraft accusations that crested at Salem in 1692.[31]

In addition to these internal challenges, Protestants throughout the English-speaking Atlantic feared Catholicism. Although Europe's Catholic revival did not directly affect British America, the colonies gave refuge to thousands of European Protestants with first-hand experience of the French Revocation of the Edict of Nantes (1685), Louis XIV's wartime devastation of the German Palatinate, and the German emperor Charles VI's expulsion of the Salzburgers and Moravians.[32] Such events suggested a life-and-death struggle between 'the pure *Religion of Jesus*'—as the Presbyterian Samuel Davies told the militia of Hanover County, Virginia, in 1755—and the forces of 'Ignorance, Superstition, Idolatry, Tyranny over conscience, Massacre, Fire and Sword and all the Mischiefs beyond Expression, with which Popery

---

[27] Bonomi, *Under the Cope of Heaven*, pp. 111–15.

[28] John Demos, 'Underlying Themes in the Witchcraft of Seventeenth-Century New England', *American Historical Review*, LXXV (1970), pp. 1311–26; Hall, *Worlds of Wonder*, pp. 114–16.

[29] Butler, *Awash in a Sea of Faith*, pp. 87–8.

[30] Joyce E. Chaplin, *Subject Matter: Technology, the Body, and Science on the Anglo-American Frontier, 1500–1676* (Cambridge, Mass., 2001).

[31] Mary Beth Norton, *In the Devil's Snare: The Salem Witchcraft Crisis of 1692* (New York, 2002).

[32] Linda Colley, *Britons: Forging the Nation, 1707–1837* (New Haven, 1992), p. 23; W. R. Ward, *The Protestant Evangelical Awakening* (Cambridge, 1992).

is pregnant'.³³ Although Davies was thinking in military terms, the struggle with Catholicism was also a battle for souls, one in which Protestant missions to the unchurched peoples of British America had a vital role to play.

Taken together, British America's weak religious institutions, widespread indifference, and popular belief in the occult meant that ministers who took up residence as parish clergy found it necessary to adopt proselytizing roles conventionally associated with missionary activity. Meanwhile, the vulnerability felt by Protestants everywhere made such challenges seem all the more urgent. Speaking in the mid-1750s of Pennsylvania's substantial German population, William Smith of Philadelphia warned that the colony's shortage of Lutheran and Reformed ministers made would-be parishioners 'liable to be seduced by every enterprizing Jesuit, having almost no Protestant Clergy among them to put them on their Guard, and warn them against Popery'.³⁴ As an opponent of the colony's Quaker oligarchy, the Anglican Smith had partisan reasons for impugning the loyalty of immigrants who supported the ruling party's candidates at the polls. But many Germans shared his concerns. The journals of the Lutheran pastor Henry Muhlenberg, who emigrated to Pennsylvania in 1742, contain numerous accounts of false prophets and the congregations they duped into supporting them.³⁵ George Whitefield warned a Philadelphia congregation in 1746, 'the rod is yet hanging over us'. Given the reality of irreligion at home and militant Catholicism abroad, Britain's only hope was 'a national reformation' that brought all its people, 'with one heart, *to observe GOD's Statutes, and keep his Laws*'.³⁶

The Protestant Awakening

By the 1740s Protestants throughout the British Empire were experiencing a reformation of sorts, a broad-based, multi-confessional revival driven in part by the activities of mission societies and evangelical networks dedicated to spreading the gospel both at home and in foreign parts. This awakening was not confined to the colonies, nor was it the exclusive preserve of evangelicals like Whitefield. In the Highlands, the Scottish SPCK—founded in 1709 as the

---

[33] Samuel Davies, *Religion and Patriotism the Constituents of a Good Soldier* (London, 1756), pp. 19–20.

[34] [William Smith] *A Brief State of the Province of Pennsylvania* (London, 1756), p. 17.

[35] Bonomi, *Under the Cope of Heaven*, p. 77.

[36] George Whitefield, *Britain's Mercies, and Britain's Duties* (1746), in Ellis Sandoz, ed., *Political Sermons of the American Founding Era, 1730–1805* (Indianapolis, 1991), p. 135.

Presbyterian Church of Scotland's counterpart to the eponymous society in England and the colonies—supported 176 schools by the 1750s, offering instruction in Protestant Christianity and the English language to nearly 6,500 Gaelic-speaking pupils.[37] The English SPCK achieved similar results in Wales, where it combined English-language instruction with the provision of Bibles in the native tongue.[38] Although the Great Awakening that swept the American colonies during the 1740s and 1750s was probably the best-known phase of this revival, its roots were both transatlantic and interdenominational, and they reached back into the closing decades of seventeenth century. The Christianizing of British America also owed more than is sometimes realized to Anglican organizations and activities.

The London-based SPG was the wealthiest and most powerful. Although the Society's founder, Thomas Bray, insisted that its purpose was not 'to intermeddle, where Christianity under any form has obtained Possession', its Anglican missionaries clashed repeatedly with Dissenters, who were numerically superior in every colony outside the Chesapeake.[39] The most dramatic conflicts occurred in New England, where the SPG built churches, forced colonial legislatures to grant Anglicans toleration, and—during the famous (or notorious) coup of 1722—induced Timothy Cutler, the Congregational rector of Yale College, to conform to the Church of England, together with two students and four nearby Congregational ministers.[40] Despite its associations with polite society, Anglicanism proved especially successful in New England's outlying districts and among the poor, prompting New Hampshire's governor John Wentworth to claim that, 'if the Church service was performed without Expense or any zealous attempts to proselyte, the People would naturally flock to it'.[41] SPG missionaries were also active in the Middle Colonies, the Lower South, and the West Indies, where they took an early lead in evangelizing both white settlers and enslaved Africans. On eve of the Revolution, Anglicans belonged to the fastest-growing colonial church, and the only one that could claim a presence from Newfoundland to the Lesser Antilles.

---

[37] T. C. Smout, *A History of the Scottish People, 1560–1830* (Glasgow, 1969), pp. 434, 436.
[38] Paul Langford, *A Polite and Commercial People: England, 1727–1783* (Oxford, 1989), p. 281.
[39] Thomas Bray, *A Memorial Representing the Present State of Religion on the Continent of North-America*, IX, quoted in Woolverton, *Colonial Anglicanism*, p. 88.
[40] Carl Bridenbaugh, *The Mitre and the Sceptre: Transatlantic faiths, Ideas, Personalities, and Politics, 1689–1775* (New York, 1962), pp. 68–77.
[41] Quoted in Woolverton, *Colonial Anglicanism*, p. 202.

Although the SPCK was a less sectarian body, its impact was equally widespread. As an indication of its multi-confessional character, the Society maintained close ties with its Scottish Presbyterian affiliate and helped sustain a German-based network that included the pietist theologian August Herrmann Francke of the University of Halle, the Lutheran mission at Tranquebar in south India, and the Salzburgers and Moravians who sought refuge in Georgia during the 1730s.[42] 'Casting my eye on a mapp of the world,' remarked the New England-born secretary of the SPCK Henry Newman in 1719, 'I [can] not help observing that Germany is near the centre of the extreams of the known habitable parts of our globe, and consequently by her situation the fittest country to invigorate the most distant nations with the most important truths.'[43] Anglicans were among the chief beneficiaries of this network. As the Jacobite rumours that haunted its early years suggest, the Society was a particular favourite of high-church Anglicans and Tories, among them Samuel Wesley and his Methodist sons Charles and John.[44] In 1718 Yale's acceptance of an unsolicited gift of books from the SPCK foreshadowed the apostasy of Timothy Cutler four years later. By the final decade of the eighteenth century the Society had founded fifty lending libraries in the colonies and sent an additional 34,000 volumes for distribution in North America and Bermuda, many by English churchmen.[45]

None of British America's dissenting churches and denominations matched these Anglican efforts in geographical reach or institutional coherence. During the SPG's initial forays, Congregationalists in New England sought closer ties with dissenting churches in London. As their numbers grew, Scottish, Irish, and German immigrants made similar efforts to stay in contact with synods, classes, and consistories in Europe. More often than not, though, such collaboration produced disagreement and, occasionally, schism. Although English Dissenters sympathized with their New England brethren, they also lectured them on the need to respect the 'Liberty of Conscience' of other Protestants, especially Quakers and Anglicans.[46] In a similar fashion, Scots Irish settlers who began migrating to Pennsylvania during the 1720s adhered to an Irish 'Old Side' Presbyterianism whose

---

[42] Ward, *Protestant Evangelical Awakening*, 302–14; Stephen Neill, *A History of Christianity in India, 1707–1858* (Cambridge, 1985), pp. 33–4, 41, 48.
[43] Quoted in Ward, *Protestant Evangelical Awakening*, p. 303.
[44] Ibid., pp. 304–5, 309.
[45] Woolverton, *Colonial Anglicanism*, p. 31.
[46] Bridenbaugh, *Mitre and Sceptre*, p. 64.

emphasis on 'local autonomy' and 'tolerance of nonessential differences' clashed with the more hierarchical, doctrinaire principles of the Church's increasingly evangelical Scottish and American clergy.[47] Between 1741 and 1758 the two factions split, with Gilbert Tennent and the evangelicals establishing their own synod at New York and college at Princeton. Even after the schism was healed, New Side evangelicals sought to limit the influence of Old Side faculty at the College of New Jersey, and in 1773 they persuaded the Philadelphia Synod to pass a 'non-importation act', effectively barring Irish clergy from Pennsylvania pulpits without the body's approval. In western Pennsylvania, where Scots Irish churches predominated, the controversy ensured that for a time three counties had no settled ministers at all.[48]

If they lacked Anglicanism's centralized, disciplined organization, Dissenters wielded two countervailing advantages during the revivals of the 1740s and 1750s. The first was a set of ecclesiastical structures that permitted local self-government and the ordination of ministers in the colonies. Unlike the Church of England, which had 'commissaries' instead of bishops and whose priests had to cross the Atlantic to be ordained by the Bishop of London, dissenting churches in British America possessed full rights of ordination and governance. As a result, Congregationalists, Presbyterians, Lutherans, and (after 1771) Dutch Reformed churches were able to replicate the essential features of their respective hierarchies in America, including schools, academies, and—by the middle decades of the eighteenth century—colleges. As the Presbyterian schism of 1741 showed, such ecclesiastical powers were occasionally the source of discord, but by the time of the American Revolution the largest colonial denominations were remarkably self-sufficient, maintaining ties to co-religionists in Europe while supplying their own clergy and settling their own rules and regulations. 'We are a Rope of Sand,' complained the Anglican Henry Caner in 1763: 'there is no union, no authority among us; we cannot even summon a Convention for united Counsell and advance, while the Dissenting ministers have their Monthly, Quarterly, and Annual Associations, Conventions, &c., to advise, assist, and support each other.'[49]

The Dissenters' other advantage was their receptivity to itinerant preaching. As the prosecution of the Connecticut evangelical James Davenport for

---

[47] Elizabeth I. Nybakken, 'New Light on the Old Side: Irish Influences on Colonial Presbyterianism', *Journal of American History*, LXVIII (1982), p. 820.
[48] Ibid., pp. 826–8.
[49] Quoted in Butler, *Awash in a Sea of Faith*, p. 197.

itinerancy showed, moderate Dissenters had little tolerance for revivalists who 'boast[ed] in another man's line' by preaching without licence.[50] Yet most evangelicals embraced itinerancy in one form or another. The most famous example was the 'Grand Itinerant' George Whitefield, who, despite his Anglican ordination and Oxford degree, opposed the Church of England's commissaries by preaching in colonial parishes without their permission, held open-air meetings that reportedly attracted as many as 30,000 people, and helped found the Methodist movement whose American branch split off in 1784 as an independent denomination.[51] Following the American Revolution, Methodist and Baptist itinerants perfected Whitefield's techniques, making theirs the fastest-growing denominations in the English-speaking Atlantic and displacing Anglicanism as the dominant church south of Pennsylvania. Unlike the Church of England's well-funded missionaries, such men typically supported themselves, maintaining farms while preaching to all that would listen.[52] As the SPG missionary Charles Woodmason complained of his frontier parish in South Carolina during the 1760s, the entire backcountry seemed to be 'eaten up by Itinerant Teachers, Preachers, and Impostors from New England and Pennsylvania—Baptists, New Lights, Presbyterians, Independents, and an hundred other Sects'.[53]

Despite their many differences, participants in British America's mid-century revivals shared a number of characteristics. The first was a pervasive willingness to be 'peddlers of divinity', and to use the British Atlantic's expanding markets to spread the gospel.[54] With their portable hierarchies and embrace of itinerancy, Dissenters were especially well suited to commercialized forms of evangelism. As Susan O'Brien has shown, the British and American revivals of the mid-eighteenth century created a 'transatlantic community of saints'—an evangelical network bound together by letters, published sermons, newspaper and magazine literature, and long-distance travel. The United Concert of Prayer, which originated during the 1730s in Scotland and England and which Jonathan Edwards helped turn into a day of thanksgiving throughout Britain's Atlantic empire, was probably the

[50] Timothy D. Hall, *Contested Boundaries: Itinerancy and the Reshaping of the Colonial American Religious World* (Durham, NC, 1994), p. 20.

[51] Woolverton, *Colonial Anglicanism*, p. 194.

[52] Raymond W. Albright, *A History of the Protestant Episcopal Church* (New York, 1964), p. 148.

[53] Quoted in Hall, *Contested Boundaries*, p. 129.

[54] Frank Lambert, *'Pedlar in Divinity': George Whitefield and the Trans-Atlantic Revivals, 1737–1770* (Princeton, 1994).

network's best-known achievement. The interconnectedness of British evangelicalism was also evident in the passages that Nicholas Gilman read to his Durham, New Hampshire, parishioners from the *Glasgow Weekly History*; the transatlantic donations raised during the 1740s and 1750s for Whitefield's Georgia Orphan House and Tennent's College of New Jersey; and the London Spa Fields Tabernacle hymn from 1742 that proclaimed 'Great things in England, Wales and Scotland wrought | And in America to pass are brought.'[55] Although Anglicanism's legal establishment made it less dependent on commercial networks, its ministers in New England and the middle colonies freely participated in this marketplace of creeds, soliciting donations for schools and missions, distributing literature through the SPCK, and competing for souls with the colonies' other churches and denominations.

The second defining characteristic of British America's Protestant missions and evangelical networks was a growing attachment to—and, often, reverence for—ecclesiastical authority. In none of the colonial denominations that experienced awakenings during the eighteenth century did lay revivalists and movements gain more than a temporary advantage. Except for the Baptists, evangelical leaders were invariably ordained ministers, whose jeremiads on the 'danger[s] of an unconverted ministry' (to quote Tennent's famous schism-producing sermon) did not mean they were in any way anticlerical.[56] Indeed, most revivals strengthened the position of their denominations' clergy and of the synods, conventions, and associations charged with supervising them. When interlopers preached doctrines with which they disagreed, evangelical clergy could be as disparaging of itinerancy as their Anglican opponents. In 1779 the Presbytery of Hanover, Virginia, founded twenty years earlier by the itinerant Samuel Davies, warned that its parishioners were in danger of being 'utterly lost by the prevalency...of many ignorant and irreligious sectaries'.[57] Even Baptists, whom students of American religion depict as typifying the eighteenth-century revivals' democratic tendencies, tried to keep popular enthusiasm within the bounds of denominational authority. Such constraints were also evident in the Society of Friends' Yearly Meetings, which, despite the Quakers' well-known toleration and anticlericalism, sought to establish mandatory positions for the

---

[55] Susan O'Brien, 'A Transatlantic Community of Saints: The Great Awakening and the First Evangelical Network, 1735–1755', *American Historical Review*, XCIX (1986), pp. 811, 828–31.

[56] Gilbert Tennent, *The Danger of an Unconverted Ministry* (Philadelphia, 1740).

[57] Howard Miller, *The Revolutionary College: American Presbyterian Higher Education, 1707–1837* (New York, 1976), p. 120.

society's 300 meetings on the conduct proper for Christians in times of war, the payment of taxes in support of military activities, and the abolition of slavery.[58]

Occasionally evangelical ministers even used the rituals of popular magic to buttress their authority, adopting the personae of 'holy men' with charismatic, supernatural powers. In the case of Whitefield, whose corpse became an object of veneration for Methodists who visited his tomb in Newburyport, Massachusetts, during the later eighteenth and early nineteenth centuries, this quasi-apotheosis occurred without his endorsement. On the other hand, Gilbert Tennent and his brothers freely claimed to have witnessed miracles, entered into altered states, and come face to face with the Devil. Although consistent with the prophetic traditions of the Old Testament and the early Church, such claims were also meant to appeal to would-be converts who, to varying degrees, still believed in magic and the occult. Satirizing this conjunction, Benjamin Franklin's *General Magazine* likened both Whitefield and the Tennents to 'Holy Necromancers'; one of Gilbert Tennent's Old Side critics was sure he had 'some cunning Art, beyond what is common to Man'.[59]

At the time of the American Revolution the effects of this Protestant revival were evident in every part of British America except predominantly Catholic Grenada and Quebec. With half a million members each, the Anglican Church and the Congregational Standing Orders were the largest mainland denominations, possessing 480 and 658 churches respectively. In New York, Pennsylvania, and New Jersey the Presbyterian Church, whose overall numbers had grown from a dozen congregations at the start of the eighteenth century to 543 churches with 400,000 adherents, was the largest denomination (and third largest in North America), while Baptists already had 498 churches, chiefly in New England and the South.[60] (In the colonies that became the United States there were about 25,000 Catholics with fifty churches in 1776, and perhaps 1,500 Jews.[61]) Only in the West Indies did Anglicans hold undisputed sway, although Methodists, Moravians, and Baptists were starting to gain converts.[62] To varying degrees, each denomination in this expansion benefited from the revival that Whitefield helped initiate, including the Church of England. American Protestants in 1776

---

[58] Butler, *Awash in a Sea of Faith*, pp. 272–3.   [59] Ibid., pp. 182–6, 188.
[60] Reich, *Colonial America*, pp. 212, 218–19, 221.   [61] Ibid., p. 223.
[62] Andrew Jackson O'Shaughnessy, *An Empire Divided: The American Revolution and the British Caribbean* (Philadelphia, 2000), pp. 29–31.

were more likely to be church members than their ancestors one hundred years earlier; their affiliations bound them as never before into a transatlantic community of missionaries and evangelicals, synods and bishops, colleges and universities, associations and councils.

African Americans

In most of British America—especially the plantation colonies of the Chesapeake, the Lower South, and the West Indies—the Protestant revival included Africans and creoles, most of whom were enslaved. The hundreds of thousands of Africans transported to the colonies after the mid-seventeenth century came from societies with their own belief systems, some based on Islam, others on religions indigenous to West Africa. Unlike Indians, whose religions persisted and, in some cases, flourished after European contact, Africans found the Middle Passage profoundly disruptive, sundering families, destroying religious hierarchies, and mixing language and ethnic groups. The details of this 'spiritual holocaust' varied considerably from place to place. In parts of North America and the West Indies, the existence of substantial populations of 'Coromantees' (the English name for the Akan peoples of present-day Ghana) enabled slaves to re-create West African obeah communities, replete with priests ('obeahmen'), coronation rituals (*ikem*), and military leaders, or 'captains'.[63] As John Thornton has shown, all three featured prominently in acts of slave resistance, including slave conspiracies in New York (1712) and Antigua (1736), and Jamaica's long-running Maroon War (1665–1739).[64] Yet, even among apparently stable communities, slavery distorted African religion, and in Virginia and South Carolina, where black majorities were smaller and the possibilities for autonomy fewer, the transformation 'forever destroyed traditional African religious systems as *systems*'.[65]

Despite the possibilities for evangelization, Protestant religious leaders and slave owners responded ambivalently to this crisis. In part, this reluctance to proselytize reflected the assumption that 'slavery was unlawfull for any Christian'—as the SPG's Anthony Gavin wrote in 1738—and that slaves

---

[63] John K. Thornton, 'War, the State, and Religious Norms in "Coromantee" Thought: The Ideology of an African American Nation', in Robert Blair St George, ed., *Possible Pasts: Becoming Colonial in Early America* (Ithaca, NY, 2000), pp. 193–6.

[64] Thornton, 'War, the State, and Religious Norms', pp. 181–200.

[65] Butler, *Awash in a Sea of Faith*, p. 130.

who converted automatically became free.[66] Although colonial legislatures passed laws barring faith-based manumissions from the mid-seventeenth century onward, the association of salvation with freedom continued to worry slaveholders, a group that included George Whitefield and the SPG. Not surprisingly, there were few Christian slaves on the SPG's own estate on Barbados.[67] The Scottish traveller Janet Schaw found a Christmas spent on Antigua in 1774 unsettling for two reasons. The first was the 'universal Jubilee' occasioned by the popular belief that 'the good Buccara God' (i.e. white man's god) would hurt any master who used 'the inhuman whip' against the island's slaves during the festivities; the second was the resulting danger of insurrection. 'It is necessary to keep a lookout during this season of unbounded freedom; and every [white] man on the Island is in arms and patrols go all round the different plantations as well as keep guard in the town.'[68]

Although such tensions remained a conspicuous feature of the Caribbean and North American landscape, two developments helped produce an upsurge in slave Christianization, starting in Virginia during the 1740s and proceeding several decades later in South Carolina and the West Indies. The first was the SPG's repudiation of Christian liberty for the doctrine that slaves owed their masters 'absolute obedience'. As Thomas Bacon observed during the 1740s, slaves were obligated to do whatever their owners commanded as if they 'did it for *God* himself'.[69] Although not all Anglicans accepted this harsh principle, the SPG's emphasis on slave obedience set the dominant tone both for its own clergy and for the Baptists, Methodists, and Presbyterians who inundated the region from the eighteenth century's middle decades. Despite their emphasis on the spiritual equality of all humanity, even Moravians preached submission for the Christian slaves who worked on their settlements in North Carolina.[70] Consequently, slave conversion came to seem much less threatening to colonial planters. Only in the West Indies (and only at the century's end) did evangelicals become an abolitionist phalanx. Yet on the eve of slavery's abolition, the humanitarian-

[66] Bonomi, *Under the Cope of Heaven*, p. 119.
[67] Philip D. Morgan, 'The Black Experience in the British Empire, 1680–1810', *OHBE* II, p. 482.
[68] Evangeline Walker Andrews and Charles McLean Andrews, eds., *Journal of a Lady of Quality* (New Haven, 1934), pp. 108–9.
[69] Quoted in Butler, *Awash in a Sea of Faith*, p. 142.
[70] Jon E. Sensbach, *A Separate Canaan: The Making of an Afro-Moravian World in North Carolina, 1763–1840* (Chapel Hill, NC, 1998).

ism of evangelicals like William Knibb of Jamaica and Antigua's Anne and Elizabeth Hart remained suspect in the eyes of many Protestants, including evangelical missionary societies in Britain and the islands' Anglican clergy.[71]

The second development was the growing receptivity to Protestant Christianity among British American blacks, especially second- and third-generation creoles, who were more likely to speak English, live in families, and have ties to local communities. Although their numbers defy precise measurement, Philip Morgan has estimated that during the final quarter of the eighteenth century blacks accounted for a third of Virginia's Baptists and a quarter of Nova Scotia's Methodists; by the century's end nearly a third of the Leeward Islands' slaves were Christian.[72] Because African Americans worshipped with whites into the early nineteenth century, the religion that grew out of this expansion was less distinctive than would later be the case, yet, even during these early years, blacks in both North America and the Caribbean accepted Christianity selectively. Because of their roles as 'religious specialists' in African traditions, women often assumed important leadership roles, ministering to the sick, maintaining church discipline, and encouraging revivals.[73] The distinctiveness of African American Protestantism was also evident in attitudes to death. Not only did slaves retain African notions of the funeral as 'the true climax of life', celebrating burials with dancing, singing, drumming, and feasting, but they adapted Christian notions of the afterlife to their own. Some thought the dead returned to Africa; others envisioned an ascent to heaven accompanied by African-style spirit guides.[74] According to Mechal Sobel, African death rituals and reverence for ancestors even influenced white religion, encouraging Southern Baptists and Methodists to reconceptualize heaven as a place of reunion 'with those we love' and to make deathbeds into scenes of ecstatic happiness and joy.[75]

---

[71] Catherine Hall, 'William Knibb and the Constitution of the New Black Subject', in Martin Daunton and Rick Halpern, eds., *Empire and Others: British Encounters with Indigenous People, 1600–1850* (Philadelphia, 1999), pp. 308, 311–20; John Salliant, 'Antiguan Methodism and Antislavery Activity', *Church History*, LXIX (2000), pp. 86–115.

[72] Morgan, 'Black Experience', p. 483.

[73] Sylvia R. Frey and Betty Wood, *Come Shouting to Zion: African American Protestantism in the American South and British Caribbean to 1830* (Chapel Hill, NC, 1998).

[74] Morgan, 'Black Experience', pp. 482–3.

[75] Mechal Sobel, *The World they Made Together: Black and White Values in Eighteenth-Century Virginia* (Princeton, 1987), pp. 223–4.

During the early nineteenth century black Christianity increasingly diverged from its white counterparts. In the United States the Baptist and Methodist churches eventually split along racial lines, with African Americans seceding from the latter denomination to form the African Methodist Episcopal Church in Philadelphia in 1816. With the exception of Barbados, where slaves and freedmen and women remained overwhelmingly loyal to the Church of England, the British West Indies followed a similar trajectory.[76] Like their counterparts to the north, black evangelical congregations in the West Indies achieved a measure of freedom from white control. In Jamaica there were two Baptist Churches by the early nineteenth century, one led by white ministers from England and affiliated with the Baptist Missionary Society in Britain, the other a 'native' denomination inspired by African American Baptists who came to Jamaica following the American Revolution. The latter Church played a key role in the Jamaican slave revolt of 1831, which, together with the rebellions on Barbados (1816) and Demerara (1823), helped swing evangelicals in Britain solidly towards emancipation.[77]

The American Revolution

Although the Protestant awakening continued well into the nineteenth century, spreading the gospel to settlers, slaves, and Indians throughout the English-speaking Atlantic, the American Revolution had several far-reaching effects on the revival's shape and character. During the war the Church of England was a favourite target of revolutionary mobs, who denounced its loyalty, defaced its chapels, and lynched its priests. Between 1775 and 1783 nearly two-thirds of the Church's ministers fled, including most of those sponsored by the SPG, and every state that had possessed an Anglican establishment before the Revolution ended the Church's privileged position.[78] On the other hand, evangelicals prospered. Although some groups baulked at severing ties with Britain—especially when, like New England's Baptists, they were a small minority—evangelicals of all stripes eventually flourished amid the civil millennialism of the new republic.

---

[76] Michael Craton, 'The Planters' World in the British West Indies', in Bernard Bailyn and Philip D. Morgan, eds., *Strangers within the Realm* (Chapel Hill, NC, 1991), pp. 360–1.

[77] Hall, 'William Knibb', p. 312.

[78] Eliga H. Gould, 'American Independence and Britain's Counter-Revolution', *Past and Present*, CLIV (Feb. 1997), pp. 107–41; Albright, *A History of the Protestant Episcopal Church*, 123–4.

Notwithstanding these disruptions, the most striking effect of the Revolution was to consolidate and intensify patterns established during the colonial era. In the United States the end of state-supported religion coincided with further efforts to strengthen denominational institutions. In 1784 the Episcopal Church received its first American bishop, Samuel Seabury, consecrated at Aberdeen by the Episcopal Primus of Scotland. With Charles Inglis's appointment as Bishop of Nova Scotia in 1787, the Anglican Communion in North America and the West Indies possessed the same ecclesiastical powers as its dissenting competitors.[79] Meanwhile, American Baptists and Methodists, blending Protestantism and republicanism, sought to curb the autonomy of their congregations and cultivate a hierarchical, respectable evangelicalism. As the history of the Baptist revivals in New England and the Canadian Maritimes shows, such efforts opened fissures between evangelicals in the United States and British North America. Even in the backwoods of Maine, Baptists suppressed their denomination's antinomian, 'primitive' tendencies. In Nova Scotia and New Brunswick, on the other hand, primitivism became the norm, giving rise to a far more 'democratized Christianity and...depoliticized religion'. 'I find none', wrote Joseph Dimock of the Baptists he met in New York and New England, 'that seem to have the life of God so pure in the soul as in Nova Scotia.'[80]

Another of the Revolution's consequences was to facilitate transatlantic collaboration through the creation of American missionary societies aligned with like-minded societies in Britain. Although some of these American ventures perpetuated the colonial tendency to replicate British originals, Protestant denominations in the United States increasingly acted as their own metropoles, working with British counterparts on terms of rough equality. The Boston-based American Board of Commissioners for Foreign Missions (founded in 1810) and the London Missionary Society (1795) cooperated extensively both in the western Pacific and in southern Africa. The same collaborative spirit was evident a generation later in the Young Men's Christian Association, whose first American chapters followed closely

---

[79] Albright, *A History of the Protestant Episcopae Church*, p. 130; Schlenther, 'Religious Faith and Commercial Empire', p. 147.

[80] George A. Rawlyck, '"A Total Revolution in Religious and Civil Government": The Maritimes, New England, and the Evolving Evangelical Ethos, 1776–1812', in Mark A. Noll, David W. Bebbington, and George A. Rawlyk, eds., *Evangelicalism: Comparative Studies of Popular Protestantism in North America, the British Isles, and Beyond, 1700–1990* (Oxford, 1994), pp. 147–50.

on the organization's founding in London (1844).[81] Even when differences interfered, as at the London conference of the Evangelical Alliance (1846) over whether to exclude slaveholders from membership, the differences arose, at least in part, from an awareness of the many commonalities shared by Protestants on both sides of the Atlantic.[82] 'America is still a land of real Protestants,' wrote Thomas Haweis of the London Missionary Society in 1812. '[T]he American colonies [sic] appear, not only rising into a vast consolidated empire, but...are, I hope, destined with us to spread the everlasting gospel to the ends of the earth.'[83]

That Haweis could write these words on the eve of the Anglo-American War of 1812–14 attests to the religious ties that continued to bind the two English-speaking empires, even as his use of the word 'colonies' is a reminder that both the United States and Britain's American colonies remained, in the suggestive words of Charles Cohen, a religious periphery 'imperfectly rendered according to European models'.[84] If the religious history of British America was distinctive, however, its distinctiveness was most apparent in comparisons with Protestantism's European metropole. As George Whitefield's career in 'three countries' suggests, the itinerant evangelism that he helped invent was ideally suited not only to America but also to the unchurched peripheries of Scotland and England—and, eventually, to the greater British frontiers of Africa, India, and Australasia.[85] In religion, as in so many other areas, the much-vaunted 'exceptionalism' of American history turns out to have been anything but exceptional.[86] Even as American denominations established their own metropolitan centres, they remained, in important respects, creatures of Britain's religious periphery. In both capacities, their impact on the British Empire was considerable.

[81] Porter, 'Church History, History of Christianity, Religious History', pp. 572–5.

[82] John Wolffe, 'Anti-Catholicism and Evangelical Identity in Britain and the United States, 1830–1860', in Noll et al., eds., Evangelicalism, pp. 190–1.

[83] Thomas Haweis, A View of the Present State of Evangelical Religion throughout the World (1812), quoted in Andrew Porter, 'North American Experience and British Missionary Encounters in Africa and the Pacific, c.1800–50', in Daunton and Halpern, eds., Empire and Others, p. 348.

[84] Charles L. Cohen, 'The Colonization of British North America as an Episode in the History of Christianity', Church History, LXXII (2003), p. 564.

[85] Harry S. Stout, 'George Whitefield in Three Countries', in Noll et al., eds., Evangelicalism, pp. 58–72.

[86] Joyce E. Chaplin, 'Expansion and Exceptionalism in Early American History', Journal of American History, LXXXIX (2003), pp. 1431–55.

Select Bibliography

JAMES AXTELL, *The Invasion Within: The Contest of Cultures in Colonial North America* (New York, 1985).

RUTH H. BLOCH, *Visionary Republic: Millennial Themes in American Thought, 1756–1800* (Cambridge, 1985).

PATRICIA U. BONOMI, *Under the Cope of Heaven: Religion, Society, and Politics in Colonial America* (Oxford, 1986).

CARL BRIDENBAUGH, *The Mitre and the Sceptre: Transatlantic Faiths, Ideas, Personalities, and Politics, 1689–1775* (New York, 1962).

JON BUTLER, *Awash in a Sea of Faith: Christianizing the American People* (Cambridge, Mass., 1990).

MICHAEL J. CRAWFORD, *Seasons of Grace: Colonial New England's Revival Tradition in its British Context* (New York, 1991).

GREGORY EVANS DOWD, *A Spirited Resistance: The North American Indian Struggle for Unity, 1745–1815* (Baltimore, 1992).

STEPHEN FOSTER, *The Long Argument: English Puritanism and the Shaping of New England Culture, 1570–1700* (Chapel Hill, NC, 1991).

SYLVIA R. FREY and BETTY WOOD, *Come Shouting to Zion: African American Protestantism in the American South and British Caribbean to 1830* (Chapel Hill, NC, 1998).

CATHERINE HALL, *Civilising Subjects: The Place of 'Race' and Empire in the English Imagination* (Cambridge, 2001).

DAVID D. HALL, *Worlds of Wonder, Days of Judgment: Popular Religious Belief in Early New England* (Cambridge, Mass., 1989).

TIMOTHY D. HALL, *Contested Boundaries: Itinerancy and the Reshaping of the Colonial American Religious World* (Durham, NC, 1994).

NATHAN O. HATCH, *The Sacred Cause of Liberty: Republican Thought and the Millennium in Revolutionary New England* (New Haven, 1977).

CHRISTINE LEIGH HEYRMAN, *Southern Cross: The Beginnings of the Bible Belt* (New York, 1997).

SUSAN JUSTER, *Disorderly Women: Sexual Politics and Evangelicalism in Revolutionary New England* (Ithaca, NY, 1994).

FRANK LAMBERT, *Inventing the 'Great Awakening'* (Princeton, 1999).

JOHN T. MCGREEVY, *Catholicism and American Freedom* (New York, 2003).

PHILIP D. MORGAN, *Slave Counterpoint: Black Culture in the Eighteenth-Century Chesapeake and Lowcountry* (Chapel Hill, NC, 1998).

LEIGH ERIC SCHMIDT, *Holy Fairs: Scottish Communions and American Revivals in the Early Modern Period* (Princeton, 1989).

W. R. WARD, *The Protestant Evangelical Awakening* (Cambridge, 1992).

3

An Overview, 1700–1914

ANDREW PORTER

From the beginning of the eighteenth century Christianity expanded as part of British culture and activities overseas on an unprecedented scale. Emigrants and temporary expatriates carried their faith abroad. Anglicans, Presbyterians, Roman Catholics, and members of other denominations recreated their churches, adapting them to new environments. In a parallel movement, driven by voluntary Protestant missionary societies, Christians and the missionaries they supported—some 10,000 by 1900—set out to evangelize or convert the extra-European world. Imperial control, colonial societies, and the missionary movement intertwined in divergent and ambiguous ways.

Home and colonial governments supported ecclesiastical and missionary expansion wherever it was likely to buttress their authority and promote social order. Nevertheless, religious dynamics proved unpredictable and often counter to imperial needs. In the white settlement colonies a religious establishment at first seemed desirable. However, more even than in Britain, the growth of denominational conflict forced governments to conclude that only a policy of religious neutrality would serve their purpose. Finding state support inadequate and constricting, churchmen too distanced themselves from political authorities. By the mid-nineteenth century formal separation of Church and State was occurring, so that religious influences began to shape imperial ties and colonial identities in less obvious ways. Although most imperial authorities initially distrusted missionary enterprise and missions rejected most if not all political involvement, both sides learned gradually that cooperation had its uses. Missions won extensive popular support at home and often acquired considerable influence with non-European communities. They could therefore not be ignored, and might be turned to imperial advantage. Missionaries came to regard secular authorities in a similarly utilitarian way. British missionary enterprise thus sometimes provided channels through which imperial controls followed; at other times it delayed annexation and colonization, or even subverted imperial authority. In many places (sometimes purposely, often unintentionally) Christian churches, British and indigenous, provided powerful stimuli to communal unity and opposition to colonial rule.

I

Eighteenth-century precedents provide many pointers to later links between missions and Empire. At various points, the settlement of North America's affairs required practical answers to serious constitutional and political questions. This was as true at the end of the seventeenth century, when the Society for Promoting Christian Knowledge (1698) and the Society for the Propagation of the Gospel (1701) were founded, as during America's fight for independence. Key questions centred on securing British sovereignty, respect for continued British colonial rule, and loyal acceptance of political obligations, without exciting colonial discontents. British leaders treated political radicalism as inseparable from religious dissent. Not surprisingly, solutions to the problems at home and throughout the Empire aimed to reinforce ties between religion, especially the established Church of England, and the State. As the SPG's charter explained,

in many of our Plantacons, Colonies, and Factories beyond the Seas... the Provision for Ministers is very mean. And many others... are wholly destitute, and unprovided of a Mainteynance for Ministers, and the Publick Worship of God; and for Lack of... such, many... doe want the Administration of God's Word and Sacraments, and seem to be abandoned to Atheism and Infidelity and alsoe for Want of Learned and Orthodox Ministers to instruct Our... Subjects in the Principles of true Religion, divers Romish Preists and Jesuits are the more incouraged to pervert and draw over Our said Loving Subjects to Popish Superstition and Idolatry.[1]

Although the charter did not explicitly mention indigenous peoples—North America's Indians—or black slaves, the term 'subjects' meant for many in the Society more than simply white emigrants and settlers. The Dean of Lincoln explained in 1702,

The design is, in the first place, to settle the State of Religion as well as may be among our *own People* there... and then to proceed... towards the *Conversion* of

---

[1] C. F. Pascoe, *Two Hundred Years of the S.P.G.*, 2 vols. (London, 1901), II, p. 932.

the *Natives*.... this is... the greatest Charity we can show... especially... to the souls of many of those *poor Natives* who may by this be converted from that state of *Barbarism* and *Idolatry* in which they now live.[2]

Equally direct concerns were expressed for the colonial slave population. The early Instructions for the missionaries set out the desired approach via 'natural religion' to instructing '*Heathens* and *Infidels*'. 'Native' was increasingly and explicitly taken to include both the Indian peoples of North America and the imported African slave population and its descendants throughout the Caribbean and the Atlantic world.

William Knox, a member of the SPG and Under-Secretary of State for the Colonies (1770–82), asserted in 1786 that 'the Prevalence of the Church of England in those Colonies is the best security that Great Britain can have for their Fidelity and attachment to her Constitution and Interests'.[3] Archbishop Secker felt

we ought to have more [missionaries] upon the frontiers; at least when it shall please God to bless us with a peace. For Missionaries there might counteract the artifices of the French Papists; and do considerable services, religious and political at once, amongst the neighbouring Indians; both which points the Society hath been heavily charged, on occasion of the present war, with having neglected.[4]

Ministers and bishops increasingly regretted their earlier limited attention to the religious life of the colonies. They moved after 1782 to provide ecclesiastical leadership for Anglicans remaining in the United States, while in neighbouring Quebec and the Maritimes, which had received more than 30,000 loyalist refugees, entrenchment of an officially supported Anglicanism was also regarded as constitutionally essential and a wise response to local needs.

However, it is easy to exaggerate the integration of Empire and Anglican missions. Congregations and clergy suffered from inadequate organization, lack of leadership, and limited resources. The Bishop of London's Commissary in Pennsylvania pointed out that

The members of our Church are not the Richest in the Place, the Riches generally centering in the Quakers & High Dutch who are very numerous & carry all before

---

[2] C. F. Pascoe, *Two Hundred Years of the S.P.G.*, 2 vols. (London, 1901), I, pp. 7–8.

[3] Vincent T. Harlow, *The Founding of the Second British Empire 1763–1793*, 2 vols. (London, 1964), II, p. 738.

[4] Frank J. Klingberg, *Anglican Humanitarianism in Colonial New York* (Philadelphia, 1940), p. 93.

them, and our Church labours under very great discouragement as we have no legal Establishment (as they have at New York) not so much as a Charter of Incorporation to enable us to manage our Business to the best advantage.[5]

Wariness, mingled with indifference to the SPG and its concerns, was the predominant attitude among officials in London. In their eyes the overwhelmingly Protestant character of British North America sufficiently guaranteed that colonial ambitions would restrict French territorial expansion. To provoke colonial religious dissent or domestic political conflict by favouring Anglicanism, even an Anglicanism stripped of its civil powers, seemed both unnecessarily provocative and politically unwise. Capturing the often easygoing expediency of the day, one governor observed of Pennsylvania's Germans, 'They fled from oppression, and after having tasted the sweets of a British Constitution, it does not seem probable to me that they will ever look back to their old masters.'[6]

Official imperial detachment from Anglican missionary ambition was modified only temporarily in particular circumstances related to Indians and colonial security. SPG efforts among the Mohawk were ignored until threat of war made their alliance strategically valuable. Then Sir William Johnson (British Commissioner for Indian Affairs, 1744–74) and the SPG missionary John Ogilvie (1749–62) worked together on New England's frontier to secure their loyalty in the Seven Years War, believing that conversion and support for the British went together, as on this occasion they did. However, as Pontiac's War of 1763–4 demonstrated, professed Protestantism and missionary contacts failed to stop treaties being broken by both sides. For some time after 1763 no more official imperial enthusiasm was shown for either Indian missions or episcopacy.

Not until the 1780s, when the imperial government found itself strategically caught between Roman Catholic dissent in Nova Scotia, Quebec's staunchly Catholic French Canadians, and the newly independent United States, did it again seek support through missionary expansion of the established Church. With the white colonists and the need to counterbalance Roman Catholicism uppermost in mind, it created bishoprics in Nova Scotia (1787) and Quebec (1793). However, local pressure for another diocese in Upper Canada was refused, and insufficient provision was made for the costs

---

[5] W. S. Perry, ed., *Historical Collections Relating to the American Colonial Church*, 5 vols. (New York, 1870–8), II, p. 260.

[6] Ibid., p. 256.

of religious establishment. The Canada Act 1791 provided only an initial endowment on the assumption that self-sufficient religious hierarchies would develop their own endowments and facilities for training local clergymen with help from colonial assemblies and local congregations.

In principle, therefore, new or revived colonial churches, combining parochial and missionary work, increasingly under the leadership of colonial bishops, were acknowledged as useful adjuncts to the civil authorities, who relied on them to underpin the imperial connection, to provide moral leadership, social cohesion, and education on a scale suited to individual colonies. This pattern of Church–State relations, framed for British North America between 1784 and 1793, was adapted throughout the colonial Empire up to the 1830s—in Calcutta (1814), and Jamaica and Barbados (1824). Supervision of Dissenters was left to the colonial authorities. Nevertheless, where populations were small, resources to support Anglican expansion more limited, and governors' powers far greater, as at the Cape and in New South Wales, imperial governments remained content with even scantier provision.

Applied unevenly, imperial principle also encountered resistance. The endowment of Protestant clergy with reserved lands, and preference for the Church of England, aimed to counterbalance the well-endowed Roman Catholic hierarchy of Quebec and to stall the progress of dissent and irreligion. Yet in every colony the mushrooming reality of denominational diversity was inescapable. Many migrant loyalists were Presbyterians or Dissenters, as were emigrants from Britain to the Canadian provinces; the religious affiliations of convicts transported to the Australian colonies were equally varied, including Roman Catholicism. Anglican self-assertion only stimulated political conflict with the denominationalism it hoped to marginalize. An articulate colonial alternative to the Anglican linking of imperial Church and State underpinned with missionary enterprise was thus elaborated, first again in British North America, then elsewhere.

In colonial North America, Baptists, Congregationalists, and Presbyterians were still less inclined than the SPG to push their missionary work beyond the boundaries of the white communities. Focusing on the close community of the religiously like-minded requiring a minister's constant attention, they were neither theologically nor institutionally committed to evangelism. The potential for revival within existing nominally Protestant communities took priority over incorporation of non-Christian peoples into the Christian world. Limited resources compelled missions to select the most promising sites, as both the Moravians from the 1730s onwards and Methodist communities superintended by Francis Asbury and Thomas Coke after 1770 demonstrated. Many people felt that Methodist rules against slavery had already demonstrated excessive partiality towards Africans, and the resentment these bred only contributed to increase hostility and resentment on the part of the colonists against Wesleyans themselves.[7] Asbury's political sense was sufficiently acute to appreciate that greater efforts to evangelize enslaved Africans could endanger the entire Methodist enterprise.

By 1790 it was widely felt that the results of nearly a century of British Protestant missionary activity had been disappointingly slight. Practical experience with evangelistic work among the heathen had bred pessimism everywhere. Nevertheless, from the confused patchwork of ecclesiastical structures and personnel, and the varied stock of theologies and missionary strategies, there were lessons to be learnt. Irrespective of denomination, missionary interests had carried little weight in contests with other agents of empire—settlers, merchants, local assemblies, colonial agents, imperial politicians—to shape the character of Empire and management of colonial society. The SPG struggled as the missionary wing of the established Church in colonial contexts. Its experience demonstrated that attempts to tie missionary enterprise to the interests of the imperial government were likely to falter. The imperial government's commitment was fickle, too vulnerable to shifting political assessments of domestic or colonial demands, and too reluctant to increase ecclesiastical power and resources, even for a national Church to rely on the secular power to sustain its missionary activities. Dissenters had long known this, and found their influence over government policies further declining after mid-century. Anglicans increasingly feared the same, and therefore began to look for alternative models of Anglican missionary enterprise.

Dissenters and Nonconformists, expecting less from colonial or imperial authorities, often felt less constrained than the SPG clergy. However, their missionary efforts suffered as much as the SPG's from a lack of effective 'denominational' or overall control. Methodists hoped to balance religious freedom and ecclesiastical order in a system of itinerant preachers, circuit organization, and annual conferences. However, where the source of missionary initiative and regulation of missionary activity should lie in such a system remained obscure. Thomas Coke found that denominational

---

[7] *The Journal and Letters of Francis Asbury*, 3 vols. (London, 1958), I, pp. 488, 498.

prejudice or inertia could easily scupper individual initiative, even though he remained a thorn in the denominational flesh. Moravians insisted on firm, even dictatorial, control of their missionaries, but undermined their policy through their requirement that every mission station be self-sufficient.

Thus eighteenth-century missionary endeavour was overwhelmingly influenced by the vagaries of individual inclination, subject only to the limited power of such central organization and authority as existed. All evangelical communities struggled to recruit missionary volunteers and prepare them for the field (if special preparation was thought necessary, which commonly it was not). Nowhere could there be found a coherent theology or practical strategy for promoting Christian missions.

II

After 1780 enthusiasts sought more purposefully to solve these intellectual and practical problems. Many Anglicans had concluded that their Church lacked both the efficiency and sympathy required for missionary enterprise. The SPCK and SPG had financed plenty of colonial clergy, garrison chaplains, and schoolmasters for Britons overseas, but missionary work with indigenous peoples remained primarily the incidental product of personal initiatives by 'pious chaplains', such as David Brown in India. Such efforts never matched those of the Moravians or the Methodists, and were rapidly overshadowed by the voluntary lay missionary societies that sprang up in the 1790s: the Baptist Missionary Society (1792); the London Missionary Society (LMS; 1795, originally non-denominational but eventually Congregational); and the Anglican Church Missionary Society (CMS; 1799). Methodists extended their operations, and the Glasgow and Edinburgh societies were both formed in 1796. Everywhere lay and Nonconformist activity was remarkable. The evangelical businessman Henry Thornton observed of the LMS in 1795,

what a striking thing it is that a Bishop of London [Beilby Porteous] is hardly able...to scrape a few hundred Pounds together for the missionary Plans in his hands among all the people of the Church Establishment & that £10,000 should be raised in such a few days by the Irregulars who are also so much poorer a Class of People than the others.[8]

---

[8] John Walsh, Colin Haydon, and Stephen Taylor, eds., *The Church of England c.1689–c.1833* (Oxford, 1993), p. 247.

The institutional Anglican Church was slow to act: lay missionaries smacked of 'Methodism' or the embarrassing and dangerous excesses of religious 'enthusiasm', and were disliked for their low educational and social standing. Moreover, objections were raised against missions to non-Europeans on practical and theological grounds, including supposed threats to imperial security from colonial subjects provoked by proselytization.

Nonetheless, by 1840 missions not only had impressively extended Britain's global presence, but had won widespread public acceptance and even official support. The CMS's early reliance on German Lutherans had given way to steady recruiting of men less likely to attract scorn. Its income averaged £58,655 per annum, derived from a wide social and geographical area. Overseas the LMS was well established in the western Pacific and South Africa, the CMS in Sierra Leone and India, the Baptists in Bengal and the West Indian colonies. Methodist and Presbyterian missions were also similarly scattered and poised for a new phase of expansion.

There is no simple causal connection in this period between religious expansion and Britain's imperial outreach. It is difficult not to be struck by the insignificance of Empire in many evangelical minds, whose thinking was dominated by the concept of an all-embracing, superintending Providence unfolding a Divine plan for the world. Although there was a certain mystery about the operations of Providence, the French and American revolutions, European wars and economic disruption provided abundant scope for millenarian speculations, based on their supposed congruence with eschatological signs in the Bible's prophetic books. In 1793 the newly founded *Evangelical Review* was in bullish mood:

That there is a time of peace, prosperity, and purity awaiting all the nations of the earth, appears evident from the prophecies and promises in the sacred Scriptures ... from a serious attention to the *signs of the times*, we may indulge the hope that this grand jubilee is at hand. The present period is a crisis replete with great events.... It seems evident that the time will come, when there will not be one nation remaining in the world, which shall not embrace the Christian religion.[9]

The new missionary societies set out to engage with Catholics in Ireland and continental Europe. The LMS and the CMS played crucial parts from 1801 in the formation of the London Society for Promoting Christianity amongst the Jews (1809). 'All three conversions, of heathens, Jews and Catholics were

---

[9] *Evangelical Magazine*, I (Oct. 1793), pp. 157–8, 162.

held together in a web of prophetic interpretation. All three, in some manner, would accompany the Second Coming and the millennium.'[10] Although Baptists and Methodists displayed less specifically prophetical enthusiasm than members of other denominations, all shared the view that in this divinely driven world it was for 'the modern missionary' to discern the means available for spreading true religion. In such a world national developments might have their place, Empire might provide an arena for providential fireworks, but no necessary priority was to be attached to either. Empire in the form of British rule was never more than one among many such means to be employed or ignored as Providence thought fit. Thus evangelicals also identified exploration, commerce, science, individual Christians, as well as the new missionary societies, among the necessary and efficacious means now available. Empire held limited potential when set within the global perspective of evangelical Christianity. Christ's death was for all mankind, as were the promises of grace and salvation. The interpretation of prophecy, the dynamic consequences of the millennium and Second Coming, the demonstration of the historical case for and against particular mission strategies, all hinged on the use of examples or evidence gathered worldwide, and on a universal outcome.

In 1812 Thomas Haweis of the LMS emphasized that missionary enterprise was no crudely national or British monopoly.[11] As CMS ties with Berlin and Basel illustrated, it was increasingly an international or ecumenical undertaking. Haweis recalled how the early LMS circular letters to foreign Protestant churches had produced enthusiastic responses. Not only had most newly formed missionary associations in Scotland become auxiliaries of the LMS, but also 'on the Continent, from places as far apart as Rotterdam and Basle, Frankfurt and Norkopping, letters of sympathy and liberal contributions came promptly to this appeal'. Contacts were made in Holland and Switzerland; an agent for the Society was established in Paris to push on the Continental work; and students trained in Berlin and Rotterdam for the Netherlands Missionary Society were taken on by the LMS for work in Java. Haweis also linked British missionary fortunes with America—'still a land of real Protestants...destined with us to spread the everlasting gospel to the

---

[10] W. H. Oliver, *Prophets and Millennialists: The Uses of Biblical Prophecy in England from the 1790s to the 1840s* (Auckland, 1978), pp. 84, 90.

[11] Thomas Haweis, *A View of the Present State of Evangelical Religion throughout the World; with a View to Promote Missionary Exertions* (London, 1812).

ends of the earth'—where the American Board of Commissioners for Foreign Missions (founded 1810) was already in contact with British societies.[12]

Providence notwithstanding, the new missionary societies recognized the necessity to establish the basic terms of their cooperation with government and adjust to local circumstances the religion they wished to impart. They began by explicitly distancing themselves from expanding colonial rule, wary of its chauvinism, secular persuasion, and commercial ambitions. Throughout the century, however, such detachment was easier for theorists or home organizers to assert than for missionaries to apply. Involvement with imperial government was difficult to avoid as missionaries soon found in India, Sierra Leone, South Africa, and the Caribbean.

In 1814 a British East India Company (EIC) chaplain, Thomas Thomason, complained, 'we have annihilated the political importance of the natives, stripped them of their power, and laid them prostrate, without giving them anything in return'. His proposed remedies were support for missionaries and an Anglican ecclesiastical establishment. His fellow chaplain, Claudius Buchanan, recommended such a religious establishment as a means of attaching colonial subjects to their government.[13] Despite the initial misgivings of officials and exclusion from certain areas—Surat and Mysore— missionaries' position slowly improved. Local resistance to their work taught them the value of staying on good terms with officials. While some administrators like Thomas Munro continued hostile, official fears of missions declined as a common interest in the transformation of colonial society became evident. William Bentinck (Governor-General of India, 1828–35) disliked the intolerance of extreme missionary lobbyists, but shared the moderate evangelicals' real commitment to missionary enterprise. As he reminded Charles Grant in 1833, 'it is Christianity, the whole Christian Church, whose cause in this heathen country we are to cherish'.[14] Missionaries impressed observers by their perseverance, good intentions, translation and educational work, and their scholarship. Episcopal support for missionary work steadily grew, and in Daniel Wilson (Bishop of Calcutta, 1832–58) the CMS had an ardent backer. Support in Britain grew still faster. Missionary publications, the British and Foreign Bible Society, and local missionary

---

[12] Richard Lovett, *History of the London Missionary Society 1795–1895*, 2 vols. (London, 1895), I, pp. 44, 75–7, 94–5, 105; Haweis, *Present State*, pp. 53–4.

[13] J. Sargent, *The Life of the Reverend Thomas Thomason* (London, 1833), p. 234; Claudius Buchanan, *Colonial Ecclesiastical Establishment*, 2nd edn. (London, 1813), pp. 37–9, 103–9.

[14] John Rosselli, *Lord William Bentinck* (London, 1974), p. 213.

associations, all improved missions' image, and contributed to the government's endorsement of their work in the 1813 and 1833 revisions of the EIC's charter.

Elsewhere, at Freetown, Sierra Leone—a community largely composed of liberated slaves from many different parts of West Africa—the CMS and Wesleyans became indispensable through the education, religion, and common language they provided. Their political authority as magistrates or village superintendents helped to make the colony governable. The obstruction missionaries met from local whites in the Caribbean and the Cape, and their persecution by planters during the Demerara and Jamaica rebellions of 1823 and 1831, aligned missions with the burgeoning anti-slavery and humanitarian movements, commensurately increasing metropolitan respect and sympathy.

This convergence of missionary thinking with official and public opinion generated an increasingly explicit association of evangelical Christianity with commerce and civilization. While missionary boards saw in wealth, stability, and expansion a divinely ordained, providential role for Britain, commercial money flowed through subscriptions to missionary societies. The private fortunes of the Clapham Sect and the establishment of the Sierra Leone Company for trading purposes rescued the evangelicals' West African settlement, the 'Province of Freedom', in 1790–2. Pacific missionaries commonly felt their survival depended on trade, and Samuel Marsden struggled vainly to persuade CMS employees in New Zealand to take subsistence agriculture seriously.[15] In the Cape Colony the LMS Superintendent John Philip felt pushed into trade by cuts in the LMS's budget and still more by the need to preserve his converts' independence from the 'system of oppression...on which the whole principle of the colonial government was conducted'.[16] Missionary coupling of commerce and Christianity meshed neatly with the growing confidence of Britain's governing classes in Britain's worldwide commercial pre-eminence and the expansion of British India. By the 1830s missions both claimed and were accorded a place in a refurbished British national identity.

---

[15] *The Letters and Journals of Samuel Marsden 1765–1838*, ed. J. R. Elder (Dunedin, 1932), pp. 232–6, 410–12.

[16] Philip to Rufus Anderson, 13 Dec. 1833, Harvard University, Houghton Library, Archives of the American Board of Commissioners for Foreign Missions, 14/1/69.

III

Missions' accommodation with the real worlds of political authority and economic activity was seen neither as inescapable surrender nor as a source of perpetual dependence. Early nineteenth-century evangelical views of imperial and indigenous authority were distinguished by their sense of self-sufficiency under Divine superintendence. Recognition by evangelicals of limiting conditions, however imposed, must always be distinguished from reliance on or subservience to them. Only through an understanding of missionaries' faith and their trust in Providence and the Bible can historians hope to explain the incurable optimism, and missions' persistence in the face of death, hardship, deprivation, and the tiny numbers of converts.

For missionaries, faith placed the Empire in perspective. 'Empire', like 'civilization', was at best something to be turned to advantage, a means to an end but equally something to be ignored or rejected if it failed to serve their purpose.

It is very well in its place [wrote Philip] to urge the civilizing influence of a missionary society. But this is not the main object of such an institution. It is not the end; it is only the accompaniment. It is a never-failing collateral, and may be used as a lawful instrument in fighting the battles of the missionary cause.

If people would but realize it, far from missions depending on Empire, the reverse was the case.

While our missionaries, beyond the borders of the colony of the Cape of Good Hope, are everywhere scattering the seeds of civilization, social order, and happiness, they are, by the most unexceptionable means, extending British interests, British influence, and the British empire... every genuine convert among them made to the Christian religion becomes the ally and friend of the colonial government.[17]

It may seem perverse for one so insecurely placed as Philip to invert the balance of power between missions and government. He did so understanding that it was the task of imperial rulers to look after Empire and, if they were wise, to facilitate missionary enterprise. Missions could generally count on the protection of Providence; the survival and success of Empire, however, were essentially uncertain.

---

[17] John Philip, *Researches in South Africa*, 2 vols. (London, 1828), II, p. 360, I, pp. ix–x.

Since the 1790s, missions had been hampered by the need for self-defence and self-justification. Having secured their initial positions, in the 1830s and 1840s they went onto the offensive. This can be seen in the performance of leading missionaries and the principal society secretaries before the parliamentary Select Committee on Aborigines in 1835–7. In the 1820s missionary defensiveness was evident in John Philip's frustrated insistence on the overwhelming need for secure, independent settlements for missionaries and their converts: 'permanent societies of Christians can never be maintained among an uncivilized people without imparting to them the arts and habits of a civilized life'. At the same time he argued, 'Agriculture and commerce can never flourish, unless private property is respected, and the laws which guard the possessions of individuals are the first principles of industry.'[18] Ten years on, this had become William Shaw's calmly stated commonsense, even conventional, wisdom. Asked if he knew 'any class of missionaries who, in their attempts to instruct the natives in Christianity, combine the principles of Christianity and civilization', Shaw responded that this 'was precisely the plan on which the missionaries of the Wesleyan society endeavoured to act'. Called to the witness stand a year later, the LMS South Seas missionary John Williams agreed.[19] The Select Committee's Report fully endorsed the role of missions as principal agents in a process of defending indigenous people against the uncontrolled rapacity of white settlers and traders.[20] The eagerness of missions to expand beyond imperial boundaries demonstrated their wish to play a similar role on a world stage, as, for example, through the societies' backing for the African Civilization Society and the Niger Expedition of 1841–2, which aimed to introduce 'legitimate' commerce to the African interior in the hope that it would displace the illegitimate trade in slaves.

Even the SPG's high-churchmen now began to jump aboard the bandwagon, establishing the Colonial Bishoprics Fund (1841) in order to extend episcopal authority and superintendence overseas. George Augustus Selwyn, consecrated Bishop of New Zealand in 1841, was the first of fifteen bishops made in the 1840s. Selwyn did not distinguish between his imperial, colonial, and missionary roles. He was a 'missionary bishop', consecrated to the task of building up the Church from its very beginning, consulting the opinions of

---

[18] John Philip, *Researches in South Africa*, 2 vols. (London, 1828), II, p. 360, I, pp. 219, 382.
[19] PP (1836) VII (538), QQ. 1116–17 (Shaw, 21 Aug. 1835), Q. 5635 (Williams, 29 July 1836).
[20] *Report from the Select Committee on Aborigines (British Settlements)*, PP (1837) VII (425).

his fellow clergy but acting essentially on his own authority inside or outside colonial territory. Highlighting the universal, global outlook of the missionary movement, the geographical limits of his diocese stretched far beyond any formal British control. Just as other missions focused on missionary stations and schools, so Selwyn elevated the cathedral and the community built around it. He shared with other denominations a sense of providential guidance and inspiration. Arriving in New Zealand in May 1842, he spoke in apocalyptic terms: 'if we know that the fulfilment of prophecy, and the completion of promises, and the growth of Christ's kingdom, all portend the coming of the end... what need we any further argument, [or] stronger motive... to devote ourselves... to this great and hopeful work?'[21] He thus launched his own Melanesian Mission in 1847.

The heady atmosphere of the decade was heightened further by other missionary initiatives, to China after the Treaty of Nanking (1842) and to southern and eastern Africa. Roman Catholic revival spawned new missions to Tahiti and New Zealand backed by French official support, adding a bitter competitive edge in the Pacific. Although the failure of the Niger Expedition was a serious setback, the missions did not allow themselves to be dragged down by it. With the aid of growing numbers of indigenous agents, Baptists, Scottish Presbyterians, the CMS, and the Methodists went ahead with new West African ventures at Badagry, Abeokuta, Fernando Po, and Calabar.

IV

The powerful conventional picture of nineteenth-century missionary enterprise as a two-pronged secular and religious civilizing mission crystallized in the years 1840–65. As conceived by the influential theorists Henry Venn in Britain and Rufus Anderson in America, the Bible, plough, and local economic growth would fuel the development of self-supporting, self-governing, and ultimately self-extending churches. The career of the missionary explorer David Livingstone and the consecration in 1864 of the liberated slave Samuel Ajayi Crowther as Bishop of the Countries of Western Africa beyond the Queen's Dominions signalled its success.

Alongside chronicled achievements, however, there was a different story to be told of frustration and lost momentum. In India, where the first systematic

---

[21] G. A. Selwyn, *How Shall we Sing the Lord's Song in a Strange Land? A Sermon Preached in the Cathedral Church of St. Peter, Exeter* (1842); id., *Thanksgiving Sermon: Preached... on his Arrival in his Diocese* (Paihia, 1842), p. 12.

statistical charting of missionary progress was established in the 1850s, the upheavals of 1857 brought home the limits of evangelical endeavours. In the West Indies enthusiasm for local ecclesiastical independence was swamped by poverty and violent rebellion in 1865. In Central and southern Africa even Livingstone's efforts ended in his abandonment of attempts to link Christianity and civilization. The movement's own historians agreed that its impetus was failing. Eugene Stock amply illustrated the declining fortunes of the missionary societies and linked them to the undermining of biblical authority by rationalism, ritualism, and Rome. 'Such a time', he wrote, 'is never a time of missionary advance.' In 1872, 'for the first time in many years ... not one single University man had offered for missionary service', and the number of missionaries maintained in India by the five largest societies fell by 12 per cent.[22] Slogans and rhetoric could neither hide the diminishing returns associated with the framework of 'Commerce, Civilization, and Christianity', nor fend off mounting criticism of missions' unjustifiable extravagance.

As in the 1790s, critics urgently demanded new ways forward. Simplicity was the keyword. The term 'missionary society' should be abandoned in favour of 'mission', and much of the societies' home organization should be dismantled. Divine provision made orchestrated fund-raising unnecessary and undesirable; subscribers should not expect dramatic visible results in return for their giving. Missions required only a small committee of referees to vet missionaries sent out, to receive donations as they were freely given, and to dispatch them to a designated head in the field with power to make decisions based on local knowledge. Links with commerce should be abandoned in favour of direct evangelization by lay preachers and teachers, both native and European. Any association of Western culture with Christianity should be minimized. Freed from the trammels of direction by home committees, and wholly non-denominational in approach, missionaries should assimilate themselves as far as possible to native ways of living. Only then would a serious impact be made on the heathen world.

This shift in strategy was not simply a response to circumstances in the mission field. It reflected developments in long-running metropolitan debates about effective evangelization, as well as a resurgence of millennial thinking. Enthusiasts began calling for a reversion to apostolic models of evangelization and enunciating pre-millennial eschatology. The dominant pattern of Protestant millennial thought before 1860 had been rooted in

[22] E. Stock, *History of the Church Missionary Society*, 3 vols. (London, 1899), II, pp. 336, 338.

Enlightenment ideas of progress. In missionary terms, it expected conversion of the world to usher in the millennium of peace, happiness, and plenty, at the end of which Christ would return to earth. The programme of 'Christianity and Commerce' was clearly aligned with this outlook. In contrast to these optimistic post-millennialist expectations, pre-millennialists matched the apocalyptic chronologies of Daniel, Isaiah, and Revelation with troubling events on earth, and concluded that very soon the world would end and Christ would deliver the Last Judgement. Only then would the millennium dawn. Pre-millennialist missionaries advocated pushing ahead with evangelism on the widest possible front, so that as many sinners as possible might have the opportunity to repent before the Second Coming. These ideas eventually found systematic expression in the China Inland Mission (CIM) established by J. Hudson Taylor in 1865, which rapidly became the second largest British missionary venture and prompted adaptations in the practice of the long-established societies.

The new 'faith missions' deliberately sought isolated and unfamiliar territory, far from European colonialism and other missions. Like inland China, many parts of Africa represented a major challenge. Despite Livingstone's expressed enthusiasm for civilization and commerce, his own example of evangelical nomadism provided ammunition for the reformers. He saw the Tswana, for example, as 'retailers of news perpetually on the move from one spot to another... This nomadic life is very favourable to the spread of the Gospel, although it is opposed to the spread of civilization'.[23]

In this spirit, Mr and Mrs H. G. Guinness launched the Livingstone Inland Mission in 1878. Other African faith missions followed in the 1880s and 1890s: the Sudan Interior Mission, the North Africa Mission, and the Congo Balolo Mission. Older societies, too, began trying the new methods. G. W. Brooke led a special Sudan Mission party supported by the CMS, modelled on the CIM and propelled by an apocalyptic pre-millennial vision.

I see no hope [he said] given in the Bible that wickedness in this world will be subdued by civilization or preaching of the gospel—until the Messiah the prince come. And to hasten that time is... the function of foreign missions... I therefore should be inclined to frame any missionary plans with a view to giving the simple gospel message to the greatest number possible of ignorant heathen in the shortest possible time.[24]

[23] David Chamberlin, ed., *Some Letters from Livingstone 1840–1872* (London, 1940), pp. 26–7.
[24] *The Mildmay Conference 1887* (London, 1887), pp. 141–8.

And it was not just 'ignorant heathen' that caught the eye of pre-millennial evangelists; Muslims and Jews again became targets.

Visible changes in the Muslim world encouraged eschatological speculation about 'the signs of the times' and stimulated study of the Bible's prophetic books. Mounting fear of Islam's alternative civilizing mission spurred on volunteers for Christian missionary work. Like the 'faith' movement, rivalry with Islam assisted the revival of missionary enthusiasm after the 1870s as the Ottoman Empire struggled for survival. A major conference on 'missions to Mohammedans' was convened at CMS House in Salisbury Square in October 1875 to plan a general forward strategy. Delaying 'new aggressive measures' in Turkey itself until the immediate crisis was over, the conference planned initiatives in Sierra Leone, Lagos, and among the Hausa. Noting the recent conference of Indian missionaries in Allahabad in 1873, the gathering asked the Missionary Conferences in Bengal and the North West Provinces to make further plans.[25]

Although 'out of our province to discuss prophetical questions', wrote the editor of the *Church Missionary Intelligencer,* 'we cannot refrain from a passing notice of the wonderful manner in which the whole question of Mohammedanism is now absorbing public attention'. Regular meetings of the Mission Secretaries Association reviewed Islam's expansion and how to combat it. More unusual were the two opportunities its members gave the Revd W. J. Adams of the London Jews Society to speak on prophetic studies and their fulfilment.[26] Finally, Gordon's death at Khartoum in 1885 brought Christian–Muslim confrontation to the forefront of imperial politics.

The faith missions had been the most striking response to the mid-century decline in missionary support and enthusiasm. For other evangelicals the future lay less in rejecting the past or mounting new kinds of missions than in reviving and adapting existing traditions. Nevertheless, the influence of the faith missions can be seen at almost every turn—in the authoritarianism and concern to protect indigenous society present in the Universities' Mission to Central Africa (UMCA); in the devastating Niger Crisis of 1888–92 and the subsequent revival of the CMS in the 1890s; in the internal conflicts of the Wesleyans over the cost of their Indian operations; and in the Scottish Presbyterians' review of educational strategies in north India.

[25] *CMI* (Mar. 1876), pp. 177–8.
[26] 'On Missions to Mohammedans', *CMI* (Jan. 1876), pp. 6–7; London Secretaries Association, minutes, vol. 5, 8 Mar. 1876 and 14 Nov. 1877, Cambridge University Library, Archives of the British and Foreign Bible Society.

V

Apart from the faith missions a new impetus in missionary strategy emerged from high-church Anglicans. The UMCA, launched with Bishop Charles Mackenzie's consecration at Cape Town in 1861, moved significantly beyond the earlier model of the SPG and the Colonial Bishoprics Fund. The UMCA prided itself on re-creating a model of the apostolic church held together by episcopal authority and ecclesiastical discipline. It was also committed to preserving traditional communities and local custom threatened by Islam and the 'debased civilization' of East Africa's coastal towns. In the practice of the UMCA, the importance attached to the possibilities of blending Anglo-Catholic Christianity with African ways intensified their theologically informed emphasis on community, authority, obedience, and discipline.

Other adaptations of Britain's high-church traditions were the Oxford Mission to Calcutta (1881) and the Cambridge Mission to Delhi (1877). The Cambridge missionaries constituted themselves the Brotherhood of the Ascended Christ and led a communal life revolving around pastoral work, evangelical preaching, and St Stephen's College. A larger number of unmarried women were drawn together into their own St Stephen's Community, initially engaged in zenana missions among secluded Indian women and later in social and medical work. The Oxford Mission, styled the Brotherhood of the Epiphany, considered there to be a surfeit of 'bazaar' preaching in Calcutta and therefore concentrated on their own schools and hostels. Increasingly they worked directly as a mission to the rapidly growing numbers of Calcutta University students. It was difficult for either mission to attain the comparative detachment from state and colonial authority achieved by the UMCA in Africa. From their beginnings they were closely connected to the SPG, which continued to play a major role in appointing and funding India's Anglican episcopate. In 1891 Henry Whitehead, already Principal of the SPG-run Bishop's College in Calcutta, was also appointed superior of the Oxford Mission, while in Delhi the Cambridge Mission took over the SPG's missionary work. Both communities began to furnish bishops for India's dioceses. Following T. V. French's appointment to Lahore in 1877, bishops and brotherhoods developed intimate ties. The Oxford Mission's policy under Bishop Johnson (1876–98) was defined by its historian as 'Do nothing without the Bishop'.[27] The missions' acquisition of city-centre sites

---

[27] George Longridge, *A History of the Oxford Mission to Calcutta* (London, 1900), p. 194; cf. pp. 66–80.

confirmed their social position and role as frequent visiting places for representatives of the Raj. They showed no sign of UMCA misgivings about the onrush of 'civilization'. Absence of obvious hostility to their activities disinclined them to question the fact of their influence. Lefroy thus commented, 'we are here to upset by God's grace their old faiths and customs, and to recreate the country in Christ Jesus; and it is only logical to suppose that we should be very much hated and objected to; only logical, but somehow hopelessly the reverse of fact'.[28] The universality of the faith was matched by belief in the utility of Oxbridge teaching transplanted to Bengal and Punjab.

This assessment was not as far removed from the UMCA's belief in missionary identification with local peoples as it might at first seem. Anglo-Catholics brought ideas of 'sympathy' and practical 'consideration' to both South Asia and Central Africa—linked to the possibility of insights the West might derive from close encounters of the religious kind. These were present in the Cambridge Mission from its foundation as a result of the influential teaching of Professor Westcott. That they lent themselves to expressions of paternalistic self-congratulation should not disguise either their novelty in the missionary world as a whole or their capacity to subvert the language of dominance and imperial control in India. In the world of Hindus and still more of Muslims, the willingness of Anglo-Catholic missions to treat the beliefs of others with some seriousness was rare. It was an assessment at the same time widely separated from the world of the UMCA. Colonial rule in India at the point of the high-church missions' arrival in the 1870s imposed far greater constraints on missionary ambitions than did those prevailing in Central Africa at the same time. The authoritarianism at the heart of the Anglo-Catholic tradition, buttressed by its social connections, could assert itself more readily under the Raj than in circumstances where colonial rule had yet to be established.

VI

Other long-established missions recovered missionary fervour through association with religious revivals at home and abroad. Methodists at work along the West African coast in 1876–8 and again in 1885 were excited by waves of religious revivalism sweeping through their congregations and

---

[28] H. H. Montgomery, *Life and Letters of George Alfred Lefroy* (London, 1920), p. 105.

attracting new members.[29] Whatever differences of understanding may have existed between cultures, missionaries found in such revivals periodic reconfirmation of the universality of both their message and their audience. Bryan Roe returned from the Lagos revival in 1885 not praising Empire but with renewed 'faith in [Africa's] ultimate, social, moral and spiritual regeneration'.[30] Fresh waves of American revivalism swept Britain in the mid-1870s, generating new currents of enthusiasm associated above all with the annual Keswick conferences after 1875 (non-denominational, but predominantly Anglican, gatherings more akin to American camp meetings than conventional conferences) and ongoing revival in the universities after 1880. Central to the Keswick experience was the prospect of a 'higher life', a state of practical holiness and sanctification. Attainable in this world through an act of faith, and signified by a second conversion, it freed Christians from all consciousness or traces of sin, effectively setting them apart from most of their fellows and opening the way to closer Christian community. Here were fresh criteria against which the reality of converts' and churchgoers' religion might be assessed.

Revivalism came as a mixed blessing to the long-standing societies. Unless they adapted their image and appeal, they appeared likely to lose many of the new volunteers to faith missions like the CIM, heterodox organizations such as the Salvation Army, or even operators on the fringes of the missionary world like the Methodist Thomas Champness's Joyful News Evangelists. The CMS found itself inundated with enquiries from volunteers, often too young or otherwise as yet unsuitable but whom it judged wise to encourage; complicated arrangements were discussed to maintain volunteers' links between CMS and other sources of recruits such as the Mildmay Institution. The new spirit of Keswick and revival had to be captured, perhaps tamed, but certainly incorporated into the everyday workings of the mainstream missionary movement. Simultaneously, Keswick itself had to be brought to take more notice of those societies.[31] The CMS's cautious acceptance of this analysis had disastrous consequences for the Niger Mission, centrepiece of the older Venn strategy. Brooke and the members of his party were deeply immersed in the revivalist stream; they brought Keswick standards to bear on Bishop Crowther and his

---

[29] Revd George Dyer to General Secretary, 21 Apr. 1876; Revds Bryan Roe and J. T. F. Halligey, letters to M. Osborn (WMMS Secretary), 8 Dec. 1885, Lagos, MMS, files 1876/10, 1885/35, 36.

[30] Revd Bryan Roe, Lagos, to Revd M. C. Osborn, [Dec. 1885], MMS, file 1885/41.

[31] Eugene Stock, 'The Missionary Element', in Charles F. Harford, ed., *The Keswick Convention: Its Message, its Method and its Men* (London, 1907).

helpers, and found them seriously wanting. Most of the African clergy and agents were alienated, many were dismissed, and the Bishop was forced into retirement. Confrontation on the Niger was generated not by a new imperialism or youthful racism, but above all by theological differences. The Niger Crisis was settled in the revivalist marketplace for missionary recruits, and the experiment with an African bishop was suspended.

Although imbibing the potentially explosive cocktail of Keswick theology, pre-millennialism, and institutional innovation, did not generally have such dramatic and destructive impact, the CMS was not alone in its difficulties. In West Africa schism rent one mission after another: Presbyterians at Calabar in 1882, Methodists and Baptists at Lagos between 1884 and 1888. Keswick enthusiasms spawned independent missions to Lagos and Freetown in 1886, 1888, and 1889. Many Lagos Christians became the target of criticisms similar to those levied at the Niger, and were no less resentful; but others displayed evidence of conversion meetings, the personal experience of salvation, and a missionary commitment of their own, which the Keswick missioners admired. Elsewhere, in Japan, East Africa, and north India, similar disputes between missionary generations and local Christians were managed with varying degrees of success.

VII

It is impossible in the space remaining to do justice to the continuing complexity of relations between missions and Empire through to 1914. It is nevertheless the variety of those relationships that must be emphasized. Notwithstanding that this was the classical period of 'high imperialism', the international networks of the missionary movement continued to expand, detaching themselves from 'Empire' as they did so. At the heart of expansionist forces stood the student missionary movement, rooted in late nineteenth-century revivalism and born of the American Student Volunteer Movement in the late 1880s. It grew rapidly to embrace the British Student Volunteer Missionary Union, the Young Men's (Women's) Christian Association, and the World Student Christian Federation. Inspired by the faith missions, Keswick's influence, and its arresting 'watchword'—'the evangelization of the world in this generation'—its most striking pre-war achievement was the great World Missionary Conference held at Edinburgh in 1910.

Just as the international, global nature of the missionary movement increasingly set it apart from national governments, so its independence gave missionary leaders greater confidence in dealing with secular authorities, including humanitarian movements. Increasingly missionaries called the humanitarian tune, with humanitarians and bodies such as the Anti-Slavery Society and the Aborigines Protection Society dependent on fluctuating missionary concern. From James Long's campaign on behalf of Bengali indigo workers in the 1850s to defence of African land rights against white and chartered company rule, and the Congo Reform Association after 1904, it was missions' capacity to arouse public feeling that gave the humanitarians political weight and compelled the imperial government to take action. Involvement in this high-level political campaigning was, as always, underpinned by the more general growth of a commitment by individual missionaries and ultimately most of their societies to the welfare of indigenous peoples. In the late nineteenth century this still embodied something of the earlier anti-slavery cause. However, it was now more often expressed in support for public works, famine relief, and medical missions, a trend that often reflected the increasing part played by women in the movement as a whole.

The willingness and capacity of the missionary movement to remind imperial authorities of their obligations was not confined to issues of indigenous rights. Missions were also seen agitating for imperial intervention to protect their own rights and freedoms. The partition of Africa gave rise to several such incidents. Demands that the British imperial government preserve missionary interests against untoward threats from the Portuguese, expanding Islam in Nyasaland, and the consequences of a British withdrawal from Uganda, were plentiful and effective. Elsewhere—for example in China and the Middle East—missions were less successful. However, the variability of their record itself demonstrates missionaries' distance from the Empire. William McCullough wrote feelingly of his experience in India:

It goes against the grain of an orthodox Imperialist like me to do anything in the way of complaining to Parliament about the Indian Government. I think our rulers here are often much injured and hampered by that sort of thing. This feeling on my part does not spring from personal bias. For from European officials in India I have never received anything better than bare civility and very often worse... I'm a missionary first and an Imperialist afterwards and I did not come out here to watch my work being stopped by 'judicial calmness'.[32]

---

[32] To Dr George Smith, 29 Nov. 1893, National Library of Scotland, MS 7839, fo. 108.

If in many places the missionary at first needed security and protection, in the aftermath of the European annexations the gradual establishment of administrative controls often caused missionaries once again to distance themselves from Empire and its overlords.

Select Bibliography

J. F. ADE AJAYI, *Christian Missions in Nigeria 1841–1891: The Making of a New Elite* (London, 1965).

JAMES AXTELL, *The Invasion Within: The Contest of Cultures in Colonial North America* (New York, 1985).

DAVID W. BEBBINGTON, *Evangelicalism in Modern Britain: A History from the 1730s to the 1890s* (London, 1988).

RUTH H. BLOCH, *Visionary Republic: Millennial Themes in American Thought, 1756–1800* (Cambridge, 1985).

PATRICIA U. BONOMI, *Under the Cope of Heaven: Religion, Society, and Politics in Colonial America* (Oxford, 1986).

HANS CNATTINGIUS, *Bishops and Societies: A Study of Anglican Colonial and Missionary Expansion, 1698–1850* (London, 1952).

JEFFREY COX, *Imperial Faultlines: Christianity and Imperial Power in India, 1818–1940* (Stanford, Calif., 2003).

ALLAN K. DAVIDSON, *Evangelicals and Attitudes to India, 1786–1813: Missionary Publicity and Claudius Buchanan* (Sutton Courtenay, 1990).

PETER M. DOLL, *Revolution, Reaction, and National Identity: Imperial Anglicanism in British North America, 1745–1795* (Madison, 2000).

ELIZABETH ELBOURNE, *Blood Ground: Colonialism, Missions, and the Contest for Christianity in the Cape Colony and Britain, 1799–1853* (Montreal, 2002).

JAMES G. GREENLEE and CHARLES M. JOHNSTON, *Good Citizens: British Missionaries and Imperial States 1870 to 1918* (Montreal, 1999).

NIEL GUNSON, *Messengers of Grace: Evangelical Missionaries in the South Seas 1797–1860* (Melbourne, 1978).

CATHERINE HALL, *Civilising Subjects: Metropole and Colony in the English Imagination, 1830–1867* (Cambridge, 2002).

ADRIAN HASTINGS, *The Church in Africa 1450–1950* (Oxford, 1994).

M. A. LAIRD, *Missionaries and Education in Bengal 1793–1837* (Oxford, 1972).

F. S. PIGGIN, *Making Evangelical Missionaries, 1780–1856: The Social Background, Motives and Training of British Missionaries to India* (Appleford, 1981).

ANDREW PORTER, *Religion versus Empire? British Protestant Missionaries and Overseas Expansion, 1700–1914* (Manchester, 2004).

—— ed., *The Imperial Horizons of British Protestant Missions, 1880–1914* (Grand Rapids, Mich., 2003).

RHONDA SEMPLE, *Missionary Women: Gender, Professionalism and the Victorian Idea of Christian Mission* (Woodbridge, 2003).

ERIC J. SHARPE, *Not to Destroy but to Fulfil: The Contribution of J. N. Farquhar to Protestant Missionary Thought in India before 1914* (Uppsala, 1965).

BRIAN STANLEY, *The Bible and the Flag: Protestant Missions and British Imperialism in the Nineteenth and Twentieth Centuries* (Leicester, 1990).

ANDREW F. WALLS, *The Missionary Movement in Christian History: Studies in the Transmission of the Faith* (New York, 1996).

C. PETER WILLIAMS, *The Ideal of the Self-Governing Church: A Study in Victorian Missionary Strategy* (Leiden, 1990).

4

Humanitarians and White Settlers in the Nineteenth Century

ALAN LESTER

Missionaries often saw themselves as an anomalous element in the Empire: striving to acquire authority over indigenous people on the one hand, while resisting aggressive colonial forces on the other. Apart from the anti-slavery movement, the most celebrated struggles between missions and secular forces were fought from the late 1820s to the mid-1840s, when missionaries and their allies posed their model of Christian, humanitarian imperialism as an alternative to the practices prevailing in the settler colonies. Three particularly fraught zones of conflict were the Cape Colony, New South Wales, and New Zealand. Although each of these distant, staggered episodes of conflict had its own local dynamics and outcomes, they were connected in debates staged by missionaries, humanitarians, and settlers. Each event was a battle in a broader 'propaganda war', fought out across trans-imperial networks of communication, incorporating such far-flung territories as the West Indies and India. At stake was the definition and determination of 'proper' relations between British colonists and their others.

While many missions blamed settlers for killing and dispossessing indigenous peoples, and also for impeding slave emancipation, evangelism, and 'civilization', settler communities sought material security and accumulation through a more forceful regulation of enslaved and indigenous peoples. Parliament's Select Committee on Aborigines (British Settlements) of 1836–7, initiated by Thomas Fowell Buxton, marshalled the testimony of missionaries spread through the colonies of settlement, and played a crucial role in situating Britain's diverse overseas colonies within a common humanitarian narrative. This narrative challenged settlers by constructing their behaviour as immoral and threatening their access to government and public opinion in Britain. However, the ambitious 'experiment' in humanitarian colonial relations that the Aborigines Committee, with its missionary informants, helped to conduct, turned out to be brief. By the mid-nineteenth century many of its own proponents were disillusioned, while its antagonists had mobilized their own network of influence to win metropolitan support. Although the humanitarian rhetoric of the missionaries retained its potency in the later nineteenth century, and certain humanitarian institutions continued to cast a critical eye over colonial behaviour, they never again mounted a comparable trans-imperial political challenge to British settler practices.

Anti-slavery, Thomas Fowell Buxton, and Imperial Humanitarian Networks

Networks of communication were critical to the construction of the Christian humanitarian world-view that many missionaries shared. They underpinned the anti-slavery movement which linked the West Indies with the United States and Britain. Key agents in the West Indies had been Nonconformist missionaries—mostly Baptists and Wesleyans—for whom slavery represented the denial of full Christian personhood. The Baptist William Knibb described Jamaica in the 1820s as a place 'where Satan reigns with awful power' while the enslaved 'sons of Africa' formed 'a pleasing contrast to the debauched white population'.[1]

West Indian planters reciprocated in kind, charging that missionaries preaching to enslaved people provided them with 'new claims for freedom' that could be appropriated and turned against the 'master subject'. Mission churches also 'provided lines of communication which were crucial to the organization of resistance', as manifested in the revolt in Jamaica in 1831. The capacity of enslaved people to revolt of their own initiative was often denied by planters, so they directed their rage at the missionaries for preaching insurrection.[2] Missionaries constituted an even larger real political threat to planter interests through their broader trans atlantic networks. Many acted as informants for the evangelical anti-slavery campaigners associated with William Wilberforce and the Clapham Sect of activist evangelicals, including Granville Sharpe, Thomas Clarkson, James Stephen, and Zachary Macaulay. After helping to bring about the abolition of the slave trade in 1807, the Sect developed an even more extensive web of evangelical connections. Concern

[1] Catherine Hall, *Civilising Subjects: Metropole and Colony in the English Imagination, 1830–1867* (Cambridge, 2002), p. 98.
[2] Ibid., p. 105.

over the progress of Christianization in the East Indies was galvanized by John Shore and Charles Grant, both East India Company officials. By the 1820s intermarriage among the Sect's founding families and new recruits had produced a 'second generation' led by Thomas Fowell Buxton.

A director of the London Missionary Society (LMS), Buxton supported the Bible and Missionary societies and the prison reform advocated by his sister-in-law, the Quaker reformer Elizabeth Fry. In 1823 he succeeded Wilberforce as head of the campaign to abolish slavery in the British colonies. As Member of Parliament for Weymouth, he articulated a wide-ranging programme of reform: 'How can I promote the welfare of others? In private, by... sparing on my own pleasure and expending on God's service. In public, by attending to the Slave Trade, Slavery, Indian widows burning themselves, the completion of those objects which have made some advance, viz. Criminal Law, Prisons, and Police.'[3]

In June 1825 the planters of Barbados lambasted the Methodist missionary William Shrewsbury for siding with insurrectionary slaves and because 'he had actually corresponded with Mr. Buxton!'[4] With prompting and help from his sister Sarah Maria, his daughter Priscilla and his wife's cousin Anna Gurney, Buxton corresponded with such far-flung missionaries as the Anglican minister Samuel Marsden in New South Wales, the Quaker missionary James Backhouse, who moved between various parts of Australia and the Pacific, and John Philip, Superintendent of the LMS at the Cape. In his own mind Buxton saw clear connections between the enslavement of African labour and indigenous peoples threatened by expanding British settlements in these places.

Great Britain has, in former times, countenanced evils of great magnitude,—slavery and the Slave Trade; but for these she has made some atonement... An evil remains very similar in character, and not altogether unfit to be compared with them in the amount of misery it produces. The oppression of the natives of barbarous countries is a practice which pleads no claim to indulgence.[5]

With missionary assistance Buxton aimed to mobilize the heart of Empire against both forms of oppression.

---

[3] *Memoirs of Sir Thomas Fowell Buxton*, ed. C. Buxton (London, 1848), p. 125.

[4] Buxton denied the correspondence; ibid., p. 155.

[5] *Report from the Select Committee on Aborigines (British Settlements)* (henceforth *Report*), PP (1836–7) VII, p. 75.

Dr John Philip and the Cape

Buxton's most prolific colonial correspondent during the 1830s was Philip in the Cape Colony. With his son-in-law John Fairbairn, editor of the Cape Town-based *South African Commercial Advertiser*, Philip denounced the policies, including pass controls and compulsory apprenticeship, which bolstered colonial masters' control over their Khoisan labour force. In 1822 he met Buxton and Wilberforce in London, and with their assistance brought his campaign to a head in 1828, the same year he published his *Researches in South Africa*, which caused a furore in the Cape and Britain.[6] During the controversy Buxton raised the issue of the Khoisan in Parliament. Two days later the Acting Governor of the Cape, Sir Richard Bourke, passed Ordinance 50 abolishing the pass laws, releasing the Khoisan from apprenticeship requirements, and acknowledging their right to own land.

British settlers established on the eastern frontier in 1820 regarded Ordinance 50 as a disaster. Thomas Stubbs, for example, denounced 'that abominable false philanthropy which made [the Khoisan] free and ruined them... They were a people that required to be under control, both for their own benefit and the public; the same as the slaves in this country.' J. C. Chase blamed 'the pious but gulled John Bull' for letting himself be duped by Philip and his allies.[7] Seemingly oblivious, Buxton moved on, backing an LMS scheme for promoting Christianization and civilization through the Kat River settlement for freed Khoisan labourers. After reading one of John Philip's letters about progress at Kat River, Buxton was seen by his daughter walking 'up and down the room, almost shedding tears of joy to hear of the prosperity and well-being of these dear people'.[8] Buxton later used the improving tale of the settlement in parliamentary debates as evidence of what might be achieved by ending ex-slaves' apprenticeships in the West Indies. White colonists, in contrast, set energetically about proving that Kat River had failed. T. J. Biddulph described it as 'the most transparent piece of humbug ever practised upon the public to serve the purposes of unscrupulous, intriguing people', and the Cape's new governor from 1847, Sir Henry Pottinger, characterized the settlement as 'a concourse of rebellious, idle

---

[6] Andrew Bank, 'The Great Debate and the Origins of South African Historiography', *Journal of African History*, XXXVIII (1997), p. 263.

[7] M. J. McGinn, 'J. C. Chase—1820 Settler and Servant of the Colony', MA thesis (Rhodes University, 1975), p. 8.

[8] Elizabeth Elbourne, *Blood Ground: Colonialism, Missions, and the Contest for Christianity in the Cape Colony and Britain, 1799–1853* (Montreal, 2002), pp. 271, 272.

paupers'.[9] It is not surprising that many of the settlement's inhabitants rebelled during the 1850–2 frontier war between colonial and Xhosa forces and that the settlement was eventually broken up by the local government. It was a story to be repeated in other settlement colonies where white farmers determined that no agricultural schemes for indigenous people should be allowed to succeed. (See pp. 270–71.)

Philip's next crusade, to prevent the extension of white settlement into Xhosa territory, also came to grief, though not without a mighty struggle. In the early 1830s British settlers were allocated land taken from the Ndlambe Xhosa chiefdom in the hope that they might act as a buffer against Xhosa raids into the Cape Colony. Having been subjected to a number of such raids by the early 1830s, prominent settlers, and notably Robert Godlonton, editor of the *Graham's Town Journal*, were beginning to orchestrate a representation of the 'typical' Xhosa as a rapacious cattle thief. Such a representation helped to legitimize calls for the Xhosa's further punitive dispossession in order to allow for the expansion of newly profitable settler sheep farms.

Philip and Fairbairn visited the frontier in 1830 and spoke with Xhosa chiefs, as well as missionaries of the LMS and Glasgow Missionary Society. Most of these missionaries would become vital channels for relaying Xhosa grievances through Philip to Buxton. By the early 1830s Fairbairn's *South African Commercial Advertiser* was increasingly coming into conflict with Godlonton's *Graham's Town Journal* as a result of their different visions of 'progress' along the frontier. The *Advertiser* saw Godlonton's programme of land appropriation and Xhosa punishment as a betrayal of Britain's civilizing and Christianizing mission. The contest between humanitarian and settler agendas in the Cape was brought to a head in the years 1834–6, when all-out war raged along on the eastern frontier. As Philip was keen to point out, the Xhosa attack that initiated the war had been provoked by a series of colonial aggressions, which the Xhosa associated with the British settler presence. Twenty-four of the settlers were killed in the first onslaught. This 'Sixth' Frontier War soon had its counterpart in a discursive war between the settlers and their evangelical critics. It became a test of strength for the post-emancipation humanitarian nexus as a whole, as prominent settlers declared that 'many of the missionaries have been labouring under the greatest delusion and although living for years amongst the Kafirs, they have not

[9] Pottinger to Grey, 16 May 1847, Grey Papers, Durham University; Biddulph's comments cited in T. Kirk, 'Self-Government and Self-Defence in South Africa', D.Phil. thesis (Oxford, 1975), p. 180.

been able to form anything like a correct estimate of the character of the people around them'.[10]

Not all missionaries in the Cape united in opposition to settler projects or participated in Buxton's humanitarian network, particularly the frustrated Wesleyan missionaries, some of whom had themselves been settlers. Bitter at widespread resistance to his evangelical efforts, the Revd Shrewsbury—the same man who had been ejected from Barbados by planters for his alleged correspondence with Buxton—declared even before the war, 'were it not that I desire to promote the salvation of their souls, I would not dwell amongst such a wretched people another hour'. Much to the embarrassment of the WMMS Directors in London, whose meetings were chaired by Buxton, Shrewsbury advocated execution of any Xhosa who had taken colonial lives and the tagging of others so that they could be monitored during 'merciful' hard labour on colonial roads.[11] The Cape Governor, General Sir Benjamin D'Urban, who had pronounced the Xhosa 'irreclaimable savages', annexed 7,000 square miles of Xhosa land before the end of hostilities and declared it open to white settlement as Queen Adelaide Province in 1835.

The Aborigines Committee

In his campaign on behalf of the dispossessed Xhosa, Buxton, prompted by Anna Gurney, took pains to ensure that what was debated was the morality of British colonization per se. He did so, first, because he had the support of the Colonial Secretary, Lord Glenelg (son of the Clapham Sect luminary Charles Grant), and secondly because he made the war in the Cape the occasion for a parliamentary inquiry into British settlement throughout the Empire. James Stephen, Under-Secretary at the Colonial Office from 1836, also had Clapham connections; his father-in-law, John Venn, was Rector of Clapham. Unsurprisingly, Buxton considered Glenelg and Stephen as allies. On hearing of the Cape frontier war, Buxton wrote to Philip, 'It will be of great importance to get the ear of the Ministers before they shall have time to form an

---

[10] *Graham's Town Journal*, 23 Jan. 1835. The word 'Kafir', sometimes rendered in other forms, such as 'Kaffir', was widely used in 19th-century southern Africa, first as a term for Xhosa-speaking Africans and later as a term for all African speakers of languages in the Bantu group. By the 20th century it had become a racial slur akin to 'nigger' and so ceased to be used in scholarly writing.

[11] Alan Lester, *Imperial Networks: Creating Identities in Nineteenth Century South Africa and Britain* (London, 2001), pp. 100–1, 134–6.

opinion on the Governor's Despatches on this subject, and one word from you in the present state of England will be enough to prevent them taking the wrong course.' Anna Gurney compiled a digest of Philip's letters for the Colonial Secretary, which Buxton anticipated would be used 'to save a nation of 100,000 beings and several flourishing missions from destruction'. Buxton also introduced Glenelg to the LMS Secretary, William Ellis, who was receiving his own independent stream of letters from Philip and the other South African missionaries.

Buxton had first agitated for a Select Committee to inquire into the humanitarian allegations about Cape frontier policy in 1834, before the outbreak of the war, asking Philip to 'furnish [him] with facts'.[12] As Chairman of the Aborigines Committee, established in 1835, Buxton had authority to investigate colonial policy throughout the overseas Empire as well as in New Zealand and the South Sea Islands, where many Britons resided. Buxton set the tone of the inquiry: 'What have we Christians done for [the indigenous peoples]? We have usurped their lands, kidnapped, enslaved and murdered themselves. The greatest of their crimes is that they sometimes trespass into the lands of their forefathers; and the very greatest of their misfortunes is that they have ever become acquainted with Christians. Shame on such Christianity!'[13] After hearing testimony from colonists, officials, and above all missionaries from the widely scattered territories, Buxton invited Philip, Anna Gurney, and Priscilla Buxton to help him write the Committee's Report.[14] It supplied the definitive humanitarian, missionary-informed, analysis of the evils of settler-led colonialism. The Report concluded that all over the globe 'the intercourse of Europeans in general, without any exception in favour of the subjects of Great Britain, has been, unless when attended by missionary exertions, a source of many calamities to uncivilized nations'.[15]

To get the Report accepted by the end of the 1837 parliamentary session, Buxton had to tone down his scathing criticisms of the Cape's colonial authorities and the British settlers. Nevertheless, the hearings had already

---

[12] Buxton, *Memoirs*, p. 361; J. G. Pretorius, *The British Humanitarians and the Cape Eastern Frontier, 1834–1836* (Pretoria, 1988), p. 12.

[13] Buxton, *Memoirs*, p. 360.

[14] Ibid., p. 415; Z. Laidlaw, 'Aunt Anna's Report: The Buxton Women and the Aborigines Select Committee, 1835–37', *Journal of Imperial and Commonwealth History*, XXXII, 2 (2004), pp. 1–28.

[15] *Report*, p. 5.

influenced Glenelg, who told Governor D'Urban, 'it is a melancholy and humiliating... truth that the contiguity of the subjects of the nations of Christendom with uncivilized tribes has invariably produced wretchedness and decay and not seldom the utter extermination of the weaker party'.[16] Glenelg then restored the short-lived Queen Adelaide Province to Xhosa chiefly rule. This act of retrocession, described by Buxton as 'life itself, and liberty, and lands and tenements to a whole nation', was to be perhaps the most significant policy initiative arising out of missionary and humanitarian influence during the first half of the nineteenth century. British settlers in the Cape accused the humanitarians and the Colonial Office of betraying them and endangering the security of the Empire as a whole. Nonetheless, Dr Thomas Hodgkin was inspired by the Committee to establish in 1837 an ongoing British and Foreign Aborigines Protection Society with Buxton as President. The Society aimed 'to assist in protecting the defenceless and promoting the advancement of Uncivilized Tribes' by guiding colonial policy through the publication of materials and the mobilization of 'popular opinion'.[17] The Committee also prompted offshoots in the colonies, with John Saunders, for instance, launching an Aborigines Protection Society in Sydney in 1838. Such trans-imperial institutional humanitarianism would continue through the remainder of the nineteenth and into the twentieth centuries, intervening critically, if not always particularly powerfully, in British colonial affairs.

Australia

Buxton and his allies had long been in receipt of communications from missionaries in the Australian colonies, which also blamed British colonists for the degradation, and worse, of indigenous peoples. James Backhouse from the Norwich community of Quakers was a close acquaintance of Buxton's relatives the Gurneys, and became a critical source of information on the colonies of the southern hemisphere. Buxton introduced him to the personnel of the Colonial Office in order to 'smooth his path' for a proposed tour of the Australian colonies with his fellow Quaker George Walker. From 1832 to 1838 the pair travelled through Australia 'for the purpose of

[16] R. Vigne, ' "Die Man Wat Die Groot Trek Veroorsaak Het": Glenelg's Personal Contribution to the Cancellation of D'Urban's Dispossession of the Rarabe in 1835', *Kleio*, XXX (1998), p. 38.

[17] R. Rainger, 'Philanthropy and Science in the 1830's', *Man*, XV (1980), pp. 707–8.

discharging a religious duty'. Their connections with Elizabeth Fry meant that transported prisoners' rights would be one crucial issue, but relations between British settlers and Australian Aborigines were also a subject of investigation. Backhouse sent copies of his reports as well as personal letters to Buxton, requesting that he lobby for 'legislative action on penal reform and policies regarding Aborigines'.[18]

Governors of Australian colonies also commissioned reports from the two Quakers, which were printed for circulation in the colonies and in Britain. The report on Tasmania was representative: 'we cannot but deprecate the short sighted policy, by which, in the Colonization of New Countries, the lands of the Aboriginal Inhabitants have been wrested from them, with little or no regard to their natural and indefeasible rights'.[19] Humanitarian members of the Aborigines Committee were naturally receptive to such representations, and the message was reinforced when the Committee interviewed witnesses and received written testimony from Australia.

The two main witnesses from New South Wales, Archdeacon Broughton and the Presbyterian minister J. D. Lang, reinforced the warning that the fate of Tasmania's Aborigines might be replicated on the mainland:

The deadly antipathy which has existed between the Aborigines and the Bushrangers of Van Diemen's Land provoked a series of outrages which would have terminated in the utter extermination of the whole race, if the local Government had not interposed to remove the last remnant of them from the island; an act of real mercy, though of apparent severity.[20]

At least, Broughton confidently declared, the survivors on Flinders Island were now 'more advantageously placed with regard to the advantage of acquiring Christianity'.[21] The voices of the 'survivors' themselves were not heard.

The directors of three of the main missionary societies, Dandeson Coates of the CMS, John Beecham of the WMS, and William Ellis of the LMS, also gave evidence on Australia, emphasizing 'the illicit intercourse of Europeans with the female Aborigines... a source of the most afflictive and distressing

---

[18] A. Johnston, 'The Well-Intentioned Imperialists: Missionary Textuality and (Post)Colonial Politics', in Bruce Bennett, Susan Cowan, Jacqueline Lo, Satendra Nandan, and Jennifer Webb, eds., *Resistance and Reconciliation: Writing in the Commonwealth* (Canberra, 2003), p. 105.

[19] Ibid.

[20] *Report*, p. 84.

[21] Ibid., p. 24.

consequences... [leading] to infanticide to a considerable extent'.[22] Information on these practices had come to Coates from the Revd W. Watson, a CMS missionary in New South Wales. The Committee's Report concluded that the effects of free British settlement in New South Wales had been 'dreadful beyond example, both in the diminution of [the Aborigines'] numbers and in their demoralization'.[23]

Missionary opinions varied about the role deliberate murder might have played in this disaster. The Committee's main informants on Australia were loath to imagine that anything like the systematic murder of Aborigines at the hands of 'respectable' Britons was being carried out (as are some contemporary historians).[24] While 'many deeds of murder and violence have undoubtedly been committed by the stock-keepers (convicts in the employ of farmers on the outskirts of the colony), by the cedar-cutters, and by other remote free settlers, and many natives have perished by the various military parties sent against them', the Report advised, 'it is not to violence only that their decrease is ascribed'. According to Broughton's evidence quoted in the final Report: 'They do not so much retire as decay; wherever Europeans meet with them they appear to wear out, and gradually to decay: they diminish in numbers; they appear actually to vanish from the face of the earth.' This conception of European influence working indirectly rather than systematically to 'diminish' Aborigines was reinforced by the evidence of Lang, also quoted in the Report: 'From the prevalence of infanticide, from intemperance and from European diseases, their number is evidently and rapidly diminishing.'[25]

Lancelot Threlkeld, who maintained a Methodist mission at Lake Macquarie, however, joined others with frontier experience in blaming relatively well-off and 'respectable' squatters (rather than the actions of colonial 'riff raff') for attempts to 'exterminate' the Aborigines persisting on 'their' land. Threlkeld had raised the ire of local settlers through his attempts to prevent the systematic abuse of Aboriginal women and killing of Aboriginal men. His 1825 report to the LMS Directors pointed out that 'no man who comes to this colony and has ground and corn can dispassionately view the subject of the blacks, their interest says annihilate the race'. According to local settlers,

---

[22] Ibid., p. 486.   [23] Ibid., pp. 10–11.
[24] G. D. B. Smithers, 'Reassuring "White Australia" ', *Journal of Social History*, XXXVII (2003), pp. 493–505.
[25] *Report*, pp. 10–11, 17.

'blacks were only a specie of baboon that might be shot down with impunity, like an Ourang Outang!'[26]

Violence around Threlkeld's station intensified over the next decade as settlers moved up the river valleys of northern New South Wales. Aboriginal resistance, typically through killing of stock, inspired exterminatory settler raiding parties. Threlkeld compiled evidence on the atrocities, which he passed on to other missionaries, officials, and members of the judiciary. He also mobilized an informal network of support following his speech to the founding meeting of the Aborigines Protection Society in Sydney. He accused newspapers such as the *Sydney Morning Herald* of 'criminality in the sight of God', for having inflamed their readership's mind against the Aborigines, warning that, 'while [editors] could shelter behind the editorial "we", that would avail them nothing when they were called to answer for their deeds "before the Judge of all" '.[27] His 1837 report to the LMS complained that a 'war of extirpation' was under way in New South Wales. Anyone who tried to speak out faced intimidation from 'lawless banditti' who defied British law 'to its very teeth'. Threlkeld won some initial sympathy from Governor George Gipps, but alienated the Governor with his next report, which implicated the colony's senior military officer for killing innocent Aborigines during a campaign along the Gwydir River valley.[28]

Although Threlkeld was unusually vocal, he proved less successful at imbricating himself within Buxton's international humanitarian network. His direct testimony did not figure in the Select Committee's proceedings. Threlkeld also managed to alienate influential churchmen in the colony, like Samuel Marsden, and even his own LMS superiors, who judged that he was spending their money recklessly and had cut him off from further funding by 1826. 'While Threlkeld could produce large amounts of information about the Awabakal people, in particular, and what he assumed was their "need" for salvation, he could not promote their cause in an appealing enough manner to ensure important moral support from Britain.'[29] This reflected not only his financial circumstances but also the contingent ways that 'truth'

---

[26] Henry Reynolds, *This Whispering in our Hearts* (St Leonards, NSW, 1998), pp. 24–46, 63–4.
[27] Ibid., p. 65.
[28] Roger Milliss, *Waterloo Creek: The Australia Day Massacre of 1838* (Sydney, 1992), pp. 609–10.
[29] A. Johnston, 'Mission Statements: Textuality and Morality in the Colonial Archive', in P. Mead, ed., *Australian Literary Studies in the 21st Century: Proceedings of the 2000 ASAL Conference* (Hobart, 2001), p. 157.

and 'knowledge' travelled from colony to metropole through the imperial networks of the day. James Read in the eastern Cape was at least as controversial a figure, yet his testimony was taken seriously and helped shape the understandings of powerful humanitarian interests because of the close relationship that his superintendent, John Philip, had forged with Buxton. Activist missionaries in Australia, such as Threlkeld and Louis Giustiniani of the Western Australia Missionary Society, lacked the kind of mediation between their local concerns and the agenda of metropolitan agencies that Philip could provide for the LMS missionaries in the Cape. The Aborigines Committee consequently chose to rely upon the more muted and restrained testimony of figures such as Broughton and Lang, who either knew little of the activities of remote 'frontier' missionaries or, in Threlkeld's case, were actually in dispute with them.

Giustiniani earned the contempt of the Swan River colonists by threatening to expose them before the 'enlightened British public, and the whole civilized world'. Without an effective conduit such as Philip, he wrote directly to Glenelg with accounts of a punitive expedition, which had taken 'revenge' for the killing of five settlers by killing and mutilating eighteen Aborigines.[30] This kind of missionary appeal provoked settler newspaper editors to forge their own trans-imperial webs of communication. In the Cape and New South Wales, for instance, editors copied extracts from each other condemning the same humanitarian 'enemies', such as Glenelg and Stephen in Britain, and the unfortunate Richard Bourke. Thanks to correspondence between the *Graham's Town Journal* and the *Sydney Morning Herald*, Bourke carried a reputation as a naive, sentimental, and 'meddling' reformer from the Cape to New South Wales. From the beginning of his tenure in Australia, Bourke found himself vehemently opposed by a vocal section of the New South Wales settlers for Ordinance 50 and other reforms at the Cape.

Though figures such as Giustiniani's testimony did not figure much in the Aborigines Committee's proceedings, it still made waves in Britain. Glenelg condemned the governor of the Swan River Colony for threatening the vengeful general destruction of local Aborigines. He had also insisted that settlers and soldiers who shot Aborigines claiming self-defence be brought to trial. In 1839 Gipps in New South Wales issued a public notice declaring 'that each succeeding dispatch from the Secretary of State [Glenelg's successor], marks in an increasing degree the importance which Her Majesty's

[30] Reynolds, *This Whispering*, pp. 85–8.

Government, and no less Parliament and the people of Great Britain, attach to the just and humane treatment of the aborigines'.[31] Although metropolitan intervention in Australia did not extend to restoration of land seized from indigenous people, it had real and unsettling effects for many settlers. As the Aborigines Committee recommended, 'Protectors of Aborigines' were appointed to each of the Australian colonies. They were to attach themselves to specific tribes and 'protect them as far as they could... from any encroachments on their property, and from acts of cruelty, oppression, or injustice, and faithfully represent their wants, wishes, and grievances' to the colonial government.[32] The intersecting roles of the Protectors and the missionaries in the colony were made clear in the Committee's Report:

> Especially [the Protectors] should claim for the maintenance of the Aborigines such lands as may be necessary for their support... The education of the young will of course be amongst the foremost of the cares of the missionaries; and the Protectors should render every assistance in their power in advancing this all-important part of any general scheme of improvement.[33]

The Myall Creek massacre of 1838 provided a test case for the effectiveness of the new measures. Eleven former convicts were tried for the murder of twenty-eight Aborigines. Despite Threlkeld's evidence of a conversation involving one of the culprits, a jury of colonists acquitted them. One of the jurors later remarked, 'I look on them [the Aborigines] as a set of monkeys, and I think the earlier they are exterminated the better. I know well they [the accused] are guilty of murder, but I for one, would never consent to see a white man suffer for shooting a black one.'[34] On Governor Gipps's insistence, seven of the settlers were retried for the murder of a child among those killed, and this time they were found guilty and hanged—an unprecedented penalty for the murder of Aborigines. Settler invective indicted not only the judiciary and the Aborigines, but also the 'ineffective' and 'misguided' missionaries who saw the Aborigines as reclaimable in the first place.

New Zealand

By 1833 concerns about the relations between Briton and Maori, generated largely by the CMS missionaries, had resulted in the appointment of James

---

[31] G. R. Mellor, *British Imperial Trusteeship, 1783–1850* (London, 1951), pp. 292–3.
[32] Ibid., pp. 291–3.   [33] *Report*, p. 83.
[34] Manning Clark, *A History of Australia*, abridged by M. Cathcart (London, 1993), p. 201.

Busby as an official British Resident in New Zealand. Busby reported that the British whalers, traders, and early settlers were provoking increased warfare and insisted that the 'miserable condition of the Maori had some claim of justice upon the protection of the British government'. He pressed Buxton to agitate for more, not less, formal British intervention.[35] The Aborigines Committee commented that 'it will be hard ... to find compensation ... for the murders, the misery, the contamination which we have brought upon [the Maori]. Our runaway convicts [and sailors, whalers, and traders] ... too frequently act in the most reckless and immoral manner when at a distance from the restraints of justice.' 'In proof', the Report continued, 'we need only refer to the evidence of the missionaries.'[36] It was correspondence from Henry Williams of the CMS and his society's Director, Dandeson Coates, that was cited most often. Coates told the Committee of an incident in 1830 when Captain Stewart of the ship *Elizabeth* and some British flax traders conspired with their Maori trading partners to lure a rival Maori chief and his followers into an ambush where many were massacred, as part of a trade deal. The Committee cited such actions, unregulated by proper authorities, as the worst form of British overseas activity.

Fearing, on advice from Williams and a former Colonial Secretary, Lord Goderich, that the Maori teetered on the verge of extinction, the Committee recommended using 'every possible method to rescue the natives of those extensive islands from the further evils which impend over them, and to deliver our own country from the disgrace and crime of having either occasioned or tolerated such enormities'.[37] As with South Africa, Glenelg was convinced by the Committee's findings of 'the necessity of some interposition by the British Government for the protection, both of the British settlers and of the natives' in New Zealand.[38]

However, even as Glenelg wrote, Edward Gibbon Wakefield's New Zealand Company was sending out its first parties of 'systematic colonizers'. Something more effective than a British Resident would be needed to regulate this much more extensive settlement. The Treaty of Waitangi, procured by the new Consul, William Hobson, followed from the Committee's prescriptions in 1840. It established Maori title, reserved large areas for exclusive Maori

[35] C. Orange, 'The Maori People and the British Crown (1769–1840)', in K. Sinclair, ed., *The Illustrated Oxford History of New Zealand*, 2nd edn. (Melbourne, 1996), p. 42.
[36] *Report*, p. 17.
[37] Ibid.
[38] Mellor, *British Imperial Trusteeship*, p. 335.

occupation, and required the Company to use state-registered channels to purchase land for settlers. Though it was an annexation rather than a retrocession of land, the Treaty seemed a humanitarian triumph comparable to the quashing of Queen Adelaide Province, and 'an experiment akin to emancipation'.[39] It was certainly upheld as a model for future settler–Aborigine relations by Australian humanitarians.[40]

However, the missionaries Henry Williams and his son Edward laid the basis for unending controversy because their English translation of the Treaty differed from the Maori version printed by the Paihia mission press. The Maori text seemed to promise the full authority of chiefs over their lands and the cession only of a more general governorship of the country. The British missionaries had played a crucial part in persuading the Maori signatories to accept the treaty by offering reassurance on this issue.[41] Settlers viewed the Treaty in yet a different light, seeing its supporters and the missionaries as placing the needs of Maori 'savages' above those of fellow Britons.[42] In the settler imagination, neither the persistent Maori claim to sovereignty nor Maori possession of the land was safeguarded by the Treaty. According to the company-financed and settler-edited *Nelson Examiner*, the Treaty did not safeguard Maori land but merely ensured that the Maori would benefit from its alienation to a more civilized race.[43]

Consul Hobson further endeavoured to pursue the Aborigines Committee's findings by supporting the CMS missionaries and appointing a Protector of Aborigines on the model already established in Australia. Through this Protectorate, 'missionary influence impinged directly on the government' in New Zealand.[44] Reluctantly, the CMS missionary George Clarke took on the role of Chief Protector in 1840, and soon found himself under pressure from the colonial government to act on its behalf in land sale negotiations with the Maori. If he did not necessarily please government

[39] C. Hall, 'Imperial Man: Edward Eyre in Australasia and the West Indies, 1833–66', in B. Schwarz, ed., *The Expansion of England: Race, Ethnicity and Cultural History* (London, 1996), p. 147.

[40] Reynolds, *This Whispering*, p. 36.

[41] Orange, 'The Maori People', p. 47.

[42] P. Moon, 'Three Historical Interpretations of the Treaty of Waitangi', *Electronic Journal of Australian and New Zealand History* <http://www.jcu.edu.au/aff/history/articles/moon.htm> (1999).

[43] *NENZC*, 12 Mar. 1842.

[44] C. H. Wake, 'George Clarke and the Government of the Maoris: 1840–45', *Historical Studies: Australia and New Zealand*, X (1962), p. 355.

officials in this role, he certainly angered settlers. From the beginning, the majority of settlers opposed the Protectorate because 'they wanted free access to the land unhindered by consideration of the native title'. Indeed, many settlers charged that the 'missionaries and "missionary-ridden" government were... villainously studying the ruin of the colony and the colonists'. Instead of protection, they demanded 'amalgamation', a term deployed by the New Zealand Company to mean the transfer of nine-tenths of the land to the settlers and the reduction of the bulk of Maori to a landless proletariat.[45]

Clarke further fuelled settler animosity by siding with the Maori over the Wairau 'Affray' in 1843, sparked by the Company's sale to British immigrants of land it had not acquired through the channels required by the Treaty of Waitangi. When the Maori chiefs Te Rauparaha and Te Ranghaeata sacked a colonial surveyor's property, a British magistrate accompanied by armed settlers set out to arrest them for looting. When they provoked a fight, in which twenty-one of them died (including one of Wakefield's brothers), British authorities put the blame plainly on the settlers for 'needlessly violating the law'.[46] Governor Fitzroy held a meeting with the chiefs in 1844 to announce that the British authorities would not be seeking revenge.[47] The settlers of Nelson, however, were more inclined to blame the missionaries—especially Clarke, who had published an address in Maori stating that both the settlers and the Maori had been 'wrong according to the laws both of God and man'.[48] Alfred Domett, writing in the *Nelson Examiner*, argued that Clarke and the missionaries stood to gain by inciting the Maori to violence, because they were engaged in the private accumulation of land and capital, ventures that would be threatened by the increasing oversight of local settler authorities. Furthermore, missionaries feared that settlers would deflect Maori attention from themselves as the sole representatives and purveyors of a superior culture. If Company-appointed bishops arrived, their own status among the Maori would inevitably diminish. A subsequent settler petition to Queen Victoria complained that 'the annual expense of the Protectorship of the Aborigines is about £3,000 a year, while not one penny is expended in protecting the settlers against the natives'.[49]

---

[45] Ibid., pp. 343–4. [46] *NENZC*, suppl., 23 Dec. 1843.
[47] J. Belich, *The Victorian Interpretation of Racial Conflict: The Maori, the British and the New Zealand Wars* (Montreal, 1989), p. 21.
[48] *NENZC*, 16 Dec. 1843.
[49] *NENZC*, suppl., 23 Dec. 1843.

Like their counterparts in the Cape and New South Wales, New Zealand settlers also used the colonial press to appeal to a more popular metropolitan readership. The *Nelson Examiner* applauded the *Times's* coverage of the 'massacre', which was itself based on articles in the *Nelson Examiner*.[50] In a comment that feminized humanitarianism, in the same way that indigenous peoples were often feminized within colonial discourses, the metropolitan and the settler papers concurred that the 'work of colonizing New Zealand' properly 'must be accomplished by the statesmanship and the management of men of common-sense—not by the old woman policies of Protectors'.[51]

Humanitarian Marginalization

By the mid-1840s a groundswell of opposition to the Christian-humanitarian model of colonization advocated by the Aborigines Committee missionaries had become evident. Colonial settlers found opinions quoted more often and their representations more willingly accepted 'at home'. Even as the dispute over the Wairau 'Affray' continued in 1843, the *Nelson Examiner* noted that its humanitarian enemies were no longer so powerful in Britain. It complained only that, 'having ceased or worn out at home', humanitarianism 'still has life and activity' in the person of government officials 'here'. 'The waves continue to roll when the storm that raised them is laid.'[52]

Christian-humanitarian discourse found its influence diminished during this period as the result of a variety of interconnected developments. Some of these developments, such as the loss of Buxton's parliamentary seat in 1837, and of Glenelg at the Colonial Office in 1839, reflected shifts in metropolitan politics. The origins of others were dispersed across a number of imperial sites. A very significant factor was widespread British disappointment at the results of emancipation in the West Indies. Abolitionists and their supporters had assumed that most freed labourers in the West Indies would progress towards 'civilization' through continued work on the plantations. The 'missionary dream', as Hall describes it, pictured sober, docile, black Christians dedicating themselves productively to the free market, post-emancipation economy of the Caribbean—'a dream which fragmented as the missionaries came to realize, to a greater or lesser extent, that they could not control the destinies of others'.[53] Within a few years of emancipation the majority of

---

[50] *NENZC*, 16 Dec. 1843.   [51] *NENZC*, suppl., 23 Dec. 1843.
[52] Ibid.   [53] Hall, *Civilising Subjects*, p. 21.

planters in Jamaica were in debt and capital was scarce. Ignoring underlying economic factors, planters blamed their distress on the desertion of roughly half of their labour force as former slaves moved off the plantations to cultivate their own small plots of land in the hilly parts of the island. William Knibb admitted that 'The new Black subjects he had envisaged were less industrious and domesticated than he would have liked.'[54] More galling for abolitionist missionaries, freed black West Indians shunned their religious authority, appropriating Christianity instead to new and syncretic forms such as revivalism, obeahism, and myalism. (See pp. 34 and 219–26.) The 'failure' of freed slaves to perform Christianity 'properly' smacked of ingratitude to their supposed benefactors. It seemed that, 'the freed people had ... reverted to African barbarism'.[55]

Despite disappointments in the West Indies, Buxton persisted in attempts to combat slavery in Africa itself and to sustain a metropolitan sense of concern for indigenous peoples. When the Niger Expedition of 1841, intended 'to attack slavery at its source' by introducing Christianity and 'legitimate commerce' to the parts of Africa most blighted by slave-trading, met disaster, the Aborigines Protection Society reflected that it had 'not attained to that magnitude and importance, or achieved those results, which doubtless [its] early friends ... might reasonably anticipate'.[56] (See p. 52.) Most other observers drew a starker conclusion: Europeans had no hope of bringing redemptive light to the denizens of a 'dark continent' which was more than capable of swallowing puny and naive humanitarian endeavours. Charles Dickens pronounced the expedition 'the prime example of philanthropic folly'.[57]

Influential commentators on colonial affairs such as Dickens, Thomas Carlyle, and Matthew Arnold (who savaged Bishop Colenso of Natal for being seduced into heresy by his Zulu congregation) helped make humanitarians figures of ridicule in mid-nineteenth-century Britain.[58] When an

[54] C. Hall, 'William Knibb and the Constitution of the New Black Subject', in M. Daunton and R. Halpern, eds., *Empire and Others: British Encounters with Indigenous Peoples, 1600–1850* (London, 1999), 320.

[55] T. C. Holt, *The Problem of Freedom: Race, Labor, and Politics in Jamaica and Britain, 1832–1938* (Baltimore, 1992), pp. 116–17, 146.

[56] Rainger, 'Philanthropy and Science', p. 709; P. Brantlinger, 'Victorians and Africans: The Genealogy of the Myth of the Dark Continent', in H. L. Gates, ed., *Race, Writing and Difference* (London, 1986), pp. 192–3.

[57] D. A. Lorimer, *Colour, Class, and the Victorians* (Leicester, 1978), p. 116.

[58] J. Guy, 'Class, Imperialism and Literary Criticism', *Journal of Southern African Studies*, XXIII (1997), pp. 219–41.

increasing proportion of the British population saw family and friends emigrate to the colonies, unrepentant humanitarians were confounded by a general swelling of sympathy for their settler foes in places where violent indigenous resistance was peaking, such as the eastern Cape in 1847–8 and 1850–2, New Zealand in 1845–6 and 1863–4, and India in 1857. During each of these episodes the metropolitan public imbibed media images of half-naked 'savages' raping, mutilating, and killing innocent Britons, as well as more intimate expressions of fear and loathing from the private correspondence of friends and relatives among the settlers overseas. The sympathy that was aroused between metropolitan and colonial Britons during such crises contributed greatly to the dissipation of humanitarian political influence after the 1840s.

The controversy over Governor Eyre's suppression of the Morant Bay Revolt in Jamaica in 1865 'crystallized Victorian thinking' about racial difference.[59] Eyre, who had been a Protector of the Aborigines in South Australia in his early career, crushed the uprising of former slaves seeking more access to land and hanged 439 of its participants, including a 'mixed-race' member of the House of Assembly. Prominent liberals and radicals including John Stuart Mill, John Bright, and Charles Darwin sought to have Eyre prosecuted, but he was successfully defended both by the island's planters and by such leading figures as Dickens, Carlyle, and Alfred Tennyson.[60] *The Times* found Morant Bay even more disappointing than the Indian Mutiny because 'its inhabitants are our spoilt children'. Though it had been claimed 'in Jamaica that the negro could become fit for self-government... Jamaica herself gainsays the fact and belies herself', the reason being that it is 'impossible to eradicate the original savageness of the African blood'.[61]

Although shifts in public opinion helped, perhaps the most direct way in which settlers won their argument with humanitarians was through being granted representative government and the right, albeit hedged by continuing but often ineffective metropolitan safeguards, to devise their own 'native policies'. Lord Durham's Report, which had first advocated the granting of self-government as a way of securing the continued loyalty of the Canadian colonies, was written only two years after the Aborigines Committee Report, in 1839. It countermanded the thrust of that prior report through much of

---

[59] C. Bolt, *Victorian Attitudes to Race* (London, 1971), p. xi.

[60] B. Semmel, *The Governor Eyre Controversy* (London, 1962); G. Heuman, *The Killing Time: The Morant Bay Rebellion in Jamaica* (Knoxville, Tenn., 1994).

[61] Bolt, *Victorian Attitudes*, pp. 76–7.

the nineteenth and twentieth centuries by placing the political fate of colonized peoples largely in the hands of locally elected settler legislatures.[62] The effect was to make humanitarian opinion in Britain largely irrelevant to the activities of colonial governance.

Governor George Grey showed in both the Cape and New Zealand how settler legislatures could help overturn humanitarian precepts 'on the ground'. During his first governorship of New Zealand (1845–53) Grey dismissed Clarke and closed down the Protectorate. In both his terms as governor (the second from 1861 to 1868) he concentrated on combating Maori sovereignty through military force. In between times he assisted in crushing Xhosa resistance on the eastern Cape frontier and entrenching British rule once more over the former Queen Adelaide Province, now known as British Kaffraria. Grey barely encountered any real opposition from the old stalwarts of the missionary–humanitarian network in either colony, while ensuring that the settlers' version of 'amalgamation' became official policy.

In the Australian colonies, by the end of the 1840s, mission stations were collapsing, having lost access to government funds because of their failure to attract settled converts. Protectorates of Aborigines were either abolished or neutered. While South Australia gave the job of protection to the police, in Western Australia the office became briefly the 'Guardian of Natives and Protector of Settlers'. The following year that office too was effectively abolished.[63] As in the Cape and in the West Indies before it, the refusal of those 'saved' by Christian humanitarians to conform to apparently universal, but in fact deeply ethnocentric, notions of 'civilized' conduct was interpreted as betraying a lack of gratitude and their incapacity to 'progress'. Even where large numbers of indigenous people were adopting Christianity, the way they adapted Christian practices and beliefs to their own needs alienated many of the original supporters of the missionary enterprise.

Humanitarian influence had by no means disappeared. Well into the twentieth century the Aborigines Protection Society and its allies continued to mobilize support in Britain and to act as guardians of the legitimacy of the Empire. Though they did little to prevent further colonial aggressions, fear of their criticism could have a restraining influence. When, for instance, during

---

[62] Julie Evans, Patricia Grimshaw, David Philips, and Shurlee Swain, *Equal Subjects, Unequal Rights: Indigenous Peoples in British Settler Colonies, 1830s–1910* (Manchester, 2003).

[63] Mellor, *British Imperial Trusteeship*, p. 312.

the Anglo-Zulu War of 1879, General Sir Garnet Wolseley confessed to his wish 'to let loose the Swazies' upon the northern Zulu, who had been insufficiently punished by the shooting of 10,000 men, he still felt obliged 'to think of the howling Societies at home who have sympathy with all black men whilst they care nothing for the miseries & cruelties inflicted upon their own kith and kin who have the misfortune to be located near these interesting niggers'.[64] In other places and at other times during the later nineteenth century, too, humanitarian mobilization could prove effective on specific issues, especially when associated with popular figures such as David Livingstone. But indignation was more often directed at African slavers or rival European colonialists like Leopold in the Congo than at fellow Britons in the colonies of settlement. Many missionaries in British colonies continued to rail against powerful local settler interests,[65] but the undercutting of the early nineteenth-century 'missionary dream'—founded on a very particular model of civilization and Christianity—and the empowerment of colonial legislatures—removed their access to the efficacious trans-imperial political network that flourished under Buxton. Though, as Andrew Porter observes in Chapter 3, 'increasingly missionaries called the humanitarian tune, with humanitarians and bodies such as the Anti-Slavery Society and the Aborigines Protection Society dependent on fluctuating missionary concern', both humanitarians and missionaries had lost the ability to challenge settler colonialism on its home ground.

Select Bibliography

ELIZABETH ELBOURNE, *Blood Ground: Colonialism, Missions, and the Contest for Christianity in the Cape Colony and Britain, 1799–1853* (Montreal, 2002).

—— *The Eastern Cape and International Networks in the Early Nineteenth Century*, Fort Hare Institute of Social and Economic Research Working Paper Series, XLIII (Aug. 2003).

NORMAN ETHERINGTON, *Preachers, Peasants and Politics in Southeast Africa, 1835–80* (London, 1978).

JULIE EVANS, PATRICIA GRIMSHAW, DAVID PHILIPS, and SHURLEE SWAIN, *Equal Subjects, Unequal Rights: Indigenous Peoples in British Settler Colonies, 1830s–1910* (Manchester, 2003).

---

[64] *The South African Journal of Sir Garnet Wolseley, 1879–1880*, ed. Adrian Preston (Cape Town, 1973), p. 71.

[65] Jeff Guy, *The Heretic* (Pietermaritzburg, 1983), pp. 193–333.

Jeff Guy, *The Heretic* (Pietermaritzburg, 1983).
Catherine Hall, *Civilizing Subjects: Metropole and Colony in the English Imagination, 1830–1867* (Cambridge, 2002).
T. C. Holt, *The Problem of Freedom: Race, Labor, and Politics in Jamaica and Britain, 1832–1938* (Baltimore, 1992).
Anna Johnston, *Missionary Writing and Empire, 1800–1860* (Cambridge, 2003).
Zoë Laidlaw, 'Integrating Metropolitan, Colonial and Imperial Histories—the Aborigines Select Committee of 1835–37', in T. Banivanna Mar and J. Evans, eds., *Writing Colonial Histories: Comparative Perspectives* (Melbourne, 2002), pp. 75–91.
—— 'Networks, Patronage and Information in Colonial Governance', D.Phil. thesis (Oxford, 2001).
David Lambert, *White Colonial Culture, Politics and Identity: Barbados in the Age of Abolition* (Cambridge, 2004).
Alan Lester, *Imperial Networks: Creating Identities in Nineteenth Century South Africa and Britain* (London, 2001).
—— 'British Settler Discourse and the Circuits of Empire', *History Workshop Journal*, LIV (2002), pp. 27–50.
G. R. Mellor, *British Imperial Trusteeship, 1783–1850* (London, 1951).
Roger Milliss, *Waterloo Creek: The Australia Day Massacre of 1838* (Sydney, 1992).
Claudia Orange, *The Treaty of Waitangi* (London, 1987).
J. G. Pretorius, *The British Humanitarians and the Cape Eastern Frontier, 1834–1836* (Pretoria, 1988).
Henry Reynolds, *This Whispering in our Hearts* (St Leonards, NSW, 1998).
David Turley, *The Culture of English Antislavery, 1780–1860* (London, 1991).
C. H. Wake, 'George Clarke and the Government of the Maoris: 1840–45', *Historical Studies: Australia and New Zealand*, X (1962), pp. 339–56.

5

Where the Missionary Frontier Ran Ahead of Empire

JOHN BARKER

In the 1790s newly formed British mission societies began sending evangelists to the far corners of the world. Thirty years later a few missions had become firmly established in the Pacific islands and Africa. Reinforcements and the entry of more denominations steadily increased the missionary presence in following years. This early work would prove to be a prelude to the colonial period, which unleashed a massive effort to convert Europe's new subjects. Yet the missionary efforts that occurred ahead of Empire had important consequences. At home, reports on the efforts in exotic locales served to elevate the missionary movement from the margins of respectable Christianity to the centre of British public life. In the mission fields the pioneers largely invented through trial and error basic practices and standards. Most importantly, they established beachheads for the later expansion of Christianity by preparing and encouraging converts who in time became the main emissaries of the Word in foreign places.

Before the mid-1870s few missionaries could have imagined that almost all the Pacific and Africa would soon become the colonial property of the Great Powers. The pre-colonial history of modern missions is of interest not just for understanding what came later but also for what might have been in the absence of European imperialism. The missionaries of the early nineteenth century conducted their labours as guests of indigenous rulers and peoples, not as colonial agents. Usually far from the protection of their government and sponsors, they relied heavily upon local populations for their security and basic material needs. Most quickly grasped that progress required patience and compromise. By the mid-century, turning necessity into a virtue, Henry Venn, the influential Secretary of the Church Missionary Society, made the rapid creation of autonomous indigenous churches the highest goal of missionary efforts. Some missions came very close to achieving this in the Pacific. While the colonial takeover would stimulate a massive expansion of missionary efforts, ironically enough it set back the goal of creating truly localized churches by many years.

This chapter focuses on developments in missions to the Pacific islands with some comparative notes on Africa in order to highlight the key interactions that shaped the early reception of Christianity on a frontier where indigenous peoples still retained autonomy over their lives. Particularly important were the interactions with local elites, which established the political limits of missionary penetration; interactions with new Christians, which refashioned imported religious ideas to local assumptions and aspirations; and interactions with other European agents on the scene, which, together with missions, conditioned the entry of indigenous peoples into the spreading economic and political hegemony of the Great Powers.

Missionaries and Chiefs

The sponsors of the first missions to the Pacific and Africa possessed an extraordinary confidence that the mere presence of the cross would win 'savage' hearts and minds from pagan darkness. The bearers of the cross were, to a large extent, men and women of modest education and means, sent out with scant provisions to distant peoples with whose languages, customs, and political circumstances they were utterly unfamiliar. Furthermore, they travelled to places where interference from European traders and adventurers had already disrupted communities by introducing new diseases and by aggravating violence between competing factions for coveted trade goods. Some missionaries were killed upon arrival, the victims of acts of vengeance against wrongs perpetrated by earlier visitors. Others fell to malaria or fled in the face of war. Those who settled down found that the act of proclaiming the gospel truth carried its own risks. A series of missionaries to the southern New Hebrides met their ends after declaring to the terrified natives that the god they represented was the source of the terrible epidemics decimating their people. Some found solace in the bottle and a few left the mission to live as natives themselves. When reading the accounts of these early days, the greatest wonder is that any missions got established at all.

Survival largely depended on carefully cultivating alliances with local leaders. Mission directors formally required their agents to submit themselves to local authorities and not engage in political activities, although few could resist offering advice to chiefs when the opportunity arose. Further, most missionaries of this period 'believed in the ultimate rightness of a monarchical form of government'[1] and succeeded in deluding themselves that the native 'kings' they encountered resembled European monarchs in terms of public legitimacy and power. Above all else, they assumed that if they could win over the elite, the rest of the population would soon follow.

By attaching themselves to one or another 'king', the early missionaries implicated themselves in long-running political contests they could scarcely comprehend and over which they had little control. The cost of association with a chief on the losing side of a conflict could be exile or sudden death. But ascendant chiefs also caused problems. Once the novelty of the missionaries' peculiar rituals wore off, and especially once they ran out of supplies and became dependent upon local people for survival, missionaries found themselves in a precarious position, at best tolerated by their patrons. In Tahiti the early missionaries were quickly reduced to rags, living in hovels, their plight made worse by the taunts of small beach communities of castaways and escaped convicts from Australia who curried favour with the chiefs by ridiculing their poverty. In New Zealand, as in southern Africa, the Maori chiefs put 'their' missionaries to work as diplomatic liaisons with European powers and to procure and repair firearms. Thus, 'the Christian community existed in the Maori world on Maori terms'.[2]

With a few exceptions, missionaries to Africa failed to win over local elites prior to the colonial period. Their early converts came mostly from the margins of society: escaped or recovered slaves, war refugees, and other outcasts and displaced people. In the Pacific islands, however, within two decades of their arrival, the missionaries witnessed a massive movement of people from all levels of society into the Church.

Most accounts date the beginnings of Christianity in Polynesia to the arrival in 1797 of thirty 'godly mechanics' sent by the London Missionary Society (LMS) to Tahiti; but a strong claim can also be made for Pomare II's decision in 1812 to become a Christian. The missionary party had tied their fortunes to Pomare's father in the mistaken belief that he controlled the island. Even within the Pomare faction they found, as John Davies complained in 1806, that there was no 'sincere desire of instruction manifested by any as to the truths of the Gospel, but on the contrary much aversion'.[3] While friendlier, Pomare II followed his father's strategy of increasing human sacrifices to the Oro cult to advance his political ambitions while engaging

---

[1] Douglas L. Oliver, *Ancient Tahitian Society* (Honolulu, 1974), p. 1290.

[2] Judith Binney, *Legacy of Guilt: A Life of Thomas Kendall* (Auckland, 1968), p. 32.

[3] John Garrett, *To Live among the Stars: Christian Origins in Oceania* (Geneva, 1985), p. 20.

in a fondness for drink and homosexual *mahu* attendants. The reasons for Pomare's change of heart remain obscure. Most likely his confidence in Oro had been badly shaken after years of fierce fighting which drove him into exile in 1808. He may also have faltered in the face of a steep population decline in the aftermath of the new diseases, alcohol, and firearms introduced by European intrusions. More positively, he became close to Henry Nott, who stayed on when the other members of the mission party had fled the fighting in 1809. In the end Pomare's choice may have been dictated less by desperation than by a shrewd calculation that the new god would provide him with a spiritual advantage. In fact, Pomare's fortunes did change upon his conversion. He won a decisive battle and for the first time united Tahiti under a single ruler. The missionaries returned to assist this unlikely Constantine who made Christianity the state religion. Tahiti became the base from which the LMS expanded steadily westward—eventually arriving in New Guinea sixty years after Pomare's conversion.

A similar scenario unfolded in Tonga. Unlike Tahiti, Tonga had once been unified under a single ruler, but civil war between the claimants of the three high titles had raged for decades, made more lethal by the introduction of firearms and castaways who knew how to use them effectively. The LMS fled the islands in 1797 after several members of its party were killed. Three decades later Methodists received a warmer reception. A young chief from the northern islands, Tāufaʻāhau, requested a teacher and then methodically put the new god through a series of tests. Having defied his own patron deity by, among other things, striking its priestess, he declared himself for the *lotu* ('Church'), ordering the destruction of spirit houses in his domain and calling for instruction in Christianity for himself and his people. Following his baptism, 'King George' consolidated the three traditional titles in his person through a mix of skilful diplomacy and bloody warfare, cheered on by the missionaries, who perceived him as a modern-day Saul engaged in a holy crusade against heathenism. Tāufaʻāhau later helped advance Christianity in neighbouring Fiji by recommending *lotu* to the warrior chief Cakobau and lending him troops to defeat his rivals.

The Fijian case suggests that the centrality of the chiefs to the acceptance of Christianity went beyond the naked exercise of power. Years before Cakobau accepted baptism, Methodist missionaries had convinced many leaders not only of the reality of the Christian god but of his superiority over their own.[4]

---

[4] Marshall Sahlins, 'Other Times, Other Customs: The Anthropology of History', *American Anthropologist*, LXXXV (1991), p. 519.

The conversion of the high chiefs signalled the conversion of the body politic because they actually embodied it. Their own authority rested upon their direct descent from the gods. In the more stratified islands the *mana* ('sacred potency') of the aristocracy was indexed by highly elaborated ritual protocols and taboos backed by spiritual sanctions and, for commoners, the threat of instant death. The *mana* of the chiefs was spectacularly displayed in Tahiti and Hawai'i through large temple complexes and flamboyant religious cults supported by a specialized priesthood. Religion legitimized the chiefs and provided 'sanctions for controlling the population and harnessing its productivity'.[5] For Pomare, Tāufa'āhau, and Cakobau, recognition of Jehovah provided spiritual legitimacy further confirmed by decisive military victories; but stability in their kingdoms depended upon the rapid re-establishment of a state religion. A variation on this theme was played out in Hawai'i after Ka'ahumanu, the favourite wife of the late Kamehameha I, who had united the islands, ended the system of public taboos on which the old religious system rested. When American Congregationalist missionaries arrived the following year, in 1820, she and her allies quickly grasped the political utility of the new religion as a means of maintaining chiefly control over the commoners. Thus the new Christian kings found themselves quite as much in need of the missionaries as the missionaries were of them.

The missionaries on Tahiti quickly took advantage of their new status by introducing a simple law code in 1819 partly based on one devised by their LMS brethren in southern Africa.[6] It legitimized Pomare II as God's chosen servant, established the sabbath as a holy day, and promulgated rules based on custom, the Ten Commandments, and evangelical morality. The code was revised almost annually, with similar laws introduced on nearby islands, culminating in an 1824 constitution establishing a parliament of chiefs, a rudimentary tax system, and a judiciary. In 1839 the missionaries implemented a similar code in northern Tonga; however, following his conquest of Tonga, Tāufa'āhau enlarged his consultations from missionaries to beachcombers, ship captains, the governor of New Zealand, and lawyers in Australia. Law codes of 1850 and 1862 reflected Christian preoccupations but also imposed a new governance structure that firmly entrenched the king's power over the aristocracy and the land. A constitution appeared 1875, written

---

[5] K. R. Howe, *Where the Waves Fall: A New South Sea Islands History from First Settlement to Colonial Rule* (Honolulu, 1984), p. 140.

[6] Neil Gunson, *Messengers of Grace: Evangelical Missionaries in the South Seas, 1797–1860* (Melbourne, 1978), p. 284.

mostly by the Wesleyan missionary Shirley Baker and based partly upon the Hawaiian constitution of 1840. Although Tonga became a British protectorate in the early twentieth century, the monarchy and the amended 1875 constitution endured.

Missionaries reached the zenith of their political influence in the newly formed kingdoms of Tahiti, Tonga, and Hawai'i, by far the most stratified of the Polynesian societies at the time of European contact. Their progress elsewhere in the region also rested heavily upon local elites, even when political structures militated against the creation of unified kingdoms. In Samoa chiefs were elected by local village and district councils, which they needed to consult on matters of governance and war. Samoa thus had a great number of local chiefs. An able and aggressive leader could accrue regional power by gaining any or all of the four most distinguished hereditary titles on the big islands of Upolu and Savai'i, but even so their authority was mostly ceremonial apart from leadership in war. Christianity spread quickly in the 1830s on a village-by-village basis. Missionaries introduced law codes but were frustrated by the tendency of local chiefs to interpret them in terms of local politics and their own ambitions. Despite repeated attempts by missionaries and intervening European powers to establish a kingdom, war between competing chiefs continued through much of the nineteenth century. A missionary kingdom also failed to form in Fiji, largely because of the enduring power of regional chiefs even after Cakobau's victories and the subsequent rapid expansion of Christianity. In New Zealand, where chiefly power was even more localized and limited, Christianity spread much more gradually, mostly following the formal annexation of the country by Britain in 1840. Progress was even slower in the Melanesian islands to the west of Fiji, where extreme linguistic and political fragmentation meant that Christianity could not be imposed from above but had to be gradually accepted from below.

K. R. Howe argues convincingly that indigenous political structures combined with chiefly ambitions profoundly shaped the forms of Polynesian societies after European contact even if 'outside influences far beyond the control of the kings and their subjects ultimately determined the fate of the royal regimes'.[7] The same, of course, was true in Africa, where powerful leaders also used their alliances with missions for political advantage. But there was a crucial difference. Few of the African elite accepted baptism and those that did, such as Khama of Botswana, did not trigger mass acceptance

[7] Howe, *Where the Waves Fall*, p. 197.

of Christianity. Missionaries in Polynesia by the early 1820s faced the daunting challenge not simply of introducing Christianity but of consolidating its hold in the general population.

Missionaries and Converts

The first agents of British mission societies left for distant posts with little guidance on how they should teach the gospel or organize local congregations once they began to emerge. Only four of the thirty missionaries (plus five wives and three children) sent to Tahiti by the LMS in 1797 were ordained ministers. Later the sending churches required most missionaries to attend a seminary, but directors continued to insist that a simple faith and skills with one's hands were the best preparation for work among the 'savage' folk of Africa and the Pacific. In the beginning, missionaries had to invent procedures and standards as they went along, a process that occasioned no end of squabbling. At first on their own initiative, but increasingly in response to directors, they reproduced in the mission fields attenuated versions of the familiar ecclesiastical structures from home, adding to them oversight and district committees as needed. Still, this left a lot of room for improvisation.

While individual proclivities and local conditions created tremendous variation, early African missions followed a markedly different path of development from those in the Pacific. In Africa most missionaries established settlements to which they recruited potential converts who lived apart from the larger population. The mission villages varied greatly in function, size, and relationship to the surrounding societies across the continent. In eastern Africa the largest mission settlements housed ex-slaves cut off from distant homelands. Many mission villages in southern Africa, in contrast, served local populations, offering refuge at times of war and the chance of employment and education at times of peace. Mission communities generally shared 'the sense that this was a place in which the European mind rather than African custom controlled the details of life—patterns of work and marriage, the shape of houses, the public practice of religion'.[8] In the early years settlements often appeared as the only practical way to introduce Christianity by combining the requirements of security with a concentration of resources and enhanced control over the residents. Over time, most missionaries would come to see the settlements as a liability, an impediment

---

[8] Adrian Hastings, *The Church in Africa, 1450–1950* (Oxford, 1994), p. 214.

to the greater task of reaching the masses. By this point, ironically enough, Africans reared in the settlements had assumed the leading role in the remarkable expansion of Christianity in the colonial period.

The pattern of mission expansion in the Pacific islands was very different. While missions eventually established head stations with boarding schools, seminaries, medical posts, workshops, and sometimes plantations, these rarely achieved the size of even the smallest African mission communities. Almost all evangelistic outreach occurred in the villages where converts continued to live side-by-side with traditionalists. In part, the absence of autonomous mission communities was the result of the limited land base on most islands, but mostly it reflected the rapid growth of mass interest in Christian instruction. To meet the demand, missionaries necessarily relinquished considerable control in two areas: first, over the direct communication of the religion to islanders and, secondly, over the shaping of Christian teachings and values in their new cultural environment.

Allied chiefs and missionaries found mutual advantage in quickly training islander evangelists to promote Christianity. Pomare II, Tāufaʻāhau, Kaʻahumanu, and other high chiefs saw islander teachers as a critical political tool to legitimize and expand their power base. While political stability was not unimportant to the missionaries, their more immediate concern was to prepare the population as quickly as possible for baptism—in their minds, literally to rescue them from eternal damnation. The scale of both the political and religious projects required the engagement of large numbers of islanders as teachers and deacons. This was especially the case in politically decentralized societies like Samoa and New Zealand, where each village insisted on having its own teacher and resisted outside control over church congregations. The eleven English missionaries who had settled in Samoa by 1839 found themselves supervising 138 teachers.[9] Similar ratios obtained in New Zealand in the 1850s, where at least 800 mostly unpaid 'native agents' worked for the two Protestant missions.[10] Even in the kingdoms, where people were familiar with centralized places of worship, the sheer numbers of islanders seeking instruction necessitated large numbers of teachers. In the early 1830s, for instance, the Hawaiʻian mission supported some 1,100 schools serving as many as 50,000 mostly adult students.[11]

---

[9] Howe, *Where the Waves Fall*, p. 241.

[10] Raeburn Lange, 'Indigenous Agents of Religious Change in New Zealand, 1830–1860,' *Journal of Religious History*, XXIV (2000), p. 287.

[11] Gavan Daws, *Shoal of Time: A History of the Hawaiian Islands* (New York, 1969), p. 90.

Islanders played a key role not just in consolidating Christianity within the new kingdoms but also in the opening of new mission fields. By the mid-1820s Tahitian converts had either deliberately or through accidental drift voyages taken the Word to the Cook Islands, Samoa, and distant Tonga. In 1822 an LMS delegation inspecting the Tahitian mission took nine converts to visit the newly established American Congregationalist mission in Hawai'i. Impressed by the persuasive role the converts played in promoting Christianity, the delegation leaders upon their return urged the creation of a native seminary to harness local religious excitement and direct it to new fields. They found a willing agent in John Williams, who had already arranged to establish converts from his base on Raiatea, near Tahiti, in the Cook Islands to the east. Over the next seventeen years Williams would do more than anyone to facilitate the use of what became known as the 'Native Agency'. After successfully settling teachers and their families in the Cooks and Samoa, Williams was clubbed to death on the beach of Erromanga in 1839 in the act of bringing Polynesian evangelists to the Melanesian islands.

The extensive employment of native 'teachers' (the term 'missionary' was reserved for whites) occasioned heated debates in the Pacific and Africa. Sceptics fretted that converts, only barely out of 'heathenism', would spread confusion or even heresy. Ignoring their own failings, they questioned whether the teachers possessed the strength of character to maintain moral discipline without missionary oversight. Still, the advantages greatly outweighed these hesitations. Teachers were far cheaper to employ than Europeans as they were expected to assume a native lifestyle requiring few supplies and small wages, if any. Islanders adjusted far more readily than whites to village lifestyles and customs, or so it was thought. In turn, the missionaries assumed that native peoples would respond more readily to evangelists who looked and acted much like themselves. Finally, although not openly acknowledged, the teachers' lives were reckoned more expendable than those of whites. Many died martyrs to the cause, especially after the push into Melanesia. In the first twenty-six years of the LMS mission to New Guinea, at least 130 out of 250 Polynesian teachers died, mostly from malaria, along with an unknown number of their wives and children.[12] The evangelization of Melanesia was built upon the graves of the Polynesian pioneers.

---

[12] Norman Goodall, *A History of the London Missionary Society* (London, 1954), p. 421.

The eagerness of so many Polynesian converts to serve as evangelists, in even extremely dangerous situations, suggests that the appearance of the Native Agency cannot be adequately explained merely with reference to the machinations of chiefs and missionaries. One must also consider personal motivations: dreams of adventure, social advancement, influence, and the promise of salvation. At a most general level, however, the rapid growth of indigenous evangelism reflected the transition of Christianity from a foreign cult to an indigenous religious movement. Decades later a similar popular movement burst from the missions in Africa, where the 'sudden vast multiplication of ... preachers and teachers had not been planned for or prepared for by missionaries. It had simply happened ....'.[13] In both places missionaries found themselves playing catch-up with a movement over which they exercised only limited control.

The emergence of the Native Agency profoundly affected social arrangements in both native societies and the mission organizations. A large number of islanders now worked, albeit at the bottom, as staff of ecclesial organizations that had no parallel in their own traditions. They voluntarily submitted to the authority of small missionary elites for training, placement, and supervision. Missionaries in turn became more distanced from direct evangelization of the masses as they assumed the ever-increasing burden of training and managing their large native staffs. All of the Pacific missions quickly set up seminaries, a few of which, like the Missionary Seminary on Maui (1831), Malua Institute in Samoa (1844), and Tupou College in Tonga (1866), won reputations for high academic standards and attracted many students. Once out of the door of the college, teachers often worked largely independently of mission supervision and support. While this could leave them vulnerable at the missionary frontier, their association with Europeans and God often proved a potent source of *mana*. Many assumed positions of great influence at home and even more so in some of the distant mission fields, such as Tuvalu, where they worked with little or no direct white supervision. Inevitably, the native pastorate came to resent their subservient position in the missions. During the 1870s Samoans forced the missionary elite on the LMS district council to cede significant authority to village deacons, many of whom were chiefs, and to ordain most teachers as pastors with the right to administer baptisms and the Eucharist.

[13] Hastings, *Church in Africa*, p. 441.

Andrew Porter observes that wherever Christianity encountered indigenous societies in the British Empire, there occurred 'a constant process of mutual engagement and two-way translation'.[14] The speed with which Christianity spread across the Pacific islands and the fact that islanders themselves were often its emissaries greatly limited the direct control white missionaries exercised over the ways the new religion was appropriated, absorbed, and redefined in local societies. Indeed, in many places the process of absorption began well before the appearance of missionaries, white or brown, as islanders encountered fragments of Christianity in the form of services conducted by naval captains, hymns sung by sailors, or rumours of the remarkable happenings in Tahiti. In the early years the appearance of the whites, in their great ships bearing awesome weapons, touched off intense speculation in the Cook Islands, Samoa, and Hawai'i, recalling ancient prophecies telling of the arrival of stranger kings bringing cataclysmic change. Not surprisingly, many islanders at first assumed that the Christian god was the ultimate source of the white man's *mana*, as displayed in his evident wealth and power. Deliberately encouraging this misconception, John Williams convinced the Samoan high chief Malietoa to accept teachers on his visits of 1830 and 1832. Not much convincing seems to have been required because by this time many Samoans had heard about missionary teachings from Tahitian visitors and during their own travels to Tahiti, Tonga, and elsewhere. One of these Samoan travellers, Siovili, gained a large cult following by prophesying the imminent return of the dead and immense prosperity for those who accepted the white man's god. For years after they began working in Samoa, the LMS and Methodist missions competed not only with Siovili and each other, but also with numerous local movements led by sailors who had been recruited and sometimes kidnapped by villagers to provide them with religious instruction. A few of these 'sailor cults' provided reasonable approximations of orthodoxy; but in other instances 'religious worship tended towards the use of a copybook as "Bible", the singing of sea-shanty "hymns", and the delivery of "sermons" in any language the preacher happened to know'.[15]

Millenarian movements emerged in many parts of Polynesia at various times in the nineteenth and twentieth centuries, but it was only in places

---

[14] Andrew Porter, 'Religion, Missionary Enthusiasm, and Empire,' in Andrew Porter, ed., OHBE III, *The Nineteenth Century* (Oxford, 1999), p. 239.

[15] R. P. Gilson, *Samoa 1830 to 1900: The Politics of a Multi-cultural Community* (Melbourne, 1970), p. 77.

where chiefly power was relatively fragmented—Samoa, western Fiji, and especially New Zealand—that they proved more than ephemeral. Even where Christianity was installed as a national religion, the early stages of conversion reflected a popular sense of momentous change. In many places zealots smashed representations of the ancestral gods, desecrated temples, and openly defied the old taboos. Crowds crushed into makeshift churches to sing praises to the new god. Most notably, they demanded to be taught the mysteries of reading and writing. The missionaries struggled to keep up with the enormous demand for spellers, vernacular translations of Christian texts, and the teachers who could provide the training to use them. The missions invested much of their resources into the work of translation, printing, and distribution. In the first year of operation the Wesleyan printing press in Tonga produced a staggering 17,000 books in the vernacular.[16] By 1845 the LMS printing press in Samoa had cranked out almost 8 million 'pages of useful reading matter', to which the Foreign and British Bible Society would soon add a Samoan New Testament and eventually the full Bible.[17] It is likely that many heeded the missionaries' contention that one's individual salvation depended upon a personal engagement with the Gospels, but the texts exuded their own powerful magic. Adrian Hastings's comment on a similar wave of enthusiasm that swept through parts of Africa in a later period is cogent: 'What was so exhilarating about the Scriptures was that they were so comprehensively supernaturalist, so supportive of belief in spirits of various sorts, and yet so manifestly useful in secular terms.'[18] Access to the Bible in the vernacular like nothing else allowed converts to engage with Christianity in their own terms. The village pastor's sermon, blending biblical stories with moral and political exhortations into a powerful rhetorical whole, gave vivid presence to God's *mana*.

Although a number of missionaries gained a deep knowledge and respect for Polynesian cultures, virtually all assumed that a full acceptance of Christianity entailed the complete rejection of the 'heathenish' past and adoption of a pious form of 'civilization' based upon British middle-class values. They engaged in a constant and often acrimonious debate over strategies for bringing this about, what local practices were compatible with Christianity, the expected pace of change, the standards for measuring the progress of

---

[16] Howe, *Where the Waves Fall*, p. 188.

[17] Richard Lovett, *The History of the London Missionary Society 1795–1895* (Oxford, 1899), p. 387.

[18] Hastings, *Church in Africa*, p. 458.

individual converts, and the treatment of those who felt short of the standards. In general, islanders were required to attend church and religious classes for a set period and to demonstrate a grasp of the essential points of the faith before receiving baptism, although in some places in the early years a mere expression of interest seems to have been enough. Baptized Christians, and to some extent the full population in the kingdoms, were presented with an ever-lengthening list of proscriptions centred on the observation of the sabbath and the regulation of moral behaviour. Miscreants and backsliders were punished by fines and sometimes beatings from the chiefs and the denial of church privileges by the missionaries. The degree of compliance waxed and waned in the mission fields, not least because the chiefs themselves ignored the rules against such things as polygyny and warfare when they became inconvenient; but in general Polynesians quickly reoriented their societies around Sunday worship and the church. While often exhilarated by the evidence of God's hand at work, the missionaries nevertheless remained sceptical that such conformance with mission rules reflected a true change of heart, the internalization of a sense of personal sin. This scepticism reached its most extreme expression in the Hawaiian mission, which so vigorously enforced its puritanical standards that after eighteen years with half the population attending church, only one congregant out of a hundred 'had been granted the privilege of communion with Christ'.[19] It was also manifested in the reluctance in all of the mission fields to ordain islanders as full ministers.

The missionaries had good reasons for doubt. Even in the Polynesian kingdoms, older religious understandings survived, often in Christian guises. The state Christianity of the kingdoms assumed a familiar form with its own taboos, temple system, and requirements for 'sacrifice' through contributions of food, labour, and eventually money. In Hawai'i commoners continued to make sacrifices to local deities at small shrines well into the Christian era. Everywhere people still made sense of their lives within a cosmology that had expanded to include the Christian god and his emissaries but which still accepted as reality ancestral spirits, sacred areas, witchcraft, magic, ancient genealogies, and founding mythologies. The outward forms of Christianity might obscure the survival of indigenous religious sensibilities for a time, but it could not destroy them.

No other organization had as wide or as deep an impact on Pacific societies in the years before Empire, and long after in many areas, as the missions. The

---

[19] Daws, *Shoal of Time*, p. 98.

cultural changes associated with Christianity affected the most intimate aspects of island societies: personal adornment, family organization, gender roles, leadership, orientations to time and space, and artistic production, to mention but a few. The missionaries imposed many prohibitions and set new standards of behaviour, but few if any would have been accepted without the active support first of the chiefs and later of islander evangelists who carried the mission regimens to more distant islands. The local forms of Christianity that emerged were hybrids combining Polynesian conceptions of hierarchy and spirituality with evangelical moralism. Visitors to Tonga in the latter decades of the nineteenth century were impressed (or dismayed) by commodious village churches, by the black-frocked native pastors exhorting their congregations during the long services to honour Jehovah and give generously to his mission, and by the melodious church choirs raising their voices to heaven. Greatly appreciated for their oratorical skills and for their educational achievements, pastors in places like Samoa and Tonga gradually occupied the spiritual centres of their communities. Local chiefs associated themselves with the pastor by serving as deacons and incorporating Christian prayers and other overt forms of the religion into their political activities. Congregations showered their pastors with lavish gifts, and the splendour of a pastor's home, along with his girth, came to be associated with God's blessing on the community as a whole. They had, in effect, taken 'the place of the priests and prophets of [the old society] as mediators with the unseen world'.[20]

The local churches, then, became key creative sites in the encounter between Western evangelical and indigenous cultures. The networks established by the missions as they expanded into new fields facilitated the diffusion of ideas, products, and practices between the islands. Some mission innovations proved remarkably population across the region. The baggy 'Mother Hubbard' dresses, for instance, initially introduced in Hawai'i to preserve Christian women's 'modesty', rapidly became the favoured costume for Pacific women anywhere they could afford the cloth. Polynesian missionaries travelling to Melanesia after 1870 introduced new crops, forms of mat-weaving, and even the *hula* dance in some places. More significantly, the form of the Christian social order they sought to establish drew largely on the example of the church in Samoa or Tonga, much to the frustration of the supervising missionaries. Like the Polynesians, the Melanesians in time would make Christianity into an indigenous religion.

[20] Garrett, *To Live among the Stars*, p. 124.

Missionaries, Traders, and Settlers in the Field

One cannot begin to make sense of the complex relationships between missionaries and other whites beyond colonial frontiers without bearing firmly in mind that the missions were, first and foremost, religious institutions. At the simplest level, the core functions of even the larger mission settlements centred upon classrooms where the essentials of the faith were taught and churches in which the faithful demonstrated their submission to God. Of course, other European Christians shared their beliefs and performed their devotions before native peoples; but only missionaries made dissemination of the religion their specialized task. At a deeper level, the religious impulse behind the missions affected not only missionaries' attitudes towards the 'perishing heathen' of the tropics but also towards their fellow countrymen both in the field and at home. Stripped to its essence, the missionary vocation rested upon a theological foundation of human similitude, belief that all humans—brown and white, female and male—were equally capable of redemption before God. The evangelical revivals of the eighteenth century had awakened a sense of eschatological urgency in the Nonconforming churches for all individuals to acknowledge their fallen natures and seek forgiveness from God. The missions were thus only one face of a religious movement that was largely concerned with moral reform and spiritual awakening at home. Harsh as missionary condemnations of indigenous cultures often were, they could be just as critical of their own failings and those of their fellow citizens. In the remarkable statistical tabulation of the religious condition of the world's people that takes up much of William Carey's evangelical manifesto of 1792, he saved his sharpest rebuke for the 'fallen Christians' of northern Europe.[21]

The assumption of human similitude at the core of the mission endeavour coexisted uneasily with the confident and often racist assumption, shared to varying degrees by almost all missionaries, of the superiority of the white 'race'. In missionary writings and in the planning behind the more ambitious mission settlements, one can detect a concerted attempt to overcome the contradiction by remaking converts into idealized versions of rural Europeans. The visionaries who created model communities like Metlakatla in British Columbia or Livingstonia in Africa saw them not simply as efficient means to 'civilize' converts but as utopian communities that

---

[21] William Carey, *An Enquiry into the Obligations of Christians to Use Means for the Conversion of Heathens* (Leicester, 1792).

simultaneously revealed the capability of non-Europeans to rise to Christian civilization and the moral failings of Europe itself. David Livingstone's famous equation of 'Christianity, Commerce and Civilization' was as much a moral rebuke of Europe as an expression of confidence in its innate superiority. All of these endeavours and fine sentiments would flounder on the missionaries' inability to convince even themselves that Pacific islanders and Africans could be their equals.

While often among the earliest Europeans to settle among indigenous groups, missionaries were rarely the first to visit or the last to remain. Following the entry of the Spanish into the region in the sixteenth century, Pacific islanders were visited by a succession of temporary visitors from naval expeditions and vessels pursuing whales, sandalwood, and bêche-de-mer. By 1800 deserters from visiting ships, castaways, and escapees from the Australian penal colony had begun to haunt the beaches, many to die from violence and drink, but others to stay as clients of chiefs. Small port settlements soon appeared in places like the Bay of Islands, Apia, and Honolulu to provision visiting ships and to participate in commodity exchanges between Polynesians and European commercial interests. While settlers remained small in number and concentrated in a few places, after the mid-century they began rapidly to acquire large tracts of land from indebted chiefs in Hawai'i, Samoa, and Fiji.

Relationships between missionaries and other whites beyond imperial authority were marked by considerable ambivalence. Missions depended on ships for transportation, mail, and provisions. They appreciated visits from naval captains both for companionship and for the aura of security lent by an association with Europe's military might. Above all, they made use of visiting ships to facilitate the trade of local products for commodities valued by the islanders as a means of winning favour from the chiefs and assuring their survival. Mission dependence on global networks of trade and military force grew and intensified. For their part, many naval captains appreciated the presence of missionaries as forces for good governance in the islands. Traders and settlers alike sought out missionaries for advice, companionship, medical care, aid in negotiations with chiefs, and as business partners.

Still the missionaries' desire to raise islanders to 'moral and useful lives' inevitably clashed with the desire of most other Europeans to find pleasure and profit in islander bodies and resources. The various codes developed by missionaries and their chiefly allies had as much to do with shielding native populations from the barbarism of whites as with leading them into 'civilization'. Ships' crews greatly resented Blue laws against public drunkenness and prostitution. In 1826 randy sailors rioted in Honolulu against restrictions on prostitution. Hiram Bingham narrowly avoided being clubbed in the mêlée. As the century progressed, the stock figure of the 'evil white man', whose debaucheries destroyed the moral fibre and body of 'innocent' natives, rivalled the witch doctor and sorcerer in mission publications as the enemy of Christian progress. For the most part, missionaries quietly if unhappily tolerated the excesses they witnessed, but on occasion some publicly protested in the colonial and metropolitan presses. Missionary correspondents employed the rhetoric of the anti-slavery movement to denounce passionately the often unsavoury methods—especially kidnapping—used to recruit Melanesian labourers for the Queensland sugar plantations in the 1880s. While they failed to end labour recruiting, their protests led to imperial interventions: reforms, better policing, and eventually a protectorate over the Solomon Islands.

The frustration felt by a sailor thwarted from easy sex was keen but temporary. Those who settled in the islands to make their fortune nurtured larger grievances against missionary 'interference', especially when it threatened their own profits. They tended to rephrase their protest into two kinds of complaint: that missionaries were hypocrites lining their own pockets while pretending to minister to the native soul; and that mission education 'ruined' the natives, either by draining all of the joy out of their lives or by encouraging the presumption that they were the equal of the white man. Neither complaint can be taken at face value, but neither should they be entirely dismissed. Missions were in part commercial enterprises. The home churches were sparing in their subsidies, forcing local missionaries to develop ways to raise funds for their own upkeep and the expansion to new fields. Beyond this, evangelicals regarded the responsible pursuit of business as a moral good, part of a bundle of cultural values they hoped to instil in their converts. All the same, the scope for missions to develop as business enterprises in their own right was very limited. The daily burden of preaching, teaching, administration, and simple survival left little time for commerce. Those individuals who demonstrated a skill for profitable initiatives were subject to restrictions laid down by society directors and, even more so, the withering criticisms of other missionaries. In the Pacific, as in most places, missionaries who developed a taste for business soon tended to give up their religious vocation.

The question of whether missions made converts more or less compliant to the settler demands, while fiercely debated, must remain a matter of conjecture. There can be little doubt, however, that the widespread acceptance of Christianity had important economic consequences. The missions served to cultivate tastes for certain European products while discouraging others, and they also served to encourage islanders to take up paid labour—when available—but never on a Sunday and much more by men than women, who became increasingly identified with the 'traditional' sphere of life. As Christianity expanded and consolidated, church members provided labour and money towards the building of hundreds of churches and the support of their pastors and own missionaries. In the 1820s the annual May meetings of the LMS in Tahiti became the occasion for Bible dramas, hymn-singing, and feasts. The festivals, which became fixtures in most of the Pacific islands, climaxed with a competition in which leading men demonstrated their *mana* through a public competition of gift-giving. During the 1860s Shirley Baker, the energetic chairman of the Methodist mission in Tonga, made the ceremony staggeringly profitable by increasing both the occasions for gift-giving and the amount by opening lines of credit against promised deliveries of palm oil. Within a decade the contributions from Tonga had grown so enormous they were effectively subsidizing the Australian Church.

The English travellers G. H. Kingsley and the Earl of Pembroke, passing through Tonga in 1871, denounced Baker's system as 'pure pillage', commenting further that 'the common name of their missionary schooner, "the Palm Oil Trader", is according to their own account, well deserved'.[22] This complaint, like those of settlers, glossed over the fact that islanders were neither just dupes nor victims but agents in their own right with their own motivations and agendas. The chiefs who enforced laws against prostitution in Hawai'i were driven not just by piety but also by a desire to assert control over commoners. The rulers of Hawai'i and Tonga made use of missionary advisers to devise constitutions not only as an acknowledgement of Jehovah but as a means of defending the sovereignty of their kingdoms in the face of a rapidly increasing presence of European commercial interests, backed by the occasional visit of a nation's warship. Islanders, of course, had entered into commercial arrangements with various traders and settlers in the first place. They were quite capable of ignoring or turning on missionaries when it served their purposes. Thus Tāufaʻāhau was led to proclaim the secessionist Free Church of Tonga in 1885 when the Australian board failed to cede control over the Methodist missions. Christianity remained central to the

---

[22] Noel Rutherford, *Shirley Baker and the King of Tonga* (Melbourne, 1971), p. 31.

evolving cultures of Tonga, Hawai'i, and elsewhere, but as the presence of other Europeans increased, the influence of missionaries steadily waned.

In the final analysis, there was no clear line between missionaries and other whites in the Pacific or in Africa. Many missionaries in the Polynesian kingdoms came to enjoy very comfortable lifestyles, with staffs of servants tending commodious houses and gardens. While most eventually returned home or settled in white colonies, others stayed, forming large families and using their local connections to advance their personal fortunes. During his furlough in England in the 1830s, John Williams promoted a plan to carry on commercial trading alongside his mission work. After his death, his son settled as a trader and American consul in Samoa. They were by no means the only ones to make such a transition. Most infamously, several descendants of the American Congregational missionaries to Hawai'i became major landowners who in 1893 helped to overthrow the Christian kingdom their predecessors had laboured to create.

Until the 1870s and 1880s missionaries were more or less 'content to live as guests' of local rulers.[23] Few anticipated the expansion of imperial powers, 'although at times they undoubtedly hoped for some sort of backing from Britain to assist and even protect them in difficulty'.[24] In the Pacific missionaries joined calls for a more visible British presence in the form of warships and consuls as traders, sailors, and settlers threatened political stability—and as Roman Catholic missionaries proved a prelude to French colonization. The declaration of a French protectorate over Tahiti in 1843 came as a particularly heavy blow to the LMS, which was expelled from the islands a decade later. All the same, prior to the years of the 'Scramble', missionaries rarely appealed to Britain to assume power over a kingdom or region. Once the race to acquire colonial territories began, however, few objected. Their main concerns, beyond a preference for a British takeover, had to do with the protection of the land rights of indigenous populations and non-interference with missionary work. In the mid-1870s the LMS missionary John Mackenzie had petitioned for a protectorate over Bechuanaland, arguing 'that nothing else could save Africans from white settler rapacity'.[25] When it appeared that Queensland might move to annex eastern New Guinea, James Chalmers urged Britain to step in to prevent a repetition of the tragic fate of the

---

[23] Kevin Ward, 'Africa', in Adrian Hastings, ed., *A World History of Christianity* (London, 1999), p. 216.

[24] Hastings, *Church in Africa*, p. 408.

[25] Ibid., p. 409.

Aborigines. Only a protectorate would do, in which land sales were severely restricted and handled by the government, white settlement discouraged, and labour recruitment for Queensland banned outright.

The Great Powers made liberal use of the rhetoric of Christian benevolence to justify their acquisition of massive colonial empires in the late nineteenth century.[26] Protection of missionaries provided a convenient pretence for French intervention in Hawai'i and Tahiti, and, to a lesser extent, for the British in parts of East Africa. When imperial representatives proclaimed a protectorate or colony, missionaries could prove useful as translators and intermediaries with the local elite. On top of this, the Christian lobby at home contributed as many or more words to public discussions of imperialism as any faction. In the final analysis, however, missionaries possessed very limited political clout. They were not an arm of the State and their work in places like Tahiti or Uganda did not in itself establish British claims or interests. In the aftermath of the Scramble, British missionaries found themselves in German and American territories as well as the British Empire. They hoped that the imposition of imperial power would put an end to incessant fighting between local chiefs in places like Samoa and halt the Arabian slave trade in eastern Africa. They hoped that areas that had been closed to them because of warfare or resistance to their presence from rulers would now be thrown open to evangelization. They hoped that all of this could be accomplished with little confrontation and loss of life. Above all, they hoped—and largely believed—that the expansion of Empire was a matter of Providence and thus mostly benevolent. If indigenous people were to lose their autonomy, at least for a time, it was in order to save them from a dark past and bitter present, for a better and brighter future. Such hopes would be severely tested in the years ahead.

Select Bibliography

JEAN COMAROFF and JOHN L. COMAROFF, *Of Revelation and Revolution*, 2 vols. (Chicago, 1991, 1997).

WILLIAM ELLIS, *Polynesian Researches* (London, 1831).

NORMAN ETHERINGTON, *Preachers, Peasants and Politics in Southeast Africa, 1835–1880* (London, 1978).

---

[26] Susan Thorne, *Congregational Missions and the Making of an Imperial Culture in Nineteenth Century England* (Stanford, Calif., 1999).

JOHN GARRETT, *To Live among the Stars: Christian Origins in Oceania* (Geneva, 1982).

PATRICIA GRIMSHAW, *Paths of Duty: American Missionary Wives in Nineteenth-Century Hawaii* (Honolulu, 1989).

NIEL GUNSON, *Messengers of Grace: Evangelical Missionaries in the South Seas, 1797–1860* (Melbourne, 1978).

ADRIAN HASTINGS, *The Church in Africa, 1450–1950* (Oxford, 1994).

TOM HINEY, *On the Missionary Trail: A Journey through Polynesia, Asia, and Africa with the London Missionary Society* (New York, 2000).

MARGARET JOLLY, ' "To Save the Girls for Brighter and Better Lives": Presbyterian Missions and Women in the South of Vanuatu 1848–1870', *Journal of Pacific History*, XXVI (1991), pp. 27–48.

DIANE LANGMORE, *Missionary Lives: Papua, 1874–1914* (Honolulu, 1989).

SIONE LATUKEFU, *Church and State in Tonga: The Wesleyan Methodist Missionaries and Political Development, 1822–1875* (Honolulu, 1974).

DOUG MUNRO and ANDREW THORNLEY, eds., *The Covenant Makers: Islander Missionaries in the Pacific* (Suva, 1996).

J. D. Y. PEEL, *Religious Encounter and the Making of the Yoruba* (Bloomington, Ind., 2000).

SUSAN THORNE, *Congregational Missions and the Making of an Imperial Culture in Nineteenth Century England* (Stanford, Calif., 1999).

6

Christian Missions and the Raj

ROBERT ERIC FRYKENBERG

It takes an elephant to catch an elephant, and a quail to catch a quail.
(Vedanayakam Sastri, Christian poet of Thanjāvur)

Rarely was the relationship between Christian missions and Empire so complex as in India. The political system that the East India Company constructed rested on the support of elite communities whose religious institutions could not be violated or treated as inferior lest their hundreds of thousands of adherents be alienated. When missionaries finally gained access to Company territories, their efforts brought counter-currents of religious renewal, social reform, and the eventual rise of nationalisms. By the same token, the advent of modem forms of Christianity opened possibilities for communities long oppressed and overshadowed by Brahmanical dominance. The paradoxical result was that Christian missions often attracted their greatest followings where their connection to imperial authority was least in evidence. Moreover, dissenting and non-British missions flourished while missions too closely connected to the Anglican establishment faltered. Even as Christians struck deep roots among peoples on the social and territorial margins of India—Dalit ('Untouchable') communities and *adivāsi* ('aboriginal' or 'tribal') communities—their influence hastened the construction (or invention) of modern, or syndicated, Hinduism and Indian nationalism, as well as Islamic revivalisms.

Missionaries who hoped the British Raj might serve as an instrument of conversion discovered that the Raj, as official policy, opposed such connections. The Raj, after all, was officially committed, both in policy and in law, to protecting all religious institutions of India. Anomalies or contradictions existed, but these in no way invalidated such detachment and 'neutrality'. Different 'British empires' had different aims. In content, culture, logic, and policy, if not style, the Indian Empire of the Company and the India Office was never the Empire of the Colonial Office.

Church, Missions, and 'Hindu Raj'

The Indian Empire was, fundamentally if not formally, a Hindu Raj. British merchants could never have established city-states at Madras, Bombay, and Calcutta without deference to local deities and rajas, as mediated through local agents and brokers (*dubashi*s). Local merchant bankers and merchant princes had served as double agents. Company forces, with sometimes as many as 300,000 sardars and sepoys, came largely from caste families that ruled agrarian villages. Without cadres of Brahman, Kayastha, and other high-caste civil servants controlling vital flows of information and revenue, no Empire would have been possible. Without collaboration, modem Hinduism could not have come into being.

The terms 'Hindu', 'Hinduism', and 'Hindutva' ('Hinduness') are modem. Non-religious denotations for things Hindu long antedated confessional meanings. In the early days of the Company, to be Hindu meant simply to be native to Hindustan. Terms like 'Hindu Muslim' and 'Hindu Christian' were not uncommon. The Empire was thus Hindu. The emergence of modem Hinduism owed much to late eighteenth-and nineteenth-century collaboration. Both Indian ('Hindu') and European ('Farangi') contributions made it so.[1] It was neither a British nor a missionary invention. Contributions made by high-caste, mainly Brahman, pandits played as decisive a part as anything done by scholars from the West. Long before the Company expanded from its coastal enclaves, local scholars had already conveyed deep insights to such missionaries as Roberto de Nobili (d. 1656), Bartholomaeus Ziegenbalg (d. 1719), and Constantius Giuseppe Beschi (d. 1747). Their studies of 'Malabarian' cultures and 'Gentoo' (or 'Hindoo') deities could not have been made without the scholarship of many local pandits. Without Company patronage, beginning with Warren Hastings in the 1770s, much ancient lore might not have been excavated, and might have perished. Missionaries also played a part. The three-volume work on 'Hindooism' published by the Serampore Baptist missionary William Ward (see pp. 202–5) merely followed the logic of codifying a single system and reifying an emerging quasi-official orthodoxy. Even as this syncretistic and tolerant ideology conveniently brought various religious systems under the imperial umbrella of Hinduism, the Company's own governments (Madras, Bengal, Bombay, etc.), on advice from their native servants, took over management responsibility for all pukka religious endowments and temples,

---

[1] John Stratton Hawley, 'Naming Hinduism', *Wilson Quarterly*, XV/3 (1991), pp. 24–34.

thereby inadvertently putting every local Hindu institution under a single, overarching structure. Tens of thousands of Hindu institutions were thereby inadvertently welded together within the imperial apparatus.

Christians had little place in this growing Empire run by a Company whose motive was profit. The first evangelical (Pietist) missionaries in Tranquebar were clapped into gaol and, but for their Royal Danish patron, would have been deported. Ever cautious and pragmatic, Company servants studiously avoided tampering with existing religious traditions. Their policies of non-interference and religious neutrality aimed to show all in India that their Raj was not Christian and did not favour missionaries. Some European servants of the Company even endowed and supported Hindu deities and temples. Although a handful of missionaries were tolerated in the eighteenth century, including Danish and German Pietists who happened to be on the ground, their efforts were not encouraged. Later, local Catholic vicars apostolic received subventions, so that their priests could serve Irish contingents within the Company's army. But the Baptist William Carey, who stirred up waves of missionary voluntarism with his *Enquiry into the Obligations of Christians to Use Means for the Conversion of Heathens* (1792), was barred from entry into Bengal. He could cross the Hugli from Serampore to Calcutta only after being hired as Professor of Oriental Languages at Fort William College. Claphamite pressure on parliament after 1792 also forced some missionary chaplains into India.

Not until 1813 was the Company's ban broken through an alliance of voluntary (missionary) agencies with free-trade opponents of monopoly. Evangelicals among the Court of Directors (led by Charles Grant) and in Parliament conducted a pamphlet war similar to the onslaught on the slave trade, which led to reinsertion of the 'Pious Clause' of 1792 into the Charter Renewal Act of 1813.[2] Thereafter, any missionary or merchant denied entry into British India could appeal directly to the Board of Control, whose Chairman could revoke actions taken by Company directors. Even so, Company authorities stood ready to summarily expel any missionary, and to punish any overly zealous officer whose tactless actions provoked social unrest. Anyone disparaging Hindu and Muslim practices as 'devilish' or 'heathen' could be admonished or even deported. Sir Thomas Munro,

---

[2] 'A Proposal for Establishing a Protestant Mission in Bengal and Behar', 17 Sept. 1787, in *Observations on the State of Society among Asiatic Subjects of Great Britain* (1792), repr. in *pp* (1812–13) X, No. 282, pp. 1–112; (1831–2) VII, No. 734, App. 1, pp. 3–92.

while Governor of Madras (1820–7), removed an officer who abused his official position by indulging in personal evangelism. When Lord Bentinck's decree of 1827 abolishing female infanticide and widow-burning (*sati*) aroused a storm, over 30,000 gentry (*bhadralog*) of Calcutta co-signed a 'Sacred Petition' complaining against the violation of their religious freedoms. Leadenhall Street and Whitehall felt duly warned.

Meanwhile, pleas by Tamil Christians for protection from persecution (1799–1806) went unheeded. How, they asked, could high officers who represented a Christian nation not offer protection to its own Christian subjects? Only after many local Christian leaders had died and the Society for Promoting Christian Knowledge (SPCK) in London again petitioned for Company protection of 'Hindu Christians' did the Company remind local authorities that religious intolerance in countries subject to its authority had never been countenanced. Since 'all sects had been permitted to follow their separate persuasions without molestation, so there could be no question that all who profess the Christian faith, whether of European, Armenian, or Indian race, should enjoy the like privilege and protection'. This failed to halt sporadic outbreaks of violence. Over 500 'native Christian householders' signed a petition, presented in March 1833, describing 'deeds... being done in support of heathenism and injustice to the poor, by the Honourable Company', which, 'like kings of old, was exempting temples from taxation, funding daily sacrifices, seasonal festivals, and reinstating devil worship'.[3] New converts were being threatened, beaten, and robbed of means of tapping palmyra trees for livelihood:

> If it were under the government of heathen kings that this injustice were shown to Christians, it would be a wonder; but that under the government of Christians and their servants, Christians should suffer injustice, and that by their means the increase of Christianity is prevented, is to us a matter of astonishment.[4]

'Native Inhabitants' of 'Blacktown' (Georgetown, Madras), on the other hand, addressed an appeal to the Governor-in-Council, pleading for protection from aggressive Christian threats against their ancient religious customs. Pleased that missionaries had been prevented from building a

---

[3] 'Humble Petition of Christian Inhabitants in the Zillah of Tinnevelly' (1833), in *Memorial of the Church Missionary Society* (London, 27 May 1853), pp. 72–8. This document was within a pamphlet submitted in connection with the Company Charter Renewal Act of 1853.

[4] Ibid.

church and school in the vicinity of their ancient temples, the petitioners ended with an expression of gratitude:

Therefore, we most humbly render our hearty thanks to your honour in Council, praying to God for your Welfare and also for the Honourable Company who are ever Benevolent... in distributing justice impartially. May the Goddess of Victory dwell on the edge of the Sword of their Warriors and let their Flag continue as long as the Sun and Moon shall endure.[5]

On 11 October 1836 the Bishop of Madras formally protested against the Government's involvement in such 'idolatrous practices' as managing properties and functions (for thousands of Hindu temples; protecting pilgrimage sites; requiring Christian soldiers to attend Hindu festivals (in violation of their consciences); forcing 'thousands of poor, defenceless peoples to leave their homes and, at the risk and even the cost of their lives' to drag great 'Temple Idol' Cars' (Rath Yatras) in processions; and turning a blind eye to hundreds of thousands of 'dancing girls' (*devadasi*s) being consigned to perpetual temple prostitution.[6] 'Disclaiming the desire, *in any degree*, to violate the liberty of conscience so fully and justly accorded to the Mahomedan and Heathen elements of the Company's empire', the Government's response was swift and ruthless.[7] Such issues were too potentially dangerous: 'great Political and State questions' could not be made liable to 'private feelings of individuals' or 'misled by excessive zeal'.[8] Bishop Daniel Corrie was publicly rebuked and General Peregrine Maitland, the Commander-in-Chief, returned to London (where he launched the Anti-Idolatry Connexion League).

In the 1840s the Governor of Madras, Lord Tweeddale, was censured and recalled for using the term 'heathen' in official communications, and for giving public support to missionaries and their schools. The Madras gentry had organized a large public meeting and sent a strongly worded memorial to the Court of Directors. A riotous tumult—so dangerous that mounted police and military were dispatched to preserve order—gathered at 'the

---

[5] Madras Public Consultations and Proceedings (henceforth MPC/P), No. 1, 4 Mar. 1818, TNA 453, pp. 759–61.

[6] Lord Bishop of Madras [Daniel Corrie] to Sir Frederick Adam, MPC/P, No. 60, 11 Oct. 1836, TNA 565, pp. 4862–4959.

[7] Ibid., p. 4871.

[8] Government of Madras to Government of India, MPC/P, No. 61, 11 Oct. 1836, TNA 656, pp. 4960–75; No. 8, Nov. 1836, TNA 657, pp. 5403–58.

rooms of Patcheapah's Institution, on Wednesday the 7th October 1846'.[9] Over 12,000 notables (*mahajan*s) of the Hindu Community of Madras affixed signatures (*chevralu*) to documents addressed to Parliament. 'Civil and Religious rights and privileges', they charged, were being violated by missionaries, abetted by pro-missionary European officials.

In the aftermath of the 'Great Mutiny' (Rebellion) of 1857, authorities both in Britain and in India blamed the 'proselytizing zeal' of missionaries. Even after the Company was abolished, in 1858, local governments, with rare exceptions, were careful not to show much public sympathy for missionaries. Particularly suspect were missionaries who sided with nationalists, Anglican prelates trying to expand ecclesiastical domains, or anyone disturbing religious institutions.[10]

Receptivity on the Margins

Over the years Christian movements fared better in areas outside the direct authority of the Raj. Beginning in south India, Christianity spread from Tranquebar to Thanjāvur, Tiruchirāpalli, Tirunelvāli, and thence to South Travancore (Tiruvanthapuram). By the late nineteenth century Christianity had spread slowly and unevenly northwards, culminating in the wholesale conversion of tribal peoples in mountains surrounding the Assam valley in north-east India.

In the century after the arrival of Royal Danish Halle Pietist missionaries in 1706, Vellalar Christian disciples from Tranquebar and Thanjāvur spread a network of chapel schools across south India. Tamil leaders initiated each expansion, which, after decades of incubation, led to movements among lower-caste peoples. 'Hindu Christians' of Thanjāvur provide a lens through which to comprehend what later happened among lower-caste Christians. The most renowned Thanjāvur Christian was Vedanayakam (Pillai) Sastriar (1773–1864), who became a master teacher and writer. Schools he served, supported by rajas of Thanjāvur, Shivaganga, and Ramnad, became so famous that Company directors subsidized them. Prominent Maratha

---

[9] *Proceedings of the Public Meeting of the Hindu Community of Madras on 7th October 1846* (Madras, 1846); *Memorial of Hindu Inhabitants of Madras Presidency to the Court of Directors, of 12th May 1847* (Madras, 1847).

[10] Susan B. Harper, *Bishop V. S. Azariah and the Travails of Christianity in the British Empire* (Grand Rapids, Mich., 2000), pp. 108–11.

Brahmans vied to have their sons enrolled. The Tamil–English curriculum provided learning beyond anything available elsewhere in India. The Saraswati Mahal Library, with its laboratory and 'Cabinet of Wonders', epitomized the Enlightenment. Vedanayakam, with reverence for Cankam culture, founded modem Tamil literature. His lyric verses extolled wonders of God's grace and wonders of science as revealed in the stars of the sky, beasts and birds of the field, cities of the world (in America, Asia, and Europe), and absurdities of inhuman behaviour. His old fellow classmate Serfoji, the Maharaja of Thanjāvur, made him 'poet laureate' (affixing Sastriar to his name).

Christianity also took root in Tirunelvāli during the 1760s, before the establishment of Company rule, when Savarimuthu Pillai, an ex-sepoy, and Rasa Clarinda, an affluent Brahmin widow, opened a chapel-school in Palayamkottai. Twenty years later Satyanathan Pillai became the first pastor–missionary of a tiny Christian community. David Sundaranandam, a Nadar (formerly Shanar) convert trained in Thanjāvur, was sent as a missionary to his own people in the late 1790s. When whole villages of Nadars turned temples into chapel-school halls, they aroused the wrath of local landlords and warlords (*palaiyakarrar*s). Chapel schools were destroyed, books were burned, and thousands lost their homes. Inspired by biblical precedents, David Sundaranandam established a 'village of refuge'. This was so successful that many similar settlements were established over the next century. After 1806 this fledgling community lost most of its leaders and continued to struggle until it caught the attention of James Hough, a military chaplain brought into Company service by the Claphamite lobby. Struck by the phenomenon of ardent hymn-singing in Tamil, he asked for help from the Church Missionary Society (CMS), who responded by sending Karl Rhenius, a brilliant if fiery Prussian military veteran with Moravian convictions, who soon became a heroic figure among Christians of Tirunelvāli.

Rhenius encouraged, instructed, trained, translated, and held dramatic public debates. His disciples, known as pilgrims, fanned out; thousands, again whole villages, turned Christian. The community doubled and trebled in size each decade thereafter. As congregations proliferated, so did chapel schools and self-help societies, with missions for the homeless, widows, and orphans. Rhenius's wife, a Ceylon-born Tamil speaker of Dutch extraction, ran schools for girls and women, teaching basic literacy and home health— setting a pattern that would soon be followed elsewhere. Teacher shortages led to recruitment of Catholics and non-Christians, some of whom also converted. High schools, colleges and seminaries, and hospitals sprang into existence as Tirunelvāli society was transformed. Again and again violent opposition occurred. Landed gentry (*zamindars*) and dominant religious figures (*pandarams*) mounted sporadic persecutions, riots, and attacks upon Christian villages. As early as 1828 a voluntary society called the Vibuthi Sangam, or Ashes Society, modelled on local Christian societies, organized efforts to thwart mass conversions. Company officials were called in to keep the peace, and missionaries were blamed for causing trouble. Local court decisions were appealed to the High Court in Madras during the 1840s. Tirunelvāli Christianity became a dominant regional culture, and a unique kind of 'Hindu Christian' communalism developed.

Christian expansion into south Travancore began with Vedamanickam. Converted in Thanjāvur while on a pilgrimage in 1799, he brought his new faith back to Mylaudy, his home village. There his success in gaining a following of several hundred provoked persecutions. While returning to Thanjāvur for help, he met William Tobias Ringeltaube. This zealous German of the London Missionary Society (LMS), then working among Nadars in Nagarkoil, accompanied Vedamanickam to his home. Within the steeply structured agrarian society of Travancore, the very existence of this small Christian community was an offence. Caste people, landlords who were Brahmans, Nayars, and Thomas Christians, were not prepared to let 'soil slaves' take liberties. That polluted people dared to declare a new faith was enough to provoke beatings and seizures. Sons were taken for corvée labour and daughters for worse purposes. Women daring to clothe their bosoms were flogged. Pukka houses were pulled down, chapel schools burned, teachers imprisoned, and sabbath worship denied.[11]

Eventually, after an incubation of fifty years, radical movements of conversion broke out. People in several communities, from non-slave castes and slave castes alike, turned Christian. Desperation, and the possibility of liberation from demons, fear, and bondage, drove these movements. Each movement began when leaders within a particular caste led their own people into the new faith. Supporting institutions and schools followed, through the assistance of missionaries (LMS, CMS, etc.). These events in turn provoked chain reactions of protest, oppression, and petitions to the authorities. Concerned over mounting disturbances, deaths, and adverse publicity,

---

[11] Robert Hardgrave, 'The Breast-Cloth Controversy: Caste Consciousness and Social Change in Southern Travancore', *Indian Economic and Social History Review*, V (1968), pp. 171–87.

British authorities in 1855 pressed for abolition of slavery. Brahman–Nayar gentry blamed missionaries. Pressures on the Maharaja mounted when Sir Charles Trevelyan, Governor of Madras, demanded remedial action. As events escalated—with conversions and demands for relief from oppression following each other—leaders within each Christian community became more assertive in opposing missionary paternalism.

Events in Tirunelvāli and Travancore set the pattern for what later happened in Telugu country, Karnataka, and places further north. Āvarna ('colourless') polluting peoples of the lowest castes and adivāsi peoples along heavily forested interior frontier escarpments began to respond when members of their own communities became missionaries among them. (See pp. 93–95 and 132–33.) As new Christian communities came into being, missionaries provided educational, medical, and social infrastructures. Away from the big cities and towns, for the most part these institutions were neither Anglican nor British.

Following twenty or thirty years of evangelism, group conversions began in Telugu country during the 1860s when a Madiga–Christian couple heard the gospel message from a relative. After baptism by an American Baptist missionary, they carried the Christian message back to their own community, leading to many conversions—with the baptism of over 2,000 in a single day. Similar movements were observed by American Evangelical Lutherans and Roman Catholics. The success of CMS, Methodist, Plymouth Brethren, and Pentecostal missions demonstrated that receptivity to Christianity did not depend on the denominational or national affiliation. One of the last large movements among Telugu peoples was led by V. S. Azariah, a Nadar missionary from Tirunelvāli, Bishop of Dornakal. A nationalist eager for the end of Empire, he epitomized the spirit of later conversion movements that have rapidly multiplied since the nations succeeded the Empire.[12]

Some of the most dramatic religious changes occurred in forested mountains around the territorial edges of Empire and in the interior wilderness areas of the interior. Particularly significant were changes among Naga, Khasi, Mizo, and Garo peoples, as also among the Karens, Chins, and Kachins of Burma. In each instance, after an apparent failure of overseas missionaries, foundations laid in the 1840s brought results thirty years later, when indigenous Christians ventured into the hazardous mountains with

---

[12] See Susan Billington Harper, *In the Shadow of the Mahatma: Bishop V. S. Azariah and the Travails of Christianity in British India* (Grand Rapids, Mich., 2000).

the Christian message. American Baptists and Welsh Presbyterians who followed took up the tasks of translating, printing, and teacher training. In the areas now known as Nagaland, Mizoram, and Meghalaya, Christianity became *the* dominant culture, even more than in Tirunelvāli. The lion's work of evangelization was done by indigenous missionaries, each speaking the gospel in his or her own mother tongue. Such events occurred in areas not yet under British rule, backed up by infrastructural aid and support from American or European, Indian, or Welsh missionaries. The intellectual and ideological roots owed at least as much to the American Midwest, Halle, and Herrnhut as to the British Isles.

In the Naga case Godhula, an Assamese Baptist, went up into the Naga Hills, well beyond the reach of imperial rule, and won hearts among the Ao Nagas of 'Old Molung'. Years later, in 1876, after Ao Nagas had been baptized in the frontier town of Shibsagar, overseas Baptist missionaries joined Godhula, helping to found a fortified village of refuge, and instigating the process which brought translations, printing presses, and schools. Eventually, Ao Naga pastors and teachers, both male and female, launched other movements that spread to Angami and Lotha Nagas. Sema Nagas turned Christian as if by spontaneous combustion—that is, without coming into direct contact with missionaries, Naga or American. They then became the most explosive evangelizing force in the region. (See pp. 93–95 and 141–44.) Although more overseas missionaries came, it was the Nagas themselves who carried on the main work of missionary expansion and whose self-supporting village congregations backed them. Even after the formation of the Naga Hills District of Assam, the region remained free from direct imperial rule. Naga autonomy, enhanced by military action during the Second World War, ensured that the Nagas would resist direct rule by India. Largely Christian and well educated, they leapfrogged into the modern world, escaping both Sanskritization and Islamization, which had occurred in areas less peripheral to the Empire.[13]

The Naga experience was repeated among Garo, Khasi, Abhor, Mishmi, Lushai, and other peoples surrounding the Assam valley, where the Ahom-Hindu cultural heartland remained largely impervious to Christian

---

[13] R. E. Frykenberg, 'Naga Baptists: A Brief Narrative of their Genesis', in Ian M. Randall, Toivo Pilli, and Anthony R. Cross, eds., *Baptist Identities from the Seventeenth to the Twentieth Centuries* (Carlisle, forthcoming); Richard Eaton, 'Comparative History as World History: Religious Conversion in Modern India', in Eaton, ed., *Essays on Islam and Indian History* (New Delhi, 2000), pp. 60–72.

influence. This same pattern, to a lesser degree, operated within the interior frontiers of Maharashtra, Gujarat, Orissa, and almost all hill regions. On geopolitical frontiers of South Asia, among *adivāsi* peoples, conversion movements of increasing volume and frequency were led by indigenous leaders, with missionary support coming mainly from non-British missionaries. Across a wide belt of forested mountain areas, from Kanya Kumari up through central India, beyond Assam, and across Burma to Thailand, conversions occurred among hundreds of separate peoples, none of whom had ever been Sanskritized or Islamicized. Having led precarious existences marked by fear and insecurity, they reinterpreted the Christian message to fit local conditions. Mission-based educational and health services reached hitherto neglected or oppressed peoples: *adivāsi* and outcasts—the impoverished, impaired, and disease-stricken. People in these areas enthusiastically welcomed the revolutionary idea that all men, women, and children were equal in the eyes of the law. It is not surprising that many of the newly literate Christians went on to higher education and then joined radical movements.

Missions and Anglican Imperialism

The process by which people turned Christian was primarily a by-product of indigenous rather than foreign agency; moreover, this was most pronounced at the lowest margins of society or in remote frontier regions of the subcontinent—as indeed in the British Empire as a whole. (See p. 8.) However, this did not prevent Western missionary societies from regarding India, along with China, as the great prizes for global evangelical activity. Consequently, in the decades after 1813, when the ban on admission to Company-ruled territories was lifted, inflows of overseas missionaries grew from a trickle to a flood. What so many missionaries accomplished is open to question. Most were not at the cutting edge of conversion movements. Not a single major movement was ever initiated by a foreign missionary. Their principal importance lay in their provision of institutional support in the form of seminaries, schools, and hospitals. However, the overseas missionary presence fuelled vexing denominational rivalries and quarrels over ecclesiastical authority.

To avoid endless conflicts over jurisdictions, inter-mission conferences led to a series of gentlemen's agreements, called 'comity'. No missionary was to work in territory already staked out by another mission. The result was a patchwork of contiguous and overlapping fields defined through a series of conferences: a General Conference of Bengal Protestant Missionaries in 1855, a South India Missionary Conference in 1858, and the Bangalore Conference of 1879. The Fourth Decennial Indian Missionary Conference, more elaborate and carefully prepared, assembled 160 delegates from twenty-six societies. Of course, there were always large numbers of missionaries from non-mainstream societies or faith missions, not to mention Catholics, who never participated in these 'ecumenical' events. Missions of Lutherans, Free Church missions, Plymouth Brethren, Salvation Army, Pentecostals, and faith societies of various kinds never agreed with comity. At the heart of many discords were relations between those Anglican societies committed to Anglo-Catholic ideas of hierarchy and establishment and other missions. (See pp. 57–58.) Many of the issues at stake were highlighted in the Rhenius affair.

At the time when Tirunelvāli country was caught up in its remarkable expansion, the CMS dismissed Karl Rhenius and replaced him with two new missionaries. Reasons for this abrupt action lay in a new ethos reflecting new ecclesiastical aspirations then rising among some Anglicans. During the eighteenth century a triangular alliance between Halle, Copenhagen, and London had existed. C. F. Schwartz, the Halle-trained Prussian who worked in the Danish Mission supported by the English SPCK, epitomized a 'soft' or informal ecumenicity. But in the 1820s the fading SPCK turned its work in India over to the Society for the Propagation of the Gospel (SPG) and the CMS. Tamil Christians leading the social revolution in Tirunelvāli had little idea of how this change was straining relations between Rhenius and Anglican authorities. The entire movement in Tirunelvāli, depending almost entirely upon locally trained pairs of ordained 'pilgrims', who, like Schwartz's 'helpers' fifty years earlier, carried the gospel to every village, rested on an 'open' ecclesiology. Tensions between Rhenius and the CMS increased after the arrival of Daniel Wilson as the Anglican Bishop of Calcutta. This first metropolitan, with a domain stretching to Australia, asserted claims to authority over all Anglican missionaries. When he rejected Tamils, whom Rhenius had recently ordained, for failing to conform, Rhenius published a pamphlet lamenting the imposition of Anglican forms upon Indian Christians.[14] In 1835 the CMS Directors summarily declared the Society's connection with Rhenius at an end.[15]

---

[14] J. Rhenius, *The Church: Her Daughters and her Handmaidens, her Pastors and her People* (London, 1835); id., *Memoir of the Rev. C. T. E. Rhenius* (London, 1841).

[15] Paul Appasamy, *Centenary History of the C.M.S. in Tinnevelly* (Palamcotta, 1923), p. 70.

Rhenius at first withdrew to Madras. But the obvious distress caused by his dismissal among Tirunelvāli congregations drew him to return. He struggled on with funds from supporters in India, Europe, and America until his death in 1838.[16] The Anglican takeover of an indigenous movement arising from the initiative of Tamil disciples of Schwartz fifty years earlier and rekindled by Rhenius's followers raised an international furore that put Anglican missionaries on the defensive. A war of pamphlets continued for two decades, while Tirunelvāli churches continued to grow along with Rhenius's posthumous stature as God's heroic 'Apostle to Tirunelvāli'.

But, even as other mission societies became embroiled in this affair, a new kind of phenomenon appeared. This was the Melpakkathar, a 'Hindu Christian' movement that broke away from all European connections, blaming Anglican machinations for Rhenius's death.[17] A precursor of later nationalisms, the Melpakkathar was a reaction to ecclesiastical missionary 'colonialism'. The Rhenius affair and its aftermath caused continuing regret among Anglicans. Robert Caldwell of the SPG, a renowned missionary–scholar who became one of the twin suffragan bishops in Tirunelvāli, lamented that 'Americans and the Germans [had done] far more for India, proportionately to their interest in it, than [was] being done by English churchmen.'[18] Statistics for 1852 showed ninety-nine Germans (many under Anglican societies) and sixty-seven Americans against only 138 Anglicans, not counting English Dissenters and Scottish or Welsh missionaries in India and Ceylon. This Caldwell saw as a 'national disgrace'. Lamenting that 'the zeal of the Germans for the evangelisation of India puts us to still greater shame' and that 'the Germans know about the antiquities of India... better than we do', Caldwell anticipated an Anglo-German rivalry that would haunt later missionary movements.

Another controversial intervention by the Bishop of Calcutta concerned caste distinctions in church. Shortly before his death Bishop Reginald Heber (1823–7) had defended caste-segregated public worship from missionary attacks, arguing that Indian Christians of different castes who sat separately were no worse than Christian masters and slaves in America or Christian gentry and servants in Europe who sat and worshipped separately.[19]

---

[16] *Farewell Letter of Mr. Rhenius to the Church Missionary Society* (London, 1836); Rhenius, *Memoir*, pp. 495–6, 497–534, 590–619; Appasamy, *Centenary History*, pp. 63–9.

[17] Appasamy, *Centenary History*, pp. 50–78.

[18] Robert Caldwell, *Lectures on the Tinnevelly Missions* (London, 1857), pp. 21–2.

[19] Reginald Heber, 21 Mar. 1826, MPC/P, TNA 620, pp. 1155–67; Thomas Robinson, *The Last Days of Bishop Heber* (London, 1830), pp. 321–5.

Bishop Wilson reversed that position by pronouncing a ban on caste discrimination in Vepery, on 12 February 1834. When Paraiyar Christians were ordered to sit on grass mats on the Vellalar side of the sanctuary, Vellalars abandoned the building and withdrew their children from the school. Later 700 of them were punished by excommunication for refusing the common cup and common bread of the Eucharist. Three thousand more in Thanjāvur suffered the same.[20] The District Magistrate of Thanjāvur was asked to flog 'Hindu Christians' for refusing to abandon caste strictures, so that one required 'professional assistance of the Surgeon'.[21] Petitions against missionary intrusions described humiliations, fines, imprisonments, and beatings.[22] Indian Christians found themselves marginalized and oppressed. Like the non-Christians surrounding them, Indian Christians resented these forms of domination.

Caste was not just a simple matter of birth (*jāti*).[23] As Vellalar Christians, Muttusami Pillai and Vedanayakam Sastri remarked that being 'Christian' was not a mere abstraction. Each Christian belonged to a family and a community on earth—with locality and specificity, face and name, *jāti* and blood (*vamsha*, 'lineage'), tongue and taste. *Jāti*, caste, intelligence, language, pollution, social ranking, and status were anything but common. At the 'Lord's Table' different beings could only 'sit together separately'. They could still enjoy 'spiritual unity' within contexts of social diversity where different peoples lived differently and separately, enjoying different status, wealth, and wisdom. Christians should be free to organize themselves according to earthbound resources and distinctions, whether of caste (India) or class (Europe).[24] However, new and radical ideas from America and Europe had

[20] 'The Humble Petition of Native Tamil Protestants of Vepery Congregation', MPC/P, TNA 619, pp. 830–41.

[21] 'Petition of Devasagayam, Mission Doctor of Tanjore', TNA 633, pp. 961–5; Resident of Tanjore [A. Douglas] to Chief Secretary, Government of Madras, TNA 622, pp. 2146–55.

[22] 'The Humble Address of Trichvay', MPC/P, TNA 633, pp. 965–8; 'Petitions from Mullathamby, Catechist, and Three Others; David Pillay, and Six Others of Tanjore', MPC/P, No. 6, 18 Apr. 1834, TNA 620, pp. 1155 ff.

[23] Nicholas Dirks, 'The Invention of Caste', *Social Analysis*, XXV (1989), pp. 42–52; id., 'Castes of Mind', *Representations*, XXXVII (1992), pp. 56–78; id., 'The Conversion of Caste: Location, Translation, and Appropriation', in P. van der Veer, ed., *Conversion of Modernities: The Globalization of Christianity* (New York, 1995), pp. 115–37.

[24] D. Dennis Hudson, ' "New Missionaries" and the Tanjore Congregation', in *Protestant Origins in India: Tamil Evangelical Christians 1707–1835* (Grand Rapids, Mich., 2000), pp. 140–72; *'Jati-tiruttalin Podium'* ['The Foolishness of Amending Caste'], *and 'Saditeratoo'* by Vedenayaga Sastree, Evangelical Poet, Tanjore 1829, British Library, Oriental and India Office Collection, MS OR 11742.

altered aspirations of missionaries in India. These now sought to impose equality, trying to mix cream with milk. They were calling for all to worship together, occupying the same seats, eating together from the same dish, drinking together from the same cup, singing together the same songs, studying together in the same schoolrooms, working together in the same fields, but wedding persons of different birth.

Thus, after a century of independence, Tamil evangelical Lutherans in Pietist congregations found themselves 'converted' overnight into Anglican Protestants—forced to read strange words (different translations), sing strange songs, and recite strange chants from an unknown Book of Common Prayer. At the same time, relations between the Anglican establishment and the Government of India were also turbulent. Bishop Wilson's scoldings of the Government for interfering 'in purely spiritual matters' were roundly rebuffed.[25]

Eventually, Vedanayakam Sastri, the most renowned Tamil evangelical of Thanājvur, who had run the school system for many years and whose status as former poet laureate in the durbar had brought glory to the entire community, was summarily dismissed. The outraged community, complaining to the Governor of Madras,[26] accused the new missionaries of committing four cruelties: (1) tampering with Tamil Scripture by replacing old versions with their own; (2) forcing integration of all Christians into one caste and excommunicating from the Eucharist all who refused to comply; (3) prohibiting flowers for festivals, weddings, and funerals; and (4) removing Tamil lyrics and Tamil music from worship.[27] When George Uglow Pope and other high-church (SPG) missionaries, attempting to 'reform' the schools that Schwartz had founded, where Vedanayakam Sastri had taught for fifty years, had even asked officials to flog 'Hindu Christians' for refusing to heed 'Church' commands, their actions damaged relations for generations thereafter.[28]

But the most audacious action of the Anglican Bishop of Calcutta was his attempt to compel Thomas Christians of Travancore to conform to Anglicanism. They saw themselves as far more ancient than the Church of

---

[25] Rt Revd Lord Bishop of Calcutta to Governor in Council, Fort St George, MPC/P, No. 3, 9 May 1834, TNA 621, pp. 1471–6. See also Harper, *In the Shadow of the Mahatma*, pp. 93–115.
[26] ' "Humble Addresses" from Soodra Christians, Complaining of Beatings, etc.', MPC/P, TNA 620, p. 1155; 622, pp. 2146–55.
[27] Hudson, *Protestant Origins*, pp. 148–72.
[28] G. U. Pope, *The Lutheran Aggression: A Letter to the Tranquebar Missionaries* (Madras, 1853).

England. 'Hindu' in culture, Christian in faith, and Syrian in polity, rituals, and doctrines, they traced their origins to the Apostle Thomas's arrival at Malankara in AD 52. Formerly merchant–warriors who wore tonsures like Nayars and Brahmans, occupied *tharavād* houses, avoided the pollution of interdining, intermarriage, or disposal of their dead, and tied *thālis* on the necks of their brides along with marriage cloths, Malankara Nazaranis were landed aristocrats. Their priesthood was hereditary, with nephews succeeding uncles. Some lineages (*vamshāvalis*) even claimed descent from Brahman converts of the Apostle, going as far back as seventy or more generations. Patriarchs of Antioch and Babylon had long vied for ecclesiastical sway over them. While Thomas Christians themselves cared little about doctrinal disputes, whether Diophysite (Nestorian) or Monophysite (Jacobite, Jakoba), the community's culture had been all but hermetically sealed for a thousand years. The Portuguese, initially welcomed as allies, had aroused resentment when their Estado da India tried to impose Catholic hegemony at the Synod of Udayamperur (Diamper) in 1599. The Archbishop of Goa, Alexius de Menezes, had cast aside Syrian institutions and burned Syrian libraries. But resistance to Catholic domination persisted. Then, in 1653, a solemn assembly of *kattanār*s (priests within the Thomas Christian Community) at Koonen Cross (Koonen Kurisu) had consecrated their own native Indian priesthood. Then, shortly after the Dutch conquest of Cochin had dramatically improved their situation, a Jakoba *metrān* (bishop within the Thomas Christian community) sent by the Catholicos of Antioch (then in Debhikr) had claimed ecclesiastical supremacy. Struggles between Antioch and Babylon, as between Orthodox Syrians and Roman Catholics, had been endemic ever after.

The first Company Residents in Travancore, Colin Macaulay (1800–10) and Sir John Munro (1811–19) were aggressively evangelical. When troops suppressed insurgencies and 'rescued' the Maharaja, Raja Rama Varma made Munro his *diwan* (chief minister). With Varma's death in 1814, Munro became virtual ruler, and displayed a partiality towards Thomas Christians that would have brought reprimands elsewhere in India. Christians, freed from compulsory service, were appointed to judgeships. Malayālam translations of Scripture were printed and placed in each church. On lands given by the Parvati-Rani, a seminary for Syrian priests was established in Kottayam. By 1816 pastors hd been brought under instruction, both in Malayālam and in Syriac; and the Metrān and CMS missionaries had taken up residence at the seminary. When, in 1816, Mar Dionysius II also died, Munro tried to influence the succession. The new Metrān, Punnathra George Kattanar, consecrated as Mar Dionysius III, then convened the Synod of Māvālikkara (1818). With missionaries sitting on each side, he told the assembled *kattanār*s that henceforth all ceremonies, doctrines, and rites were to conform with Scripture (as interpreted by missionaries). Konaṭṭu, a leading *malpān* ('instructor'), stood up to warn that the changes were too rapid. Already, due to missionary pressure, too many schools had been opened, clergy had been made to marry, images had been removed, and the reading of Scripture each Sunday in Malayālam had become almost mandatory.

After the retirement of Munro in 1820 relations deteriorated—both between Hindus and Christians, and between Anglican missionaries and Syrian clergy. Hindus turned their resentments upon both Thomas Christians and missionaries. After Mar Dionysius III died in 1825 and Philipose Malpān was elected as Mar Dionysius IV, Christians lost their government positions. The new Resident was not sympathetic; and even as fresh quarrels broke out between Malankara and Antioch, with opposed parties of Thomas Christians claiming Patriarchal support, resentments against missionary interference boiled over. The conciliatory Bishop Heber having died, Bishop Daniel Wilson came to Travancore and took a harder line. He so outraged the community with his presumptions that, at the Māvālikkara Assembly in 1836, they totally rejected Anglican ecclesiastical authority and reaffirmed their ancient tradition. All formal connections between Thomas Christians and Anglicans abruptly ended, with struggles over Kottayam property henceforth aggravating the rupture.

Thus, after three decades of Anglo-Syrian collaboration, two evangelical groups of Thomas Christians emerged: an insignificant Anglican branch tied to the CMS, and a much larger branch that stayed staunchly within the Thomas Christian tradition. While fierce battles continued to rage over doctrine and leadership, the dominant Thomas Church gradually grafted reform doctrines onto ancient institutions. Hostility to Anglican domination never extinguished reform within the Church. New schools continued to multiply, and literacy increased. After 1888, when the Mar Thoma Evangelistic Association was founded, its missionaries reached out to lower-caste peoples, ashram-like settlements were established, and Maraman, in Kerala, became famous for its great annual conventions.[29]

---

[29] At least six communities claim Apostolic Tradition: Orthodox Syrians (two branches); Malankara Catholics (Syrian Rite); the Independent Syrians of Malabar (Kunnamkulam); the Church of the East (Chaldaean); Mar Thoma; and St Thomas Evangelicals (two factions).

Catholic Recovery and Expansion

Of all the competitors Anglicans might have feared, the Catholics long seemed the least likely to succeed. After upheavals in both Europe and India, Catholic institutions had suffered disruption, decline, and dissension. The suppression of the Jesuits in 1773 had left many congregations abandoned. When Capuchin attempts to acquire Jesuit properties in India failed, Missions Étrangères de Paris, with only six missionaries in Pondicherry—three elderly and infirm (one a bishop) and three novices—had struggled to avert extinction. The French Revolution, Napoleonic Wars, occupation of Rome, weakened papal authority, and failing communications and funding from Europe had left local priests, many half-trained, to fill the void.

Three centuries of Catholic expansion seemed to be in jeopardy. Missionaries belonging to Catholic orders, with considerable autonomy from Lisbon or Rome, had once gone forth from monastic and collegial citadels into the countryside outside of the Estado da India. Fisherfolk along the coasts, such as the Paravars and Mukkavars, had turned Catholic, in defiance of Hindu and Muslim rulers. The Jesuit 'Brahmans' Roberto de Nobili and Constantius Giuseppe Beschi had established a Catholic presence in Sanskrit scholarship. 'Caste' people from respectable families, such as Brahmans, Vallalars, and Kammas, had become Catholic in towns all along both coasts of the peninsula. Yet, ongoing disputes between the Padroado Rial (the right of Portuguese royal patronage) and the Vatican's *propaganda fide* (created 1622) endangered all these achievements. Despite Portugal's decline in world power and flagging zeal in Lisbon, claims of the Padroado Rial had not weakened. While suffragan sees in Cranganore, Cochin, and Mylapore had lain vacant for decades, papal missionaries moving into areas under Padroado authority were being thwarted. Agents of vicariates apostolic still aroused fierce resistance. Catholic institutions languished, and many flocks remained untended.

Change began in the 1830s, when Cardinal Cappellari of *propaganda fide* became Pope Gregory XVI. The plight of Catholics in India prompted him to establish new vicariates apostolic—in Madras (1832), Bombay (1833), Calcutta and Ceylon (1834), the Coromandel Coast (1835), and Pondicherry and Madurai (1836). Within a century the map of Catholic India showed twenty-eight bishops, twenty-five within the Madras Presidency.[30] The restored

---

[30] Kenneth Ballhatchet, *Caste, Class and Catholicism in India: 1789–1914* (Richmond, 1998), p. 5.

Society of Jesus (Jesuits) returned to Madurai (1837). New dioceses, *within* domains of the Padroado but answering to *propaganda fide*, challenged Padroado institutions. Next, by the decree *Multa Praececlare*, Pope Gregory boldly asserted papal supremacy over all Catholics in India. Henceforth, any area within the diocese of Mylapore not assigned to a vicar apostolic was to come under the new vicariate of Madras. Neglected parishes in Cranganore and Cochin were assigned to the vicariate of Malabar. The Archbishop of Goa would no longer have authority outside Goa.

But it was one thing to make such pronouncements and another to implement them. With centuries of experience among 'country priests', padroadists had perfected skills of delay and obfuscation. They hoped, thereby, to outlast this Pope and then 'turn' his successor.[31] Even after 1846, when Pius IX ascended the Holy See and after the Concordat of 1860, disputes continued. Only after a series of synods under Clément Bonnand, Bishop of Pondicherry and Vicar Apostolic of the Coromandel Coast, did real changes occur. Foundations were laid—for a comprehensive educational system, stretching from villages to institutions of higher learning, and for the training of a native Indian clergy within an English-speaking Indo-British world. The significance for Catholicism in India of the formation of the Catholic Hierarchy of India in 1886 can hardly be exaggerated.

The most constructive initiative of Bishop Bonnand was to come to terms with the Raj. Catholic disputes settled by the British ended most interventions from Goa or Rome. Repeal of the Test Acts in 1828 and the Catholic Emancipation Act of 1829 had removed most legal disabilities for Catholics throughout the Empire. Irish immigration to England and other parts of the Empire was making Catholicism a more normal part of the denominational scene than had been so for three centuries. Once English-speaking Irish vicars apostolic arrived, padroadist versus propagandist disputes could be turned over to the Raj for adjudication. In turn, the Raj 'devised a Protestant-style principle to the effect that a change of jurisdiction was possible if a majority of local people wanted it. Such proposals prompted official investigation, and the Company frequently became involved in local affairs of the Roman Catholic Church.'[32] In short, Catholic institutions and missionaries within the Indian Empire, like other non-British missionaries, flourished as never

---

[31] Robrecht Boudens, *Catholic Missionaries in a British Colony: Successes and Failures in Ceylon, 1796–1893* (Immensee, 1979).

[32] Ballhatchet, *Caste, Class and Catholicism*, p. 5.

before. Having no illusions or pretensions to being part of the establishment, either ecclesiastical or imperial, they could carry on with their programme beneath the radar of official sensitivities.

Educational Infrastructure

Although missionaries were not the primary agents of religious conversion, they did provide the primary vehicles of literacy and learning. Ziegenbalg's charity school (*dharmappallikkādam*) in Tranquebar spread rapidly as a model for increasing literacy between 1728 and 1731.[33] After Rajanayakam, the captain (*servaikāran*) of the royal guard in Thanjāvur, arranged to bring a school into the kingdom under a royal land-grant (*inām*), a fully ordained Tamil pastor–teacher named Aaron arrived, and the process of introducing model schools, presses, and libraries underwent amazing expansion. This continued and spread to all of India. By 1835, for example, 261 village congregations in Tirunelvāli district had enrolled 2,882 children, 159 of them girls, in a hundred schools, two secondary schools, and a seminary for pastor–teacher training.[34] By the end of the century missionary school systems stretched from Kanya Kumari to Karachi and Kohima. At each mission station, or compound, a boarding school received pupils from feeder schools in surrounding villages. After 1854 these school systems, already funded by voluntary missionary societies in American and Europe, received supplemental grants-in-aid from local governments. The language of instruction was vernacular, with English introduced at higher levels. Local Christians, initially under European supervision, did most of the teaching. Many missionaries, in effect, became colonial administrators, with staff and teachers depending on foreigners for pay or pensions.

At the apex of missionary efforts were institutions of higher learning. In virtually every city they attracted non-Christians. Antedating government-run institutions, the impact of these on Hindu (*bhadralok*) and Muslim (*ashrāf*) elites was often greater than among Christians. These schools included such important institutions as William Carey's Serampore College (1818), Alexander Duff's College (1830), Bishops College (1824) in Calcutta, John Wilson's College (1835) in Bombay, John Anderson's Christian College (1838) in Madras, and Forman Christian College (1865) in Lahore. Later came

[33] Hudson, *Protestant Origins*, pp. 20–1, 93–4, 101.
[34] Edward Sargent, in *Proceedings of the South India Missionary Conference, held at Ootacamund, April 19th–May 5th, 1858* (Madras, 1858), pp. 12–14; Rhenius, *Memoir*, p. 357.

institutions for women: Sarah Tucker College (Palayamkottai), Lady Doak College (Madurai), the Women's Christian College (Madras), Kinnaird College (Lahore), and Isabella Thoburn College (Allahabad). These became elite institutions and, as such, catered heavily to the highest classes, training suitable brides for aspiring and upwardly mobile Indian gentlemen.

The language of instruction in colleges was English, not because of Macaulay's famous Minute on Education, but because successive echelons of 'Hindu' notables, civil servants, and professionals demanded it. On the other hand, almost all missionaries, especially those who wanted to break down caste barriers and untouchability, opposed the use of English, clashing unsuccessfully with high-caste Hindus in the coastal cities of Madras, Calcutta, and Bombay.[35] By the late nineteenth century theologically liberal missionaries were beginning to replace or equate 'conversion' with 'civilization' as their primary goal. Many extolled 'Hindu' civilization, searching it for 'Christian' elements derived by 'natural revelation'. For upper-class, intellectually eclectic educators, such as William Miller of Madras Christian College, the Christian task was to permeate Indian society with Christian principles, thereby influencing the elites who had taken to Western education in such droves. The task for missionaries was to increase dialogue and mutual understanding. This kind of thinking, called 'fulfilment theory', gained wider acceptance, especially among upper-class missionaries in the colleges. (See pp. 16 and 267.)

The last frontier of missions in the Indian Empire was Punjab, where communal feelings between Hindus, Muslims, and Sikhs were raw. Few Christians had been there prior to the 1840s. British and American missionaries moving there and establishing institutions in collaboration with Indians found many preconceived notions breaking down. By then, two-thirds of missionaries were women. Universal claims clashed with local dilemmas of gender, race, and imperial privilege. When multiracial institutions and principles of equality challenged social hierarchies, missionaries had to compromise and negotiate—with Indian Christians, officials, critics, patients, students, and staffs at their institutions. Upper-class, university-educated missionaries wanting to influence Hindu and Muslim gentry found themselves, ironically, striving for the oppressed, poor, and stigmatized.

---

[35] R. E. Frykenberg, 'Modern Education in South India, 1784–1854', *American Historical Review*, XCI (1986), pp. 37–65; id., 'Macaulay's Minute and the Myth of English as a "Colonialist" Imposition upon India', *Journal of the Royal Asiatic Society*, 2 (1988), 1–11.

Rising nationalist sentiments and communalism exposed inner conflicts. Dilemmas faced those who saw that missions might not outlive imperial rule, and for those who sympathized with nationalist aspirations, such dilemmas were never fully resolved.

Among converts to Christianity, as with earlier Christian elites in the south, what was notable was the tenacity with which they preserved traditional culture and avoided, or even spurned, ways of the West. Maulvi 'Imad ud-din strove to communicate with his own (*ashrāf*) people.[36] Pandita Ramabai insisted that she was a 'Hindu Christian'.[37] Narayan Vaman Tilak, in his life pilgrimage (*parampara*), strove to reconcile his Sanskritic heritage with emancipation of the oppressed and marginalized, ending his years as a *bhakta sannyāsi* (wandering ascetic). Sadhu Sundar Singh, declaring that 'Indians need the Water of Life, but not the European cup,' became a wandering *bhakti* mendicant and avoided missionary churches.[38] What many Christians of India, elite and non-elite alike, most abhorred was any colonial or 'compound' mentality of dependency and subservience, most of all as manifest in educational and ecclesiastical institutions.

Conclusion

All Indian Christians knew that their religious identity could never supersede other identities that were grounded in history and culture. Traces of this dilemma never disappeared. On one hand, ceaselessly revolving around each inner conflict—Indian or Westerner, Catholic or evangelical, Anglican or Nonconformist (Dissenter), Mar Thoma (Syrian) or Nazarani, Jakoba or Nestorian, Brahman or Vallalar or Nadar, conservative or liberal—was the problem of birth or caste (*jāti*). The historical and theological dimensions of this problem remain to this day. Unity and diversity, polarities and contradictions, acceptance of a common humanity without repudiation of lineage distinctions, have persisted everywhere—before, during, and after Empire.

---

[36] Avril A. Powell, ' "Pillar of a New Faith": Christianity in Late Nineteenth Century Punjab from the Perspective of a Convert from Islam', in Robert Eric Frykenberg, ed., *Christians and Missionaries in India: Cross-cultural Communication since 1500* (London, 2003), 223–55.

[37] Her *High-Caste Hindu Woman* (London, 1887, 1888, 1984) made her world-famous. See 'Pandita Ramabai Sarawati: A Biographical Introduction', in *Pandita Ramabai's America*, ed. Robert Eric Frykenberg, trans. K. Gomes (Grand Rapids, Mich. 2003), pp. 1–54.

[38] A. J. Appasamy, *Sundar Singh: A Biography* (London, 1958); Rebecca Parker, *Sadhu Sundar Singh: Called of God*, 7th rev. edn. (London, 1930); C. F. Andrews, *Sadhu Sunder Singh* (London, 1934).

Christians in India suffer a double dependency, a dual identity that seems indelible. On the other hand, often hovering over Indian Christians was the obvious 'foreignness' of missionaries—aliens, agents of change, disturbers of the status quo. Clashes between alien and indigenous, foreign and native, were more than religious or theological. They were cultural, political, and psychological. When Christians, both alien and native, were opposed by political regimes, they found common ground and mutual support. But when alien Christians, whether missionaries or officials, found common ground, Indian Christians suffered colonial domination. Yet, the work of missionaries—agents belonging to hundreds of missionary societies from overseas—rarely benefited from colonialism. Pre-colonial, non-colonial, and anti-colonial missionaries, taken together, outnumbered colonial missionaries.

British missionaries who strove for an Anglican establishment were the least successful of all. British missionaries from Nonconformist missionary societies suffered from being identified as part of this same 'alien' shadow of colonial rule (whose minions often despised them). Among British missionaries who were anti-colonial, none were less acceptable in the colonial establishment than the Salvation Army. The position of Catholic missionaries, being predominantly non-British (French, Italian, Irish, etc.), and of non-British evangelical (or Protestant) missionaries, whether from North America or northern Europe, remained ambivalent. Ambivalence towards the Raj persisted among missionary recruits from lower classes. Faith missions, operating mostly beyond ordinary systems of ecclesiastical control, could also be ambivalent. (See pp. 55–56.) To sum up, from the first Portuguese Catholics to the late colonial missionary friends of Gandhi there were always prominent missionaries prepared to challenge or ignore the imperial system and their own ecclesiastical authorities.

Thus there can be no easy summary of the relations between missions and colonialism. Hitherto there has been too much emphasis on linkages and too little attention paid to indigenous agency, impacts of conversion, reactions to conversion (or to counter-conversion), and indigenous movements. Much of what really happened still lies hidden from the gaze of historians. Social forces straining against each other in historical silence, due to our ignorance, were no less (nor more) implacable for hitherto lying beyond that gaze. Furthermore, profound tensions existed between the imperial system and established religions of any sort. In India 'secularism' has always meant 'non-interference' and 'neutrality'. It never resembled secularism in the West, nor did it ever imply separation of Church and State. Rather, it denoted even-handed acceptance of all religions. This rendered an Anglican establishment impossible. While India's peoples, Hindu and Muslim, accepted the existence of an Ecclesiastical Department, they most certainly resented favouritism or discrimination.[39] The imperial Mahāchakra, or great Wheel of State, could not remain balanced for long if some supporting spokes were broken or missing. The anomaly of missions and Empire lay in the fact that each religious system had to be, in some measure, as 'free' from imperial control or favour as every other system.

Select Bibliography

KENNETH BALLHATCHET, *Caste, Class and Catholicism in India, 1789–1914* (Richmond, 1998).

H. K. BARPUJARI, *The American Missionaries and North-East India (1836–1900)* (Guwahati, Delhi, 1986).

SUSAN BAYLY, *Saints, Goddesses, and Kings: Muslims and Christians in South Indian Society, 1700–1900* (Cambridge, 1989).

JEFFREY COX, *Imperial Fault Lines: Christianity and Colonial Power in India, 1818–1940* (Stanford, Calif., 2002).

FREDERICK S. DOWNS, *History of Christianity in India, V5, Northeast India in the Nineteenth and Twentieth Centuries* (Bangalore, 1992).

ROBERT ERIC FRYKENBERG, ed., *Christians and Missionaries in India: Cross-cultural Communication since 1500* (London, 2003).

J. W. GLADSTONE, *Protestant Christianity and People's Movements in Kerala: A Study of Christian Mass Movements in Relation to Neo-Hindu Socio-religious Movements in Kerala, 1850–1936* (Trivandrum, 1984).

KENNETH INGHAM, *Reformers in India: An Account of the Work of Christian Missionaries on Behalf of Social Reform* (Cambridge, 1956).

S. KAROTEMPREL, *The Impact of Christianity on the Tribes of Northeast India* (Shillong, 1994).

KOJI KAWASHIMA, *Missionaries and a Hindu State: Travancore, 1858–1936* (Delhi, 1998).

STEPHEN NEILL, *A History of Christianity in India (1707–1858)* (Cambridge, 1985).

GEOFFREY A. ODDIE, *Hindu and Christian in South-East India* (London, 1991).

---

[39] Chandra Y. Mudaliar, *The Secular State and Religious Institutions in India* (Wiesbaden, 1974); Franklin A. Presler, *Religion under Bureaucracy: Policy and Administration for Hindu Temples in South India* (Cambridge, 1987), pp. 1–35.

E. DANIEL POTTS, *British Baptist Missionaries in India, 1793–1837: The History of Serampore and its Missions* (Cambridge, 1967).

AVRIL A. POWELL, *Muslims and Missionaries in Pre-Mutiny India* (Richmond, 1993).

JULIUS RICHTER, *A History of Missions in India* (Edinburgh, 1908).

RICHARD FOX YOUNG, *Resistant Hinduism: Sanskrit Sources on Anti-Christian Apologetics in Early Nineteenth Century India* (Vienna, 1981).

7

New Christians as Evangelists

PEGGY BROCK

The spread of Christianity through the British Empire depended only in the first instance on European missionaries. Very soon local agents, themselves recent converts to Christianity, came to outnumber foreign-born missionaries in almost all mission fields. The 10,000 official missionaries employed by British societies at the turn of the twentieth century may have represented a high-water mark of European evangelism, but that figure is dwarfed by the legions of missionaries drawn from local communities across the Empire.[1] In Africa conversions of large numbers only began when locally recruited Christians constituted a critical mass.[2] Any discussion of missions and Empire that ignores the armies of non-European evangelists grossly misrepresents the grass-roots dynamics of Christianization. If, as some assert, the missionary movement was part of a larger imperial project of cultural colonialism, it is important to recognize that the footsoldiers of the advance were the indigenous preachers. Mission statistics affirm their existence but rarely do we hear their voices. These 'new Christian' men and women not only proselytized among their own communities, but also volunteered to take their message to peoples of different cultures and languages.[3] They communicated their own understandings of Christianity based partly on what missionaries had taught them and partly on their own cultural assumptions. Those who evangelized among distant peoples not only carried messages forged during the development of European Christianity, they often carried technical, social, and political concepts from their own cultures with

---

[1] Andrew Porter, 'Religion and Empire: British Expansion in the Long Nineteenth Century, 1780–1914', *Journal of Imperial and Commonwealth History*, XX (1993), p. 372.

[2] Richard Gray, *Black Christians and White Missionaries* (New Haven, 1990), pp. 80–1.

[3] The term 'new Christian evangelist' denotes people who, having accepted Christianity, attempted to persuade others to adopt the new religion. It lacks the negative connotations of 'native evangelists' and the political freight of 'indigenous evangelists'. These evangelists were not necessarily native or indigenous to the communities to whom they preached.

them such as new forms of housing, village organization, and cuisine.[4] If they were agents of imperialism, then they were double agents. Their known world did not include the imperial metropole or even its peripheral centres. What they knew well were their own societies and cultures embellished by superficial understandings of Christian Europe.

Most knowledge of the historical experience of new Christian evangelists comes through the filter of mission reports. Louise Pirouet's study of black evangelists in Uganda exemplifies the problems raised by such sources. We can know what they did, but remain removed from their lived experiences.[5] Some indigenous agents, however, have left records in their own words. J. D. Y. Peel has found reports from Yoruba evangelists from the inception of the Church Missionary Society (CMS) mission in 1845.[6] E. Palmer Patterson and Susan Neylan have used the writings of Tsimshian and Nisga'a Christians to investigate religious change in the Pacific north-west of Canada.[7] The South Pacific provides a relatively rich source of texts as islanders took to Christian evangelism in greater numbers than elsewhere, and several recorded their experiences.[8]

First-hand accounts by new Christian evangelists reveal the complex realities of people experiencing revolutionary change in their spiritual and material worlds. Neylan's analysis of Tsimshian writings uncovers 'diverse expressions of what it meant to be Christian. Tsimshian uses of both indigenous and Christian modes to describe conversion span the entire "outside–inside" spectrum, and ultimately demonstrate not just "inbetweenness" but the multiple identities of Native missionaries.'[9] New Christians who became evangelists put themselves in an ambiguous relationship to their own

---

[4] David Wetherell, 'From Fiji to Papua: The Work of the "Vakavuvuli" ', *Journal of Pacific History*, XIII (1978), pp. 153–72; Sione Latikefu, 'Pacific Islander Missionaries', in Doug Munro and Andrew Thornley, eds., *The Covenant Makers: Islander Missionaries in the Pacific* (Suva, 1996), pp. 17–40.

[5] Louise M. Pirouet, *Black Evangelists: The Spread of Christianity in Uganda 1891–1914* (London, 1978).

[6] J. D. Y. Peel, *Religious Encounter and the Making of the Yoruba* (Bloomington, Ind., 2000), pp. 589–90.

[7] E. Palmer Patterson, 'Native Missionaries of the North Pacific Coast: Philip McKay and Others', *Pacific Historian*, XXX (1986), pp. 22–37; Susan Neylan, *The Heavens Are Changing: Nineteenth-Century Protestant Missions and Tsimshian Christianity* (Montreal, 2003).

[8] Doug Munro and Andrew Thornley, 'Pacific Islander Pastors and Missionaries: Some Historiographical and Analytical Issues', *Pacific Studies*, XIII (2000), pp. 1–31.

[9] Neylan, *Heavens Are Changing*, p. 130.

communities. They were, as Peel also notes, both insiders and outsiders.[10] Most, although not all, adopted some traits of cultural outsiders along with their Christian beliefs. European clothing was a common marker. Housing, food, bodily decoration (or lack of it), as well as Christian religious observance might single out Christians from non-Christians, but were not always firm indicators of religious adherence. Evangelists almost by definition stood in judgement on their fellows, as their aim was to change beliefs, religious practices, and moral standards. They cherished a sense of superiority over those not yet enlightened by the word of God.

While some new Christians visibly improved their material circumstances by aligning themselves with missions, those who became evangelists stepped outside the social hierarchy of their own societies. Their insider–outsider status depended on the success of their preaching. Evangelists might begin despised and marginalized, but as their following grew, so too did their status and material circumstances. Some who went to foreign communities were invited and quickly attained status as teachers, or even as alternative sources of authority and power; others had to work hard to gain acceptance.[11] They used a variety of evangelical strategies to convey their message to non-believers by translating indigenous concepts into Christian equivalents,[12] Christianizing customary rituals,[13] or advocating the destruction of pre-existing rituals and beliefs.[14]

The heart of this chapter concerns texts produced by new Christian evangelists who left first-hand accounts of their lives. These men (unfortunately, accounts by women are even rarer[15]) came from different regions of

[10] Peel, *Religious Encounter*, p. 589.

[11] Donovan Williams, *Umfundisi: A Biography of Tiyo Soga 1829–1871* (Lovedale, 1978), p. 5. Missionaries from Fiji, Samoa, and Tonga expected special treatment from other western Pacific societies; Sione Latukefu, 'The Impact of South Sea Islands Missionaries on Melanesia', in J. A. Boutilier, D. T. Hughes, and S. W. Tiffany, eds., *Mission, Church and Sect in Oceania* (Lanham, Md., 1978), pp. 91–108; Charles W. Forman, 'The Missionary Force of the Pacific Island Churches', *International Review of Mission*, LIX (1970), pp. 215–26; Clement Marau, *A Story of a Melanesian Deacon, Written by Himself*, trans. R. H. Codrington (London, 1905), p. 75.

[12] Jay Miller, *Tsimshian Culture: A Light through the Ages* (Lincoln, Nebr., 1997), p. 143; Neylan, *Heavens Are Changing*, p. 131.

[13] Geoffrey M. White, *Identity through History: Living Stories in a Solomon Islands Society* (Cambridge, 1991), p. 108.

[14] Pirouet, *Black Evangelists*, p. 198.

[15] A rare example of a female new Christian who has left some record of her life is Srimati Sona Murmu, a Santal woman in India. The Danish missionary P. O. Boddington wrote a biography, *Sona: The Life and Deeds of a Christian Santal Lady*, based on reminiscences he had

the Empire. All were committed Christians who used the Bible as the authoritative source of their Christian teaching. Some had encountered Christianity as children and were inducted into its teachings and mores over many years. Others had a very brief training before absorbing aspects of Christianity which they then communicated to others. Some learned about Christianity in their own, or a closely related, tongue. Others were taught in English, but preached in their own language or the language of the people they were evangelizing. Most writings of new Christian evangelists have not been readily accessible, only coming into the public domain in the last thirty to forty years through the painstaking work of historians who have tracked down the manuscripts lodged in widely scattered archives. Some were translated soon after they were written; others have presented formidable problems for recent scholars, who have had to grapple with discontinued orthographies and grammatically ambiguous texts. Commenting on one such text, Marjorie Crocombe, notes:

> Maretu was not an easy writer to understand. His handwriting was cumbersome and irregular, and he did not understand punctuation or divide the narrative into paragraphs. Nor was he always sure what constituted a word. In some cases a single word was divided into two, and in others several words were joined into one. There were also many words and letters within words omitted.[16]

Five new Christian evangelists have been selected because of the richness of their first-hand accounts. Each was originally introduced to Christianity by missionaries from other parts of the British Empire, the United States, or Europe. They in turn took their version of Christianity, modified by their own cultural understandings, to the communities they taught. Tiyo Soga, a Xhosa man from the brutal frontier war zone of South Africa, kept a journal intermittently from 1857 to 1870. His other writings include letters to his mission society (Foreign Missions of the United Presbyterian Church) and articles for a Xhosa mission magazine.[17] Soga had a thoroughgoing Christian education in Scotland and returned to southern Africa as an ordained

---

persuaded her to write. See Peter B. Anderson, 'Revival from a Native Point of View: Proselytization of the Indian Home Mission and the Kherwar Movement among the Santals', in J. M. Brown and R. E. Frykenberg, eds., *Christians, Cultural Interactions, and India's Religious Traditions* (London, 2002).

[16] Maretu, *Cannibals and Converts*, ed. and trans. M. T. Crocombe (Suva, 1983), p. 16.

[17] *The Journal and Selected Writings of Rev Tiyo Soga*, ed. Donovan Williams (Cape Town, 1983).

minister with a Scottish wife. Arthur Wellington Clah, a Tsimshian who lived in British Columbia, maintained a diary from the late 1850s until 1910.[18] After a few months of schooling from an Anglican missionary, Clah began making diary entries in idiosyncratic English. Maretu and Ta'unga were Rarotongans of the Cook Islands in the South Pacific. Maretu, who never left the Cook Islands, wrote an autobiography in his native language.[19] Ta'unga attended a mission school where he learnt to write in Rarotongan in an orthography developed by the missionaries. He used this limited orthography to write about his evangelism in the Tuauru language of New Caledonia, where he spent some of his working life. Moses Tjalkabota was a western Arrernte from central Australia, who dictated an account of his life to the Lutheran missionary F. W. Albrecht in the 1950s.[20]

All five men were first-generation Christians[21] born into unsettled times in the nineteenth century. Four of them were introduced to Christianity by missionaries as children. Clah, who grew up in a Tsimshian village by a Hudson's Bay Company trading post, did not gain access to Christian teachings until he was 26 or 27. The first Europeans Tjalkabota met were the Lutheran missionaries who established the Hermannsburg mission. Although Soga had visited Europe, and Clah had a taste of Canadian town life in Victoria, British Columbia, they, like the other three, lived mainly among their own people. Four of them were formally affiliated to Protestant mission societies. The fifth, Clah, had also been closely associated with Protestant missionaries but never formally aligned himself with a church. He would exhort his own family, the people in his village, and the peoples, including occasional Europeans, whom he met as he went about fishing, hunting, trading, and mining. Soga, after his sojourns in Scotland, proselytized among the Xhosa and other groups in his region. Ta'unga alone had to learn a new language in order to preach in New Caledonia to people who were culturally and (as he noted) physically different from his own people.[22]

---

[18] Arthur Wellington Clah diary, Wellcome Library for the History and Understanding of Medicine, London, WMS Amer 140/1–72.

[19] Maretu, *Cannibals and Converts*, p. 15.

[20] 'Moses Tjalkabota', in Paul G. E. Albrecht, *From Mission to Church, 1877–2002, Finke River Mission* (Adelaide, 2002), app. 2.

[21] Soga's and Maretu's fathers were nominal Christians, but never baptized.

[22] Describing the people of Tana (Vanuatu), 'They are black and quite small...have a wild appearance and evil-looking faces' (*The Works of Ta'unga: Records of a Polynesian Traveller in the South Seas, 1833–9*, ed. and trans. R. G. and Marjorie Crocombe (Canberra, 1968), pp. 21–2).

Tjalkabota could only visit people within walking or donkey-riding distance of his home in central Australia.

The accounts these local missionaries left behind them come as close as modern scholars are likely to get to the spirit that animated the key agents of missions within the British Empire.

Tiyo Soga

Soga's journal mixes mundane commentary about people attending class and Sunday services with doubts about his own ability to preach and observations on Africans he encountered. His writings clearly reveal his insider–outsider status. Not only did he have a Scottish wife and a European lifestyle, he had not gone through male initiation ceremonies and, therefore, was not regarded by many Xhosa as a mature man.[23] Although these factors militated against his identification with other Africans, including the Xhosa, he also suffered from racial discrimination, particularly after his return to South Africa.[24]

His evangelical programme did not feature accommodation to British rule, and he saw no cultural impediment to Xhosa acceptance of Christianity. Though Soga made distinctions between Christians and heathens, he found both receptive to his itinerant preaching among thirty communities located up to 23 miles from his Emgwali mission.[25] He was impressed by considered questions put to him by non-believers. On one occasion when he had reprimanded 'my poor benighted country-men' for wearing painted blankets and ornamentation useless to 'an immortal being like me', they responded by asking him questions about sin. Would an infant who died be considered sinful and be cast into hell? Would a person who had sinned a short time be forgiven? Soga replied that a merciful God would not cast the infant into hell, but there was 'no possibility of escape to any who have once entered the regions of evil'. A few years later he challenged some fellow countrymen to explain why they did not accept Christianity. A senior chief responded that such knowledge should have come from their forefathers if it was so important; it should not have been withheld from them. Soga pointed out that neither had their forefathers known the white man's metal spades,

---

[23] Williams, *Umfundisi*, pp. 5, 19.   [24] Soga, *Journal and Selected Writings*, pp. 2–3, 6.
[25] Entry for 1 Jan. 1860, in Soga, *Journal and Selected Writings*, p. 28; Williams, *Umfundisi*, p. 64.

hoes, and blankets.[26] He used both reasoned argument, based on his knowledge of Xhosa society, and diabolical threats of punishment in the afterlife to reinforce his Christian message. These discussions suggest that the people to whom Soga preached did not connect technological innovations with Christianity, unlike many people in other parts of the Empire. They also worried that this religion was not being incorporated into existing belief systems in an appropriate manner.

Soga treated their nuanced responses seriously, and addressed their often unstated reservations. He could claim to be one of them and present himself as an example of the benefits of being a Christian. Yet he could be as judgemental as the harshest of European missionaries: criticizing slavish adherence to superstitions such as rainmaking or killing witches. From an imperial perspective the most striking aspect of Soga's texts was his nationalist belief that Christianity could unify the battered and divided Xhosa people, even though in the short run the division of Africans into Christians and non-Christians had the potential to undermine chiefly authority.[27] He strongly believed that, while Christianity could not tolerate some aspects of their culture, it posed no threat to their African identity. Soga's education outside the continent made him conscious of his identity not only as a Xhosa, but also as an African. Rejecting the European view of Africans as doomed to extinction, he argued that God gave Africa to Ham and all his descendants, and that God would ensure that they stayed there. He recognized that Africans depended on European missionaries to spread Christianity, but they had to resist the European vices that inhibited human progress and enlightenment.[28]

Maretu and Ta'unga

People of the South Pacific region, particularly the eastern island groups, responded rapidly to Christian evangelism. Hundreds volunteered to become evangelists. Charles Forman has estimated that 895 missionaries left Fiji, Samoa, the Cook Islands, the Solomon Islands, and Tonga to proselytize in Papua New Guinea, the Solomon Islands, Vanuatu (New Hebrides), and Kiribati and Tuvalu (Gilbert and Ellice Islands).[29] Many

---

[26] Entry for 17 July 1863, in Soga, *Journal and Selected Writings*, p. 36.
[27] Soga, *Journal and Selected Writings*, pp. 71, 173.   [28] Ibid., pp. 38–9, 178–82.
[29] Charles W. Forman, 'The Missionary Force of the Pacific Island Churches', *International Review of Mission*, LIX (1970), pp. 215–26; Munro and Thornley, 'Pacific Islander Pastors', p. 2, estimate that at least 1,500 Islanders went as pastors to other islands from 1819 to the 1970s.

more preached in their own or neighbouring communities. Many of these pioneer missionaries did not survive the violence and diseases they encountered, particularly in the western Pacific. Of the LMS Islander pastors sent to Papua New Guinea between 1871 and 1885, almost half died.[30] Ta'unga, a Rarotongan, was one of the few evangelists to return from New Caledonia.

One of the most attractive aspects of Christianity for Pacific Islanders was its association with reading and writing.[31] Elekana, a Rarotongan missionary who arrived on the Tuvaluan island of Nukulaelae after being blown off course, was welcomed when the islanders realized he could read the Bible. He distributed pages of his book to help them read. 'Day after day old and young men, and women came, requesting me to spell and read to them, and begging for part of my book. Soon none of my book was left.'[32] The hunger for literacy—even symbols of literacy such as pages of a book—crops up in many of the autobiographical writings of first-generation Christian evangelists in the Pacific region. Two of the most detailed personal accounts to have been published come from the pens of Maretu and Ta'unga, both trained by Charles Pitman of the LMS.

Maretu's narrative, while strongly influenced by his Christianity, reveals more about the societies in which he lived than many of the other surviving autobiographies. A telling comparison is the hagiographic life of the Tongan Joel Bulu, who evangelized in Fiji. This 'autobiography' was written down by a missionary, based on conversations the two had conducted over a period of time. It presents a formulaic account of the young Bulu, 'quaking with fear and weeping in great anguish', finding God, and then risking his life to spread the Word among violent cannibals.[33] Maretu's writings, in contrast, make insightful observations about functioning societies, their hierarchical nature, their social relationships, the traumatic effects of Christian teachings, the awful impact of introduced diseases, and the tensions between evangelists from different island groups. His account of cannibalism is more ethnographic than a representation of evil: 'No one ate human flesh during times of peace; it was only in times of war.... Pigs, matured *kava* plants and fish

---

[30] Munro and Thornley, 'Pacific Islander Pastors', p. 8.
[31] Charles W. Forman, *The Island Churches of the South Pacific: Emergence in the Twentieth Century* (Maryknoll, NY, 1982), p. 90; Bronwyn Elsmore, *Mana from Heaven: A Century of Maori Prophets in New Zealand* (Auckland, 1999), p. 15.
[32] M. Goldsmith and D. Munro, 'Encountering Elekana Encountering Tuvalu', in Don Rubinstein, ed., *Pacific History: Papers from the Eighth Pacific History Association Conference* (Mangilao, 1992), pp. 25–41, 28.
[33] Joel Bulu, *The Autobiography of a Native Minister of the South Seas* (London, 1871), p. 23.

poison were substituted for human sacrifices in times of peace, for to eat human flesh then was an offence against the rules of the *ariki* and *mataiapo*.[34] Maretu worked among his own people in the Cook Islands because Charles Pitman would not release him for service in more distant places. His opportunity for independent action did not arise until 1839, when unrest broke out on the neighbouring island of Mangaia, where Tahitian evangelists had been working. Later Maretu travelled to the islands of Manihiki and Rakahanga before returning to Rarotonga. Ta'unga, on the other hand, left Rarotonga in 1842 for New Caledonia, whose people looked strange to him, spoke an unfamiliar language, and practised customs he did not understand. On his arrival he maintained an ethnocentric distance:

These people are a very strange kind of people. They walk about without clothing, both men and women. The latter are indeed more degraded than the former. It is, they say, what they are accustomed to from of old. They are just the same when they sleep. They make a fire in their huts then they lie down and sleep by the side of it.[35]

Ta'unga's account demonstrates that evangelism could be a dangerous and life-threatening commitment. Sometimes the evangelists were blamed for epidemics that were rife among the New Caledonians; or jealous chiefs wanted them killed. European traders tried to undermine them by claiming that the new religion did not come from Europe, but was being disseminated from Samoa and Rarotonga.

Threats to evangelists' lives eventually became so severe that the mission society insisted they leave; Ta'unga was sent to Mare and other islands in the Loyalty group. Here his main protagonists were Samoans who had previously established a mission to the islanders. Ta'unga was again confronted by strange cultural practices, particularly cannibalism, which he described in some detail: 'When the enemy is taken, they grab him and chop him up in pieces and give him to the womenfolk who carry him back to their houses.' In contrast to Maretu's unembellished description of cannibalism among his own people, Ta'unga claimed that it was not only victims of war that were eaten, but that New Caledonians were so depraved that family members ate each other.[36] Ta'unga was writing for a missionary audience, which possibly accounts for his lurid descriptions of evil customs. He told Charles Pitman, 'The customs of these islands are innumerable. I have not written about all of

[34] Maretu, *Cannibals and Converts*, p. 33. [35] *Works of Ta'unga*, p. 34.
[36] Ibid., pp. 91–2.

them, lest you should not approve of these matters, and perhaps you may not be interested.'[37]

When Ta'unga went back to New Caledonia in an effort to resume his interrupted work, he found the village where he had lived burnt out and deserted. The threats of violence had been carried through. Instead of continuing with pioneering evangelism, he spent twenty-one years on Manu'a in Samoa ministering to an established Christian community. At first he remained aloof from the villagers, who thought him an inferior substitute for the European missionary they wanted, but by the time he left Samoa there were many celebratory legends told about him, including oral accounts which survived into the late twentieth century.

The autobiographies of new Christian evangelists in the Pacific reflect their willingness to sacrifice their lives for the privilege of preaching to the unconverted. All accounts from Pacific Islander evangelists are cast in heroic mode, where failure and danger are ever present. Clement Marau from the Bank Islands in Vanuatu recounted his early despair on the island of Ulawa when he tried to convert a whole village: 'at first I began wrong, beginning with a great number of people at once, and failed entirely; whereas afterwards I came to see that it is a good thing to begin with one person rather than many'.[38] While frequently discouraged by their lack of success, they retained a sense of their superiority over non-Christians. Evangelizing among those who were at least nominal Christians was not considered a challenge. Fijian evangelists in Papua were fascinated by the prospect of physical danger. The two Rarotongans also sought out perilous situations. The Fijian evangelist Poate Ratu described cannibalism among the Papuans: 'They cut up the victims like one does fish.... They are not baked whole, as at one time with us; so if you hear of one of us being killed, you would know that we were not baked in an oven, and roasted, but that we were grilled in small pieces over a fire.'[39]

Although early islander missionaries worked in societies relatively untouched by colonialism, they showed an awareness of cultural issues. Far from accepting the hegemony of overseas missionaries, many declared they were better suited to converting their fellow islanders than Europeans. Having so recently experienced the evils of heathenism themselves, they believed

[37] Ibid., p. 111.
[38] Clement Marau, *A Story of a Melanesian Deacon*, trans. R. H. Codrington (London, 1905), p. 75.
[39] Wetherell, 'From Fiji to Papua', pp. 158, 163.

they were better placed to understand and discourage unsavoury customs.[40] They had the advantage of understanding the social and political structures of the communities. However, when Polynesians from societies with inherited chiefs went to the western Pacific communities where the political hierarchies were more fluid, they had great difficulty devising effective evangelical strategies.[41] Latukefu argues that even in these circumstances, and despite their sense of superiority, new Christian evangelists in New Guinea were culturally closer to the people than European missionaries. They participated in village feasting, and readily became absorbed into the clan system of the locals.[42] However, they never totally shook off their outsider status of being associated with innovations, and remained vulnerable to physical attacks.

Evangelists introduced customs from their home societies, but their main aim was to communicate their version of religious truth. Whether they preached a more violent message has been a matter of debate. Some historians have argued that European missionaries emphasized the God of love and the softer side of Christianity, whereas the new Christian evangelists focused on God's retributive role and tried to instil the fear of hell.[43] The writings of the evangelists belie this generalization. When Maretu showed the people of Manihiki how to build a lime kiln, they lit the fire and exclaimed, 'Oh Maretu. I suppose the fire of the god of darkness down below is something like this!' Maretu replied that the fire, which was the anger of God, would die if all people believed in Jesus Christ.[44] His preaching emphasized Jesus' sacrifice, not God's wrath. Ta'unga criticized a fellow evangelist for underplaying the love of God in his preaching. He himself balanced the hard and soft sides of Christianity: 'The crucial things are the anger of God and boundless love. Because of his anger with man for his committing sin, souls went down to hell, but because of his great love, God brought men back from the fire, and the souls reached heaven.'[45]

Preachers not only lauded the new religion but also delighted in exposing the inadequacy of people's existing beliefs. They used rhetorical devices to

---

[40] Marau, *Story of a Melanesian Deacon*, p. 46.

[41] Wetherell, 'From Fiji to Papua', p. 159.

[42] R. Sinclair, 'Samoans in Papua', in Marjorie Crocombe, ed., *Polynesian Missions in Melanesia* (Suva, 1982), p. 20.

[43] Forman, *Island Churches of the South Pacific*, p. 94; Niel Gunson, *Messengers of Grace: Evangelical Missionaries in the South Seas 1797–1860* (Melbourne, 1978), p. 225.

[44] Maretu, *Cannibals and Converts*, p. 172.

[45] *Works of Ta'unga*, p. 6.

show how Christianity could answer questions about the origins of human existence, the soul, and sin, which local religions did not address, as well as the impotence of these religions in the face of epidemic diseases and natural catastrophes. A common evangelical strategy was the destruction of people's idols and sacred places.[46] Ta'unga insisted that a chief who had embraced Christian prayer must burn the effigies of his old gods. Marau destroyed all the idols of the people of Ulawa and burned down their sacred grove to prove they had no supernatural powers.[47] Maretu recounted how the two Tahitian evangelists who brought Christianity to his own community led the villagers in the destruction of the *marae* ('religious grounds') and idols. Maretu's own intervention in burning his father's *marae* saved his father from a fatal illness. There were other forms of destruction and renewal. When Maretu baptized twenty people on Manihiki, he gave the children biblical names. Soon everyone in the community wanted to be baptized so they could acquire a new name, a social act seen as creating bonds of commitment between the people, the missionary, and his god.[48]

The accounts of Ta'unga and Maretu do not conform to bipolar models of the encounter between European cultural colonialism and indigenous cultural response. New Christians did not simply parrot a European message but communicated their own understandings of the Bible. They transmitted aspects of their own cultural heritage along with ideas received from foreign missions. They encouraged people to cover their bodies,[49] to move into centralized villages, and to adopt new technologies. Sometimes they learned skills and knowledge from their host community. Thus Pacific Christianity was associated with a wide range of multidirectional cultural and intellectual exchanges. Some of these anticipated British imperial control and even facilitated its imposition: in Fiji and New Zealand, British government negotiations with indigenous elites were assisted by the existence of large polities formed in response to the work of missionaries and new Christian evangelists.

Arthur Wellington Clah

Clah was one among many Tsimshian, Nisga'a, and other First Nations people who proselytized among societies along Canada's Pacific coast.

[46] Sinclair, 'Samoans in Papua', p. 20.   [47] Marau, *Story of a Melanesian Deacon*, p. 68.
[48] Maretu, *Cannibals and Converts*, p. 160.
[49] Marau, *Story of a Melanesian Deacon*, p. 65.

CMS records list 358 native lay teachers (men and women) in the North Pacific Mission between 1865 and 1901.[50] Methodist records list 635 native preachers in the same region between 1883 and 1900, as well as native exhorters, stewards, leaders, and assistants.[51] Although it is unclear how many of these Christians actively proselytized, the figures suggest that the nascent churches relied heavily on the support of new Christians to garner support. The CMS missionary William Duncan began his mission to the Tsimshian people in 1857. As in other regions that proved immediately responsive to Christianity, the coming of a new religion had been predicted by prophets. Duncan and the missionaries who followed him were relatively late arrivals on the coast. Fur traders had been active in the region since the late eighteenth century, and in 1831 the first Hudson's Bay Company trading post was established. Missionaries were not the first or sole point of European contact but interlopers in a well-established trading relationship.

A number of the evangelists on this coast, stretching from Victoria on Vancouver Island to Alaska, have left accounts of their lives.[52] However, the diary of Arthur Wellington Clah—a daily record maintained from his late twenties through old age—overshadows all these writings. It is of great value, not only because it covers such a long period, but because it was maintained on a day-to-day basis. Unlike most autobiographical writings it is not retrospective, nor is it addressed to a church, mission society, or one of their representatives. Clah remained largely independent of such organizations. While new Christians in many regions of the British Empire took it upon themselves to spread new religious understandings, it was unusual for people without institutional support to make and keep written records.

Clah may have been a unique record-keeper, but other aspects of his life were rooted in his own Tsimshian society. Like most new Christians throughout the Empire he received no stipend or support from the communities to which he preached. He combined evangelism with the everyday activities of fishing, hunting, and trading that dominated his existence.[53] His writings suggest he was untroubled by the insider–outsider status that unsettled other new Christian evangelists. Many of his activities frankly aimed at increasing his prestige and status among the Tsimshian.[54] He

---

[50] Neylan, *Heavens Are Changing*, pp. 284–5.   [51] Ibid., p. 74.
[52] Ibid., pp. 147–59.   [53] Patterson, 'Native Missionaries', p. 35.
[54] Peggy Brock, 'Building Bridges: Politics and Religion in a First Nations Community', *Canadian Historical Review*, XXIV (2000), pp. 159–79.

took pride in operating independently of Euro-Canadian missionaries, insisting that his authority came directly from God:

Since our God father telling in my heart to stapeth [stop] every thing we do. I can told all people to nock [knock] up given [giving] big feast and stop given away all property to our chiefs. I told all people to stop everything wrong [that] makes God angry. I believe our God is strong[,] for Lord Jesus Christ defend out [our] since [sins].[55]

He encouraged communities to scorn slavish dependence on missionaries and to forge their own links with God.

Neither does Clah's account of his life conform to the conversion narratives commonly found in mission records (see pp. 155–56). He did not experience a sudden transformation from heathen to Christian. It is not even clear at what point he first identified himself as a Christian. The earliest references to Christ and God appear after he experienced a near-catastrophe at sea. He perceived God as a force who could save believers from the natural elements and disease. Later in the diary God also appears as chastising sinners.[56] Punishment might be experienced as 'bad luck' resulting in hunger and unemployment, or death from disease. Salvation expressed itself in equally simple terms: 'He take care my live [life] always Save my soul[,] give all food I use[,] so I feel happy for Him for all Blessing.'[57] While Pacific Islander evangelists expressed fear of hell, Clah was preoccupied with the here and now. His diary steers clear of the confessional mode common among many missionaries; rarely does he dwell on moral lapses or tribulations to be overcome.[58] His descriptions of his activities and those of the people around him include his own drunkenness, fighting, and sexual temptations. In 1867 he records taking a second wife.[59] In 1869 he kidnaps a relative of a man who had not repaid a debt.[60] Clah rarely seems to suffer moral compunction following these lapses from Christian standards of behaviour.

He judged other people more severely, particularly those who maintained what he called the 'old fashioned ways'—the status-enhancing activities and rites of passage of the north-west Pacific coast peoples. There was a rather fine line, however, between what Clah considered un-Christian, or bad, behaviour and what he found acceptable. Clah criticized the competitive, status-enhancing activities of chiefs who staged feasts (potlatches)

[55] Clah diary, 23 Dec. 1873, WMS Amer 140/5.
[56] Ibid., 14 Aug. 1879, WMS Amer 140/6.
[57] Ibid., 5 Aug. 1879, WMS Amer 140/6.
[58] Neylan, *Heavens Are Changing*, 134, 163, 167.
[59] Clah diary, 27 June 1867, WMS Amer 140/2.
[60] Ibid., 16 Apr. 1869, WMS Amer 140/2.

celebrating marriages and inheritance of chiefly positions, yet he hosted many feasts himself. Sometimes he justifies these as Christian feasts, but at other times they are time-honoured Tsimshian celebrations for a newly built house, or success in hunting or trading. In 1876 a Methodist missionary deeply offended Clah by asking him and others to reclaim property they had given away, thus incurring a reciprocal obligation (an integral part of potlatches): 'We [He] having no right to ask about our property. Because we no promise to take our property back after few days. We give to the poor for we called [call it] present is no right to going to friends house and ask things back. In our law give things back in feast house not to taking back for nothing.'[61] This incident illustrates Clah's insider status as a Tsimshian, as well as his readiness to criticize non-Christian Tsimshian, missionaries, and other Euro-Canadians. He felt particularly aggrieved that missionaries did not follow their own teachings about the sabbath and demanded money from their congregations.

Clah expressed a keen sense of the injustices perpetrated by the settler government of British Columbia, which, by the 1880s, was impoverishing his people through alienation of Tsimshian land. He railed against both government agents and the missionaries who, he believed, were in league against the 'poor Indians'. He was also aware of the wider imperial forces arraigned against colonized peoples: '... I think everything about our place that whit [white] man taking away from us. It was Queen Victoria gaven [who gave] away to everyone so we losted [lost] our land.'[62] At the end of the diary for 1881 Clah returns to the theme of land theft, drawing a moral contrast between Britain's abolition of slavery and its toleration of dispossession: 'As I want to know what English people wants sell out our land. As I had [heard] some body says Boston people [Americans] not right sell out Black people and I have heard Queen tont [don't] wanted [want it] so now what is the reason Queen sell our land.'[63] Clah spent many years trying unsuccessfully to reclaim land that he believed had been taken from him and his wife's family. While it is tempting to cast him as an early anti-imperial nationalist, he also hankered after the approval and praise of missionaries and other Euro-Canadians in authority, insisting that he be treated as an equal, not a servant or employee. He was deeply offended when a Euro-Canadian patronized him by addressing him in Chinook, the trading jargon, rather than

---

[61] Clah diary, 12–13 Jan. 1876, WMS Amer 140/6.
[62] Ibid., 19 Aug. 1881, WMS Amer 140/15.   [63] Ibid., end of volume, WMS Amer 140/15.

English. He recounted dreams he had in which missionaries came up to him and shook his hand, or in other ways acknowledged him as an equal.

A drive to preach to 'blind hearts', people who had not encountered Christianity, is omnipresent in the journals. Clah would preach to anyone who would listen to him, whether fishing, mining, or working in fish canneries.

I don't want preach amongs[t] our Christianity [Christians] I want preach all pline [blind] friends some stranger amongs[t] us who not interested words of god they wanted to be Christian. Some time I help the friends everywere where were I travel round preach them sometimes in the Name of our lord Jesus Christ some I teach them how to prayer and song.[64]

While he preferred to seek out unconverted people, Clah would also preach and pray with Christians. If offered a house to preach in, he would hold a meeting there; if not, he would hold prayer meetings outside. Occasionally he would preach in a church, although he did not treat church buildings as evidence of religious adherence. His Christianity was mediated by neither priest nor institution, being founded on what he regarded as a direct relationship with God. After his break with William Duncan, he viewed himself as an active competitor of the Anglicans, Methodists, Salvation Army, and other Protestant denominations in British Columbia. While receptive to new religious and technological ideas, he also maintained a steadfast independence in the face of the colonial forces which rapidly followed the introduction of Christianity to his region of the British Empire.

Moses Tjalkabota

Tjalkabota's story of his life in central Australia begins with his Arrernte childhood: travelling with his parents to hunt and gather food, assembling with larger groups of relatives in good seasons, learning to fear attack by neighbours, and eventually discovering that missionaries with strange animals had come to his region. Tjalkabota's life and early encounters with Christianity differ in fundamental ways from those of the Xhosa, Tsimshian, and Pacific Islanders. There were no villages where the missionaries could establish a base. They had to build a mission and wait for the Arrernte to

---

[64] Ibid., 24 June 1883, WMS Amer 140/20. See also Peggy Brock, 'Two Indigenous Evangelists: Moses Tjalkabota and Arthur Wellington Clah', *Journal of Religious History*, XXVII (2003), pp. 348–66.

come to them. Tjalkabota recounts how men hid women and children before approaching the mission alone. They rejected the gifts of bullock meat and flour the missionaries gave them, alert to the possible dangers of strangers in their midst.[65] After a time the men made return visits, eventually taking women and children with them. Nonetheless, the main focus of Arrernte life continued to lie outside the mission. Tjalkabota would return to the mission periodically, attending the school, then leave to travel with his grandfather and other family members.

When he began attending school, a rift developed with the adults, who maintained an intellectual distance from the missionaries. The boy decided to remain permanently at Hermannsburg, while his parents continued their mobile lives. The rift became more pronounced when Tjalkabota was baptized. His father and other men of the older generation could not comprehend that their children had allied themselves to an alternative source of sacred power. Tjalkabota recalled conversations that suggest they viewed baptism as another form of initiation ceremonies and Christianity as another route to religious knowledge, potentially compatible with their own beliefs. When Tjalkabota accused them of being heathens, people without religion, they were bemused. The young man also challenged the rainmaking abilities of the old men, and questioned their accounts of creation.[66] He claimed to have ridiculed their most deeply held beliefs.

Moses' text presents his evangelizing as a series of intellectual engagements with his protagonists. He does not mention any attempt to change the way people lived, the food they ate, or their dress. To the Lutheran missionaries clothing was a marker of civilization. They gave the young Tjalkabota clothes and a blanket when he first visited the Hermannsburg mission. But clothes did not mark a transformation in his life, which came only with his acceptance of the Christian God and the rejection of his parent's beliefs.[67] He describes one incident at the mission when the men performed a religious dance. The missionaries disrupt the ceremony, ripping off the men's decorations, accuse them of being children of the devil and heathens, and demand they put their clothes back on. But the men refuse until all the community have seen the sacred markings on their bodies.[68] In recounting this incident Moses does not take the outsider's view that associated nakedness with savagery and the primitive; rather he emphasizes its religious significance.

[65] 'Moses Tjalkabota', p. 243.   [66] Ibid., pp. 275–6.
[67] Ibid., p. 249.   [68] Ibid., p. 247.

Most of his preaching was directed not to his father's generation, but to younger people who were growing up in the colonized world of cattle and sheep stations. He travelled around the stations talking to the stock workers and their families. Peter Bullah, one of the first Aboriginal men to be ordained as a Lutheran pastor, remembered Moses Tjalkabota's evangelism: 'One day an old man came to Henbury [cattle] station, old blind Moses. He taught us the word of God. Many people heard God's word at that place.'[69]

Unlike Clah's diary, which is anchored to a chronology reckoned by the British calendar, Tjalkabota's account is driven by a sense of place. Despite having spent much of his life at Hermannsburg, in the township of Alice Springs, and at the Jay Creek ration depot, he talks mainly about journeys: childhood journeys with his family and evangelizing trips after the onset of blindness. He describes in detail the routes he took, naming the places he passed by, where he slept along the way, and the things he 'saw'. In this and other important ways his text conforms to Arrernte cultural forms rather than any Lutheran missionary template. At the same time there can be no doubt that it is the testimony of a deeply committed Christian who seems never to have been riven by doubts. Thus, an insider–outsider dichotomy is not clear-cut in Tjalkabota's text. Unlike Tiyo Soga, who suffered in the eyes of his fellows by not having passed through essential rites of passage, Tjalkabota was an initiated man. However, he deliberately placed himself outside Arrernte religious traditions, denigrating religious objects such as *tjurunga* and helping to desecrate a site sacred to his ancestors.[70] At the same time he was also a cultural broker, a translator of Christian texts into Arrernte, and a source for anthropologists and others seeking information about Arrernte cultural and religious practices.

As a witness to the process of colonization, Tjalkabota was ideally situated to comment on the impact of Empire. He does not do so, perhaps because it was not imposed by overt war and conquest. He experienced the advent of the new order as a series of apparently unconnected intrusions. First came the German Lutheran missionaries when he was about 5 years old. Later other outsiders came to build a telegraph line, followed by pastoralists and miners. These colonial developments revolutionized Arrernte life, but Tjalkabota's narrative does not bring them to the foreground. His spiritual and

---

[69] Peter Bullah, 'Peter Bullah's Story', in Albrecht, *From Mission to Church*, pp. 211–13.
[70] Jacqueline Van Gent, 'Changing Concepts of Embodiment and Illness among the Western Arrernte at Hermannsburg Mission', *Journal of Religious History*, XXVII (2003), p. 340.

physical journeys from the Arrernte cosmological universe into the colonized landscape of twentieth-century Australia receive little comment. Tjalkabota appears to have viewed himself as protected by God from the violence of the early colonial era. On one occasion people were amazed to see him arrive in Alice Springs in a stranger's truck:

'That white man is continually chasing us with a rifle. Moses, why did you come with him? He is forever threatening us with a rifle.'
I said, 'God himself protects me on the road, so that people cannot harm me.'
They said, 'So it is with God that you travel about so confidently.'[71]

Unlike Soga and Clah, Tjalkabota's text avoids criticism of colonial society, presenting himself as under divine protection as God's messenger.

Conclusion

There is a hidden history of mission and Empire that is only partially disclosed in written records. European mission societies and missionaries were conduits for the spread of Christianity from Europe, but they would have failed in their endeavours if indigenous people at the periphery had not created their own channels of communication to direct the flow of evangelism beyond the mission stations into the villages and hinterlands of the Empire. Mission statistics in many regions indicate the gigantic scale of this localized Christian evangelism, but few accounts present the perspective of the new Christians. Those accounts we can access suggest there was a strong impetus among first-generation Christians to introduce others to their new-found spiritual world. But these new Christian missionaries were for the most part far removed from the European metropole of the mission organizations. Their knowledge and understanding of the metropolitan culture—in European terms, civilization—was at best superficial.

Many of these evangelists encountered Christianity before the full impact of colonialism was felt by their societies. In some instances, the Arrernte for example, missionaries provided their first experience of distant outsiders. In other regions the missionaries followed traders who had established relationships with indigenous groups over many decades. Whatever the circumstances in which Christianity was introduced, the first generation of Christians who became evangelists may have functioned as agents of an

[71] 'Moses Tjalkabota', pp. 293, 296–7.

ideology closely associated with Britain and other European powers, but that was not the way they viewed themselves. They were embedded in their own societies as critics of existing religious beliefs, practices, and moral codes. The basis of their critique was their understanding of the Bible, not an unfavourable comparison between their own culture and a faraway metropolitan society most of them had never experienced. Their evangelical strategies were grounded in the political structures and cultural standards of the societies among whom they preached. While European periodicals and propaganda portrayed mission operations as a Manichaean contest between Christian civilization and paganism, evangelists on the ground were profoundly shaped by the cultures around them. It could not have been otherwise, given the vital role of new Christian evangelists in spreading religious knowledge.

The accounts considered in this chapter plainly display salient characteristics of their cultures. Tsimshian admired oratory and were impressed by the display of material accumulation: attributes very much epitomized in the career of Arthur Wellington Clah. Moses Tjalkabota's life and preaching reflected the mobile nature of Australia's central desert societies, where a church was the dome of heaven and material accumulation was neither an aspiration nor a possibility. Moses' religious authority was based on his knowledge of the Scriptures and his general wisdom. His blindness probably added to this aura. Thus the first-hand accounts of each of the five evangelists are predicated on the values of their birth cultures and the people among whom they worked. Missionaries from Europe approached potential converts with no knowledge of their language or culture and made many mistakes as they tried to impose their values. Local evangelists did not make these mistakes. When they challenged ingrained beliefs and practices, they did it knowingly.

Being embedded in local communities also had disadvantages. Sometimes these evangelists were ignored or vilified by host societies precisely because they were *not* agents of Britain. Although Britain did not generally perceive the mission enterprise as part of the imperial agenda, many indigenous people seeking access to trade, technologies, and the political and military support of the outsiders wanted European missionaries. Thus the relationship between Empire and mission is more complex than it appears when attention is concentrated on European personnel. Local circumstances were a decisive influence on the relationship. Some new Christian evangelists became critics of Empire. Others influenced their people to turn to

Christianity as a protection against the havoc wreaked on them by violence, introduced diseases, and the pressures of modernity.

Select Bibliography

PEGGY BROCK, ed., *Indigenous Peoples, Christianity, and Religious Change*, *Journal of Religious History*, XXVII (2003).

—— 'Two Indigenous Evangelists: Moses Tjalkabota and Arthur Wellington Clah', *Journal of Religious History*, XXVII (2003), pp. 348–66.

CHARLES W. FORMAN, 'The Missionary Force of the Pacific Island Churches', *International Review of Mission*, LIX (1970), pp. 215–26.

ROBERT W. HEFNER, ed., *Conversion to Christianity: Historical and Anthropological Perspectives on a Great Transition* (Berkeley, 1993).

MARETU, *Cannibals and Converts*, ed. and trans. M. T. Crocombe (Suva, 1983).

'Moses Tjalkabota', in Paul G. E. Albrecht, *From Mission to Church, 1877–2002: Finke River Mission* (Adelaide, 2002), app. 2.

DOUG MUNRO and ANDREW THORNLEY, eds., *The Covenant Makers: Islander Missionaries in the Pacific* (Suva, 1996).

SUSAN NEYLAN, *The Heavens Are Changing: Nineteenth-Century Protestant Missions and Tsimshian Christianity* (Montreal, 2003).

J. D. Y. PEEL, *Religious Encounter and the Making of the Yoruba* (Bloomington, Ind., 2000).

ANDREW PORTER, 'Religion and Empire: British Expansion in the Long Nineteenth Century, 1780–1914', *Journal of Imperial and Commonwealth History*, XX (1992), pp. 370–90.

TIYO SOGA, *The Journal and Selected Writings of Rev. Tiyo Soga*, ed. Donovan Williams (Cape Town, 1983).

DONOVAN WILLIAMS, *Umfundisi: A Biography of Tiyo Soga 1829–1871* (Lovedale, 1978).

8

'Trained to Tell the Truth':
Missionaries, Converts, and Narration

GARETH GRIFFITHS

Missionaries invested an inordinate amount of energy in producing written material. Apart from the obvious priority given to the primary aim of conversion—such as printed Bibles and catechisms in the languages of their intended audiences—missions utilized the whole range of media of their day from print and colour reproduction tracts to screen technology (magic lantern slides). Personal accounts of the newly converted in the form of life stories and autobiographies were particularly widespread. They are among the earliest texts in colonial languages that feature the lives and experiences of colonized peoples. Such accounts were important to the colonized subjects themselves, to the missionaries who wrote them down, and to the Christians readers at whom they were aimed.

As one might expect, the texts were censored through complex systems of patronage and control.[1] What missionaries wrote in their personal diaries, or even in the daybooks of the mission stations, differed significantly in tone and content from accounts submitted to mission headquarters. Mission journals also rewrote such material for their pages, imposing further filters. Shifting from the voice of the native subject to the pen of the mission recorder was only the first step in a long process of control exercised over the record of the lives of their converts. These texts provided the principal lens through which home audiences viewed the imperial world beyond colonial homelands and so decisively shaped the attitudes by which colonized cultures were judged. Despite the profound limitations on personal agency involved in their production, they were also among the earliest means by which the subjects of the imperial venture could communicate some of their own views to those who had invaded their lands and to their fellow

---

[1] Anna Johnston, 'Adam's Ribs: Gender, Colonialism, and the Missionaries, 1800–1860', Ph.D. diss. (Queensland, 1999).

colonized people. Eventually, they would even be employed to speak to other colonized people across linguistic and cultural divides. Mission texts, like other texts in the colonial languages, could thus be both an instrument of oppression and a means of resistance, depending on the circumstances of their production and dissemination.

While societies expended much energy on material for use in the mission field, at least as many of their publications were aimed at encouraging interest and financial contributions from the home audience. By the end of the nineteenth century mission presses rivalled secular publishers and printers in volume of output and had adopted many of the secular presses' genres, forms, and discursive features. This was only to be expected until such time as a significant literate local audience of converted 'natives' existed in the mission field, a phenomenon that came late—usually after the control of evangelistic effort had passed from the hands of Euro-American missionaries into those of local converts. Even then a legacy of mission conventions persisted, partly because institutional control of the publishing remained in overseas or expatriate hands.

Gauri Viswanathan emphasizes that conversion did not necessarily mean a total deculturation, even when it was a massively disruptive event.[2] Since converts frequently continued as an active part of their communities, they retained a significant degree of agency. While acting upon their own society as agents of change, they also brought the values and viewpoints of that society into their dealings with the converting society. The great majority of converts discarded neither their pre-existing culture, nor the totality of their previous identity. Viswanathan emphasizes that new Christians worked for change in two directions. While acting as forces for modernization among their own people, they could simultaneously act as forceful critics of the Euro-American Christian societies—a phenomenon exemplified by such converts as the Revd. Attoh Ahuma and J. E. Casely Hayford in West Africa, and Ham Mukasa in East Africa. The case was quite different when converts had been previously ripped from their cultures, as was the case of the 'recaptives'—people freed from slave ships and caravans through the intervention of British imperial officials. Seldom did they return to their own communities, being consigned instead to artificial communities peopled by other recaptives, who often spoke different languages and practised different

---

[2] Gauri Viswanathan, *Outside the Fold: Conversion, Modernity and Belief* (Princeton, 1998), p. xi.

customs. For these converts the only convenient vehicles for communicating their stories were the languages and texts controlled by missionaries, texts whose forms were profoundly limiting. However, as these new communities began to succeed in converting people from the established undisrupted African communities, the processes described by Viswanathan in the Indian context slowly come into play.

This chapter employs close analysis of receptive life stories and personal conversion narratives produced from the 1870s to the 1920s to demonstrate that, even in the most unfavourable circumstances, the voices of the colonized subjects cannot be completely suppressed. The necessity for a narrow focus in such a detailed textual investigation has led this chapter to focus on East and Central African sources dating from about 1870, though the occasional passing reference to texts from West Africa might suggest that in a fuller analysis of such texts a wider range of examples might usefully be compared. The texts reveal how narrative conventions operated to contain the 'native voice' they claimed to express, while, paradoxically, that very act of containment inscribed a record of its presence and even its actual operation in the choices and narrative strategies of the texts themselves. Although the voices of the missionized 'subjects' may seem to have got rather lost in these ventriloquized texts, read against the grain they reveal traces of the silenced voices of the converted colonized subject. Such is the case in West Africa of J. B. Danquah's work, which set out to rehabilitate and reaffirm the value and effectiveness of Akan traditional culture, law, and even religious thought in, for example, *The Akan Doctrine of God: A Fragment of Gold Coast Ethics and Religion*. In East Africa there are comparable cases, such as Jomo Kenyatta's work on the Kikuyu in texts such as *My People of the Gikuyu and The Life of Chief Wangora*. That these figures, both leading nationalists and anti-colonial fighters, felt able to publish in mission series shows how complex were the relations between this generation of African leaders and the missions, and how they felt, even in the 1940s when these texts were published, that mission presses were effective tools for communicating their ideas, if only in indirect and subtle ways. Read in this way, the life stories form an interesting and revealing accompaniment to the self-authored texts discussed by Peggy Brock in Chapter 7 and even the more radical texts by mission-educated nationalists which mission presses produced in the lead-up to decolonization.

These early 'ghosted' accounts of native life and conversion are sometimes openly stated to be the product of the missionary pen, but at the same time purport to give the 'true' account of the life of these subjects, 'as told to' a mission amanuensis. In fact, a dominant concern of these texts is the claim to authenticity. That discloses the troubled awareness the missionary amanuensis had of exercising controlling power over the agency of the colonized convert, a power at odds with the missionaries' stated aim to free these converts. The strenuous assertions of authenticity also reveal uneasiness about the missionary's role in the imperial process. It is clearly problematic to discuss overall how much the mission 'patron' exercised direct control over such texts. In some cases the control was almost total, to the extent that the 'subject' of the text was simply the passive pretext for the authorization of the mission amanuensis's own ideas and attitudes. However, from the earliest period even these ghosted texts allow their subjects' voices to disturb the stereotypical imperial presentation of them and their culture. Of course the missionary discourse of a savage, barbarous, 'dark', and benighted heathenism continued to condition these accounts, but the very presence of this stereotype creates in the gaps and silences of these texts an awareness of its enabling, silenced, and repressed opposite. The question these early conversion accounts pose is what agency, if any, the native subjects of mission texts authored by missionaries on their behalf could achieve within the boundaries of mission literary forms and narrative conventions which still largely represented them. Can the very silences and repressions of these early accounts in which missionary authors speak for the native subject reveal the nature of that control and so reveal through the rents in the veil of a dominant discourse the disturbing presence of the hidden subjects of the tale? And is the repressed desire for control and power of the missionary amanuensis also revealed within the very forms which they create and impose on their subjects, rendering their condition, too, as part of these text's occluded subject?

This is not to claim that the forms of mission narrative examined here were present in all missions. Imperial mission conversion narratives and forms are legion and diverse. The question posed here is simply, how far does the mission text of the high imperial period enable us to assert the existence of a paradigmatic relationship between missionary and native convert lodged within mission narrative form itself? Does it expose the hidden subject of their narrative choices and rhetorical structures, namely the voices of the enunciated colonized native subjects and of their missionary enunciator and the relations between them?

Many narratives published by missionaries in East Africa take the form of 'release' narratives: stories that purport to tell the 'unvarnished tale' of slaves purchased by missionaries, or rescued from slavery by the British Navy and brought to missions where missionary amanuenses write down their life stories. A typical example appeared in *Central Africa*, the journal of the Universities' Mission to Central Africa (UMCA) in 1884, entitled 'The Story of a Nyassa Boy, as Told by Himself'. As with so many similar tales, the actual missionary 'author' claims only to be the 'translator' and/or recorder. 'The following story of a Nyassa boy's life and wanderings, up to the time when he was received by the Mission, was written out by himself in the Swahili language... There is no reason, from the character and ability of the lad to doubt the story.' Though 'allowance must be made for the fact that he was certainly very young, perhaps ten or twelve years of age at most, when first carried away from his home. He is now probably eighteen years of age.' Elsewhere the author asserts, 'It is the story of an intelligent boy who has been seven years at the Mission Schools and risen to be a teacher and to promise well for future usefulness.' The final proof for the 'translator' of the truth of the story is the closeness with which it conforms to existing ideological and narrative expectations. In a classic early statement of the conventions of the release form, he offers one final proof of authenticity.

Lastly, the substance of the story is not only typical of the experiences of hundreds, even thousands, of East African children, but of some intrinsic interest as a picture of the state of society and operations of the slave trade in the Eastern Lake district. The stages may be distinguished as follows: first, the normal state of the Nyasa tribes, war among themselves, and war with their common enemies; next, the sequel of war, the passing of the captives from owner to owner, until they fall into the hands of Arabs forming large caravans for conveyance to the coast; then the long march down to the coast, with all its hardships and terrible cost of human life; lastly, the attempt to ship the slaves to meet foreign demands, their capture by an English man-of-war, and the final consignment of a portion of them to the care of the Universities' Mission.

There could hardly be a clearer statement of the essential features of the 'narrative' mission texts embraced as the 'typical' life of the now freed, once enslaved, convert. It is followed by a renewed assertion of truthfulness on the part of the missionary recorder. 'In translation, care has been taken in no way to make any substantial change in the story, only to render it in simple and readable English.' The assertion is disingenuous. Not only had the 'author' of the original Swahili version been a pupil of the mission for seven years by the time of its composition, but he had become a trusted teacher. In the process of becoming literate in Swahili, and probably having a spoken if not written knowledge of English as well, he would have absorbed the ideological determinants of mission narrative. Thus, while there is truth in the basic facts recorded in the release narrative—experiences common among freed slaves at the mission—the transformation of those experiences into a text was inextricably bound up in the narrative form which focused, shaped, and ordered the raw events that were related. This is a more profound 'translation', which precedes the mere act of transferring narratives from one language to another, or even from a source oral narrator to a missionary-authored written text. By the time this story was published in 1884, the form of the release narrative that shaped it had long been established as the template for all such life narratives.

Women were often the authors of mission accounts of African life and experience, partly because many of the journals which printed them had began as children's journals. Thus, in the case of the UMCA they appear mainly in the journal *African Tidings* (originally *Children's Tidings*) rather than in the society's official journal, *Central Africa*. The audience for these stories quickly spread beyond young people as the adult readership broadened to include less educated members of the home congregations who responded to the human appeal of these stories of native life couched in personal rather than official discourse. There was, of course, the appeal of the exotic. The window this kind of account opened for home readers into what they assumed to be the 'true' world of the native, a world recognizably human but tinged with a frisson of horror, gelled with the seemingly perennial taste for the combination of the shocking and the moral, providing them with both a justification for their interest and a sense of satisfaction in their own superiority to the cultures depicted. In this respect the mission journals helped disseminate the wider ideology of imperialism, notwithstanding their unintended effects when read as potential counter-discursive texts. Since the texts examined here emerged from an area later absorbed into the British Empire (Tanganyika–Zanzibar), they are relevant to the wider story this volume seeks to tell. But since this part of Africa attracted attention from several European powers—France, Belgium, Germany, and Britain—and the missionaries came from many nations, the narrative conventions embodied in the texts they produced appear not to be rooted in any particular national culture. They clearly share a broader set of concerns. There was, of course, to some degree a shared culture of mission representation of Africans in this period. However, one must be equally mindful that crucial differences existed in individual missions. In the same way, it is arguable that the similarities these texts display were rooted in the broader structures of imperial control itself, structures common to all the nations engaged in the colonization of Africa, despite their differences in detailed practice.

Thus conversion narratives of an identical kind also occur in the journals of the Catholic society operating in the whole Central and East African region, the Pères de Saint Esprit, or Spiritans, as they came to be more familiarly known, and their accompanying nuns, the Sœurs de Sacré Cœur de Marie, who looked after the rescued girl slaves (it was deemed unseemly for male missionaries to be in charge of females). For similar reasons, by the mid-1880s a substantial force of laywomen were managing the Anglican UMCA reception house at Shangani Point and the girls' training establishment at Mbweni. Unlike women in some other Protestant missions, these High Anglican women were mostly spinsters who remained unmarried and who lived in all-female communities, in effect if not in name an order of Anglican nuns. These unmarried women missionaries, Catholic and Anglican, were often the channels through which the voices of Africans telling their tales were translated. This was especially so in the case of the UMCA, whose missionary laywomen were often from a very highly educated upper-class background, making them perhaps more inclined to engage in this kind of 'literary' work. The UMCA women were frequently independent, intellectual women who resisted the restrictions of a late nineteenth-century marriage. Mission work in East Africa, India, and China offered such women a more independent existence than a late Victorian marriage afforded. While in other Protestant missions marriage to a fellow missionary was sometimes a precondition for acceptance, even then the status and isolated location of these missionary couples afforded women more authority and a broader scope for the exercise of their talents than was usual at home. It was perhaps to be expected that such women would take an interest in the expressions of the voiceless subjects to whom the condition of their gender bound them in coils of sympathy and fellow feeling.

In 1896 the Spiritans' journal printed an example of the classic 'release narrative' which indicates clearly how exactly the Catholic missionaries at Bagamoya reproduced the narrative template employed by their Anglican rivals in the region. The 'Histoire d'Angelina' recounts the story of a woman who comes to beg food in a famine.[3] She is told the mission has only enough

---

[3] *Annales Apostoliques*, XLII (April 1896), pp. 77–79; my translation.

food to feed the hungry abandoned children it has taken in and instead is given some advice on how to trade in the local material of the forest to people in the hills for maize and bananas. She returns to tell her story, together with a present of a magnificent woven mat that she has made, clearly a product of the skills she learned as a result of the mission advice. She relates how she was born near Lake Nyasa, and was captured, 'stolen from my parents, like so many others, an Arab from Zanzibar bought me'. The phrase 'like so many others' declares the generic quality of the tale, which the narrator is at no pains to hide, since its stereotypical nature is part of its design and the foundation of the claim it makes on its intended audience of mission supporters at home. After an account of maltreatment rendered in the usual generalized terms, she goes on to tell of her escape and how she learned about the fathers at the mission to which she fled to find the familiar sanctuary. 'Under the protection of the Mission I found happiness. I was instructed in the religion of our Dear Lord Jesus, and baptized.'

Another revealing narrative in the standard mould is 'Ambimoya; or, The History of a Young Slave, Told by Himself'.[4] In this case the identity of the amanuensis, R.P. (Reverend Pere Le Roy, later Mgr Le Roy, a significant figure in the Spiritans' African mission), is incorporated into the text. Although the narrative includes few details of the process of the telling, it emphasizes the slowness of the procedure, a feature whose significance will emerge in later discussion of this process of relating and recording the testimonials of the converts. In this case the subject, Patrice Ambimoya, is a Christian child who in earlier times 'has accompanied Mgr. De Courmont on all his travels'. Perhaps the arduous character of one particular journey—'We were still walking, as long as the sun lightened our way, until our legs refused to carry us any further'—and the unusual intimacy inspired the lengthy conversation that ensues, at least in this textual dramatization of the event. 'Gradually a conversation began and Patrice told us his story at length'. This dramatization forcefully claims the authentic voice through the conventions of reported speech: 'I begin', said Patrice. Despite these signifiers of an 'authentic' voice and the unusual amplitude and detail the text affords, it remains confined within the narrative convention of what is by now a classic, well-established form of slave capture and release through Christian conversion.

Patrice, we are told, was born near Ungindo. The grammar and syntax suggest that the stealing and enslavement of children in this inland location

---

[4] *Annales Apostoliques*, VI (Apr. 1887), pp. 71–6.

were so widespread as to be universal conditions. 'Where I come from they steal children.' The central event of his enslavement, foretold if not almost predestined by the narrative structure, is fulfilled: 'The thief seized me. Put me into a sack made from palm leaves and stuffed my mouth with maize paste to smother my cries.' The plethora of similar details serves to reinforce the concrete existence of the source narrator, whose substantive life story the narrative purports to relate. Against such detail is ranged the enveloping narrative patterning into which all such stories are now enfolded, a process of containment, as much, one suspects, for the convert who is their source as for the missionary who is their scribe. That Patrice Ambimoya is an older child and not a recent convert may indicate that he has told this story more than once, indeed, that his life and its memory have been shaped, as in all narratives of the past, by the expectations and conventions of the forms into which they are cast, which in turn were shaped by the audiences for which they are intended. In any case, following more details, including extended dialogues between the narrator and his parents, Patrice is captured and sold. There follows a riveting, gruesome account of the caravan journey to the coast to Kiloa (Kilwa), along with conversations between Patrice and his various owners. These are far more precisely distinguished than is usual in these narratives; one is 'a great Arab, Abdallah bin Seliman'. These acknowledgements of the different qualities of individual Arab slave owners, differences usually disguised in these texts by a generalized, pejorative characterization and by the use of the generic term 'Arab' or 'Mussulman' in place of individual names, make this a fascinating example of the edges and boundaries of the standardized release narrative genre. This text is also one of the few mission accounts to acknowledge the historical reality that Arabs were not just slavers but also potential rivals in the conversion of their captives: 'An Arab with a white beard appeared, looked me over, asked me some questions, and bought me: "Don't cry," he said, "in ten days we'll leave for Mascate, you'll come with me, you'll be taught the Koran, and God willing you'll be a good Muslim." ' For a moment the potential rupture between the viewpoint of the subject of the text and its mission recorder is glimpsed. Of course this textual fissure soon closes. The good master dies and Ambimoya is again sold, but this time he is rescued by the missionaries. However, the presentation of this event once again allows a leakage of unstandardized material into the form of this account of rescue. Ambimoya is terrified since he has been warned while at Kiloa that the white-robed fathers are slavers whose slaves are summoned to service in their 'stone house' by cords, which are attached to them and to the bed of the White Ones (the Spiritans). 'These Whites have houses of stone, and in these houses a type of chair that is like a bed. All their slaves are lodged in adjoining rooms, tied with ropes that are attached to the White's bed. When he wants a slave he pulls on the rope, without disturbing himself, and the slave arrives.'

No wonder Ambimoya is terrified. 'That is why I said to myself "I am lost" upon seeing the Whiteman approach.' This little vignette is clearly designed by the missionary amanuensis to illustrate false ideas about the missions promulgated by the Arab slavers to prevent slaves from seeking the sanctuary of the mission. The preamble is again very revealing. Ambimoya, we are told, has been warned thus by his fellow slaves: 'There are Whites who are wickedness itself, and you should never speak to them concerning yourself, or concerning your village.' The story the missionary amanuensis records is clearly meant to disprove this assertion, showing that Ambimoya can and does speak openly to his new mission friends. But at a deeper and ironic level the warning against revealing anything of oneself or one's society to these intruders may have an unintentional force in a text and form whose ultimate goal is the conversion of the subject and the transformation and 'civilization' of their cultures. At such moments the suppressed, 'disordered' perceptions of the unreconstructed narrated subject seem about to erupt into open discourse. Almost, but never quite. In the end even the least well-policed 'authentic' testament must conform to the mission's ideological and narrative patterns. Thus, for all its fascinating detail and moments of textual fracture, the narrative closure is as inevitably fixed by the form as in the most simple example of the genre, ending as early release narrative demands at the moment of baptism ('You have brought me to Bagamoya, you have taught me to work, to read, to wash my soul through baptism, and here I am').

Meanwhile, when the good Arab master dies, the narrator piously notes that it 'is the Good Lord who wished it thus; otherwise where would I be today?' In fact, one might conclude by his own earlier account that had he in fact been taken as a slave to 'Mascate' (Muscat) by this master, been taught to read and converted, his experience might not have been profoundly different from what occurs when he is converted by the white missionary (Le Blanc). The fissures in this version of the release narrative suggest alternative narrative outcomes that lurk within and behind the story that eventually is recorded. Now the further possibilities of reading the text, as counter-discourse for example, may be more easily perceived. The story of

Ambimoya reveals how much the mission amanuensis needed to suppress or transform the oral narrative to enable the officially acceptable version of the 'truth' of the convert's experience to be recorded.

Another elaborate example of how such processes operate, entitled 'Panya', appeared in the pamphlet series Stories of Africa, which, although it is undated, was published sometime in the first decade of the twentieth century.[5] This product of the Anglican UMCA mission on Zanzibar recounts the rescue of a 9-year-old girl, Panya, from Arab slavers. The exceptional interest of this tale lies in its foregrounding of the process by which the paradigmatic narratives of the tracts were produced through a controlled transmission of story from 'subject' to 'author'. This example clearly shows how hollow were the claims of the mission amanuensis to be a simple, objective recorder of lives. Panya's tale starts with the customary claim that it is 'as told' by its subject herself to A.F., a female missionary at the Mbweni Training Establishment in 1894–5. Panya had been released from an Arab dhow in April 1893. Her 'conversion' had occurred in the interval between the release and the finding of 'peace' and baptism at Mbweni, a process that is made an explicit subject of the narration. Also explicit is the degree to which this transformation and reconstruction is intertwined with the production of the allegedly unmediated 'true' textual narrative of Panya.

The text describes an elaborate training process centred on control of the child's perception and memory. 'I remembered Panya's story,' A.F. observes, 'and I gave her fair warning I should expect it to be ready in a week.' A.F. had taught Panya Swahili but was surprised to find that she had also picked up some knowledge of English. 'I found if I didn't want the Little Pitcher to enjoy all my talks with the other ladies, she must be sent away before we began.' This aside makes plain that A.F. must have translated the Swahili original of Panya's oral narrative into English, a fact that might otherwise have gone unnoticed. Communication then was to be a controlled process, with information flowing from A.F. to Panya only if the missionary chose. Panya, A.F. tells us, had to be 'trained to tell the truth'. That complex process of training is then described, the purpose of which was to determine the 'truth' of Panya's story.

---

[5] A version of the story was first printed in *African Tidings*, XCVI (Feb. 1896), pp. 110–11 and XCVII (Mar. 1897), pp. 120–22. Its reworking in this collection a decade or more later shows how little mission presses cared about the date or provenance of accounts or their relevance to changing circumstances in the field.

And now Panya began to tell the truth sometimes. I found she very much disliked having to say afterwards what she ought to have said first, when she had told a lie. At first she only cared a little, but I think each time she cared more, and the last time she lost her temper; in fact, we both did considerably, and she gave me a lot of trouble. But when I came up a long time afterwards, and found her lying with her face pressed down upon the concrete floor, and saw that sympathizing friends were met by silence and kicks, if they came too near, I said to myself, 'Good, we have learnt something at last'. And from that day forward she began to try to speak the truth.

The idea that Panya's anger expressed her frustration at having to modify her story to fit the expectations of her listener and the structure required by mission release narratives does not seem to occur to the amanuensis A.F.

Only after this complex process of control has been narrated is 'Panya's story' told. By this time, of course, the identification of Panya as its controlling agent and A.F. as a mere neutral recorder implicit in the phrase 'as told to' has been exposed as a determining fiction. The story which we now hear is not that story of 'misery' which the 'men and women' of the mission heard from Panya's lips during her illness, but a reorganized, probably bowdlerized, version. What aspect of her story has been altered or suppressed and for what motives? It is possible to speculate that the 'unvarnished tale' described, among other things, a sexual relationship between the child and the slaver. The slavers' sexual abuse of children could not be recorded in the evangelical tracts because of the sensitivity of its intended audience and the negative impact this might have on the mission presentation of Africans as 'innocent victims'. Of course, for late Victorian readers no female victim of sexual abuse could ever be rendered as 'innocent', however traduced and pressured. Whatever adjustments were required of this and other kinds to ensure the 'truth' of Panya's story before it could be released, what this long process of negotiation and control finally produces bears the hallmark of the by now paradigmatic release narrative. Thus A.F.'s struggle with Panya to get her to 'tell the truth' resulted in a narrative that fulfilled all the patterns of the well-established mission narrative of release and conversion. This provides a telling comment on the interchangeability of the concepts of 'training' and 'truth-telling' by which both the subject and the scribe of the text are profoundly overdetermined.

Panya goes on to relate how at 3 years old she went from Uganda to 'live among the Nyamwezi' (how or why is not explained). She is approached by a man who 'carried me away to the houses of his people, and then that deceiver took me away to another house and sold me'. She is sold on until she ends at 'Saadani (an Arab town on the coast, nearly opposite Zanzibar) and we stayed there two months (meaning some little time)'. These internal glosses are interesting both in terms of their stress on the text's intended audience, the 'home' audience, which needs to be 'informed', and, even more significantly, as evidence of the intrusive 'voice' of A.F. even within the narrative we are offered as an accurate 'transcription' of Panya's 'own' tale.

And we went on from Saadani just the same, only we went in a boat. It was a very large boat, so high that I could not climb up into it by myself. And we stayed in the boat, and we slept in it at night; but the man who had bought me loved me and took care of me in the boat, till one day we landed near a town.

At this juncture an Arab steals her and she is smuggled out of the town on another dhow. After she has been beaten for screaming, Panya's ear is cut off and fed to a dog. Eventually an English gunboat rescues her. The rest of the story concerns her reception and settlement 'in great peace and quietness' at Mbweni. This last phrase suggests none of the complex tensions between Panya and the rescuing missionaries recorded in A.F.'s long preamble. Thus the text reveals the complex, palimpsestic nature of the construction of this text vis-à-vis alternative and more complex 'truths' the tale cannot voice. The tale reveals remarkable open evidence of the process of construction involved in the making of paradigmatic texts of the nineteenth century release narrative, a process that later examples ignore. This may reflect the different practices of the missionary transcribers, but it may also reflect the different instrumental functions of the text with regard to the mission project and the audience it addressed in the different periods of the mission text's production.

The UMCA mission worker Alice Foxley, who worked at the mission on Zanzibar from 1894 until 1911, was almost certainly A.F. because she was the only person at Mbweni in 1894 with those initials. A.F. authored numerous other contributions to mission journals during Foxley's period of residency in Zanzibar, but none appeared after her departure. It may be that the self-revealing discussion of the processes of text production reflected unconsciously an essential sympathy felt by women for the controlled nature of their subjects, though this must remain merely speculative. For whatever reason, it is to a woman missionary, Alice Foxley, that we are indebted for one of the most revealing accounts of the personal life and narrative of an African convert and of the processes by which it was recorded.

Over the course of several decades a shift can be discerned from the texts narrowly focused on the anti-slavery campaigns in the region to the emergence of forms addressing wider concerns. Later texts retailing the experiences of converted natives were designed not only for a home audience but also for a growing body of converted Africans literate in both African languages and English whom the missions wished to provide with appropriate reading matter. These later texts (especially those produced after the First World War) address different concerns, notably those of 'backsliding' by converts under the pressures on these converts of the societies from which conversion has purportedly removed them. That this shift reflected a change in the target audience is confirmed by the fact that the daybooks that have survived at the missions at Bagamoya and at the Anglican Cathedral on Zanzibar regularly record struggles with backsliding converts in entries as early as 1870. Similar accounts appear only rarely in the *published* records until the audience for these publications include literate native converts, perhaps because struggles with backsliding and errant converts held little appeal to a 'home' audience, which needed to hear tales of success to ensure their continued contributions to mission funds. Despite the different emphasis of these later texts and their shift to the concerns of a local target audience, they remain strongly controlled by a process of editing or recording by mission amanuenses. Consequently, they remain equally problematic expressions of the actual concerns of Africans.

The series Little Books for Africa, issued by the Sheldon Press, an imprint of the Society for the Promoting of Christian Knowledge in the late 1920s and early 1930s, typifies the reading materials produced by missionary presses in the period between the wars for congregations of African Christian converts.[6] The series lays frequent claim to African authorship, with titles including the words 'autobiography' or 'as told by himself'. A number of texts are even attributed to specific individuals, thereby implying that they were directly authored by Africans. Despite the increasing claims to be 'authentic' and 'unmediated', the process of transmission and transcription continued to be very problematic, as an investigation of the provenance of the texts being circulated as late as the 1920s and 1930s as 'authentic' life accounts of African converts will reveal.

---

[6] All the titles in the Sheldon series discussed here are lodged in the British Library.

The Sheldon series includes *Ways I Have Trodden*, subtitled *The Experiences of a Teacher in Tanganyika Told by Himself*.[7] The translation is dated 1932; however, since the text is translated from German, it clearly had a pre-war origin. The collapse of the time frame between the events and the republication is again passed over without comment. This may be because, as with the earlier accounts of pre-Christian and pre-mission Africa recorded in the early release narratives, the point of these stories is to emphasize the unchanging, negative side of African life for those not converted and so saved. Even in the late 1930s they anachronistically conjure up an Africa riven by tribal divisions, warfare, and intertribal enslavement. Moreover, their form retains the features of classic release narratives. A war occurs; the protagonist (male or female) is captured and enslaved, and then sold to slavers. They escape. They are taken into the mission. They are healed in body. They are baptized. These late published stories confirm the view of the African past currently favoured by the mission societies, presenting as they do an essentially anachronistic picture of warfare and enslavement.

Another production of the Sheldon series was *Stories of Old Times: Being the Autobiographies of Two Women of East Africa (Narwimba and Chisi-Ndjurisiye-Sichayunga)*.[8] Subheadings set out the narrative structures that shape the 'life' of the African subjects: 'Childhood', 'Stolen from Home', 'Slavery', 'Escape', 'Marriage', 'Ill-Treatment', 'Death of my Husband', 'I Marry Again', 'The Sin of Senga', 'Utengule (the Mission Station)', 'Baptism'. This final chapter concludes with the two sentences 'I was baptized on August 1, 1914. I have finished.' The narrative contains its lives within a frame of representation in which the African past—presented as violent, arbitrary, and brutal, especially in its treatment of women—is redeemable only by Christian conversion. The African 'life' is defined in these terms, and the arrival at the state of conversion is literally the 'end of life', that is to say they are not just born again but literally disappear from narrative possibility. The convert's life displays no continuity with the past, nor does it connect to a post-conversion present. No indication of how conversion affects the subjects subsequently is aired, nor of how it changes their relations within and towards African society. In the same way the colonized state of recent

---

[7] *Ways I Have Trodden: The Experiences of a Teacher in Tanganyika Told by Himself*, trans. and abridged by Margaret Bryan from the German of Elise Kootz-Kretschmer (London, 1932).

[8] Elise Kootz-Kretschmer, *Stories of Old Times: Being the Autobiographies of Two Women of East Africa (Narwimba and Chisi-Ndjurisiye-Sichayunga)*, trans. and abridged from German (London, 1932).

African history also disappears, overwritten by a determining myth of unchanged and unchangeable heathenism to which only conversion can bring an end. To account for this one might postulate that these pieces dealing with the African 'past' are meant to act as contrasts, and one must ask if they are not preaching (literally) to the converted since by the time they were published or republished in the inter-war years they were dealing with matters decades out of date. Indeed in cases such as *The Story of Dorugu*, set in Nigeria and recorded by the same J. F. Schön who was Samuel Crowther's superior on the 1841 expedition up the Niger–Tshadda, the time lag is obviously much longer.[9] The overriding purpose is to contrast post-conversion African life with the brutish and savage African past from which the present congregations, descendants of these early converts, are now happily released. It is the present Christian congregation that is now the text's determining audience, replacing the 'home' audience for which the earlier release narratives were primarily published. Although the ostensible theme of the text remains conversion, its principal aim is not to encourage new conversions but to confirm the present, already converted audience in its superior status and correctness of belief, and to reinforce its identity as a people saved from darkness.

In some of these later narratives the 'rescue' and conversion theme extends beyond actual enslavement to metaphorical enslavement by ignorance and heathenism. The release is from the demands of their communities and the 'pagan customs' to which they may be tempted to return. In *The Tale of Rachel Dangilo*, also from the Sheldon series, the burden of its narrative concerns post-conversion trials. Although Rachel, the heroine, has her leg saved by the mission doctor after her release from slavery, where she has been tortured, the text stresses that this is not the central miraculous event. The real miracle is her conversion, since even after the operation she remained lame and in pain throughout her life. The main body of the narrative recounts a series of temptations to return to the pre-Christian community structure. Rachel is praised for following the Bible injunction to 'forsake all others and follow me'. Those she forsakes include even her parents. This

---

[9] *The Story of Dorugu*, selections from *Magana Hausa* by J. F. Schön (London, 1932). *Magana Hausa* was first published in Hausa in Berlin in 1857, translated into English by Schön himself in 1885, and revised by Charles E. Robinson in 1906. Both these earlier English collections from which *The Story of Dorugu* is taken were published by the SPCK, who therefore had the English-language rights when they abstracted this story from the collection for the Little Books in Africa series in 1932.

allegory of excision from 'pagan' life clearly aims to arm converted people against temptations to regress into 'pagan ways'. The fact that such regression also involves a rejection of traditional and customary practice is, of course, ignored or even seen as beneficial. Since, as Viswanathan and others have pointed out, conversion need not and often does not involve deculturation and may, indeed, act to stimulate a critical attitude to the society and values of the converting culture as much or even more than of the convert's own culture, the politics of these late publications may be seen as part of a powerful attempt to justify the destructive impact of missions and the larger imperial enterprise within which such cultural onslaughts are embedded.

Although this chapter has concentrated on mission texts about conversion, especially the release narrative that served a variety of evangelical purposes in different historical periods, it has argued that the texts provide a paradigm of the kind of control involved in all imperial narratives. Indeed, as a polemic and instrumental form, mission narratives may be especially prone to such control. The release narratives are ranged alongside other related mission genres in these early to mid-twentieth-century mission series, including the 'lives' which claim the status of a full autobiography, since the amanuensis is removed from the narration. An example (this time from West Africa) in the Sheldon series is *The Life of Aaron Kuku of Eweland Born 1860–Died 1929 By Himself*. This 'autobiography' is nevertheless remarkable for the extent to which it replicates the narrative structures of the earlier missionary tales of 'release' through conversion, as witnessed by its subheadings: 'Childhood', 'The Ashanti War 1869–70', 'The Report of the War to the King', 'How I Was Nearly Killed', 'Three Months with Pagan Priests', 'I See my Father', 'Flight', 'The Return to the Ewe Country', 'At Home', 'The Death of my Wife and How I Revenged her Death', 'I See my Mother and Relations Again', 'I Become a Christian', 'My Work as Evangelist', 'How I Teach'. Despite its more sophisticated shape and a time-frame extended again beyond the moment of conversion, the basic account of pre-mission and pre-colonial African life in these later narrative forms continues to stress its disruptive and barbaric nature. This late mission genre of the exemplary life of the famous convert retains the basic evangelical Christian pattern of sin and redemption derived from the earlier narrative form, incorporated now into this overtly historicized 'autobiographical' form. The title claim to first-person authentic authorship disguises this ongoing control, and here, unlike in the earlier examples discussed, the absence of the amanuensis from the text, far from removing the fundamental narrative control implicit in the form, serves only to disguise more successfully the control exercised by the form and by the institution which maintains and produces it, the mission press.

For all their self-consciously 'liberal' surface and overt praise for the individual achievement of exemplary African converts in these late narratives, African traditional societies are still presented in many of these later mission texts as wholly negative. Intertribal warfare is the 'cause' of the enslavement of the Africans either directly, when they are sold as captives, or indirectly, when they are separated from their families as a result of the disruptions caused by warfare. *The Life of Aaron Kuku of Eweland* continues to structure its story along the established narrative spine of the 'release' form, which has become the standardized, seemingly now inescapable, way of framing any mission-generated African life story even in the late colonial period. Before Africans could fully subvert such controlling mission forms and redirect them to new ends, the narrative forms themselves needed to be substantially reworked and their audiences redefined. In particular, the forms of the ethnography, or 'history', and of the 'exemplary life' needed to be released from the narrative spine inherited from the 'release' form of the conversion narrative culminating in baptism and personal salvation. It needed to be directed away from the salvation of the individual subject towards the preservation and development of the social group and culture he or she represents. In addition the audience of mission-educated 'readers' needed to be perceived not simply as converts but as modern Africans, eager to hear their past presented in positive and affirming ways. Thus Jomo Kenyatta's 1942 text *The Life of Chief Wangombe wa Ihora*, which was itself published by a mission press, displays a clear intention to counter the presentation of the past in missionary exemplary lives as 'nasty, brutish and short'. In Kenyatta's text the mission genre of the exemplary life is employed for a much more radical end, divesting itself of concern with conversion as the narrative conclusion or even its principal subject. Now the form is appropriated for the purpose of establishing and celebrating communal African identity as an alternative model for the future of the peoples of Africa. In this thoroughly appropriated form of the mission genre of the exemplary African life narrative Wangombe wa Ihora is presented as a self-sufficient leader whose example provides his people with the strength to resist enemies and also the insight to be able to form alliances with them. The account records how Wangombe negotiates a peace with the Maasai. The wars of Africa in which he is involved are presented not as the brutal tribal encounters featured in earlier mission texts, but as conflicts analogous to European warfare, with causes rooted in similar processes of expansion, economic interest, and cultural pride, able to be resolved by negotiation between peoples. Kenyatta also records how, at the end of his life, Wangombe warns his people to beware the Europeans and to 'learn their clever way of talking for it is by using your wisdom that you may safeguard your country'.[10] The subject of the mission text is now exhorted to resist control by taking over the form rather than allowing the form to take them over. These late texts thus seek to reverse the flow of control across the site of the early mission genre and text.

As this account of these earlier texts has also tried to illustrate, even at the height of that textual control, when the native subject of the text had little or no agency through the control of his or her own representation, the very act of the mission amanuenses engaging discursively with the native 'other' created texts which always threatened to escape the control they sought to embody. In the silences and spaces of the classic accounts of the salvation and conversion of the native subject we may now discern personal and cultural engagements which could never be fully contained within the lineaments of the mission text conventions. Speaker and spoken stand revealed in these texts as intimate enemies, bound together in a linked if unequal process of self-definition. The missionary writing down the life of her native convert expressed and revealed the limitations and boundaries of her own subjectivity even in the act of rendering mute the unacceptable truths of that subject's unmediated expression.

Select Bibliography

J. B. DANQUAH, *The Akan Doctrine of God: A Fragment of Gold Coast Ethics and Religion* (London, 1944).

GARETH GRIFFITHS, *African Literatures in English—East and West* (London, 2000).

—— and JAMIE S. SCOTT, eds., *Mixed Messages: Materiality, Textuality, Missions* (New York, 2005).

—— and JOHN V. SINGLER, eds., *J. J. Walters's 'Guanya Pau: The Story of an African Princess'* (Toronto, 2004).

---

[10] Jomo Kenyatta, *My People of Kikuyu and The Life of Chief Wangombe wa Ihora.* (London, 1942), p. 63.

Isabel Hofmeyr, *The Portable Bunyan: A Transnational History of 'The Pilgrim's Progress'* (Princeton, 2004).
Mary Talor Huber and Nancy C. Lutkehaus, eds., *Gendered Missions: Women and Men in Missionary Discourse and Practice* (Ann Arbor, 1999).
Anna Johnston, *Missionary Writing and Empire, 1800–1860* (Cambridge, 2003)
Jomo Kenyatta, *My People of the Kikuyu and The Life of Chief Wangombe wa Ihora* (London, 1942).
Brian Stanley, ed., *Christian Missions and the Enlightenment* (Cambridge, 2001).
Gerhardt Stilz, ed., *Colonies, Missions, Cultures in the English-Speaking World: General and Comparative Studies*, ZAA Studies, XII (Tübingen, 2000).
Gauri Viswanathan, *Outside the Fold: Conversion, Modernity and Belief* (Princeton, 1998).

9

Women and Cultural Exchanges

PATRICIA GRIMSHAW AND PETER SHERLOCK

Robin Winks complained in volume V of the *Oxford History of the British Empire* that women's studies had made a negligible impact on imperial history. Scholars of gender and women's experience had done little to transform the broader field. Moreover, their debates had been conducted 'in a side area, as though the issues had been marginalized'. Nonetheless, he predicted that the quantity and scope of the work on women was bound to grow—as indeed it has.[1] Certainly the first four volumes of the *Oxford History of the British Empire* are barely touched by contemporary feminist scholarships (a fault partially repaired by the companion volume *Gender and Empire*).[2] Mainstream histories of Christian missions have paid even less attention to women and the insights of feminist scholars. Even academic mission histories have slighted women's experiences. This absence is remarkable, for since the proliferation of feminist critiques of humanities and the social sciences in the 1970s, much ground-breaking work has been completed on the role of women in missions and Empire. This chapter maps the trajectory of historical writing about women in missions from its origins in hagiography to current work informed by post-colonial theoretical insights. It delineates key findings, points to omissions requiring attention, and attempts to evaluate the significance of such studies for the field as a whole.

Resources for the history of missionary women over the last two centuries are diverse and dispersed, reflecting the wide variety of experience depending on marital status, age, personal capacity, and the possibilities for women's work offered by different denominations. Recent scholarship on women enhances our understanding of missions as a whole, probing the complex ways by which women within the mission household economies promoted

---

[1] Robin W. Winks, ed., *OHBE* V, *Historiography* (Oxford, 1999), p. 665.
[2] Philippa Levine, ed., *Gender and Empire*, OHBECS (Oxford, 2004). A notable exception is Rosalind O'Hanlon, 'Gender in the British Empire', in Judith M. Brown and W. Roger Louis, eds., *OHBE* IV, *The Twentieth Century* (Oxford, 1999), pp. 379–97.

the conversion, education, and training of indigenes in Western forms. Another part of the story is the gradual emergence of white women as professionals deriving satisfactions as salaried workers, albeit not among their own compatriots but among indigenous peoples in exotic sites. The recognition of both women's agency and the fundamentally gendered nature of the mission enterprise is integral to the future of imperial history and the history of missions.[3]

In 1907 a British schoolmaster, Charles Hayward, compiled a volume on missionary heroines as examples to the Christian faithful. One vignette described the tragic but triumphant life of Mrs Johnston, wife of the Wesleyan Methodist missionary George Johnston, who served among African slaves on plantations of the West Indies from 1807 to 1811. On the eve of her voyage from England, Mrs Johnston declared herself yearning 'to carry the Glad Tidings to the slaves and may God bless my labours'. She cheerfully faced the trials she knew were in store, confident that in God's sight the soul of one man, however wretched and despised, was equal to any other. She found hardship beyond her imaginings. On her deathbed, stricken in Dominica with 'swamp fever', she urged her husband to persevere in the grand cause: 'My motto is: "A sinner saved by grace. A brand plucked from the fire".' George Johnston informed his mission society that his deceased wife had contributed valiantly to the mission, including ably filling his place when he was away on Sundays: 'both the Church and myself have suffered'. She had been 'a true help-meet for me in body and in soul'.[4]

From the outset of the expansionary era of British missions in the late eighteenth century missionaries and mission organizations acknowledged the significant work of women. By the late nineteenth century white women outnumbered the men in imperial missions as wives, teachers, nurses, and nuns, not only from Britain and British ex-colonies such as Canada and Australia, but also from the United States and continental Europe. Hayward's collection was designed to show how women like Mrs Johnston worked heroically until old age or death, converting, educating, and ministering to the bodily needs of non-Christian people the world over. Although married women were not officially commissioned as missionaries, they were all expected to work where and when they were able. They are under-represented

---

[3] For an overview of gender and missions, see Patricia Grimshaw, 'Faith, Missionary Life and the Family', in Levine, *Gender and Empire*, pp. 260–80.

[4] Charles F. Hayward, *Women in the Mission Field* (London, [c.1907]), pp. 12, 16, 18.

in archives, because, unlike their husbands, they had no obligation to submit reports and journals. Single women, on the other hand, sustained the same commitments as the men. Mission journals printed news about them and mission wives as a means of interesting the Christian public, especially fund-raisers, in the broader work.

Although women figured in anecdotal fashion in early institutional and popular mission histories like Hayward's, their activities were not subjected to serious scholarly analysis before the Second World War, and the writing of mission history was largely left to educated Christian laymen outside academia. From the mid-twentieth century, when professionally trained scholars took an interest, the absence of women from mainstream accounts was notable. A recent historiographical survey of mission histories notes that most historians ignored women's experiences.[5] It was acknowledged that male missionaries had wives, who kept house, entertained visitors, taught local women, and often died prematurely; despite single women's greater potential agency, their special concerns were often presented as anomalous, and in any case they often married and disappeared from view into the marital household. Because women's letters went mainly to relatives rather than to society headquarters, they are under-represented in mission archives, a problem compounded by a lack of conceptual frameworks for representing the wives' existence. Women's daily work was relegated to the margins and divorced from the broader narrative of the establishment of missions, which centred on conversion and the nurturing of new churches.

Two developments in humanities research outside the area of mission history aroused scholarly interest in the domestic arena of missionary work. These were the rise of a new kind of feminism and a shift within anthropological scholarship away from examining non-European cultures to the study of cultural exchanges. From the 1970s feminists promoted the case for the inclusion of women in mainstream history to a sceptical male-dominated profession. Rather than studying exceptional 'women worthies', the new generation of scholars sought to centre women in their disciplines. Mainstream history focused, they suggested, on a taken-for-granted search for meta-narratives dealing with political and economic transformations and the actors—almost always men—associated with them. Feminist scholars countered this paradigm on a number of fronts: women were often closely connected to these stories but were ignored; most of the

---

[5] Norman Etherington, 'Missions and Empire', *OHBE* V, pp. 303–14.

significant questions about how and why changes took place and their outcomes relied on inappropriately marginalized cultural and social histories in which women figured equally with men; finally, gender, or the relationships of men and women, constituted an analytical category concomitant with class and race, and should substantially inform any history. The new women's history would offer a usable past not only to women, but also to men, as the discipline transformed the meta-narrative to develop inclusive human perspectives.

Mission history remained largely unaffected by this movement until the 1980s, as few scholars in the area had been affected by feminist theory. Moreover, some new works on female missionaries perpetuated the mode of missionary propaganda by seeking to rescue forgotten women from obscurity and demonstrate their significance. Thus, in her 1988 overview *Guardians of the Great Commission*, Ruth Tucker wrote: 'it is a credit to women missionaries around the world that the influence of Christianity on the family and on the role of women in the home has had significant impact—especially in some non-Western cultures, where women have traditionally had a very low status in society'.[6] The first works to argue that the missionary enterprise had played a critical role in transforming the whole of society emerged from the United States, whose feminist historians took a greater interest in women and religion than those of other Western nations. Jane Hunter's *The Gospel of Gentility* and Patricia Hill's *The World their Household* were particularly influential in exploring the attraction of missions and laying out a framework for research. North American scholars such as Dana Robert have continued to lead the field in examining white women missionaries as historical agents.[7]

Also in the 1980s, anthropologists and a new breed of social historians began to write about missions as a prime site wherein the records of daily behaviour could be studied. Those with an ethnographer's eye set about examining women's daily rounds, their support for male missionaries, and single women's agency, as dramatizing European ideas of femininity to local

---

[6] Ruth A. Tucker, *Guardians of the Great Commission: The Story of Women in Modern Missions* (Grand Rapids, Mich., 1988), p. 118.

[7] Jane Hunter, *The Gospel of Gentility* (New Haven, 1984); Patricia Hill, *The World their Household: The American Women's Foreign Mission Movement and Cultural Transformation, 1870–1920* (Ann Arbor, 1985); Dana L. Robert, *American Women in Mission* (Macon, Ga., 1996); id., ed., *Gospel Bearers, Gender Barriers: Missionary Women in the Twentieth Century* (Maryknoll, NY, 2002).

people. These scholars established a narrative of women in the mission field to set beside the general male accounts. This work sees missions as a key site for observing cultural conflict—one in which gender relations and the household were crucial battlegrounds. Much of this ethnographically driven historical work has focused on British, Australian, and American missions in the Pacific. Diane Langmore's 1989 study of missionaries in Papua focused on men and women, both Protestant and Catholic, in order to expose the gendered underpinnings of missions. In the same year Patricia Grimshaw's *Paths of Duty: American Missionary Women in Nineteenth-Century Hawaii* appeared together with an influential collection of historical and anthropological chapters, *Family and Gender in the Pacific* edited by fellow Australians Margaret Jolly and Martha Macintyre. A most significant collection on women and missions with a strong focus on Africa emerged in 1993 from collaboration between historians and anthropologists—one that accorded equal weight to missionaries and to the indigenous subjects of mission.[8] Six years later a similar collection demonstrated in its statement of purpose how the field of study had developed:

We focus on missions first because missionaries usually worked closer to local communities than other colonial agents, often with a moral agenda that provided a broad critique of local gender regimes. Further, because of their concerns with women, children, and family, missionary groups were more likely than others to include Western women among their workers and thus to face more immediately the destabilizing challenges that colonial experience posed to their own ways of organizing relations between women and men.[9]

This collection also reflects a third development in the study of women and missions, which is the use of mission archives to explore the relation between gender, race, and Empire. Since the late 1980s feminist scholars have been forced to respond to post-colonial critiques questioning the role of white women as agents of mission enterprises. Were women's historians bent on discovering white women's significance in Empire-building to valorize their

---

[8] Diane Langmore, *Missionary Lives: Papua 1874–1914* (Honolulu, 1989); Patricia Grimshaw, *Paths of Duty: American Missionary Wives in Nineteenth-Century Hawaii* (Honolulu, 1989); Margaret Jolly and Martha Macintyre, eds., *Family and Gender in the Pacific: Domestic Contradictions and the Colonial Impact* (Cambridge, 1989); Fiona Bowie, Deborah Kirkwood, and Shirley Ardener, eds., *Women and Missions: Past and Present: Anthropological and Historical Perceptions* (Oxford, 1993).

[9] Mary Taylor Huber and Nancy C. Lutkehaus, eds., *Gendered Missions: Women and Men in Missionary Discourse and Practice* (Ann Arbor, 1999), p. 1.

roles? Should they not instead be engaged in teasing out white women's complicity with white men in sustaining colonial power structures at the expense of indigenous people? Post-colonial historians linked mission women directly to the exercise of colonial power and the treatment of colonized peoples. Missions as a whole were recast as a destructive enterprise in which white women played a part. The influence of post-colonial studies can be seen in Ruth Compton Brouwer's study of Canadian Presbyterian women in Indian missions, where success in conversion and cultural transmission was directly related to exploitation of local crises such as famine or disease and the subsequent removal of children to mission stations. Similarly, Myra Rutherdale's magisterial *Women and the White Man's God* shows how ideas and practices determined by competing concepts of gender and race affected all those involved in the mission encounter in Canada, not only white female missionaries.[10]

Inspired by the theoretical work of Edward Said and other studies of the impact of colonialism on the colonizers, historians such as Antoinette Burton, Judith Rowbotham, and Susan Thorne focus on linkages between events in the metropole and the overseas Empire, for example, between British women's attempts to advance their own emancipation through a slanted representation of the colonial 'others' who were to be 'liberated' and converted.[11] Catherine Hall's *Civilising Subjects: Metropole and Colony in the English Imagination 1830–1867* (2002) casts a fresh light on the work of humanitarians in Britain, and the interactions between British and colonial vested interests. Her study stresses the racialized and gendered grounding of missions in the metropole and in the West Indies, in ways that foreshadow a complete reintegration of mission history into imperial history. Each of these revisionist historians has emphasized that women's contributions to missions were an integral part of the wider movement whereby women of the nineteenth and twentieth centuries asserted the significance of domesticity and the private sphere, while striving for greater autonomy. Thus, women missionaries carried a

---

[10] Ruth Compton Brouwer, *New Women for God: Canadian Presbyterian Women and India Missions 1876–1914* (Toronto, 1990); Myra Rutherdale, *Women and the White Man's God: Gender and Race in the Canadian Mission Field* (Vancouver, 2002).

[11] Antoinette Burton, *At the Heart of Empire: Indians and the Colonial Encounter in Late-Victorian Britain* (Berkeley, 1998) and *Burdens of History: British Feminists, Indian Women, and Imperial Culture, 1865–1915* (Chapel Hill, NC, 1994); Judith Rowbotham, ' "Soldiers of Christ?" Images of Female Missionaries in Late Nineteenth Century Britain', *Gender and History*, XII (2000), pp. 82–106; Susan Thorne, *Congregational Missions and the Making of an Imperial Culture in Nineteenth-Century England* (Stanford, Calif., 1999).

European feminine and domestic agenda of Western modernity to indigenous peoples, exemplifying new knowledge, technologies, and practices that were revolutionizing their home societies.

Women's historians justify singling out women as a discrete subject in history by pointing to the distinctive trajectory of their lives and the need for a wholesale revision of our notion of what topics are appropriate objects of historical study. These objectives are amply illustrated in studies of the life experiences of married women in mission households. Although, from the earliest days of the missionary enterprise, women believed they were called to enter the mission field by the same evangelical imperatives that prompted men to leave the British Isles, they were not treated in the same manner. White middle-class women across the Empire were prompted to consider missionary service by the growing body of literature on 'missionary heroines', which simultaneously encouraged the raising of funds by women to support the missionary cause. This literature frequently constructed the subject of missionary efforts as savage, depraved, and ignorant, while portraying the white woman as an adventurous and brave soul who overstepped the boundaries of home and hearth, sacrificing family life to bring the light of the gospel to the unenlightened. Indigenous girls were represented as in desperate need of moral rescue through the provision of domestic education and basic literacy. Meanwhile, the representation of women who died on the mission field in tragic circumstances constructed a valiant image of martyrdom that further confirmed the validity of female missionary work. Women missionaries thus made a substantial impact upon the imaginations of generations of children in Britain and the settler colonies.[12]

Only in the nineteenth century did women begin to enter the mission field in significant numbers, first as mission wives, and then in their own right, reluctantly accepted by the major missionary societies (sometimes in the hopes that they would marry widowers in the field and hence retain valuable men in place) or through small, single-purpose societies. By the middle of the nineteenth century a wife was considered a necessary asset for the would-be missionary, even though married women were neither directly commissioned by the societies nor paid a separate wage. Furthermore, single women missionaries in organizations such as the London Missionary Society (LMS)

---

[12] Burton, *Burdens of History*; Judith Rowbotham, ' "Hear an Indian Sister's Plea": Reporting the Work of Nineteenth-Century British Female Missionaries', *Women's Studies International Forum*, XXI (1998), pp. 247–61, and 'Soldiers of Christ', pp. 82–106.

were expected to resign their commission upon marriage, even as they carried on as voluntary workers.[13]

Wives were expected to work, and work they did, but the method and mode of their work distinguished them from male missionaries, who pursued conversion through preaching, teaching, and negotiation: work more easily recognized in a capitalist society as deserving financial remuneration. The work of missionary wives took place within a household economy of pre-industrial times, work designated as auxiliary to that of men, but which was nevertheless essential to the maintenance of European domestic family life, to the creation of a Christian community, and to the wider cause of proselytization. Missionary wives performed manifold duties in respect to sexuality, childbearing, and child-rearing; housewifery, ranging across obtaining food, cooking, cleaning, sewing, nursing the sick, maintaining a vegetable garden, keeping poultry, and growing vegetables to training and supervising others to assist in these tasks; and furthering the mission work which brought in their husbands' stipends. Mission societies also expected wives to take on the additional tasks of teaching local women and children the skills of European domesticity (however foreign to their own culture) and to teach reading, infused, of course, by spiritual truth.

This burden is well represented by the life of Marianne Williams, an exemplary missionary wife who worked with her husband, Henry, at the Paihia mission in New Zealand (established in 1823). Prior to departure she had studied nursing, as well as the Moravian missionary principles of education. Once located in the Bay of Islands, she exemplified European family ideals, raising eleven children of her own, dispensing medicine and hospitality, and attempting to domesticate indigenous women by running a school for Maori girls, bringing them into her home to learn cooking, needlework, and the art of housewifery. Yet her attempts to impose her version of womanly behaviour met with resistance: Maori simply walked out of her home if she berated them verbally, leaving her without aid in what was a large household even for missionary families. Although Williams could control her own body and those of her children, she had to battle, cajole, and frequently acknowledge complete failure in her attempts to get Maori women to dress and behave as Europeans in accordance with her vision of the outward signs of Christian belief. As Kathryn Rountree observes, at the

---

[13] Deborah Kirkwood, 'Protestant Missionary Women: Wives and Spinsters', in Bowie *et al.*, eds., *Women and Missions*, pp. 25–31.

core of her work as a missionary wife was the colonization of the bodies of Maori as a preparation for the colonization of their souls.[14]

The perceived need of male missionaries for companionship and domestic support, together with underlying fears of sexual misconduct, quickly made a wife a necessary asset, leading some mission societies to provide men with suitable companions just prior to departure. The controversy surrounding the early nineteenth-century LMS missionaries who married or had liaisons with indigenous women in southern Africa was a reminder of the perils single men posed for missionary societies, which relied for finance upon a culture increasingly intolerant of interracial marriage.[15] And if single women faced one major threat to their independent work in the early phases of a mission other than finding themselves swiftly transformed into wives, it was their co-option to the role of right-hand help to the hard-pressed mission wife and mother whose urgent need, in the absence of sisters and mothers, for Western skilled help was bottomless. Moreover, single women who arrived at mission stations against all odds in the period prior to the 1880s found the alternative of marriage quickly pressed upon them since few men ever contemplated staying in the field unless they could marry there. Single women often released single or recently widowed men from the labour of returning to the home base to acquire a wife, or the disappointment of abandoning their calling altogether. James and Matilda Ward arrived on Thursday Island in the Torres Strait as Moravian missionaries in 1890. Before long their colleague Nicholas Hey had married Mrs Ward's sister Mary Ann and the two women could model European gender order; although after James Ward's death Matilda continued on, working in her own right under the auspices of the Victorian Presbyterian Women's Missionary Union alongside her sister and brother-in-law.[16]

Because childbearing frequently undermined their constitutions, the health and energy of wives were more deeply affected than their husbands by migration to new and challenging communities and cultures. Wives were held responsible for sustaining a model household and an exemplary family, which increased their personal insecurity. Missionaries had to cope with difficult living conditions, often at odds with their socio-economic

---

[14] Kathryn Rountree, 'Re-making the Maori Female Body: Marianne Williams's Mission in the Bay of Islands', *Journal of Pacific History*, XXXV (2000), pp. 49–66.

[15] Julia Wells, 'The Suppression of Mixed Marriages among LMS Missionaries in South Africa before 1820', *South African Historical Journal*, XLIV (2001), pp. 1–20.

[16] E. C. Dawson, *Missionary Heroines in Many Lands* (London, n.d.), ch. 8.

background, and come to grips with being self-reliant in every matter from erecting a suitable house to finding food and water. Improvements to their residences might come at the cost of goodwill, however, if local people viewed them more as wealthy and powerful masters rather than as the mere purveyors of the gospel. But improved conditions were the basis of good health for women and young children if they were to be anything other than a burden and worry for the mission. Mortality of wives and their babies was high, and those who survived the early years could be plagued by ill health for decades. Mary Hill and her husband, Micaiah, worked for the LMS at Berhampur in Bengal from 1824 to 1847, during which time two of their children died. Mary suffered from exhaustion owing to her work as a nurse and schoolteacher and the hardships of finding suitable accommodation in an unaccustomed climate.[17]

Raising children according to European custom was very difficult. The lack of money, food, the trappings of domesticity, and the company of other Europeans imposed a constant strain on mothers who sought to communicate British culture to their own children as well as to the objects of the missionary enterprise. Servants might be employed in the mission house, who spoke their own language to missionary children, and might win greater affection than their parents could. For these reasons missionary parents often sent their children to boarding schools in their country of origin to assure a successful future—good marriages for the girls, and professional employment for the boys. The pain of separation from children imposed another burden on wives like Mary Hill, who felt compelled to send her eldest son back to England on account of his frequent illnesses.

The mission field severely strained the gendered division of labour between husband and wife thought appropriate in British societies in the nineteenth and early twentieth centuries. While men might occasionally take on temporary roles as carers for children and the sick in the absence of women, their wives frequently left the domestic realm for more public activities. This was especially so prior to the arrival in the 1880s of large numbers of single women missionaries, as wives ran schools and instructed indigenous women on the skills of European housewifery from cooking to sewing. At times any semblance of Victorian domestic ideology disappeared in practice, despite the belief that this was the model that Christian converts

---

[17] Valentine Cunningham, 'God and Nature Intended you for a Missionary's Wife', in Bowie et al., eds., *Women in Missions*, pp. 85–105.

should imitate. Some wives found themselves alone in charge of entire missions stations. The British Columbian bishop William Ridley was forced to go to Ottawa in 1884 and then to England to deal with a disobedient Church Missionary Society (CMS) missionary. His wife, Jane, stayed behind to run the vacant Hazelton mission station through the Canadian winter. After death she was eulogized for her bravery in stepping outside the boundaries of feminine activity, and for her apparent success in working among the Tsimshian people.[18] The pattern was repeated across the Empire, as husbands departed for extensive periods of itinerant preaching, leaving wives to replace them in mission churches. In the 1890s two Fiji missionary wives, Minnie Burns and Lydia Brown, even went so far as to preach in their husbands' absence.[19] Wives quietly contributed to these activities, even when beset by pregnancies, miscarriages, and the need to nurse the sick. No matter their skills or load, if wives were to gain official approval, however, they needed to maintain a modest, self-deprecatory demeanour that translated into virtual invisibility in mission reports and that might one day be praised in the obituary columns. By proving they could survive both physically and culturally on colonial frontiers, missionary wives helped pave the way for the employment of women as missionaries in their own right. There was, however, stiff resistance to the concept of appointing women missionaries throughout the nineteenth century, which restricted the opportunities available to most unmarried women. In the 1840s Bishop Wilson of Calcutta famously objected 'in principle to single ladies coming out unprotected to so distant a place with a climate so unfriendly, and with the almost certainty of their marrying within a month of their arrival... the whole thing is against apostolic maxim, "I suffer not a woman to speak in the church" '.[20]

While the major missionary societies continued to debate the subject of women as professional evangelists throughout the late nineteenth century, a range of smaller organizations did offer opportunities. The Society for Promoting Female Education in the East, founded in 1834 as a response to the concern of both missionaries and the Ladies' Society of Calcutta, and the Indian Female Normal School and Instruction Society (1859) were two such groups, employing women as schoolteachers, while the unmarried relations of male missionaries might accompany their brothers and fathers to the

---

[18] Rutherdale, *Women and the White Man's God*, pp. 54–6.
[19] Claudia Knapman, *White Women in Fiji 1835–1930: The Ruin of Empire?* (Sydney, 1986), pp. 65–6.
[20] C. F. Pascoe, *Two Hundred Years of the S.P.G.* (London, 1901), p. 617.

mission field. A major change in mission policy on women occurred in 1878, when, despite public criticism, Hudson Taylor engaged single female missionaries from Britain and the colonies to work in teams for his China Inland Mission.[21] Once women had been admitted to the major missionary institutions, their numbers rapidly multiplied. It is a central if unacknowledged fact of mission history that by the end of the nineteenth century the largest group of missionaries were not clergy or married couples, but single women. In 1909 the CMS had 1,390 European staff on its books, 414 of whom were clergymen, 152 laymen, 386 missionary wives, and 438 single women.[22] For these latter women, missionary work offered a viable alternative to marriage, based on the same principle of self-sacrifice to a higher cause, while for would-be doctors and teachers, missions offered career prospects not available at home.

Two factors gave missionary organizations compelling reasons to facilitate women's participation in proselytization in the second half of the nineteenth century. First, a large number of single women felt called to leave Britain, the United States, and the British settler colonies to spread the Christian gospel; and they were able to call upon the particular support of other white women as fund-raisers. Secondly, the major missionary societies recognized that women could go to places inaccessible to men and thus attempt new forms of proselytization.

The catchphrase of women's missionary endeavours from the mid-nineteenth century to the First World War was 'women's work for women', as both a justification for and description of their work in the field. The female missionary organizations pursued the ideology of separate spheres of activity, focusing on the tasks of teaching girls, domestic training, modelling Victorian and Edwardian womanhood, providing medical care in the form of nursing, and entering exclusive female spaces. Recruitment of female missionaries could be class-based in a way that selection of male missionaries generally was not. The LMS Ladies' Committee interviewed applicants for mission service and discriminated between them on the basis of educational qualifications and the ability to maintain ladylike qualities in a foreign

---

[21] Margaret Donaldson, ' "The Cultivation of the Heart and the Moulding of the Will...": The Missionary Contribution of the Society for Promoting Female Education in China, India and the East', in W. J. Sheils and Diana Wood, eds., *Women in the Church: Studies in Church History*, XXVII (London, 1990). On debates over female missionaries, see Sean Gill, *Women in the Church of England* (London, 1994), pp. 174–81.

[22] G. Gollock, *The Story of the Church Missionary Society* (London, 1909), p. 46.

land.[23] 'Women's work for women' and the educational ideal behind the civilizing mission were most clearly articulated in the various attempts to gain access to the zenana in colonial India. Here missionary strategy shifted, as the belief that women needed to be 'rescued' was replaced by the view that women were the key to changing the whole moral system of a society. If missionaries could enter the zenana—forbidden to European men—then Christianity and civilization would filter down to the peoples of India through their elite women, paralleling the role assigned to middle-class women by Victorian evangelical ideology. One result was the establishment of mission organizations solely for women, such as the Baptist Church's Zenana Missionary Society (1867) and the Church of England Zenana Missionary Society (1880). Not only did their special work justify the recruitment of female missionaries, it also positioned them as crucial to the spread of the gospel and required them to be drawn from the middle classes of the British Empire.[24]

The sign of success for female missionaries—and the imperial ideal—could thus be reduced to the extent to which they planted European ideals of gender behaviour. On the one hand, practices such as polygamy or widow-burning would be attacked by male administrators and female activists in both the colonies and Britain. On the other, women would introduce female education to secondary level. Heather Sharkey has demonstrated how the CMS mission in northern Sudan received continuing support from Britain despite achieving only one convert in sixty years as it was seen to have successfully established girls' schools and improved the status of women.[25]

Nevertheless, the path for white women's employment in the mission field was not always smooth. In the late nineteenth century the emphasis on zenanas made it difficult for many women to take up mainstream mission work with the Baptist Missionary Society.[26] Scottish male missionaries in South Africa opposed the education of girls in mission schools beyond basic

[23] Jane Haggis, ' "A Heart that Has Felt the Love of God and Longs for Others to Know It": Conventions of Gender, Tensions of Self and Constructions of Difference in Offering to Be a Lady Missionary', *Women's History Review*, VII (1998), pp. 171–92.

[24] David Savage, 'Missionaries and the Development of a Colonial Ideology of Female Education in India', *Gender and History*, IX (1997), pp. 201–21; Maina Chawla Singh, *Gender, Religion and the 'Heathen Lands': American Missionary Women in South Asia, 1860s–1940s* (New York, 2000), pp. 118–22.

[25] Heather Sharkey, 'Christians among Muslims: The Church Missionary Society in the Northern Sudan', *Journal of African History*, XLIII (2002), pp. 51–75.

[26] Brian Stanley, *The History of the Baptist Missionary Society* (Edinburgh, 1992), p. 232.

domestic training, thus obviating the need for female teachers as their own wives could undertake this duty.[27] Similarly, the fund-raising efforts of British women were more often directed towards supporting all missions, not just activities of women. The New South Wales Presbyterian Women's Missionary Association initially desired to raise money for female missionaries, but as they could not identify specifically feminine objectives, they had to divert their efforts to supporting all Presbyterian missions.[28] Women seeking opportunities for careers in teaching or medicine that did not exist at home often met frustrating obstacles. Jane Waterston, the Scotswoman who became South Africa's first female doctor, complained in the 1870s about being relegated to 'women's work' despite having studied at Sophia Jex Blake's London School of Medicine for Women for the specific purpose of practising medicine on the mission field.[29] Just as single male missionaries posed a potential threat to the moral codes and domestic arrangements promoted by the churches, single females could provoke debate. This ranged from the perennial accusation that single women were likely to get married and cease the mission work they were originally employed to do, to the thornier problem of authority. While women could work with other women, what authority might they exercise over men? Marion Fairweather's experience with the Canadian Presbyterians' Central India Mission illustrates the problem. After she arrived at Indore in 1877, her involvement in a wide range of activities, including visiting and socializing with the local Hindu elite women, meant she was effectively doing work equal to any male lay missionary. However, she was recalled to Canada in 1879 and dismissed in 1880 after rumours that she had had an affair with the mission's male founder. The fallout from this incident led to a preference for married males in this mission, not only because of the security in matters of morality this apparently offered, but also because Fairweather's operational independence had unbalanced the precarious negotiation of authority between male and female missionaries in favour of the women.[30]

[27] Natasha Erlank, ' "Raising up the Degraded Daughters of Africa": The Provision of Education for Xhosa Women in the Mid-Nineteenth Century', *South African Historical Journal*, XLIII (2000), pp. 24–38.

[28] Judith Godden, 'Containment and Control: Presbyterian Women and the Missionary Impulse in New South Wales, 1891–1914', *Women's History Review*, VI (1997), pp. 75–93.

[29] L. Bean and E. van Heyningen, eds., *The Letters of Jane Elizabeth Waterston 1866–1905* (Cape Town, 1983).

[30] Brouwer, *New Women for God*, pp. 131–5.

A few exceptional women were able to take charge of their own missionary activities successfully by citing evangelical imperatives. 'Missionary heroines' such as Amy Carmichael in India and Florence Young in the Pacific founded entire organizations and institutions, travelled beyond the frontiers of colonial settlements, and negotiated with indigenous peoples independently of male administrators or missionaries. The most celebrated of these women (her image appears on a Scottish banknote) was Mary Mitchell Slessor, who went to Calabar with the Scottish Presbyterian Mission in East Nigeria in 1876. Unusual in her working-class background, she qualified by studying at night school while teaching in Dundee. Her work focused on building schools for African students and encouraging what would now be described as community development. She believed that Christianity would be received when people had acquired the educational skills and economic freedoms necessary to enable them to appreciate the Bible. She raised the eyebrows of male missionaries and colonial officials because of her close relations with indigenous peoples; the local Efik leaders encouraged her to carry her work beyond the colonial frontier. She maintained an unusual degree of autonomy through her ability to raise money in Britain independently of her mission organization. Simultaneously, she confronted the Efik over what she perceived to be abusive treatment of women, children, and slaves, urging the abolition of polygamy and establishing refuges for women and children who left their husbands and fathers. In 1883 she adopted the first of many Efik girls, and, despite being a single white woman, was by the 1890s known as Ma Akamba (Great Mother). Despite the claims of some missionary propaganda, Slessor's achievements lay not so much in numbers of converts as in her communication of knowledge that helped the Efik respond more effectively to the impact of British colonialism.[31]

Other single women might be less adventurous, but, as mission culture changed in the twentieth century, gained recognition by male colleagues. Female missionaries were finally able to develop an established professional identity which expanded beyond the private sphere after the Edinburgh Missionary Conference of 1910 created guidelines for their selection and training.[32] This was a profound change, as the work undertaken by male and female missionaries was now much less differentiated. In previous

[31] W. H. Taylor, *Mission to Educate: A History of the Educational Work of the Scottish Presbyterian Mission in East Nigeria, 1846–1960* (New York, 1996), ch. 7.

[32] Rhonda Anne Semple, *Missionary Women: Gender, Professionalism and the Victorian Idea of Christian Mission* (Woodbridge, 2003), p. 2.

generations the cultural exchanges embodied in the missionary encounter had been far more focused on the communication of knowledge from men to men and women to women.

Brouwer's study of three Canadian women working in different arenas of mission work demonstrates their increased recognition by male missionaries compared to their nineteenth-century predecessors, together with their new role in transmitting knowledge and culture from Western to non-Western societies. The new, professional missionary frequently held authority over indigenous men as well as other women, and, rather than communicating domestic practices alone, might pass on medical technology and skill or theological learning as part of a broader process of modernization.[33] An increasing sense of professional identity empowered some women to determine for whom they would work, what they would do, and where they would do it. Miss Corbett, who worked in Darjeeling for the Scottish Presbyterian mission in the eastern Himalayas, was the only qualified teacher at the mission, and by 1908 had expanded her school to 300 students. She therefore asked for her work to be confined to the primary school, where she felt her expertise lay, exempting her from instructing at the mission's teacher-training institute. When the Women's Association for Mission denied her request, she joined another mission where her vocation could be fulfilled.[34]

From the 1920s, as part of the new responsibilities formally accorded to women, some missionaries were now ordained as ministers in the Protestant churches or deaconesses in the Anglican Church. Depending on the beliefs and attitudes of their superiors, some were allowed to act as the sole minister in charge of new congregations, a role they could not usually take up at home. This was especially the case in southern China, Hong Kong, East Africa, and some remote rural areas of Australia, New Zealand, and Canada. Yet the authority of missionary women remained as contested as it had been in the nineteenth century, and in turn affected the role of women in the churches of Britain, North America, and the settler colonies, as female missionaries with wide experience in preaching and leadership were effectively demoted upon repatriation. Many Australian women who trained for the CMS at Deaconess House in Sydney were sent to places such as the Anglican missionary diocese of Central Tanganyika, where in the 1930s and 1940s the Australian bishop George Chambers used his authority to promote women's work on the mission field. Yet when these women returned to

---

[33] Ruth Compton Brouwer, *Modern Women, Modernising Men* (Vancouver, 2002).
[34] Semple, *Missionary Women*, pp. 148–9.

Sydney, they could no longer preach or take up representative roles on decision-making bodies, leading to an anomalous gap between white women's authority at home and abroad.[35]

One of the less understood areas of research in missionary history is the work undertaken by Catholic female religious around the world. Like single women and missionary wives, nuns did not conform to established structures of domestic life, but at the same time they could not perform European household ideals of marriage, housewifery, and child-rearing. Unlike members of male orders, they had to overcome restrictions on movement outside their communities, which made mission work impossible until the nineteenth century, when new orders for women were instituted. Well into the twentieth century financial dependence and subordinate status constrained the work of missionary nuns.[36]

The most challenging new research on women and missions has centred on the activities of indigenous women, both as subjects and as agents of mission, and their gradual emergence as leaders in the new churches. Three areas of research have arisen as the voices of Third and Fourth World women begin to be heard in the halls of academia. First are studies of exceptional women who converted to Christianity or used mission education to proceed to leadership positions in their own and in other societies. Secondly, attention is being to be paid to the crucial role of Christian women in expanding and leading new churches in Africa, Asia, and the Pacific. Finally, historians are beginning to write accounts of how indigenous women might respond to and resist the interventions of white missionary women, being variously compelled to live under foreign conditions, or adapting knowledges that were useful to them and rejecting those which were not. Within all these fields, the outcomes of the missionary enterprise for indigenous women have varied with the nature of colonialism in each region and the dynamics of power between colonizers and colonized. Like much of the earlier work on women and missions, interest in the role of women of colour as agents of mission was first taken up in North America with study of African American women who travelled from the late nineteenth century to southern and western Africa to spread Christianity.[37] In the British imperial context,

---

[35] Muriel Porter, *Women in the Church* (Melbourne, 1989), p. 53.

[36] Hilary Carey, 'Subordination, Invisibility and Chosen Work: Missionary Nuns and Australian Aborigines, c.1900–1949', *Australian Feminist Studies*, XIII (1998), pp. 251–67.

[37] Sylvia Jacobs, 'African-American Women Missionaries and European Imperialism in Southern Africa, 1880–1920', *Women's Studies International Forum*, XIII (1990), pp. 381–94.

early studies of indigenous women missionaries focused on India, where educational efforts combined with class dynamics to produce female leaders within Church and government. One of the most notable was Pandita Ramabai (1858–1922), a Brahman woman known as a scholar of Hinduism who famously converted to Christianity in 1883 while living at the female religious community at Wantage, in Berkshire. For the remainder of her life she promoted education for women and preached a distinctive version of Christianity in India as a way of enhancing the status of women in patriarchal societies of any kind.[38] Like the maverick Mary Slessor, however, Ramabai has been singled out because she was exceptional, at times obscuring other stories.

As the explosive growth of Christianity in Asia, Africa, and the Pacific is better studied, the role of women as grass-roots supporters and leaders is coming to be acknowledged, although much more work remains to be done on this topic. Enabling the numerical rise of Christians has been the work of Bible Women and the adaptation of organizations such as the Mother's Union, now a backbone of the Anglican Church in Africa and a key social institution.[39] Just as indigenous men began to emerge as leading clergy and bishops in the 1950s, so too women followed twenty years later. Some of the earliest Anglican female clergy in the world appeared in Africa when Bishop Festo Kivengere ordained four women as deacons in Uganda in 1972. During the 1980s in the Torres Strait Islands and northern Australia, senior indigenous women were appointed as church elders or ordained as clergy largely to work among other women.[40]

Perhaps the most significant new histories of women and missions are those that focus on the diverse active responses made by indigenous women to the missionaries. In the Pacific, for example, missionary women's attempts to impose European domestic behaviour met with mixed results. Mrs Gunn's efforts to teach sewing and home-making to women in Vanuatu in the 1880s and 1890s were successful in terms of imparting skills, but her desire that they

[38] Padma Angol, 'Indian Christian Women and Indigenous Feminism, c.1850–c.1920', in Clare Midgley, ed., *Gender and Imperialism* (Manchester, 1998), pp. 79–103; Meera Kosambi, 'Multiple Contestations: Pandita Ramabai's Educational and Missionary Activities in Late Nineteenth-Century India and Abroad', *Women's History Review*, VII (1998), pp. 193–208.

[39] Deborah Gaitskell, 'Whose Heartland and Which Periphery? Christian Women Crossing South Africa's Racial Divide in the Twentieth Century', *Women's History Review*, XI (2002), pp. 375–415.

[40] John Harris, 'Anglicanism and Indigenous Peoples', in Bruce Kaye, ed., *Anglicanism in Australia: A History* (Melbourne, 2002), p. 243.

should produce artefacts that could be sold or otherwise used to support the mission work was wholeheartedly rejected.[41] In Kenya missionary efforts at evangelization through schooling met some success in the early twentieth century as women and men perceived education as a means of social mobility, yet were reversed from 1929 when missionaries attacked female circumcision outright. Ninety per cent of Kikuyu adherents left the mission until a variety of compromises were reached including some communities in which new Christians themselves provided church circumcisers.[42]

Recent works on this aspect of missions are necessarily based on painstaking oral history. Some make use of family connections to the subjects of mission education. Maina Chawla Singh's account of American women in South Asia is informed by an awareness of how Indian and Bengali women were selectively adopting and adapting the knowledge taught by the missionaries to their own ends, an awareness derived from her own mother's schooling in a mission-run college.[43] Others use oral narratives to uncover otherwise unrecorded stories about the integration and adaptation of European Christianity to indigenous cultures. The work of Christine Choo has thus revealed the existence of a remarkable Aboriginal order of nuns, the Daughters of Our Lady, Queen of the Apostles, at Beagle Bay in Western Australia in the 1940s. This demonstrates the variety of outcomes for indigenous women who attempted to maintain a traditional identity while converting to Catholicism, who negotiated oppressive mission structures on the one hand, yet also had to cope with loss of lands, forced relocation, and the stringencies of hostile state legislation on the other.[44]

Given the substantial body of work on women and gender concerns in missions, we might in conclusion reflect further on their relative lack of impact on mainstream narratives of mission histories. First, many of the women who have written these accounts have turned to the topic not because they are centrally engaged in religious or mission history generally, but because they are pursuing paths that women took per se. They did not therefore engage with the central concerns of the main practitioners for

---

[41] William Gunn and Mrs Gunn, *Heralds of Dawn: Early Converts in the New Hebrides* (London, 1924).

[42] Tabitha Kanogo, 'Mission Impact on Women in Colonial Kenya', in Bowie *et al.*, eds., *Women in Missions*, pp. 165–86.

[43] Singh, *Gender, Religion and 'Heathen Lands'*.

[44] Christine Choo, *Mission Girls: Aboriginal Women on Catholic Missions in the Kimberley, Western Australia, 1900–1950* (Perth, WA, 2000).

whom mission history was a priority. Many such scholars took different questions as their starting point, about women's position in nineteenth- and early twentieth-century modern history. They linked women missionaries to examinations of women and colonialism, and saw mission women as the bearers of ideas of modernity both in the careers they pursued and in the skills they attempted to transmit to the protégés they adopted. They themselves, while by no means consciously feminist, exemplified how ordinary middle-class women might adapt the opportunities that modernity presented to their own benefit, how the imposition of domestic ideals, the creation of institutions and organizational structures involving women, their education and medicine, their lessons in the authority of men reveal that Western activities in the East were not solely about white men conquering the world. The impact of modernity on colonialism, and on women as agents and subjects, has not been a major interest of mission historiography; hence this whole strand of missionary history remains marginal.

Work on women and gender in mission contexts still has the capacity to inspire continuing research and encourage other historians to consider ways towards greater inclusiveness. Meanwhile, indigenous scholars from the ex-colonies will themselves increasingly command their own voices in the field, through methodologies of their own choosing, and the historians of the West, female and male, will in turn learn more fully from them of the nature of the mission project and the understandings of new churches.

Select Bibliography

FIONA BOWIE, DEBORAH KIRKWOOD, and SHIRLEY ARDENER, eds., *Women and Missions: Past and Present: Anthropological and Historical Perceptions* (Oxford, 1993).

RUTH COMPTON BROUWER, *Modern Women, Modernizing Men* (Vancouver, 2002).

—— *New Women for God: Canadian Presbyterian Women and India Missions 1876–1914* (Toronto, 1990).

CHRISTINE CHOO, *Mission Girls: Aboriginal Women on Catholic Missions in the Kimberley, Western Australia, 1900–1950* (Perth, WA, 2001).

JEAN COMAROFF and JOHN L. COMAROFF, *Of Revelation and Revolution, I, Christianity, Colonialism and Consciousness in South Africa* (Chicago, 1991).

PATRICIA GRIMSHAW, 'Faith, Missionary Life and the Family', in Philippa Levine, ed., *Gender and Empire*, OHBECS (Oxford, 2004), pp. 260–80.

—— *Paths of Duty: American Missionary Wives in Nineteenth-Century Hawaii* (Honolulu, 1989).
CATHERINE HALL, *Civilising Subjects: Metropole and Colony in the English Imagination 1830–1867* (Cambridge, 2002).
MARY TAYLOR HUBER and NANCY C. LUTKEHAUS, eds., *Gendered Missions: Women and Men in Missionary Discourse and Practice* (Ann Arbor, 1999).
MARGARET JOLLY and MARTHA MACINTYRE, eds., *Family and Gender in the Pacific: Domestic Contradictions and the Colonial Impact* (Cambridge, 1989).
DIANE LANGMORE, *Missionary Lives: Papua, 1874–1914* (Honolulu, 1989).
DANA L. ROBERT, ed., *Gospel Bearers, Gender Barriers: Missionary Women in the Twentieth Century* (Maryknoll, NY, 2002).
MYRA RUTHERDALE, *Women and the White Man's God: Gender and Race in the Canadian Mission Field* (Vancouver, 2002).
RHONDA ANNE SEMPLE, *Missionary Women: Gender, Professionalism and the Victorian Idea of Christian Mission* (Woodbridge, 2003).
MAINA CHAWLA SINGH, *Gender, Religion and the 'Heathen Lands': American Missionary Women in South Asia, 1860s–1940s* (New York, 2000).

10

Language

PAUL LANDAU

Nearly all the world's alphabets are elaborations of a Semitic orthography from Canaan or Egypt. Medieval missionaries brought the Roman version to Europe, and in the modern era evangelists carried it to other continents. Inevitably the British Empire became a party to this dispersion as it grew to administer a quarter of the world's population, but its subjects received their basic education from clerics. Such was even the case in Bengal, where the East India Company funded Hindu and Muslim schools. The alphabet invariably spread through religious teachings.

It was inevitable that Christian missionaries would be interested in language and literacy. Most of them believed that reading was a direct route for grace. On a daily basis, they tested their pupils with recitations and essays, and many of them composed and translated catechisms, prayer books, hymns and Bibles, primers, and spelling books. All such texts asserted that one must acknowledge God, that Christ died for everyone's salvation, that master and servant are both welcome in church, that you are a sinner, that there is life after death. At the same time, as missionaries knew, the Empire's peoples used their texts as they wished. Some of them regarded 'the book' as a charm or form of medicine, while others thought literacy was something that might come from a dream or vision. Hymns might be sung to praise nationalist politicians or beer. Even before missionaries lost their monopoly on the Empire's presses, 'print culture' had expanded beyond their reach.

Missionaries also wrote histories, genealogies, ethnographies, dictionaries, and grammars of 'their' people, for Europeans to read. Some such material became part of the heritage of ethnic and nationalist movements, while at the same time fuelling the concept of the 'tribe', the favoured sub-unit of imperial governance for African and Pacific peoples. For instance, civil cases entailed appeals to 'native law and custom', preferably written down, which turned history into a kind of eternal repetition. The dispersal of stereotypes in images and texts, coupled with racial science and administrative logistics, further imprinted this problematic concept in written histories. Yet tribes only resembled one another at a distance, differing greatly in what they stood for. The odd decision of French missionaries in Lesotho to use *li* for a syllable elsewhere written as *di*, for example, marked King Moshoeshoe's family dialect as a language, seSotho. Nearby a new affiliation emerged in an urban context, in which 'Shangaan' migrant labourers used the missionary Henri Junod's rendering of 'Amatonga' language, which was then taken up by black clerks and other 'Tsonga' professionals. Both Tsonga and Sotho became 'tribes' in apartheid South Africa.[1]

The commonness and consistency of Christian texts in newly alphabetic languages helped produce national identifications from the inside, among readers. Externally, the state was also more likely to recognize literate people with an administrative district and a magistrate. But the alphabet could also provide a forum for division. Mission presses, from Morija in southern Africa to Serampore in Bengal, both underwrote and challenged community identities. When missionaries encountered literate elites schooled in Arabic or Sanskrit, their teaching of English and their publications in vernaculars were rightly seen as destabilizing. Imperial officials were often leery of 'educated natives'.

This chapter examines the effects of the evangelical concern for language, translation, and literacy. To begin, a consideration of Yorubaland in Nigeria and Kikuyuland in Kenya demonstrates how colonized people used Christian-inflected languages in their nationalist projects. Contrastingly, examples from Oceania show how the comparative impulse in missionaries' scholarship could enfeeble subject peoples. In India, in multi-confessional and urbanized Bengal, literate elites played off one another in competing translational projects. Perhaps surprisingly, there, as well as in South Africa, early contests over the lexicons for divinity—a preoccupation of missionaries—left an indelible mark on populist movements later on.

Literate Nations: Yoruba and Kikuyu

What people do gives significance to what they say and write. Missionaries approached their work in this spirit, and looked for behaviours they might

---

[1] Benedict Anderson, *Imagined Communities*, 2nd edn. (New York, 1991); Roger Chartier, *The Cultural Uses of Print in Early Modern Europe* (Princeton, 1987); Patrick Harries, 'Exclusion, Classification and Internal Colonialism: The Emergence of Ethnicity among the Tsonga-Speakers of South Africa', in Leroy Vail, ed., *The Creation of Tribalism in Southern Africa* (London, 1989), pp. 82–117.

undermine. In Yorubaland they interrupted ordinary people's *orisa* sacrifices and stigmatized the tools of the *babalawo*, the *ifa* divination specialist, as Satan's things. In place of the *babalawo*'s attempt to access knowledge, they offered religious texts; in place of personal rites they advocated a 'washing' in the 'blood of the lamb', a sacrifice recapitulated in Communion. J. D. Y. Peel shows how such interactions permitted Christian nationalists to unite the 'Yoruba' in a communal identity. It is not that the prejudices that Oyo and other city-states bore one another were erased. Instead, Yoruba—originally a Hausa word used about Oyo—was produced as a sensibility worth competing for from the inside.

The Yoruba seized the status the Bible offered all nations of the world, just like Europeans had done, and interpreted Christianity as their own. They submitted *olorun* as 'the living God' and *eshu*, the trickster, as Satan. While God's wisdom contended with that of the *orisa*, eventually Moses became 'an Ibaden warlord', and *oduduwa* was demoted to Yoruba ethnic founder. Their modernizing ideal tapped Muslim (Hausa) as well as Christian traditions of literacy; Samuel Crowther's Yoruba dictionary of 1843 even chose the word 'alufa' ('Muslim cleric') for Christ's own priesthood. Literate Brazilian and Cuban entrepreneurs and evangelists further moulded Yoruba identity, as they did other cults and ethnicities on the shores of the 'Black Atlantic'.[2] The evangelical pan-Africanist Orishatukeh Faduma (b. William Davis) hypothesized that God had always been a universal conception even in *orisa*, which further explained concordances. James Johnson's *Yoruba Heathenism* (1899) and Samuel Johnson's monumental *History of the Yorubas* (1897) both made sense of the past as a prelude to contemporary Yoruba assertiveness.

The following 'myth' told by a senior diviner for royalty about a 'brother' of Olorun (God?) named Ela concerns literacy and *ifa* divination. Ela was 'the father of the diviners. In the morning all the Whitemen used to come to Ela to learn how to read and write, and in the evening all his African children, the babalawo, gathered around him to memorize the Ifa verses and learn divination. Ifa taught them to write on their Ifa boards...'. The verse continues: Muslims turned the Ifa boards into wooden writing tablets, and

---

[2] Adrian Hastings, *The Construction of Nationhood: Ethnicity, Religion and Nationalism* (New York, 1997); Lorand J. Matory, 'The English Professors of Brazil: On the Diasporic Roots of the Yoruba Nation', *Comparative Studies in Society and History*, XLI (1999), pp. 72–103; J. D. Y. Peel, *Religious Encounter and the Making of the Yoruba* (Bloomington, Ind., 2000); Stephan Palmié, *Wizards and Scientists: Explorations in Afro-Cuban Modernity and Tradition* (Durham, NC, 2002).

Christians, into slates and books. Yoruba culture is in this way asserted to lie behind even the inscription of Yoruba nationalism.[3]

On the other side of Africa, among the hearty farmers of Kenya's central highlands, the introduction of Christianity likewise accompanied the formation of a broader identity. Previously, political organization was 'local government gone mad', according to John Lonsdale, a zone of masculine competitiveness, much as was the case in Yorubaland. Mutual comprehension meant contestation. Again similarly God was already known by Muslim traders, this time Swahili ones, and 'Ngai'—the word for God in the Kikuyu Bible—was a loan word (Maasai).[4] The first generation of students, called *athomi*, or 'readers', made these ideas 'Kikuyu'. *Athomi* joined their pre-colonial codes of obligation and work to a new narrative of the self, one 'prefigured' in the Bible: 'endurance, improvement and salvation'.[5] Their translations supported their argument for recognizing an *ituika*, the lapsed tradition of once-per-generation rupture and independence. The 'readers' called letters of the alphabet 'cuts' or 'stripes', so their writing itself evoked the act of 'chopping trees', the emblematic work of mature Kikuyu masculinity. By altering orthography to fit Anglophonic conventions, by espousing textually anchored truth, *athomi* helped make their own political project 'thinkable'.

The 'readers' held their Kikuyuness in a universalizing idiom. This was so even when it came to clitoridectomy and circumcision rites. In a well-known debate the African Inland Mission (AIM) denounced clitoridectomy, and *athomi* stood by it. The readers pointed out that the Bible describes the Virgin as a *muiritu*, a circumcised woman. They allied with their non-Christian kin, thus joining them as fellow Kikuyu, against the AIM 'loyalists', the missionaries and some senior men. At another point the AIM favoured mandatory clitoridectomy for pubescent girls, done 'surgically', through chiefs' authority. In both cases *athomi* supported the sanctity of the female-controlled domain of reproduction against intervention, and did so

---

[3] William R. Bascom, *Sixteen Cowries: Yoruba Divination from Africa to the New World* (Bloomington, Ind., 1980); Moses N. More, *Orishatukeh Faduma: Liberal Theology and Evangelical Pan-Africanism, 1857–1946* (Lanham, Md., 1996).

[4] Richard Waller, 'Kidongoi's Kin: Prophecy and Power in Masaailand', in D. M. Anderson and D. Johnson, eds., *Revealing Prophets* (London, 1995), pp. 28–64.

[5] Derek Peterson, *Creative Writing: Translation, Bookkeeping, and the Work of Imagination in Colonial Kenya* (Portsmouth, NH, 2004); John Lonsdale, 'Kikuyu Christianities: A History of Intimate Diversity', in D. Maxwell, ed., *Christianity and the African Imagination* (Leiden, 2002), pp. 157–97.

in the name of Kikuyuness. In his Kikuyu ethnography *Facing Mount Kenya* (1938) the future president Jomo Kenyatta put forth more of the same associations. Ngai was always already God; *irua* for girls (clitoridectomy) is likened to surgery, and an icy river becomes their anaesthetic. Their instruction is like a 'school', and the genital-cutting is done with the 'dexterity of a Harley street surgeon'. Thus Kikuyu registered in the family of nations.[6]

The Mau Mau insurgency of the 1950s again contested Kikuyu ethics, albeit with weapons, and again Christian language played a role. Presbyterian students erased the name 'Jesus Christ' from their hymnbooks and pencilled in 'Jomo Kenyatta'. The African Independent Pentecostal Church, adopting the Bible as their sole doctrinal authority, permitted *irua* and wrote out a genealogy for themselves going back to the apostles. *Athomi* taught English and writing in independent schools. The government closed them, and banned anti-AIM hymns, if to little effect. Surely it was enormously empowering that Ngai turned out to be omnipotent, but an omnipotent being is often a content being. In the end, as Kikuyu Christianities multiplied, and as Ngai expanded his realms, Kikuyuness no longer entailed access to open land and honourable work. John Lonsdale has argued that Christianity 'clarified' the nature of being Kikuyu, its 'base metal', and that Mau Mau furthered the same process through violence. But Mau Mau was also about land and freedom, which Ngai could not himself bring.[7]

Pacific Translations

The first Pacific islanders' interactions with Europeans were 'dialogues of the deaf' held offshore or on the beach. James Cook described how in 1769 a Maori man went about Cook's ship 'touching this and that ... [when] any new thing caught his attention he shouted as loud as he could for some

---

[6] David Sandgren, *Christianity and the Kikuyu* (New York, 1989), pp. 73 ff.; Jomo Kenyatta, *Facing Mount Kenya* (London, 1938), p. 140; B. A. Ogot, 'Politics, Culture and Music in Central Kenya: A Study of Mau Mau Hymns, 1951–1956', *Kenya Historical Review*, V (1977), pp. 275–86; John Lonsdale, ' "Listen While I Read": The Orality of Christian Literacy in the Young Kenyatta's Making of the Kikuyu', in L. de la Gorgendière, ed., *Ethnicity in Africa: Roots, Meanings and Implications* (Edinburgh, 1996), pp. 17–53.

[7] V. Neckbrouke, 'Onzième Commandment: Étiology divine, église independente au pied du Mont Kenya', *Nouvelle Review de Science Missionaire*, XXVII (1978), pp. 316 ff., Lynn Thomas, *Politics of the Womb: Women, Reproduction, and the State in Kenya* (Berkeley, 2003); Bruce Berman and John Lonsdale, *Unhappy Valley: Conflict in Kenya and Africa* (Athens, OH, 1992), pp. 265–504; Lonsdale, 'Kikuyu Christianities', p. 161.

minutes without directing his speech either to us or to any one of his countrymen'.[8] Such a performance implied the existence of a script or formula, a shadow text that a prayer book might replace. Thirty-four years later, on Christmas Day 1813, Samuel Marsden preached his first sermon to New Zealanders, drawing on Luke 2: 10, and no one understood him either, the preacher admonishing them 'not to mind that now'. The field of comparative Oceanic religion began with these incomprehensions. Thomas Kendall, in Marsden's Anglican mission, was the first literate practitioner.[9] With the assistance of northern *hapu* chiefs, he produced a Lord's Prayer and a grammar, following the method 'laid down in the Sanscrit Grammars' of Christian linguists in India (more about which below). Kendall tried to distinguish identities from concepts. The wife of a culture hero could not be the Virgin Mary, but the word 'atua' could express 'the Divinity', because *atua* was not a personage. Apparently Maori as in Tangata Maori already meant 'we autochthones' in the eighteenth century. Prayer books and portions of Scripture were translated, '*w[h]akamoari*', meaning 'us-ified' into 'the language of New Zealand'. In 1837 William Colenso of the London Missionary Society (LMS) completed a New Testament, the *KoTeKawenata-Hou*, standardizing the northern dialect.[10] It was from this time that 'Maori' became an ethnicity, and that white settlers' numbers grew, soon to eclipse them.

In general the Pacific posed a great challenge: hundreds of languages each with tiny numbers of speakers; vast and turbulent seas separating populations; ritualized violence and hostility on individual islands. While most share a basic grammar, their lexicons differ greatly. It was and is common for adults to know two or three of them. In Papua New Guinea some 760 languages have been counted, a third of which have fewer than 500 speakers; several dozen are spoken by a village's worth of fishwives. Thus it was not possible to follow the example of Colenso with the northern *hapu* 'Maori'.[11] The Anglican pioneer George Selwyn began his mission by teaching himself to read Maori aboard ship, with a copy of Colenso's *KoTeKawenataHou*—or

---

[8] Nicolas Thomas, *Cook* (New York, 2003), pp. 53, 65.

[9] Alfred Penny, *Ten Years in Melanesia* (London, 1888), p. 16.

[10] Personal communications from Doug Munro (in 1990), Courtney Handman, Marie-Paule Robitaille, and (for the Maori quotation) Ross Clark and Mark Laws.

[11] Illaitia S. Tuwere, 'What Is Contextual Theology? A View from Oceania', and Sr. Keiiti Ann Kauongata'a, 'Why Contextual?', *Pacific Journal of Theology*, sec. 2, XXVII (2000), pp. 7–20, 21–40.

rather, he taught himself to read the *KoTeKawenataHou*—and at 'St Johns' on Norfolk Island he studied for two weeks with a local man translating a bit of Scripture into his vernacular version. Then he learnt that the man's dialect was limited to half the southern tip of the island. Ultimately the solution Selwyn found was the same that Marsden adopted: the daily work of resident missions would be assigned to indigenously 'Pacific' pastors who could settle and learn languages related to their own. (See pp. 135–36.) The result was great variety in linguistic practices and strategies in evangelism.

In Melanesia two creole languages eventually predominated: the 'Motu' of the colonial police (which first drew personnel from Motu Island), and 'Pisin Tok', pidgin talk, which emerged among Pacific migrant workers on Samoan coconut plantations. People learnt them in addition to their natal tongue, and neither became a national identity. When Melanesian Christians shouted 'I know the one true God' to identify themselves to other boats, they used the English word 'God'. As Pacific pastors are aware, it was missionaries' desire to communicate in English that brought Oceania as a concept into being.[12] In many cases, 'government and church seem to have been blended and overlaid' in South Pacific societies. In the Loyalty Islands antagonistic Catholic and Protestant factions of chiefs, abetted by competing missionaries, repackaged their conflicts as 'religious wars'. Their pastors later disseminated their understandings of Christianity westward. Lay evangelists on Tuvalu used hymns 'inappropriately' and formed their own 'ekalesia'. After a Solomon Islands pastor–chief, Soga, extended his dominion by preaching against local raids and killings ('headhunting'), the title Soga was taken by paramount chiefs. Anglicans in the Solomons associated themselves with a *vunagi kiloau*, or 'church masters' council—Soga II competed with one—much as a *samaj* ('society') of elders and churchmen emerged among the Rishi (Untouchables) of the Ganges plain, and much as cattle-owning Christians occupied kingships in central and southern

---

[12] David Hilliard, *God's Gentlemen: A History of the Melanesian Mission, 1849–1942* (St Lucia, Qld, 1978), p. 34; David Hanlon, 'God vs. Gods: The First Years of the Micronesian Mission in Ponope', *Journal of Pacific History*, XIX (1984), pp. 41–59; Michael Goldsmith and Doug Munro, 'Conversion and Church Formation in Tuvalu', *Journal of Pacific History*, XXVII (June 1992), p. 51; D. C. Laycock, 'Melanesian Linguistic Diversity: A Melanesian Choice?', in R. J. May and Hank Nelson, eds., *Melanesia: Beyond Diversity*, 2 vols. (Canberra, 1982), I, pp. 33–6; Jeremy Beckett, *Torres Strait Islanders: Custom and Colonialism* (Cambridge, 1987).

Africa. Authority and Christianity spoke the same language, and tended to overlap in many parts of the Empire.[13]

It fell to Selwyn's junior colleague Robert Codrington to attempt the first broad-based study of Oceanic languages in the 1860s. Not only did Codrington compile the Police (*Pai*) *Motu* dictionary, but he also mastered the rudiments of forty other languages, writing a massive comparative grammar. Codrington's texts established the Oceanic meaning of *mana*, a word found everywhere, even in New Zealand, as 'an invisible spiritual force or influence' deriving from the ancestors; 'the Melanesian mind is entirely possessed by the belief' in *mana*, 'a supernatural power or influence'. Pacific religion was all about *mana*, its pursuit and deployment. In his 1911 study *History of Melanesian Society* the anthropologist W. H. R. Rivers also accepted *mana*, after conducting his research aboard the Anglican mission ship *The Southern Cross*, his main informant the son of a 'native pastor'. Raymond Firth, in *Tikopia* (1940), further Christianized its meaning as 'soul substance'.[14]

Recent scholarship suggests *mana* originally meant only that something 'worked', with nothing spiritual in it. According to Roger Keesing, it connoted 'to be efficacious', as opposed to *drevi*, 'useless'. In this view, Pacific missionaries brought *mana* into being as a spiritual concept so they could replace it with a Christian alternative. *Mana* was about ambition and the exertion of will, whereas grace, which the Christian cherished, was something one received. It was *mana*'s inscription in this opposition that made it exterior and receivable, and requiring faith. Codrington seems to have harboured doubts about *mana*'s spirituality, but it was his study *The Melanesians* that defined it so, effectively casting Pacific people's efforts to be powerful in life, to have 'juice', as a superstition.[15]

---

[13] Anne Salmond, *Two Worlds: First Meetings between Maori and Europeans, 1642–1772* (Auckland, 1991), p. 112; K. R. Howe, *Nation, Culture, and History: The 'Knowing' of Oceania* (Honolulu, 2000), p. 14; Geoffrey M. White, *Identity through History: Living Stories in a Solomon Islands Society* (Cambridge, 1991), pp. 94 ff.; Tom Dutton, 'The Missionary Response to Language Division: The Papuan Example', in May and Nelson, eds., *Melanesia*; Cosimo Zene, *The Rishi of Bangladesh: A History of Christian Dialogues* (New York, 2002), pp. 142–7.

[14] R. Codrington, *The Melanesian Languages* (Oxford, 1885), p. 52; R. Codrington and J. Palmer, *Dictionary of the Language of Mota* (London, 1896), 66; R. Codrington, *The Melanesians: Studies in their Anthropology and Folklore* (1891; repr. New Haven, 1957), pp. 188, 121; George Stocking, Jr., *After Tylor: British Social Anthropology, 1888–1951* (Madison, 1995).

[15] Roger Keesing, 'Rethinking *Mana*', *Journal of Anthropological Research*, XL (1984), pp. 137–56; Malcolm J. Ruel, *Belief, Ritual and the Securing of Life: Reflective Essays on a Bantu Religion* (Leiden, 1997).

Pacific people also wrested control of Christian language themselves. Although the first Maori baptism occurred in 1825, by the 1860s nearly all Maori represented themselves as normative Christians, regardless of what missionaries thought. On the East Coast, the Revd William Williams found Maori eager to internalize Christian ideas, and he was crushed when his church later lost nearly all its members to the Kereopa, the local manifestation of the great Pai Marire insurgency in 1865 (See pp. 82–83 and 226–27.). In many respects, however, Kereopa was quite close to Maori Christianity, though it was politicized differently. Even the 'Maori high god', Io, was apparently adapted from Scripture. As J. Z. Smith argues, it derived from a Taranaki Maori's vision of Gabriel in September 1861, at a critical juncture in the insurrection. From that point on Io appeared as the equal and opposite protagonist to the 'God' of the Southern Cross. The name was a refitting of Ihowa, or Jehovah. As Smith aptly remarks, *homo religiosus* is essentially *homo faber*.[16]

The Baptists of Bengal

Captain Cook's *Voyages* inspired an apprentice cobbler in Northampton, William Carey, to seek a missionary career in Tahiti. Initially rebuffed as a 'miserable enthusiast', Carey co-founded the Baptist Missionary Society (BMS) in 1792 and went to India the following year. He settled at Serampore, under Danish protection, because the British East India Company barred him from their territory, believing that missionaries would subvert order. In fact the Company disciplined the Governor of Madras for using the word 'heathen' in his correspondence and posted offerings at major Hindu shrines. India, although denied parity with the West, was not viewed as lacking in structure or civilization as were Africans and Pacific peoples.[17] Carey, William Ward, and Joshua Marshman were known as the Serampore

---

[16] Kay Sanderson, 'Maori Christianity on the East Coast', *New Zealand Journal of History*, XVII (1983), pp. 166–84; Jonathan Z. Smith, *Imagining Religion: From Babylon to Jonestown* (Chicago, 1982), p. 92.

[17] Brian Stanley, *The History of the Baptist Missionary Society, 1792–1992* (Edinburgh, 1992); W. Carey, *An Enquiry into the Obligations of Christians to Use Means for the Conversion of the Heathen* (1792; repr. London, 1961); Eustace Carey, *Memoir of William Carey* (Boston, 1836), p. 68; John Clarke Marshman, *The Life and Times of Carey, Marshman, and Ward*, 2 vols. (London, 1859); Daniel Potts, *British Baptist Missionaries in India, 1793–1837* (Cambridge, 1967), p. 124; Gauri Viswanatha, ' "Coping with (Civil) Death": The Christian Convert's Right of Passage in Colonial India', in Gyan Prakash, ed., *After Colonialism* (New York, 1994), pp. 198–200.

Trio. (See p. 108.) Their families created a super-domestic unit, sharing their finances and possessions. Carey's involvement with indigo plantings at Mudnabati served both economic necessity and the principle of self-sufficiency. The constraints and prejudices of caste reminded him of the class snobbery he knew in England. The Trio handed out pamphlets and accosted upper-caste Brahmans in 'debates' that were soon found to be intolerable.[18]

Unlike the Pacific or Africa, in India there was a profound literate tradition in Nagari and a prior history of language work. The first European Christians had arrived in 1498 to find an existing population of Thomas Christians. In 1706 Danish Protestant missionaries reached Tranquebar in the south. The Jesuits wrote an influential 'Q. & A.' dialogue in vernacular Bengali in 1599, and a Portuguese Bengali grammar appeared in 1743. After Clive's conquest of Bengal, the work accelerated. The Revd William Jones wrote a Persian and Sanskrit grammar in 1771 and 1786. Warren Hastings hired pandits to compile 'Hindu law' from all the shastric literatures, their output supervised by Nathaniel B. Halhed, which produced the *Code of Gentoo Laws* in 1768; Halhed also wrote a Bengali grammar in 1778, Father Paulinus, Sancto Bartholomeo one in 1790, and H. P. Foster a dictionary in 1802.

Carey appears to have worked on his many Bible translations with but little reference to these predecessors. His first was Bengali, in 1802. With it he embarrassed the cosmopolitan pretensions of the BMS's fund-raising by baldly translating 'baptize' as 'immerse' in Bengali. He argued that the word 'baptiso', John the Baptist's act, meant 'immerse' in Greek, and so constrained him in his choices. Carey's diary shows him obsessed with language, disciplined, and scholastic. From dawn to starlight he typically prayed, translated, studied an Indian language with a pandit, studied Greek and Hebrew on his own, practised his Sunday homiletics, and then prayed again.[19] New missionaries in Calcutta did not like being directed by the Trio, which separated from the BMS in 1827. Even after forty years in Bengal, detractors noted, Serampore had only forty-three converts in good standing.

---

[18] Brian Stanley, 'Some Problems in Writing a Mission History Today', in Rosemary Seton and Robert Bickers, eds., *Missionary Encounters: Sources and Issues* (London, 1996), p. 46; Stanley, *History of the Baptist Missionary Society*, p. 67; and Geoffrey A. Oddie, 'Constructing Hinduism: The Impact of the Protestant Mission on Hindu Self-Understanding', in R. Frykenberg, ed., *Christians and Missionaries in India: Cross-cultural Communication since 1500* (London, 2001), p. 169.

[19] Carey's letters in *Periodical Accounts Relative to the Baptist Missionary Society*, vols. I–V (London, 1800–15), vol. V, p. 490.

Carey employed teams of pandits of diverse backgrounds, most of them non-Christian and English-speaking. They knew about God, Jesus, and Muhammad from their own contacts. Once it became clear that many of Bengal's languages were related to one another and to Sanskrit, it remained to translate the Bible into Sanskrit. This was done in 1810 and became an *ur*-text for Serampore, paralleling the Greek Septuagint's relationship to the Standard Bible. None of the translations remained in use for as long as the Sanskrit, their interpretative linchpin; and it fell into desuetude after only thirty years. Carey's system produced Oriya, Hindi, Assamese, Hindustani (Urdu), Marathi, Pashto, and Punjabi translations of the New Testament in the decades that followed. Among Carey's dictionaries, the Marathi is really a smallish lexicon, ordered in Nagari according to roots which could be located in Sanskrit; the definitions are English. Several of the Bibles were criticized as structurally erratic, their sentences formed according to English grammar. Carey, however, also wrote Indian-language grammars, beginning with Bengali (1805), and he revised his Bibles in subsequent printings.[20]

In 1811 Serampore's press published William Ward's long book *An Account of the Writings, Religion, and Manners of the Hindoos*, a work revealing of the Trio's perspective. Instead of seeing Hinduism from within, riven as it was by competing movements of reform, Ward viewed it from the outside, a totality he divided into unequal compartments: literature, philosophy, architecture, prayers, medicine, cults, sacrifices, law, astronomy, etc. Ward argued theologically against Hindu ideas, and also highlighted their 'impurity and cruelty'.[21] Hinduism's idolatry was 'disgusting', especially in condoning sexual outrages and featuring ecstatic pain. Ward called *sati*, or widow-burning, an offence against humanity, and decried the withholding of education from women. It cannot be denied that compared to the *alufa* and the imam, Christian missionaries were more apt to welcome girls into their classrooms. Most of all, Ward discerned in Hindu myths that the eternal and omnipotent God is given by many names, with none of them adequate. Some parts of him are represented as Brumhu ('both the clay and the potter', 'invisible', 'perfect'), others are not. Ward used 'Brumhu' (or 'Brahma', 'Brahmo') as a name for God, but specific narratives were rejected, for

[20] W. Carey, *A Dictionary of the Mahratta Language* (Serampore, 1810); Stanley, *History of the Baptist Missionary Society*, pp. 57 ff.; Stewart Gordon, *The Marathas, 1600–1818* (Cambridge, 1993).

[21] W. Ward, *An Account of the Writings, Religion, and Manners of the Hindoos*, 2 vols. (Serampore, 1811), I, pp. 1, xxxvii.

instance that Brumhu 'lusted' after his own daughter. In other respects Vishnu, who came before Brumhu, or Krishna or Shiva were like God.[22]

The *Account* derived from the Trio's conversations with Serampore's translators. One 'educated Brahman' told Carey, 'God was a great light, and as no one could see him, he became incarnate under the three-fold character of Brumha, Beesho, and Seeb.' Such were 'errant beliefs' about God associated with 'their own deities'. In other words the Trio was fashioning a single godhead from scraps of Hindu lore, literature, and law. For example, Carey's Marathi dictionary defines a single word as 'the staff or beam of a plough' and 'The Lord, God'. Secondarily, God (defined as 'he who fixes the situation of all') is nested among derivations of the root signifying pedestal, temple, heaven, sacred, idol, providential, revelation, and fate. The result of all such work was to translate prior mythology and customs as a set of mistakes, or lies, behind which one might glimpse a vestige of higher truth without a single sufficient appellation.

Serampore is recognized as the fountain of Indian vernacular publishing largely through the efforts of Brahman translators about whom little is known.[23] They worked on Joshua Marshman's *Dig-Darshan* ('Signpost'), the precursor of the *Samachan Darpan* ('News Mirror'), from 1818, a pioneering Indian newspaper. Vidyalankar and Ram Basu were two of the translators; Ram Mohun Roy was briefly another. Vidyalankar became a leading exponent of anti-reformist Hindu orthodoxy, and Ram Mohun Roy became the father of modern Hindu reformism. In a process reminiscent of Yoruba, Kikuyu, and Maori situations, Roy drafted the translated God into a prior Hindu tradition, 'returning' to the 'great light' behind specific Hindu incarnations (the very corruptions Ward denounced). Roy adhered to Unitarianism aside from denying the expiatory nature of Christ's death, and he launched his organization Brahmo Sahba ('council' or 'congress') by filing a deed to build a church.[24] Renovation had long been a dimension of Hindu intellectual life, and for a while one could be a Hindu Christian; complementarily, the idea arose that Hindus 'had their own distinctive... *religious*

---

[22] Ibid., I, pp. cxi, cxl, 81–4.

[23] Carey to Ryland, 14 Oct. 1815, in *Periodical Accounts Relative to the Baptist Missionary Society*, vol. V, pp. 163–6; see also pp. 338 and 482.

[24] David Kopf, *The Brahmo Samaj and the Shaping of the Modern Indian Mind* (Princeton, 1979); R. E. Frykenberg, 'The Construction of Hinduism at the Nexus of History and Religion', *Journal of Interdisciplinary History*, XXIII (1993), pp. 523–50; Richard F. Young, *Resistant Hinduism: Sanskrit Sources on Anti-Christian Apologetics in Early Nineteenth Century India* (Vienna, 1981).

system', or *dharma*.[25] In 1843 Debendranath Tagore changed Roy's organization to the well-known progressive Brahmo Samaj (Transcendent Deity Society). The Ramanandis, a sect devoted to Rama (Vishnu), rejected caste and proselytized among the poor; they spread the Hindi version of the Ramayana, which Carey and Marshman had translated into English, in the newly cost-effective medium of movable type. Other reformers made Krishna into a masculine, righteous deity, projecting the triumphal colonial strength of Christianity back into the Hindu past, 'updating' Roy.[26] And there remained Serampore's Brumhu, his light now clear of Vedic particularities.

The Tswana: How Ancestor Became God

Missionaries in Bengal helped usher into being new social identities with familiar lexical material. This section traces how missionaries turned a single concept, 'ancestor' (*modimo*, pl. *badimo*), into God, and looks at the reverberations of this translation. The account here differs from previous scholarship, not least in contextualizing the particular interactions through which translation happens.[27]

Today the word 'Tswana' denotes both a language and an ethnic identity. Originally the term (*-chuana*) appears to have meant to be 'similar'. As in Kikuyuland and Yorubaland, a common field of comprehension meant a common field of conflict. Tswana patriarchs fought to keep their populations in 'proper Bechuana towns' where authority and production could be recouped. They made alliances through marriages, including with Korana, the Khoe-speaking people of the Orange River. They rustled cattle, killed one another in raids, and absorbed their scattering peoples, always seeking to establish themselves—with their penumbral genealogies—as rulers.[28] At the

[25] Oddie, 'Constructing Hinduism', citing Cynthia Talbot, 'Inscribing the Self: Hindu–Muslim Identities in Colonial India', *Comparative Studies in Society and History*, XXXVII, 4 (1995), pp. 692–722.

[26] Ashis Nandy, *The Intimate Enemy: Loss and Recovery of Self under Colonialism* (New Delhi, 1983), p. 26.

[27] For other interpretations, see Lamin Sanneh, *Translating the Message: The Missionary Impact on Culture* (Maryknoll, NY, 1989), pp. 171 ff.; David Chidester, *Savage Systems: Colonialism and Comparative Religion in Southern Africa* (Charlottesville, Va., 1996); Jean and John L. Comaroff, *Of Revelation and Revolution*, 2 vols. (Chicago, 1991, 1997), I, pp. 214 ff., II, pp. 76, 110 ff.; William Worger, 'Parsing God: Conversations about the Meaning of Words in Nineteenth Century South Africa', *Journal of African History*, XLII, (2001), pp. 417–47.

[28] Robert Ross, *Adam Kok's Griquas* (Cambridge, 1976); Elizabeth Elbourne, *Blood Ground: Colonialism, Missions, and the Contest for Christianity in the Cape Colony and Britain, 1799–1853* (Montreal, 2002), pp. 220 ff., 320 ff.

end of the eighteenth century cultural, new religious, and racial pluralisms entered Tswana territory from the colonized parts of the Cape Colony. Tswana people often outnumbered the métis people they joined for military protection, who often spoke seTswana. Records show also the interpenetration of ex-slaves, Korana, and San (Bushmen) with Tswana, and the existence of markets in ivory, beads, captives, and iron involving foreign partners. Dutch-speaking 'bushmen' (with cattle) accompanied Tswana leaders on diplomatic missions. Christianity flowed through these various patriarchies like electricity as they vied for guns and trade, legitimacy, safety, and wealth.

In 1813 John Campbell of the LMS, together with a party of local evangelists and Griqua 'captains', including Adam Kok, arrived at Dithakong. They came to parley with Mothibi, the Tswana 'chief' of 'the Bachapees' (meaning thus: ba- (people of) Tlhaping, the eponymous kingly ancestor), and the 'Bastard Captains' living under his authority. As Mothibi was away hunting, Campbell decided to talk to some royal women.

Mahooto the queen...was averse to our going away [before Mothibi returned]...we explained to her the nature of a letter. Mr. [William] Anderson showed her one he had got from his wife...that Adam Kok had brought it, yet did not know anything that was in it...by the use of the wax[.] The bible was lying on our table, which gave rise to our explaining the nature and use of a book, and particularly that book. That it informed us of God who made all things; of the beginning of all things which seemed to astonish her very much, and many a look was directed toward the bible.

In the complex multilingual conversation that followed, missionaries may have noticed someone speaking the word 'moreemo' (ancestor: *modimo*), because Campbell henceforth used it to name God. So did the Revd James Read, who had consecrated the status of many of the region's most powerful evangelists. Read held up the Book and said gravely, 'The people that lived in darkness have seen a great light; light has dawned on those who lived in the land of death's dark shadow,' and again all this, even 'death's dark shadow', had to be (doubly) translated. Mahutu posed questions that had 'previously occurred to her'. She asked, 'Will people who are dead rise up again? Is God under the earth or where is he?'—showing clearly that she too viewed the matter under discussion as concerned with ancestors and death.[29]

As late as 1827 it was not established that this Tswana term (*modimo*) would become the regional signifier for God. Korana and 'Bastard' or 'Griqua' (métis) power brokers on the high veld saw no profit in the

---

[29] Campbell to the Secretary of the LMS, 27 July 1813, CWM, LMS In-letters, 5/2/D.

translation; in 1812 a Khoe-speaking interpreter equated 'mooléemo' with the Dutch word for 'devil', and Mothibi himself spoke the Kora native to his mother and his wife.[30] The Griqua accompanying Campbell made Mothibi nervous, who greeted Campbell by saying, 'you needn't have brought Captain Kok with you for safe passage'. Métis people were the dominant power on the high veld. Jan Hendricks, for instance, besides being a deacon and pastor for the LMS, was a magistrate of the fledgling Griqua polity. Mothibi was nonetheless persuaded to receive 'the teaching' by the following exercise. The Revd Anderson asked Mothibi the names of his 'predecessors in government', wrote them down on a scrap of paper, and read them aloud, ostensibly to demonstrate the power of writing. From Mothibi's point of view, the recital was a public inscription of his own descent from legitimizing ancestors back to the recognized founder–king, Tlhaping, *and logically*, to the very 'ancestor' that Anderson offered as the greatest king of all. Mothibi reiterated his position in the new lineage in his response: 'Let the missionaries come. I will be a father to them.'

In the complicated politics of the frontier, the mixed Cape-descended 'Captains' living nominally under Mothibi subsequently raised objections, probably to the Christian 'Basters' who would come with any missionary. Over the next three years Mothibi stalled the LMS, but a fresh band came to implore Mothibi to keep his promise, including a West Indian (Corner), Cupido Kakkerlak, at least one Tswana Christian, and several of Kok's men. In 1816 Jan Hendricks and James Read settled beside Mothibi's town with twenty-nine parishioners and their families from the Griqua town of Bethelsdorp. During one of his early services Read discovered that many of the 'chiefs' (*dikgosi*) thought 'modimo' was a way for Read to refer to himself. Thereafter Hendricks took over the preaching.[31]

As Christianity expanded, 'modimo' developed further usages. Not only could it signify a missionary, but also power, past kings, the station of one's ethnonym, or even a living king whose rule united a nation. Ancestors involved the powers of collective action and patrimony, so 'a cow with a wet nose', a breeder that might produce wealth and (therefore) human dependants, was 'ancestor'. A woman who married among Mothibi's people claimed to speak to *modimo* daily, demanding gifts of livestock for her

---

[30] William J. Burchell, *Travels in the Interior of South Africa* (repr. London, 1953), 550.

[31] Karel Schoeman, ed., *The Mission at Griquatown, 1801–1821* (Griquatown, 1997), p. 17; Schoeman, *The Griqua Captaincy of Philippolis, 1826–1861* (Menlopark, 2002), pp. 13, 24; Elbourne, *Blood Ground*, pp. 197–206.

blessings. A freelancing preacher, Stephanus, disseminated what missionaries called a 'false' theology in advance of their own work. (See p. 144.) 'Modimo' became a contested notion in common speech. A woman caught stealing meat from a Kora captain explained herself by saying, 'she could not help it, as *modimo* told her to'. By this did she mean 'ancestor' or 'The Ancestor' (God)? How could one know, with no definite article 'the' in the Tswana language? In time it became clear that Mothibi's alliance with 'teachers of the message of (the) ancestor' had not paid off. While guns helped him in battle, he remained vulnerable to guerrilla attacks and in 1820 had to repair to the Griqua statelet of Andries Waterboer, who superintended his own version of an LMS church.[32]

A Methodist missionary, Samuel Broadbent, brought further complications, coming from Ceylon, where he felt he had seen 'diabolic ceremonies' and 'demon-worship'. As he travelled through the disturbed frontier zone of the Dithakong ('Lattakoo') region, patriarchs threw themselves at his feet, begging his party to keep close by, holding hostages, taking their cattle. His colleague Thomas Hodgson even witnessed cannibalism born of starvation. Although virtually all his papers were incinerated in 1824, a lexicon survives. Relying on a métis Dutch-speaking interpreter, Broadbent rendered 'Badeem' (*badimo*, ancestors) as 'the Devil', and, as he had in Ceylon, he diabolized South Africa's 'heathendom', shaping antitheses of his own prescriptions into 'naturally occurring' instances of traditional religion. Broadbent altered the spelling of the root (*-dimo*) from its appearance in 'God', which was 'Mulimo or Mudeemo' in the same list, to '-deem' as if 'badeem' were a one-off singular on its own. The LMS missionary Robert Moffat initially agreed, commenting that 'badimo' had no plural. (In the Pacific 'atua' had embraced a competitive pantheon before becoming God.) Broadbent's first attempts at public preaching in Tswana avoided the word 'modimo' itself. Instead he read out his version of the Lord's Prayer, with its deployment of 'father'. He asked a group 'of the more intelligent' villagers to repeat after him, a rote recitation without any evident content:

Hara oa rona u mo ligudimong ('Father, our, who art above.') I then asked, whether they knew who was meant by our Father above? *No*, was the general answer; we do not know who you mean. Addressing one of our cattle watchers by

---

[32] Hoyt Alverson, *Mind in the Heart of Darkness: Value and Self-Identity among the Tswana of Southern Africa* (New Haven, 1978), pp. 125–6, 178; Journal of Thomas Hodgson, CWM, WMMS.

name, Roboque ['Broken'], don't you know who it is we speak to in these words? He burst out in laughter; no, said he, I have no father above![33]

One did have fathers, not above, but below, where the dead were buried. Yet Broadbent would not say, 'Our father who art below'. Instead he propounded a kind of camouflaged genealogy:

I was at a stand for a moment, but soon replied, You know that we exist, and descended from our progenitors, and they from theirs, and so on to the first of human kind; but who gave them being?' Several voices answered, '*Mudeemo*'. I then spoke of the earth and heavens, and remarked they also had a beginning and must have had a producing cause, for you know, from nothing, nothing can proceed; who then, I further asked, is the great first cause of all? Again they replied, *Mudeemo*.

'Who had the most power, the most long ago?' elicited the answer, 'An ancestor!' Having orchestrated a comprehensible dialogue, how far would Broadbent go in making God more like an ancestor? He and his colleagues were already alarmed by the word's variety of uncontrolled uses. A visitor called the Revd Hodgson 'Modimo', clapping his hands, in appreciation of how he had drop-forged lead shot in a water bucket. It was not clear whom missionaries were talking about when they spoke of Modimo. 'Has he hair as we have?' people asked Moffat. 'Have you seen him?' 'Modimo' was shouted in pain, said of clever people, even fast horses. Most troubling, confided Broadbent in his diary, was that people made the 'traditionary [*sic*], though inconsistent statement of Mudeemo proceeding from beneath some mountain', though it is unclear if one ancestor or one of many might so proceed. Broadbent preached mostly about 'father', 'king', and 'king of kings', and he hoped missionaries would adopt the term 'Jehovah'. But if people said 'tell me about a/the ancestor', one necessarily obliged, while stressing that 'there was, and could be but one, *Mudeemo*, [and] that He is Eternal...'.

The dominant personality among South African LMS agents in the field was Robert Moffat, who, at the time he sent Broadbent his translation of John 1, seemed well on the way to a definitive version of the rest of the Gospels. Moffat used 'Modimo' to mean God, although he nursed doubts, seeing the indigenous idea (not his comprehension of it) as ambiguous, an 'unknown force' below ground.[34] Further he considered using a word built

---

[33] Samuel Broadbent, 'Reminiscences', notebook 'Second Part', CWM, WMMS, Missionaries' Papers, box 600 and following.

[34] Moffat to LMS, 16 Apr. 1819, CWM, LMS In-letters, 8/1/A.

on 'great', possibly 'mogolo' or 'mogologolo' (a doubling for emphasis), which would have made God a cognate of the term chosen by Nguni speakers (*unkulunkulu*). Broadbent felt Moffat still lacked sufficient command of Tswana, a judgement confirmed by Mrs Moffat even in 1827; that year Moffat went to remedy his deficiency by moving up-country for four months, living in the company of non-Christian Tswana companions in a remote cattle-post settlement.[35] The following year he finished the translation of Luke, completing the initial phase of missionary endeavours to refer to God with Tswana concepts.

In the end, the term for ancestor indeed came to mean God. Future missionaries would supply narratives for this Modimo, displacing specific lore about Tswana pasts in favour of a history common to everybody (but known best by Christians). Henceforth Tswana people would read their own ancestral histories as versions of the Bible's stories of Ancestor's reign, in Exodus and Acts, and in terms of texts such as *The Pilgrim's Progress*. The relationship between Modimo and historical kings ceased being denotative and became metaphorical. Modimo was the 'greatest king'. Missionaries and new Tswana Christians agreed there would be no plural for 'Modimo', which received its own special noun-class (1a); ancestors (*badimo*) became the plural 'demons' (pl., cl. 2, not 2a) and had no singular form. As Toril Moi remarks, 'the power struggle intersects in the sign'. In retrospect, the 'pre-colonial' Tswana 'modimo' became the imperfect version, a 'remote' and 'half-known' god.[36]

The appearance of Moffat's 1839 New Testament in 'Sechuana' was a watershed also in another sense. As the first African-language Bible it opened the way for dozens of others which disseminated Christianity and alphabetic literacy throughout much of sub-Saharan Africa. And although subsequent 'South African Tswana', Sotho, and Pedi Bibles appeared, the Moffat 'Sechuana' version remains in use today. The Bible became a source book for the ethnic identity 'Tswana', which would grow to number in the millions, and supplied the basic vocabulary to Isaac Schapera's œuvre of genealogies, in which ancestor names become tribes, and ancestor rites a depoliticized religion.[37]

---

[35] Chidester, *Savage Systems*, pp. 184 ff.; Ross, *Adam Kok's Griquas*, p. 24.

[36] Toril Moi, *Sexual/Textual Politics: Feminist Literary Theory* (London, 1985), cited by Janice Boddy, *Wombs and Alien Spirits: Women, Men, and the Zar Cult in Northern Sudan* (Madison, 1989), p. 310; contrastingly, Comaroffs, *Revelation*, I, pp. 218, 337 n. 27.

[37] I. Schapera, *Handbook of Tswana Law and Custom* (Oxford, 1940), and *Ethnic Composition of Tswana Tribes* (London, 1952).

Missionaries, Language, and Identities

Missionaries' collective engagement with other languages shaped theology, nationalism, and national reformist movements throughout the Empire. Not only did the bureaucratic machinery of imperialism rely on missionaries' language work; subject peoples, when they wanted to be heard and understood by the colonial state, represented themselves in ways the Christian state could grasp. It is clear that missionaries' interaction with indigenous modernizers was at least a two-way street. James Read committed adultery with a deaconess at the Bushman mission at Bethelsdorp and was suspended in 1817. The missionary who worked most closely with Ram Mohun Roy in Bengal, the Revd William Aden, became a freethinker in Calcutta. Thomas Kendall, the linguist in New Zealand, left the ministry and married a Maori. Apparently there was a danger in half-known logics: one might get converted out of Christianity instead of converting others into it.

A missionary in alien surroundings typically looked for familiar practices, rituals, and concepts, and learned words for them: divination, ancestor, effectiveness (*mana*), etc. Often he split such words in two: one remaining the heathen target of his efforts at replacement, perhaps for generations, while the other named the intended replacement itself. Thus in Kongo, 'nkisi' was lifted from its position in local symbologies of fear and success, and used in two ways: as 'fetish object' (among non-Christians) and, as a written and spoken word, as 'holy', its veritable opposite, among Christians. Badimo had to descend to hell so Modimo could rise to heaven. In Zambia, Anglicanism appeared to mirror the way a secret society (*dini*) operated; when Anglicanism became a religion and a church for Chewa people, alongside the original secret *dini*, the word adopted for a religion or church was again 'dini'. Of course Christian movements not only spoke in familiar terms, but took up new ones: Zambian Watchtower (Jehovah's Witnesses) followers called those who refused baptism 'wasatani', 'devils', and in Ghana Ewe Christians embraced the dualist vision of heathen ways as Satan's and Christianity as God's, because the Devil could be a useful guide, a partner ferrying them into the new dispensation.[38] Good translation is an art. The New Caledonian missionary Maurice Leenhardt took fifteen years to render the Gospel of Matthew in the Houailou tongue, determined not to ask converts to parrot

---

[38] John Janzen, 'Tradition of Renewal in Kongo Religion', in N. S. Booth, ed., *African Religion: A Symposium* (New York: 1977), pp. 69–115; Richard Stuart, 'Anglican Missionaries and a Chewa Dini', *Journal of Religion in Africa*, X (1979), pp. 46–69.

ideas before they could make sense of them. In considering how to translate 'propitiatory', he let go of violent sacrifice as a font of analogies altogether, and translated a word meaning 'healing leaf' as 'Christ's blood'.[39]

Even such contextualization was unavoidably partisan. Each term, 'olorun' and 'eshu', 'nkisi', 'dini', 'io' and 'mana', 'ancestor' and leaf, became a kind of prism through which different viewpoints vied for hegemony, and by which different constellations of people elevated competing usages. Now, Robin Horton has argued that in Africa pre-Christian religions were mostly about 'explanation–prediction–control'. Following his view, the notion of the high god emerged in colonized societies not primarily due to missionaries but because local explanatory and magical paradigms failed to account for the changing world. 'Face to face' societies were intellectually 'closed'; they valued custom over innovation.[40] In departing from this somewhat (Sir J. G.) Frazerian model, I have paid attention to the intersection of missionaries' aims with genuine political forces and stratagems. *Tapu*, or ancestor-propitiation, did not fall into neglect because of inherent flaws in their host cultures, but because of guns, wells, corvée labour, racial thinking, and extractive bureaucracies, in a word, imperialism. Whether murder and feasting are religions or crimes is always a political matter.

Finally, for scholars, missionaries' involvement with translation and publication has bred a body of knowledge managed in part by post-colonial practitioners, for instance 'African traditional religion', which revalues diverse rituals as expressions of an overarching religious orientation proleptic of the essential ideas in Christianity and Islam. Crucially, missionaries' interventions produced an unprecedented number of newly constructed written languages and millions of readers for them. Missionaries' lasting textual imprint has also been to primitivize and tribalize peoples in their own histories, construing their pasts as enchanted or superstitious. Not only popular insurgencies, but the forces of diffusion and oppression, have (re)occupied Christianity's vocabulary. The legacy of missionaries' engagement with the languages of the Empire is not an entirely uplifting one.

---

[39] James Clifford, 'The Translation of Cultures: Maurice Leenhardt's Evangelism, New Caledonia, 1902–1926', *Journal of Pacific History*, XXV (1980), pp. 2–20.

[40] Norman Etherington, 'Missions and Empire', *OHBE* V, *Historiography* (Oxford, 1999), p. 330, for a brief and sympathetic review of Robin Horton's work, with a bibliography.

Select Bibliography

JOHN BARKER, ed., *Christianity in Oceania* (Lanham, Md., 1990).

ATHALYA BRENNER and JAN WILLEM VAN HENTEN, eds., *Bible Translation on the Threshold of the Twenty-First Century: Authority, Reception, Culture and Religion* (London, 2002).

PEGGY BROCK, ed., *Indigenous Peoples, Christianity, and Religious Change*, Journal of Religious History, XXVII, special issue (2003).

DAVID CHIDESTER, *Savage Systems: Colonialism and Comparative Religion in Southern Africa* (Charlottesville, Va., 1996).

GREG DENING, *Islands and Beaches: Discourse on a Silent Land: Marquesas, 1774–1880* (Honolulu, 1980).

CLEMENT DOKE, 'Scripture Translation into Bantu Languages', *African Studies*, XVII (1958), pp. 82–99.

BRONWEN DOUGLAS, 'Encounters with the Enemy? Academic Readings of Missionary Narratives on Melanesians', *Comparative Studies on Society and History*, XLI (2001), pp. 37–64.

ROBERT FRYKENBERG, *Christians and Missionaries in India: Cross-cultural Communication since 1500* (London, 2001).

JACK GOODY, *The Domestication of the Savage Mind* (Cambridge, 1978).

BARRY HALLAN and J. OLUBI SODIPO, *Knowledge, Belief, and Witchcraft: Analytic Experiments in African Philosophy*, 2nd edn. (Stanford, Calif., 1997).

DON KULICK, *Language Shift and Cultural Reproduction: Socialization, Self and Syncretism in a Papua New Guinea Village* (Cambridge, 1992).

PAUL LANDAU, *The Realm of the Word: Language, Gender and Christianity in a Southern African Kingdom* (Portsmouth, NH, 1995).

BIRGIT MEYER, *Translating the Devil: Religion and Modernity among the Ewe in Ghana* (Trenton, NJ, 1999).

DOUG MUNRO and ANDREW THORNLEY, 'Pacific Islander Pastors and Missionaries: Some Historiographical and Analytical Issues', *Pacific Studies*, XXIII/3–4 (2000), pp. 1–31.

J. D. Y. PEEL, *Religious Encounter and the Making of the Yoruba* (Bloomington, Ind., 2000).

DEREK PETERSON, *Creative Writing: Translation, Bookkeeping, and the Work of Imagination in Colonial Kenya* (Portsmouth, NH, 2004).

VINCENT RAFAEL, *Contracting Colonialism: Translation and Christian Conversion in Tagalog Society under Early Spanish Rule* (Durham, NC, 1993).

LAMIN SANNEH, *Translating the Message: The Missionary Impact on Culture* (Maryknoll, NY, 1989).

WILLIAM A. SMALLEY, *Translation as Mission: Bible Translation in the Modern Missionary Movement* (Macon, Ga., 1991).

Andrew Thornley, *Exodus of the I Taukei: The Wesleyan Church in Fiji, 1848–74* (Suva, 2002).

Peter van der Veer, ed., *Conversion to Modernities: The Globalization of Christianity* (New York, 1996).

Michael W. Young, 'Commemorating Missionary Heroes: Local Christianity and Narratives of Nationalism', in Ton Otto and Nicolas Thomas, eds., *Narratives of Nation in the South Pacific* (Amsterdam, 1997), pp. 91–132.

11

New Religious Movements

ROBERT EDGAR

Movements of reformation, renewal, and innovation have historically accompanied the spread of Christianity to different parts of the world. This is particularly true of the British Empire, where colonized peoples interrogated, challenged, reinterpreted, and assimilated Christianity. Sometimes the vehicle for challenge was an established mission church, but at other times it was a new religious movement. In colonial Africa and New Zealand independent churches took many forms: challenges to mission denominations; spirit churches that addressed health concerns; religious movements that responded to land conquest; and millenarian movements that appeared to challenge the colonial state.

Declarations of Independence

Colonized peoples challenged mission Christianity in the late nineteenth century through the founding of independent churches. The racist and domineering leadership of many European missionaries and their condemnations of African cultural practices often precipitated these first painful schisms. Some splits took place before colonial rule. In Nigeria cultural and leadership disputes precipitated African breakaways from Methodist, Anglican, and Baptist missions in Yoruba areas of the Niger delta. In 1888 David Brown Vincent split from the American-sponsored Baptist Church in Lagos to establish the Native Baptist Church. Africanizing his name to Mojola Agbebi, he challenged Baptist doctrine forbidding polygyny and argued for an autonomous African church freed from the 'apron strings of foreign teachers'. Several years later a breakaway from the Church Missionary Society (CMS) primarily stemmed from its treatment of Bishop Samuel Crowther, one of the few Africans in a leadership position. European missionaries marginalized and humiliated Crowther before his death, and the CMS hierarchy refused to select an African as his successor. Disaffected members challenged Crowther's persecutors by establishing the United Native African Church.[1] In both cases the disputes had nothing to do with doctrine or liturgy; the new churches were mirror images of the mission churches but with one important difference: they had African leaders.

In southern Africa, where white settlers intruded more directly on black lives, there were hundreds of schisms. In 1892 at Kilnerton Institution near Pretoria, Mangena Mokone, who sought 'to serve God in his own way', left the Methodist fold after acrimonious disagreements with European clergy over paltry wages for black ministers, the Church's persistence in segregating meetings of blacks and whites, and the unwillingness of white clergy to allow their black counterparts in leadership posts.[2] By naming his group the Ethiopian Church, Mokone embraced one of the clearest expressions of identification with an African home of early Christianity. After Mokone learned of the African American African Methodist Episcopal Church (AME) through a relative studying at Wilberforce, an AME college in America, he, Jacobus Xaba, and James Mata Dwane journeyed to the United States in 1895 to meet AME officials and returned to implant the Church in South Africa. In 1898 the AME solidified its base in South Africa when Bishop Henry McNeil Turner's whirlwind tour of the Cape Colony and Transvaal doubled the number of AME members. Numerous congregations, schools, and an annual conference were established. However, Turner could not prevent the restless Dwane from returning to mainstream Christianity a few years later to found the Order of Ethiopia, a semi-autonomous branch of the Anglican Church. The AME was not in fact an independent church, and its mission philosophy differed little from European missions. AME missionaries assumed that African Christians desired to acquire Western skills and education as an essential part of becoming civilized, but were convinced that African American clergy could do a much better job than Europeans. Indeed, the AME founded a number of schools in South Africa and sponsored about 100 southern African students for higher education, mostly in African American colleges in the United States. The AME strove to displace, not expel, whites, but their activities were still regarded as a distinct threat to the control of European missionaries, who appealed to colonial officials to bar AME missionaries from entering their territories. Although

---

[1] J. B. Webster, *The African Church among the Yoruba, 1888–1922* (Oxford, 1964).

[2] James Campbell, *Songs of Zion: The African Methodist Episcopal Church in the United States and South Africa* (New York, 1995), p. 117.

AME bishops sought to demonstrate that they were in fact loyal to the British Crown and not spreading a gospel of revolution, AME ministers were invariably branded subversives and identified with seditious 'Ethiopianism'. In Barotseland in Northern Rhodesia, Willie Mokalapa broke with the Paris Evangelical Mission Society (PEMS) over his pay and conditions of service and joined the AME in 1903, winning the support of the local Lozi elite and Lewanika's ruling family through the AME's emphasis on education. However, PEMS missionaries successfully lobbied the British South Africa Company to issue a proclamation prohibiting other AME missionaries from entering the territory. The AME did not reappear in Northern Rhodesia until the 1930s, when it attracted considerable support from educated Africans in rapidly growing copperbelt towns.

Cultural misunderstandings underlay an acrimonious split in Kenya between Kikuyu Christians and the Church of Scotland Mission (CSM) and the American-sponsored African Inland Mission (AIM).[3] The white missionaries derided certain elements of Kikuyu culture as 'incompatible with Christianity', particularly the circumcision ceremony, a rite of passage for teenage boys and girls. Although the missionaries decided that male circumcision could be performed by hospital doctors, in the late 1920s they fiercely condemned female circumcision as barbaric and 'sexual mutilation' and demanded that church members forswear it. Colonial officials, who had studiously avoided taking a position on these issues, enacted a law in the early 1920s that restricted female initiation periods to two months—a measure whose real intent was to ensure that the flow of labour to white farms was not interrupted by ceremonies. However, when the controversy intensified later in the decade, officials tried to moderate mission policy by limiting the oath against female circumcision to teachers and allowing those who rejected the circumcision prohibition to have access to schools.

Most Kikuyu valued circumcision ceremonies for bringing initiates into the larger community as adults and reinforcing patriarchal dominance. Banning them was further proof that colonizers planned to expropriate more Kikuyu land. The prohibitions touched off a mass exodus from the missions and split Kikuyu church members into the minority *kirore* ('fingerprint'), who were prepared to sign the oath, and the Agikuyu karing'a ('pure

---

[3] Francis Githieya, *The Freedom of the Spirit: African Indigenous Churches in Kenya* (Atlanta, 1997), and David Sandgren, *Christianity and the Kikuyu: Religious Divisions and Social Conflict* (New York, 1989).

Kikuyu'), who rejected the pledge. Dissidents withdrew their children from mission schools and refused to attend church. A stanza of 'Muthirugu', a popular protest song of the time, encouraged secession.

> I am going to break all friendships
> The only friendship I shall retain
> Is between me and Jehovah.[4]

They established the African Independent Pentecostal Church and the Kikuyu Independent School Association in 1934, and explored ways to address a glaring weakness in their new church's structure, how to ordain their own clergy. A few years later a solution was found through Archbishop Daniel William Alexander of the African Orthodox Church (AOC) of South Africa, whom dissidents persuaded to visit Kenya and to ordain individuals to lead the independent church.

Cultural issues also shaped the formation of Maori churches in New Zealand, but, unlike African independent churches, most Maori churches defined themselves as complementary to established mission denominations. Because mainstream missions established separate Maori church wings under European control, the independent churches embraced a liberatory message and carved out space for personalized styles of worship. However, many of their congregants still retained membership in their original churches. The Church of the Seven Rules of Jehovah, founded in the late 1890s, peaked during the First World War. It opposed *tohunga* (Maori religious figures consulted on matters of well-being and illness) and strove to unite all Maori tribes under one Christian institution. Recognizing the Church of England as the mother church, it patterned its worship services, building styles, clerical hierarchy, and observance of a Sunday sabbath after the Anglicans. However, because Maori culture did not sanction eating the body and drinking the blood of a divine figure, the Church did not celebrate the Holy Sacrament.[5]

Churches of the Spirit

Because so many indigenous religious specialists specialized in healing, the first Western missionaries were closely questioned on Christianity's relation

---
[4] Githieya, *Freedom of the Spirit*, p. 87.
[5] Bronwyn Elsmore, *Mana from Heaven: A Century of Maori Prophets in New Zealand* (Tauranga, 1989).

to health. People expressed particular concern about devastating diseases, such as smallpox, measles, plague, and influenza, that accompanied European conquest. They asked whether missionaries were superior to traditional practitioners in controlling these diseases. This challenged missionaries, who rarely addressed health concerns in their ministries and neglected scriptural references to healing and caused many people to prefer healer–prophets who invoked spiritual forces. Some of these healers incorporated traditional techniques, while others favoured Christian-based methods.

Measles and influenza swept through mid-nineteenth-century New Zealand, killing thousands more Maori than *pakeha* (Europeans). In 1860 *pakeha* and Maori populations both numbered roughly 75,000, while three decades later the Maori population had declined to fewer than 45,000.[6] Many Maori concluded that their *atua* ('gods') could not protect them from the stronger European *atua*, who had sent the epidemics as punishment for Maori who clung to their old faith. Old Testament verses describing how Jehovah inflicted plagues on worshippers of false gods reinforced this interpretation. Te Hara rose to prominence as a healer after the spirit of one of her dead children and Moses appeared in a vision, directing her 'to heal the sick and diseased'. She combined the traditional practice of placing patients on heated stones and medicinal herbs with a prayer imploring Christ's assistance. Other healers stressed that belief in the European god, Atuaniu, paved the way to good health and urged Maori to discard the traditional ways in favour of 'Christian practices'. The Wahi Tapu (Sacred Places) movement blamed sickness on ancestral spirits opposed to Christianity. Wahi Tapu's solution was to recite scripture while building a fire and cooking and eating special foods to cleanse an area of *tapu*.

In contrast to the healing movements of the nineteenth century, twentieth-century prophet–healers like Mere Rikiriki firmly rooted their spiritual messages in Christian idioms. Although she came from a family of *tohunga*s, she exhorted her followers to embrace Christianity. Her Holy Ghost Mission (Te Hahi o te Wairua Tapu) preached the 'Holy Spirit's agency as a mediator between God and man'. Mere Rikiriki's prediction that a gifted prophet would appear was realized when her nephew Tahupotiki Wiremu Ratana answered God's call to service during the devastating influenza pandemic of 1918.[7] Though many converted Maori interpreted this disease as a sign of

---

[6] Ibid.
[7] J. M. Henderson, *Ratana: The Man, the Church, the Movement* (Wellington, 1963).

disapproval from Maori gods, Ratana preached instead that the gospel would bring people back to Jehovah. As the *mangai*, a mouthpiece of God, he set out 'to cure the spirits and bodies of his people'. Known as the Maori Miracle Man, he engaged in faith-healing at Ratana Pa, his headquarters, and on a circuit around New Zealand. Those whom he healed had to sign an oath accepting their belief in the Holy Trinity and rejecting the Maori beliefs to which he attributed influenza and other devastating diseases. Although the non-denominational Ratana Church he founded in 1925 was repudiated by the Church of England, by the mid-1930s it counted about 20 per cent of the Maori population as adherents. Unlike many prophet–healers, Ratana increasingly shifted his energies to secular matters, devoting his time to establishing schools and leading Maori to reclaim their rights enshrined in the Treaty of Waitangi of 1840, moves that reflected a general shift by Maori leaders from religious to secular authority. Ratana handpicked men who successfully stood for four Maori seats in Parliament to promote the land issue and win additional land rights.

When the influenza pandemic of 1918 killed an estimated 2 million people in Africa, a newspaper described Lagos, Nigeria, as 'a veritable city of the dead' and colonial officials shut down churches to prevent 'dangerous gatherings'.[8] The pandemic spurred the formation of Aladura (a Yoruba word for 'one who prays') churches, whose members invoked the Holy Spirit to receive the healing, prophecy, and the blessings of God. Church members also inveighed against demons, ancestral spirits, and *orisa*, Yoruba deities who interceded between the high God and humans. The first Aladura church is attributed to Joseph Shadore, an Anglican who established a prayer group within his church to 'offer spiritual help against the plague', and his relative Sophia Odunlami, who renounced traditional and modern medicine in favour of healing through drinking blessed water. Their prayer group, Precious Water, broke with the Anglicans in 1922 and renamed itself Faith Tabernacle after an American Pentecostal group. The church was popular among African government clerks and traders, who used their personal networks to found branches in administrative centres.[9] During the Great Depression it received a boost from mass healings conducted by Prophet

---

[8] J. D. Y. Peel, *Aladura: A Religious Movement among the Yoruba* (London, 1968), p. 60.

[9] Robert Cameron Mitchell, 'Religious Protest and Social Change: The Origins of the Aladura Movement in Western Nigeria', in Robert Rotberg and Ali Mazrui, eds., *Protest and Power in Black Africa* (New York, 1970), pp. 458–96.

Joseph Babalola (Baba Aladura). The British, worried by Babalola's pronouncements against taxation, sentenced him to six months in gaol for violating a law against witchcraft accusations. A young Yoruba girl, Christiana Abiodum Akinsowon, founded another healing church following a bubonic plague epidemic in Lagos in the mid-1920s, adopting the name Seraphim after angels appeared to them. Another Aladura leader, Joseph Oshitela, split from the Anglicans in 1929 and initiated a ministry that stressed faith-healing and the gift of prophecy. Although Oshitela aroused suspicion because some of his pamphlets contained anti-colonial and anti-tax messages, British officials decided not to prosecute him.

Many southern African spirit churches formed connections with American Zionist and Pentecostal healing churches.[10] John Alexander Dowie, who founded the Christian Apostolic Church in 1896 and established his headquarters at Zion City near Chicago, Illinois, stressed divine healing free from doctors and medication; he strictly prohibited his followers from eating pork or using alcohol and tobacco. Dowie's message was spread to South Africa through Johannes Buchler, P. L. Le Roux, and Edgar Mahon. Following the 1906 Azusa Street, California, Pentecostal revival meetings held by the African American preacher William Seymour, American evangelical couples exposed to Dowie brought the Azusa Street message to South Africa. Pentecostalism was institutionalized with the formation of the Apostolic Faith Mission (AFM) in 1908, which quickly won followings among both Afrikaners and Africans. While early meetings were interracial, the movement soon split into white and black wings.

One white Pentecostal leader, Edgar Mahon, who maintained ties with the black community, tolerated polygyny and advised his followers, 'Enter ye into the Ark with your wives and children; the Lord wants all of you. Repent.' Mahon's AFM representative in Basutoland, Edward Tau, better known as Edward Lion, took his admonition to heart and repented on many occasions. Around 1910 he began baptizing people in the Caledon River on the Orange Free State–Basutoland border, acquiring a reputation as a healer. After Lion founded his 'Headquarters for the World' seven years later at a site called Zion City in Basutoland, the AFM suspected him of separatist tendencies and eventually severed all links after charging that he had fallen prey to

---

[10] David Maxwell, 'Historicizing Christian Independency: The Southern African Pentecostal Movement c.1908–1960', *Journal of African History*, XL (1999), pp. 243–64, and Bengt Sundkler, *Zulu Zion and Some Swazi Zionists* (London, 1976).

'hubris' and was expecting his followers to treat him with 'divine reverence'. Although Lion maintained amicable relations with local chiefs and headmen, colonial officials took umbrage with his ministry. A district officer reported that Lion attracted 'all the blackguards in the country, and his village appears to be a general refuge for runaway wives'.[11] Indeed, his Zion City defied both British and chieftaincy, but not for long. Lion's downfall came after he practised sexual healing on a young woman and her father came to demand compensation for Lion's liaison. When Lion beat him, officials seized on the incident to try him in the courts of the Paramount Chief and the Resident Commissioner and expel him from Basutoland in 1927.

Migrant workers and itinerant preachers took advantage of the openness of colonial boundaries to spread the Pentecostal–Zionist message to rural areas. African evangelists spread the AFM to Southern Rhodesia in 1915. When the influenza pandemic hit three years later, African religious leaders provided explanations and treatments that were comprehensible in traditional terms. They could dispense medicine, identify witches abetting the evil, and direct people to perform sacrifices to the ancestors at the Mwari shrine. However, when these methods failed to halt the pandemic, many turned to Pentecostalism, whose emphasis on healing and miracles provided an alternative. There is a direct connection between the AFM, the influenza, and the emergence of the two most successful Shona healer–prophets, Johane Maranke and John Masowe.[12] After receiving the Holy Spirit in 1932, Maranke acquired the power to heal through laying his hands on people. In the manner of John the Baptist, Maranke carried a staff for performing miracles. This conformed to a belief in Apostolic circles that they had to receive the power of 'divine authority' from God because European missionaries had withheld it from them. Maranke enjoined his followers to abandon their protective medicine horns and ancestor worship, and shun the malevolent *shavi* spirits.[13] At first his African Apostolic Church

---

[11] Colin Murray, 'The Father, the Son and the Holy Spirit: Resistance and Abuse in the Life of Solomon Lion (1908–1987)', *Journal of Religion in Africa*, XXIX (1999), pp. 341–86.

[12] T. O. Ranger, 'The Influenza Pandemic in Southern Rhodesia: A Crisis of Comprehension', in David Arnold, ed., *Imperial Medicine and Indigenous Societies* (New York, 1988), pp. 172–89, and id., 'Plagues of Beasts and Men: Prophetic Responses to Epidemic in Eastern and Southern Africa', in T. O. Ranger and Paul Slack, eds., *Epidemics and Ideas: Essays on the Historical Perception of Pestilence* (Cambridge, 1992), pp. 241–68.

[13] M. Daneel, *Old and New in Southern Shona Independent Churches, I, Background and Rise of the Major Movements* (The Hague, 1972), pp. 57–8.

(also known as Vapostoris) was limited to Maranke's extended family, but soon it spread to the Maranke Reserve and then to six neighbouring countries. In Maranke's home area government officials tolerated the church, but in other districts officials and chiefs regarded him as a madman and restricted the movements of Vapostori evangelists. Shoniwa Moyo founded the Apostolic Sabbath Church of God after being summoned by God to be a prophet, changing his name to John Masowe because God called him to perform like John the Baptist and because he had gone into the wilderness ('masowe' is the Shona word for wilderness) to pray. Claiming that he died and was resurrected three days later, Masowe positioned himself as a messiah for Africa and prepared his followers for the imminent end of the world. Calling on the Holy Spirit to enter his body, Masowe emphasized his healing ministry and his ability to identify sources of witchcraft.[14]

Although the Pentecostal–Zionist churches spawned many branches, some healing churches such as Isaiah Shembe's Nazareth Baptist Church developed independently. While still a Wesleyan, Shembe dreamed that a man came to him and read from Mark 16: 18–19, declaring that those who are believers 'will lay the hands on the sick, and they will recover'.[15] Shembe founded his church in 1911 with headquarters at Ekuphakameni ('The High and Elevated Place') in the Inanda Reserve on the outskirts of Durban. Some people, observing that Shembe's grandfather had been a diviner and healer, commented that his actions resembled those of a diviner. However, he emphasized that his calling to ministry came not from the ancestors (as would a diviner), but from God. While acknowledging Jesus Christ as saviour, he stressed the primacy of God the Father over God the Son.

Women were especially drawn to spirit churches because they recognized their prophetic gifts. Following a vision of an imposing church with twelve doors which she took to be the Temple of Jerusalem on Mount Zion, the charismatic healer Ma' Nku left the Dutch Reformed Church for the AFM before establishing her own St John's Apostolic Church near Johannesburg. When her prayers imbued water with healing properties, so many people flocked to her that she had to install a water-pump for mass healings and baptisms. However popular Ma' Nku and other women prophets were, their movements, either during or after their lifetimes, were eventually headed by

---

[14] Clive Dillon-Malone, *The Korsten Basketmakers: A Study of the Masowe Apostles, an Indigenous African Religious Movement* (Manchester, 1978). Masowe's church subsequently moved to Botswana and South Africa and finally to Kenya.

[15] Absolom Vilakazi, *Shembe: The Revitalization of African Society* (Johannesburg, 1986).

men, who structured a male-dominated hierarchy. The 1954 constitution of the Church of the Lord accepted women as prophets and preachers, but prohibited them from entering the altar sanctuary and, following 1 Corinthians 14: 14, required them to remain silent during services. Although spirit churches typically fit a patriarchal mould, women still found ways to carve out personalized spaces. In the Roho churches founded in the 1930s in western Kenya, hymns inspired by the Holy Spirit were the provenance of women, whose singing created an 'expressive domain' that men could not control. They built on the *lang'o* spirit possession cult that was predominantly made up of women and featured ecstatic song and dance. In the aftermath of their founder's violent death in 1934 Roho women composed songs boldly proclaiming that they were the backbone of the movement. One hymn proudly asserted, 'we are women of war, we are women of fire'.[16] As these Christian soldiers roamed the countryside, their rapturous songs heralded their approaches to communities.

The healing practices of Zionist churches in southern Africa resonated with displaced and dispossessed women (and men) who drew connections between their own bodies' well-being and their marginalization in a rapidly changing society controlled by whites. Jean Comaroff argues that 'the notion of the body at war with itself' and the 'focus upon "healing" as a mode of repairing the tormented body' became a metaphor for 'the oppressive social order itself'. According to Carol Muller, in Shembe's church, 'barrenness becomes a symbol for fragmentation of the social order' and the inability of women and men to procreate.[17] Hence, Shembe's Ekuphakameni attracted women and girls precisely because he set aside housing specifically for them and paid special attention to guarding their bodies and fertility. Shembe also established a secluded church meeting for women at the time—from evening on the thirteenth day of each month to the morning of the fifteenth—when women were believed to be most fertile.

In Southern Rhodesia women worried about fertility could consult Mai Chaza, who, in the mid-1950s, established her Guta re Johova (City of God) at a village near Salisbury. Her control of land within the white urban areas appealed to newly urbanized landless women who eked out marginal

---

[16] Carolyn Hoehler-Fatton, *Women of Fire and Spirit: History, Faith, and Gender in Roho Religion in Western Kenya* (Oxford, 1996), pp. 195–202.

[17] Carol Ann Muller, *Rituals of Fertility and the Sacrifice of Desire* (Chicago, 1999), p. 240; Jean Comaroff, *Body of Power, Spirit of Resistance: The Culture and History of a South African People* (Chicago, 1985), p. 25.

existences in towns. Renowned for success with people possessed by *shavi* spirits, Mai Chaza opposed the use of traditional medicines and expected her followers to give up money and tobacco. Barren women seeking her help had to bring their husbands and marriage certificates and to be screened by male assistants.[18]

Promised Lands

As historic guardians of the land, prophets played innovative roles in resistance and adaptation to European colonialism. Many drew valuable inspiration and examples from the Old Testament. Between 1860 and 1900, when Maori were dispossessed of much land, prophets inspired by the Old Testament flourished on the North Island of New Zealand.[19] When settler expansion belied belief that the Treaty of Waitangi would protect them against expropriation, the Maori launched several wars of resistance. Observing European missionaries serving as chaplains in the British army or abandoning their mission stations, many Maoris questioned their sincerity and were drawn to the prophets' messages. Identifying with the Old Testament search of the Israelites for freedom from bondage, Maori religious leaders concluded that they, too, were a chosen people and had a covenant with God.[20] Maori prophets divided into two camps: those who acted in the manner of *tohunga*s and those who incorporated Christian beliefs. Most of the latter were Christian converts whose followers had turned against the British missionaries. Te Ua had been baptized in the Methodist Church and served as a low-level teacher in mission schools. In 1862 after the angel Gabriel appeared to him, Te Ua founded the Pai Marire (Good and Peaceful) movement grounded in the belief that Jehovah and angels would protect Maori land and force the *pakeha* back to their homelands. Te Ua cosmology incorporated not only Jehovah, but also Rura and Riki, Maori sky deities, and Ripe, a bird that conveyed divine messages between heaven and earth. Its central ritual involved marching around a sacred pole uttering prayers.

---

[18] Timothy Scarnecchia, 'Mai Chaza's Guta re Jehova: Gender, Healing and Urban Identity in an Independent Church', *Journal of Southern African Studies*, XXVII (1997), pp. 87–105.

[19] Jean Rosenfeld, *The Island Broken in Two Halves: Land and Renewal Movements among the Maori* (University Park, Pa., 1999).

[20] The Old Testament was fully translated into the Maori language by 1858. Later Mormon missionaries reinforced the idea of a Chosen People by identifying the Maori as descendants of a lost tribe of Israel.

Te Ua also brought in the New Testament by invoking the Holy Spirit of Acts 2: 1–4. His movement started on the west coast of the North Island and spread rapidly around the island. Although he preached peace and reconciliation, some of his apostles, the Hau Hau, adopted a more militant line when war resumed in 1863. Believing the *hau*, or wind spirits, would shield them from bullets, they carried on an armed struggle against the British for several years. Te Ua, however, remained steadfast in his message of peace; after being captured by the British in 1866, he accompanied Governor George Grey on a tour aimed at persuading rebels to surrender.[21]

Another prophet, Te Kooti Rikirangi, had been baptized and educated at a CMS mission. Although he had publicly sided with government forces against the Hau Hau, suspicious officials charged him with spying and banished him with 300 others to the distant Chatham Islands. In exile the archangel Michael appeared in a vision to Te Kooti, assuring him that the Maori were a chosen people whom Jehovah would deliver from bondage and dispossession. After escaping in 1868, Te Kooti led a guerrilla campaign for many years in Urerewa Reserve before disappearing into a remote area. Never captured, he was finally granted a state pardon in 1883. The religion he founded was known as Ringatu (Upraised Hand), a sign of blessing, and specialized in healing through laying on hands. Believing a new faith to be essential because the missionaries had distorted Scripture to suit colonial aims, Ringatu adopted the new set of Scriptures which God had revealed to Te Kooti. The Ringatu church observed a Saturday sabbath and offered prayers to God but without the mediation of Jesus Christ.[22]

Xhosa chiefdoms on the front line of colonial conquest in nineteenth-century South Africa also spawned prophets. Visionaries such as Nxele and Mlanjeni relied on Xhosa religious precepts to rally their people against European intrusion, while Ntsikana, regarded as the first Xhosa Christian convert and prophet, preached accommodation with colonial power. However, by the end of the nineteenth century Afrikaner settlers and British colonists had conquered roughly 93 per cent of South Africa and consigned Africans to impoverished rural reserves, small pockets of land scattered about the countryside. In 1913 the Natives Land Act virtually froze the land division between blacks and whites, and became a burning issue as thousands of Africans forced off the land migrated to urban centres. Some black

---

[21] Paul Clark, '*Hau Hau*': *The Pai Marire Search for Maori Identity* (Auckland, 1975).
[22] Elsmore, *Mana from Heaven*.

religious leaders responded by adopting a strategy of defensive segregation, establishing 'holy villages' or 'New Jerusalems' in which their devoted followers could find safe havens, even if for a brief time, from European oppression.

To the prophets, Zion Cities functioned as natural extensions of Zionist and Pentecostal religious teachings—gathering places for their followers devastated by land shortages. Ignatius Lekganyane, the prophet–healer who founded the Zion Christian Church in 1925, made Moriah (near Pietersburg (Polokwane) in the northern Transvaal) the centre of an annual Passover festival that now attracts millions of his church's adherents. Moriah was considered the church's central sacred space free from white domination and interference, while each local congregation developed its own sacred space. Isaiah Shembe applied the same concept of sacral space, using church offerings to purchase 38 acres for his principal sanctuary, Ekuphakameni, centre of his healing ministry and site of an annual three-week assembly in July. To his amaNazaretha faithful, Ekuphakameni was both an earthly Zion and a court of heavenly worship. Shembe bought more than twenty other parcels of land and rented them to individuals. He instilled a disciplined work ethic embedded in a church liturgy that advised: 'Never be idle. It is a sin to be lazy. A busy person is like a dog which survives by begging food from human beings.'[23] Shembe's mission directed his preaching at Zulu traditionalists hostile to the Christianity of mainstream missions. With his acceptance of polygyny and the authority of parents over children as well as husbands over wives, Shembe appealed to Zulus anxious to uphold patriarchal values. He presided over his followers like a Zulu chief, meting out punishments and choosing when to hold ceremonial dances. Housing at Ekuphakameni resembled a traditional pattern of Zulu royal residences with separate spaces for men and women and maidens 'secluded' in an area much like the *isigodlo*.

The ministry of other religious leaders, such as A. A. S. Le Fleur, stressed the search for land. In 1861–2, 3,000 Griquas had trekked to Griqualand East with Le Fleur's father-in-law, Adam Kok, only to see their fortunes ruined by white land speculators and settlers. In 1889 Le Fleur saw a vision of God directing him to collect Kok's bones and reunite the scattered Griquas. Known among the Griqua as Die Kneg (Servant) and for his predictions, he served a five-year gaol term for an abortive rebellion against white rule.

---

[23] Elizabeth Gunner, *Man of Heaven and the Beautiful Ones of God: Writings from Ibandla lamaNazaretha, a South African Church* (Leiden, 2002), p. 45.

By the First World War he was advocating self-help schemes for his people. In 1917 he trekked with about 800 people from Griqualand East to Touws River in the western Cape. Although his plan to develop a prosperous farming community failed dismally and his followers dispersed, he escaped conviction for defrauding them. Retaining his reputation as the Griqua's 'New Moses', he continued his quest to uplift the community. He worked through the long-established Griqua Independent Church and eventually founded a settlement for his followers at Kranshoek, near Plettenberg Bay, that is still a site for pilgrimages.[24] Resentment over lost lands also fuelled the Samuelite movement which emerged among the Seleka Rolong at Thaba 'Nchu, an African reserve near Bloemfontein that allowed private land ownership. After Samuel killed his brother Tshipinare in 1884 during a dispute over the succession to their father, Chief Moroka, Samuel went into exile, settling eventually with his supporters at Motsiloje in north-eastern Bechuanaland. More people joined them after passage of the Natives Land Act. Although reclamation of lost land was never a realistic prospect, around 1923 Henry Morolong, an independent preacher, fuelled millennial expectations that Samuel was soon returning to vanquish Tshipinare's supporters at Thaba 'Nchu.[25]

The South African government suspected the political implications of these 'movements' but did not aggressively confront them as it did in the case of Enoch Mgijima, who, like the New Zealand prophets, identified his followers with the Old Testament Israelites. When Halley's comet blazed across the sky in 1910, he had a vision of an impending war that would come from the East.[26] Shortly after the influenza pandemic arrived in late 1918, another vision led him to call his followers to await the end of the world at his holy village, Ntabelanga (Mountain of the Rising Sun), in Bullhoek location in the eastern Cape. Although the Israelites claimed they were gathering to observe their annual Passover festival, local officials worried that many were building permanent dwellings. Lacking the manpower to enforce the law against the disciplined, uncompromising defiance of the Israelites, they

---

[24] Henry Bredekamp, 'The Dead Bones of Adam Kok', in P. Faber, ed., *Group Portrait South Africa: Nine Family Histories* (Cape Town, 2003), pp. 132–55; Robert Edgar and Christopher Saunders, 'A. A. S. LeFleur and the Griqua Trek of 1917', *International Journal of African Historical Studies*, XV (1982), pp. 201–20.

[25] Paul Landau, 'The Spirit of God, Pigs and Demons: The "Samuelites" of Southern Africa', *Journal of Religion in Africa*, XXIX (1999), pp. 313–40.

[26] Robert Edgar, *Because they Chose the Plan of God: The Story of the Bullhoek Massacre* (Johannesburg, 1987).

called in the national government. Neither inducements nor threats would budge the Israelites, who proclaimed they were following the dictates of God, not the state. Officials, in their turn, suspected a plot to organize a wider rebellion. What else could explain Israelite men with knobkerries and ceremonial swords performing disciplined drills in martial formations before and during services? Misinterpreting these established features of Israelite ritual as preparation for warfare, officials decided to expel the Israelites from their holy village, lest their resistance damage the image of European invincibility. Eight hundred police with rifles and machine guns suffered only light casualties during the twenty minutes required to overcome the assegais and knobkerries of the Israelites at the battle of Bullhoek on 24 May 1921, where 200 Israelites perished.

New Heavens and New Earths

The Bullhoek massacre highlights a recurrent theme in the histories of new religious movements in colonial situations. Colonial officials generally accommodated these movements as long as they operated within orthodox religious boundaries or limited their challenges to mission denominations. However, once they adopted beliefs that appeared to transgress political boundaries and question the legitimacy of colonial authority, officials usually misinterpreted the religious messages and aggressively confronted these movements, often with tragic consequences. Millenarian movements, with their visions of an impending end of the world, their unwillingness to compromise, and their rigid division of society into the saved and the damned, particularly vexed secular officials, whether during or after the colonial period.[27]

In Central Africa the greatest religious challenge to Pax Britannica was Watch Tower (after 1931, Jehovah's Witnesses), founded in the 1870s in America by Charles Taze Russell. He predicted that Armageddon would follow Christ's return to earth in 1914. African migrant workers in mining compounds and domestic service imbibed Watch Tower's message and spread it throughout southern Africa. Watch Tower's leading salesmen of

---

[27] Though some historians see these churches as precursors to anti-colonial movements, nationalist movements and independent churches emerged more or less at the same time, and independent churches usually distanced themselves from nationalist parties. See T. O. Ranger, 'Religious Movements and Politics in Sub-Saharan Africa', *African Studies Review*, XXIX (1986), pp. 1–69.

salvation in Central Africa, Hanoc Sinwano and Elliott Kenan Kamwana, both Free Church of Scotland members, had worked as labour migrants in Cape Town. There they had received Watch Tower's message from Joseph Booth, a one-time Baptist missionary in Nyasaland whose egalitarian views on African autonomy put him at odds with most European missionaries. Returning to Nyasaland in 1908, Kamwana preached that colonial taxes and labour recruitment represented a form of witchcraft. His revivalist campaign promoted mass baptisms by immersion as protection against evil, while those who refused to be dipped were labelled 'wasatani or devils'.[28] The Watch Tower message offered a searing indictment not only of specific colonial abuses but also of white rule itself. As Karen Fields has put it, Kamwana's words offered 'an intelligible ideology' for his followers that the forces of good and evil were engaged in mortal combat, and that colonial officials undermined and corrupted the religious authority of white missionaries and African traditional rulers alike. This 'satanic alliance', he declared, between mission churches and colonial officials had to be destroyed. His incendiary preaching sparked conflict with civil authorities. He was repeatedly deported to remote areas of Nyasaland and ultimately exiled to the Seychelles islands in 1915. That same year Watch Tower was banned in Nyasaland and two years later in Southern Rhodesia.

Although the outbreak of world war in 1914 was not precisely the millennium Watch Tower adherents expected, it brought enormous trauma to Africans in Central Africa as colonial officials increased their demands. The war radicalized John Chilembwe. After being taught by Booth and schooled at an African American theological seminary in Virginia, Chilembwe returned to Nyasaland to found the Providence Industrial Mission.[29] A firm believer in Booker T. Washington's gradualist philosophy of industrial education, he was a model of respectability. (See pp. 267–71.) However, he grew increasingly critical of the abusive treatment of African tenants and labourers on European plantations. He was further angered when British officials imposed additional taxes and threw hundreds of thousands of African soldiers and porters into the fight against the Germans in East Africa. With a small band of conspirators, he hastily launched a rebellion in early 1915 against British rule and European plantation owners. He likely knew that his

[28] Karen Fields, *Revival and Rebellion in Colonial Central Africa* (Portsmouth, NH, 1997).
[29] D. D. Phiri, *John Chilembwe* (Lilongwe, 1976); George Shepperson and Thomas Price, *Independent African: John Chilembwe and the Origins, Setting and Sign of the Nyasaland Native Rising of 1915* (Edinburgh, 1958).

uprising was doomed to failure, but thought it worthwhile to 'strike a blow and die' in the manner of one of his heroes, the American abolitionist John Brown. Kamwana, in contrast, refused to join the plot on the ground that Jehovah was about to usher in the millennium. Chilembwe's rising alarmed colonial officials, who recognized that their 'thin white line' was stretched to the limits. Northern Rhodesia's Chief Justice Macdonnell believed Watchtower had exposed 'our fragile... hold over these people, and, at times, one saw the abyss opening'.[30] Officials voiced fears that they had little or no control over the black evangelists and mission schoolteachers who assumed key positions at mission stations after white missionaries were called up for military service. These teachers undermined the efforts to enlist Africans, and inspired black soldiers and police to challenge the colonial order. As a result African employees of mission stations and Watch Tower evangelists were singled out for persecution. In September 1918 two Watch Tower members were arrested for resisting an order to serve as porters and for inciting others to follow suit. Their defence was straightforward: they would not 'serve two masters—God and man'.[31]

In South Africa the Bullhoek massacre created a government security psychosis which put any new prophet under extreme suspicion. Nontetha Nkwenkwe, a middle-aged Xhosa widow with grown children, fell deathly ill during the 1918 influenza pandemic and learned in a vision that this disaster was God's punishment for the sins of her people. They must turn away from drunkenness, adultery, and circumcision.[32] An illiterate, Nontetha preached Scripture from the palms of her hands, calling on her faithful to convert to Christianity, attend schools, and prepare for doomsday. Clearly, Nontetha was not preaching sedition; if anything, her teaching suggested accommodation rather than resistance to white rule. However, white officials, fearing another Bullhoek showdown, tried to remove her from the scene. Though she had broken no laws, a magistrate declared her mentally ill, and in 1922 she was committed to a nearby asylum. When followers continued to visit her, officials removed her to a Pretoria mental hospital. Even then her followers organized two remarkable 'Pilgrimages of Grace', setting out on foot on a 600 mile journey to visit her. Hospital psychiatrists, who admitted that she posed

---

[30] Edmund Yorke, 'The Spectre of a Second Chilembwe', *Journal of African History*, XXXI (1990), p. 380.

[31] Ibid., p. 387.

[32] Robert Edgar and Hilary Sapire, *African Apocalypse: The Story of Nontetha Nkwenkwe, a Twentieth Century South African Prophet* (Athens, OH, 2000).

no physical threat to anyone, nonetheless accepted the State's view that she must be locked away lest she agitate her followers and create problems. When she died in 1935, authorities refused to surrender her body to her family and buried her in an anonymous grave in a pauper's field.

Official misperceptions also plagued the Kikuyu Kanitha wa Roho (Church of the Holy Spirit) in Kenya.[33] In 1926 Moses Thuo and Joseph Ng'anga felt themselves miraculously filled with the Holy Spirit that called them to prophetic ministries. They appropriated the name 'arathi', a word for diviners or prophets who had an intimate relationship with Ngai, the Creator God. But their interpretation of *arathi*, reflecting their reading of the Old Testament, diverged from traditional precepts. They saw God not as a remote figure, but as one who engaged in the daily affairs of humans and sided with the oppressed and downtrodden. It was logical for *arathi* to relate their own experience of colonialism with the Israelites, a chosen people destined to be delivered from bondage. Their eschatology preached that a day of redemption was coming in which the British colonizers would be expelled from Kikuyu lands. *Arathi* scorned not only colonial rule, but also aspects of both traditional and mission-taught values. They attacked witchcraft and ritual sacrifices to the ancestors and Ngai, while condemning the missions for corrupting African customs and introducing modern trappings such as clothes, shoes, and money. The *arathi*'s autonomous value system was based on their own rendering of biblical precepts. Although the movement supported Kikuyu independent schools and churches, it saw these institutions as too closely identified with Western ideas and values. For their part, Kikuyu independent church members distrusted *arathi* and gathered intelligence about its activities for colonial officials. Colonial officials, who initially dismissed *arathi* as 'pseudo-religious fanatics', grew alarmed after observing *arathi* men carrying bows and arrows and double-edged swords. The *arathi* justified arming themselves for defensive purposes because a prophecy predicted that a great war was imminent. Colonial officials closely monitored their activities, and, in 1934, prohibited *arathi* meetings and gaoled anyone contravening the regulation. In February 1934 police killed three *arathi*, including Ng'anga, during a skirmish in the Ndaragu forest. Thuo, on the other hand, lent his support to the Kikuyu Central Association, although few of his followers joined him.

[33] Francis Githieya, 'The Church of the Holy Spirit: Biblical Beliefs and Practices of the Arathi of Kenya, 1926–1950', in T. Spear and I. Kimambo, eds., *East African Expressions of Christianity* (Athens, OH, 1999), pp. 231–43; Githieya, *Freedom of the Spirit*.

One of the last major Maori prophets, Rua Kenana, came to prominence after further *pakeha* land grabs on North Island. Between 1892 and 1900 almost 3 million of the 7 million acres held by Maori were sold off to white settlers. When Rua was tapped by God, he declared that he was fulfilling Te Kooti's prophecy before his death in 1893 that a prophet would appear in the East to carry on his work and that Rua had a special mission to address the land crisis: 'If your wish', Rua told God, 'is for me to save my people, I won't help, but if it is to save this land, then I shall carry out this task.'[34] Claiming that the Holy Spirit spoke through him, Rua called his movement Wairua Tapu (Holy Spirit) movement and his followers Israelites. Male Israelites wore their hair long in the style of the biblical Nazarites. Rua's campaign to redress land inequities led him to make a bold prediction that the British monarch, Edward VII, would arrive in Gisborne, Rua's home town, on 26 June 1906 and present £4 million to buy back all of the alienated Maori land. Rua persuaded his adherents to journey to his home to await this millennial happening. His message especially resonated with Maori contract workers on white farms or in occupations such as sheep-shearers, ploughmen, and fencers. A thousand or so of the faithful responded to the call. Rua's predictions about expulsions threw the white community into a panic. When rumours spread that the Israelites possessed firearms, the government targeted Rua as the fomenter of armed rebellion through the Tohunga Suppression Act in 1907. After King Edward failed to materialize, Rua led his followers to land he owned in the nearby Urewera Reserve and founded his own community. His New Jerusalem was near his birthplace at the base of the sacred mountain Maungapohatu (Mountain of Stone), whose caves held the bones of Maori ancestors. Rua's Israelites escaped the tragic fate of Mgijima's Israelites in South Africa. As a landowner he was able to exchange a parcel of his land with the government in order to gain additional land for his community. However, the government still perceived him as a rabble-rouser and, in 1915, arrested him for selling liquor without a licence. After serving a one-year gaol term, he failed to respond to additional charges and further inflamed the situation by admitting to an official that he hoped the Germans would win the First World War. In April 1916 a police force sent to arrest him for sedition clashed with Rua and his Israelites. Two Israelites were killed and three more wounded.

---

[34] Peter Webster, *Rua and the Maori Millennium* (Wellington, 1979), p. 158.

Prophetic churches continued to trouble the colonial state right up to the eve of independence. In September 1953 Alice Lenshina, an illiterate woman in her early thirties living in Bemba territory, Northern Rhodesia, emerged from a coma and announced that she had died and been resurrected. Christ had shown her a true Bible specifically for Africans, from which she drew a puritanical moral code prohibiting beer-drinking and tobacco-smoking, polygyny, traditional dances, sorcery, and divination. Several years after her baptism in a Presbyterian mission, she founded the Lumpa (To Be Superior) Church, which attracted adherents away from Presbyterian and Catholic congregants. Some of her appeal lay in her offer of protection from witchcraft by administering a powerful medicine, a practice similar to the *bamucapi* cult that had entered Bemba territory from Nyasaland several decades before. Although Lenshina expressed no political aspirations, her church recognized only her authority and was antagonistic to both the colonial regime and mission churches. The Lumpa Church became an independent force, establishing villages throughout the region. The Church collected tribute from chiefs, and her deacons (*badikoni*) harassed people who did not pay. Its principal leaders were teachers who had lost their jobs after colonial officials upgraded teachers' standards. Many women were attracted to Lenshina because she portrayed herself as a mediator between earth and God, a traditional women's role, and stressed the sacredness of home and marital purity and harmony.[35] In 1959 colonial officials brought conflict to a head by sending police to expel illegal residents at Kasomo. The following year Lenshina went to teach at the copperbelt; in her absence, many of her followers lent their support to the nationalist political parties leading the struggle for independence. When Lenshina returned home several years later, she enjoined her followers not to participate in politics. However, after the 1962 election produced the territory's first African government, the United National Independence Party, featuring Bemba leaders such as Kenneth Kaunda and Simon Kapwepwe, clashes between her female followers and male party members regularly broke out. Lumpa members perceived themselves in a life-and-death struggle for survival, and it did not matter whether they were confronting white or black rulers. As independence neared in late 1964, several incidents escalated into confrontations with government forces between June and October in which over 1,500 church

---

[35] Hugo Hinfelaar, 'Women's Revolt: The Lumpa Church of Lenshina Mulenga in the 1950s', *Journal of Religion in Africa*, XXI (1991), pp. 99–128.

members died. Conflict between Church and State would survive the end of Empire.

Select Bibliography

JAMES CAMPBELL, *Songs of Zion: The African Methodist Episcopal Church in the United States and South Africa* (New York, 1995).

M. DANEEL, *Old and New in Southern Shona Independent Churches, I, Background and Rise of the Major Movements* (The Hague, 1972).

ROBERT EDGAR and HILARY SAPIRE, *African Apocalypse: The Story of Nontetha Nkwenkwe, a Twentieth Century South African Prophet* (Athens, OH, 2000).

BRONWYN ELSMORE, *Mana from Heaven: A Century of Maori Prophets in New Zealand* (Tauranga, 1989).

KAREN FIELDS, *Revival and Rebellion in Colonial Central Africa* (Portsmouth, NH, 1997).

FRANCIS GITHIEYA, *The Freedom of the Spirit: African Indigenous Churches in Kenya* (Atlanta, 1997).

ELIZABETH GUNNER, *Man of Heaven and the Beautiful Ones of God: Writings from Ibandla lamaNazaretha, a South African Church* (Leiden, 2002).

CYNTHIA HOEHLER-FATTON, *Women of Fire and Spirit: History, Faith, and Gender in Roho Religion in Western Kenya* (Oxford, 1996).

DAVID MAXWELL, 'Historicizing Christian Independency: The Southern African Pentecostal Movement c.1908–1960', *Journal of African History*, XL (1999), pp. 243–64.

ROBERT CAMERON MITCHELL, 'Religious Protest and Social Change: The Origins of the Aladura Movement in Western Nigeria', in Robert Rotberg and Ali Mazrui, eds., *Protest and Power in Black Africa* (New York, 1970), 458–96.

CAROL ANN MULLER, *Rituals of Fertility and the Sacrifice of Desire* (Chicago, 1999).

J. D. Y. PEEL, *Aladura: A Religious Movement among the Yoruba* (London, 1968).

D. D. PHIRI, *John Chilembwe* (Lilongwe, 1976).

T. O. RANGER, 'The Influenza Pandemic in Southern Rhodesia: A Crisis of Comprehension', in David Arnold, ed., *Imperial Medicine and Indigenous Societies* (New York, 1988), pp. 172–89.

JEAN ROSENFELD, *The Island Broken in Two Halves: Land and Renewal Movements among the Maori* (University Park, Pa., 1999).

DAVID SANDGREN, *Christianity and the Kikuyu: Religious Divisions and Social Conflict* (New York, 1989).

GEORGE SHEPPERSON and THOMAS PRICE, *Independent African: John Chilembwe and the Origins, Setting and Sign of the Nyasaland Native Rising of 1915* (Edinburgh, 1958).
BENGT SUNDKLER, *Zulu Zion and Some Swazi Zionists* (London, 1976).
ABSOLOM VILAKAZI, *Shembe: The Revitalization of African Society* (Johannesburg, 1986).
PETER WEBSTER, *Rua and the Maori Millennium* (Wellington, 1979).

12

Anthropology

PATRICK HARRIES

'Anthropology was born of the marriage of foreign missions and modern science,' wrote W. C. Willoughby confidently in 1913.[1] Edwin Smith, another leading missionary anthropologist, repeated this assertion eleven years later. 'Social anthropology might almost be claimed as a missionary science,' he declared, 'first, on account of its great utility to missionaries, and second, because the material upon which it is built has so largely been gathered by them.'[2] When Smith wrote these lines, missionaries' sturdy tribal monographs lined the shelves of the new university departments of social anthropology, their articles filled a range of journals, and they were about to play a leading role in the funding and organization of the new discipline.[3] Yet within ten years the age of the missionary anthropologist was in decline and his, rather than her, contribution to the discipline quickly faded. This chapter explores the emergence and decline of missionary contributions to anthropology.

Missionaries as Commentators on Indigenous Society

Missionaries contributed some of the earliest works of anthropology, ranging from Jean de Léry's *Histoire d'un voyage en terre du Brésil* (1578), which Claude Lévi-Strauss described as the first work of ethnography, to the classics of François-Xavier de Charlevoix and Jean-Marie Lafitau, Jesuit missionaries in early eighteenth-century Canada. European philosophers turned to such missionary texts to find evidence in support of their explanations for such phenomena as the origins of language or the development of private property. Missionaries were obliged to become skilled propagandists

---

[1] W. C. Willoughby, review of *Life of a South African Tribe*, IRM (1913), p. 588.
[2] E. W. Smith, 'Social Anthropology and Mission Work', *IRM* XIII (1924), p. 518.
[3] Henk J. van Rinsum, 'Edwin W. Smith and his "Raw Material": Texts of a Missionary and Ethnographer in Context', *Anthropos*, XCIV (1999), pp. 351–80.

to raise funds for their costly evangelical endeavours and gladly supplied metropolitan thinkers with the data on the place and evolution of humanity in the world.

In the early nineteenth century this genre of literature, focusing on travel and description, grew appreciably in size, introducing tens of thousands of readers to the diverse habits and customs of a wide range of peoples. Missionary bulletins, journals, magazines, religious tracts, and Sunday school literature carried a good deal of information on the customs of people in need of evangelical attention.[4] Photographs were used from an early date to raise the awareness of supporters at home and to solicit funds. Owing to the predominant missionary concern to propagate the gospel, there was a tendency to portray the customs of native peoples as an obstacle to civilization and, hence, as a worthy target for the ministrations of metropolitan Christians. Alternatively, indigenous people were portrayed as victims of the despotism of their rulers, slave traders, or, merely, the weight of custom and community. However, some missionaries developed an exposé literature aimed at denouncing the injustices to which their congregants, real and potential, were subjected by colonial rule. As missionaries became familiar with local customs, governments increasingly called on them to provide information on the people among whom they lived. When colonial governments tried to impress the rule of law in frontier areas, this information grew to include descriptions of local customs, evidence on how best to supply the labour market, or simply suggestions on how to solve 'the native problem'.

By the third quarter of the nineteenth century many missionaries were eager to display their observations of native peoples before a more scholarly readership. The large and growing number of geographical society journals and the first anthropological journals provided a natural home for articles on ethnographic subjects. Missionaries also began to publish books on customs and beliefs of various peoples. Books such as Fritz Ramseyer's *Quatre ans chez les Achanties* (1876) painted a vivid picture of the dark forces faced by evangelical Christians in Africa and remained a key text in missionary propaganda for the next hundred years. During this 'heroic age' of evangelical expansion, many other missionaries contributed to the view that 'heathen' customs were of diabolical inspiration. In an age of growing racism,

---

[4] N. J. van Warmelo, *Anthropology of Southern Africa in Periodicals to 1950* (Pretoria, 1977); T. Barringer, 'Why Are Missionary Periodicals (not) so Boring?', *African Research and Documentation*, LXXXIV (2000), pp. 33–46.

these texts buttressed the view that non-European peoples were fixed at lower levels of evolution and that only missionary supervision could bring about their spiritual and secular salvation.[5]

Other work presented a more favourable picture of indigenous societies. *Les Bassoutos* (1859) by Eugène Casalis, a French Protestant missionary in South Africa, provided an enlightened description of the 'habits and customs' of the Basotho. Henry Callaway and John Colenso, both bishops in the Anglican Church, produced pioneering work in the fields of Zulu religion and folklore. Jeff Guy has drawn attention to the importance of William Ngidi, Colenso's assistant, in delineating features of Zulu religion and persuading the bishop to accept some African beliefs and practices that were unacceptable to his Church. David Chidester, on the other hand, holds that Callaway and Colenso 'invented' African religion through a discursive strategy built on analogies drawn between modern African beliefs and those of the Old Testament and ancient Europe. For Guy, and Colenso himself, the bishop's Christianity was strongly influenced by the authentic religiosity of the Zulu people; for Chidester, that religiosity was constructed by Europeans who, confronted by new concepts of deep time and biblical criticism, were eager to extend their knowledge of history beyond the 6,000 years contained in the Bible. Educated churchmen in the outposts of Empire sought—and found—reflections of their own morality and belief systems, and a universality of religion in the behaviour and practices of primitive people. However, in the process they created ('invented' or 'imagined') rather than 'found' many non-European religions.[6] Missionaries certainly spent a good deal of time looking for a Supreme Being in the languages of the communities they encountered. Yet frequently they ended up finding only vestiges of this figure in their searches and, in the process, convinced themselves that local religious beliefs had degenerated from the monotheistic stage recounted in the Bible.[7] Other missionaries believed they could find vernacular terms for a Supreme Being in native languages, and with these terms, proof of an evolved, almost natural, religious consciousness in primitive societies.

[5] Revd J. G. Wood, *The Natural History of Men* (London, 1868), p. 53; Revd William Holden, *The Past and Future of the Kaffir Races* (London, 1866).

[6] D. Chidester, *Savage Systems: Colonialism and Comparative Religion in Southern Africa* (Cape Town, 1996), chap. 4; Jeff Guy, 'Class, Imperialism and Literary Criticism: William Ngidi, John Colenso and Matthew Arnold', *Journal of Southern African Studies*, XXIII (1997), pp. 219–41.

[7] Eugène Casalis, *Les Bassoutos; ou, Vingt-Trois Années d'études et d'observations au sud de l'Afrique* (Paris, 1859), p. 298; Henry Callaway, 'On the Religious Sentiment amongst the Tribes of South Africa', *Cape Monthly Magazine*, N S VIII (Feb. 1880), pp. 92 ff.

But many of their colleagues, often in the same missionary society, believed they had merely invented a name for God by infusing local words with their own, Christian meanings. (See pp. 206–11.)

Virtually all missionaries adhered to a common belief in the biblical narrative of a single origin of humankind. This put them in the opposite camp to that of the polygenists, who held that humankind had many origins and that its races were the equivalent of zoological species. Monogenist missionaries gathered in the Aborigines Protection Society (founded 1837), which was concerned with human rights, and the Ethnological Society of London (founded 1843), which was concerned with science. In Africa they threw themselves into the moral crusade of the anti-slavery movement. This cocktail of humanitarian care and scientific curiosity underlay much of the missionaries' interest in the workings of aboriginal societies. During the third quarter of the nineteenth century missionary texts grew in sophistication and scale. By this stage, too, the rise of evolutionist theory as the key to understanding led 'scientific' theorists to look more closely at the elements of humanity on the outskirts of Empire. Johan Bachofen in Basel, Lewis Henry Morgan in the United States, Edward Tylor and, later, James Frazer in Oxford turned to missionary writings to recover a picture of aboriginals who seemed to represent an unrecorded stage in Europe's history. A relationship quickly developed between missionaries and metropolitan experts whereby the men in the field, like collectors in the natural sciences, supplied the professionals at home with the evidence needed to classify and compare cultures. By tracing the vestiges, or 'survivals', of previous cultures found in current practices, these early anthropologists believed they could detect the course of humanity as it progressed from one stage of evolution to another. Bachofen claimed to find evidence of an earlier, 'matriarchal' stage of development in missionaries' reports on the special relationship in some African societies between a son and his mother's brother and descriptions of female 'Amazon' warriors. Armchair anthropologists could piece together these remnants of earlier cultures and construct, in much the same way as palaeontologists with a few bones, an earlier stage of human existence. Bachofen remarked with some irony that he had undertaken all his fieldwork 'in his slippers', and Tylor and Frazer, famously for later generations, never crossed the Mediterranean. The missionaries' role as fieldworkers in the pursuit of knowledge provided a new sense of purpose and a link with influential centres of knowledge and power at home. The rise of anthropology as a science also caused many missionaries to reconsider the culture of primitive peoples in new ways. As the beliefs and practices of aboriginal peoples became a focus of science, their culture was viewed increasingly as an object of legitimate interest rather than a product of diabolical agency or a sign of human decadence. Some missionaries shifted their attention away from the dark, gothic practices and unspeakable rites that called for Christian intervention, towards appreciation of the spiritual and spontaneous disposition of aboriginal peoples.

Most missionaries were content to play the junior partner in modern science by reporting on the customs of natives and to see their observations incorporated into the works of the experts at home. However, there were exceptions. Lorimer Fison, a Methodist missionary in Fiji, collected folklore in the 1860s and corresponded with Max Müller and Lewis Morgan. He went even further during a stay in Australia by classifying kinship terminology in such a way as to elaborate on Morgan's evolutionary schema. He and his colleague A. W. Howitt showed that Australian Aborigines had their own marriage rules and gave their own meanings, filled with implicit rights and obligations, to different, classificatory members of the 'family' or group. Most importantly, Fison stressed the importance of the community in Aboriginal life. Individuals had no say in marriage strategies, which, he pointed out, were decided on by the tribe, or the class within the tribe, to which the individual belonged. Fison went on to show that one of the communities he described practised an extremely early form of marriage. In this community people formed promiscuous liaisons within their group while, in the second group he studied, people had 'advanced' from the stage of 'group marriage' to one in which marriages were entered into between partners. The next stage in the evolution of marriage practices was also manifested in this group by the existence of marriage by elopement. By choosing to enter into this form of marriage, women placed their individual interests above those of the community. This not only showed an 'advance' in the growth of individualism; it also indicated an evolution towards patriarchy as marital rights were transferred from the group to the husband. Fison's work combined research in the field with theory. It seemed to unveil Aboriginal communities as remnants of a lost past that provided a living picture of the long evolution of humanity. By situating these groups on an evolutionary scale, he indicated how they should be governed. Experts in the metropole praised Fison's contribution to the advancement of anthropology.[8]

[8] George Stocking, *After Tylor: British Social Anthropology, 1888–1951* (London, 1996), pp. 17–34; Patrick Wolfe, *Settler Colonialism and the Transformation of Anthropology* (London, 1999), pp. 94–5.

Fison encouraged other missionaries to gather ethnographic data, particularly the Oxford-educated Anglican missionary Robert Codrington, who arrived in Melanesia in 1863. (See p. 201.) Codrington was appalled by the ravages brought to isolated island communities by labour-recruiting, imported liquor, and other elements of European civilization. This led him to regard contemporary evolutionist theories with scepticism and, instead, to construct an ethnography based on careful personal observation. Codrington brought a critical eye to his 'fieldwork' by questioning the bias of his Christian and non-Christian informants, and by interrogating the deep importance of translation. He was particularly concerned to give the native point of view by transcribing verbatim accounts of their beliefs and practices. This led him to look behind the 'superstitions' of the natives for a system of religious belief that he described as 'mana', a supernatural power distinct from Tylor's notion of animism. Codrington and Fison developed a critical ethnography that was not subservient to the theories of the experts with whom they communicated in England and America. But whereas Fison organized his work around the concept of evolution, Codrington wrote in a pre-evolutionist register that avoided explanation or that attributed change to the early migrations of population groups.[9]

Missionaries in many parts of the Empire shared Fison's interest in folklore. Their work in the fields of translation and transcription necessarily drew them into the oral literature of these communities. Following the lead of philological experts in Europe, many missionaries believed that linguistics and folklore could indicate the level of development of the natives just as effectively as the structure of kinship. There was no consensus on these issues. Some missionaries thought the languages and oral literatures of aboriginal communities rich and creative expressions of an original mindset, while others regarded them as degenerate remnants of a former, higher stage of evolution—or as childlike products infused with sin and immorality. Those influenced by romanticism saw in native languages and folklore a reflection of primitive, pre-Christian purity, the soul of a people, and a creative genius and morality that had a specific contribution to make to the evolution of humanity. Missionaries played a vital role in capturing on paper languages and folklores that were threatened with extinction by the rising tide of modernity.

[9] Stocking, *After Tylor*, pp. 34–46; S. Sohmer, 'The Melanesian Mission and Victorian Anthropology', in R. MacLeod and P. F. Rehbock, eds., *Darwin's Laboratory: Evolutionary Theory and Natural History in the Pacific* (Honolulu, 1994).

There were differences of opinion over the plasticity of folklore. Was it, as the romantics believed, a true reflection of the soul of a people, or merely a creative product shaped and formed by the changing context in which those people lived. There was debate over whether folklore needed to be copied verbatim from elderly representatives of the tribe or whether it could be collected by students and Christian converts. Despite these differences of opinion, virtually all missionaries saw folklore as a window to the beliefs, values, and morality of native communities. It thus served to provide a linguistic group with beliefs and practices that distinguished its culture from that of its neighbours. In this way, the missionaries in the field distinguished tribes, nations, and peoples as clearly defined groups on which they reported to the philological experts at home. These professionals then compared the different languages and grouped them into linguistic families in much the same way as natural scientists gathered related species of animals and plants into a common genus. This was a way of filling space with manageable units; but it was also a powerful new means of explanation. As the borders of Empire expanded, the State's concern with native peoples shifted from frontier policing to administration and control of newly subject peoples.

Unfortunately, many scholars came to treat the names of linguistic categories not just as terms applied to specific facts they had grouped together, but as facts themselves. The same process occurred in the natural sciences when collectors 'uncovered' relationships between species they saw as either God's handiwork or the product of the laws of nature. This way of looking at the composition of the animate (and inanimate) world obscured the degree of human invention and imagination required to assemble languages and related folklores, or, for that matter, species of butterflies or beetles. However, this approach had the great advantage of providing the world with a regular order by placing individuals in groups that could be situated in both time and space. The reification of an idea (a linguistic category invented by human beings) into a social group (a natural tribe or race) had important political consequences.

At the turn of the twentieth century peripatetic missionaries were driven by their intellectual background, and by the nature of their work, to lump tribal peoples together in generic groups such as 'the Kaffirs' or 'the Bantu'. Books on these subjects, with their sweeping claims about the natives, initially enjoyed a wide popular appeal. But it was the splitters, concentrating on narrow tribal groups, who came to dominate the emerging discipline of anthropology. Missionaries gradually covered the Empire with a patchwork of tribal studies; through their published works and museum exhibitions, they popularized this perception of the tribe as the natural social unit for 'primitive' and 'savage' peoples. In the metropole this work gradually won the support of both professional anthropologists and missionary societies. Progressive missionaries moderated their condemnatory approach to aboriginal cultures and, instead, sought to select and understand certain practices as a legitimate basis on which to build new and authentic forms of Christianity, education, and politics.

The conquests that accompanied the spread of Empire also required a thorough knowledge of aboriginal cultures. In some areas, like the Gold Coast, the colonial government was willing to invest time and money in this task; but in other areas, such as South Africa in the years after the Anglo-Boer War, missionaries initially shouldered this role, particularly through their participation in the South African Association for the Advancement of Science. In 1907 this association called on the South African states to preserve the observations made by missionaries and others before 'the advance of civilization began to obscure and even obliterate all true traditions, customs and habits of the South African peoples'. These would soon be 'irrevocably lost' as the missionaries died out or became frail, the committee warned in its annual report, which mooted the establishment of a Central Ethnographical Bureau for the British colonies of South Africa and stressed that success depended on the willingness of missionaries to participate in the collection of artefacts and data.[10]

Calls for evangelical enthusiasm to be reinforced by anthropological understanding culminated in 1910 when Commission IV of the World Missionary Conference debated this point in Edinburgh. The issue was of vital importance for the many young practitioners, who were calling for Christianity to be built on the positive aspects of indigenous culture. This perspective won the day at Edinburgh when the Conference called on each mission society to embark on a scientific study of the population inhabiting its field of operation. J. H. Oldham, an Oxford graduate and former missionary in India, was a leading force in propelling the missionary movement towards greater concern with social and political issues. He had played a major role at Edinburgh, served as Secretary to the Conference Continuation Committee and, in 1912, founded the *International Review of Missions*. At a

---

[10] *Report of the South African Association for the Advancement of Science* (1908), pp. xxiv–xxvii.

time when missionaries were still destroying shrines and killing sacred pythons in Tanganyika, and burning protective charms on the Witwatersrand, this journal saw anthropology as a tool that would enable missionaries to understand the cultures, and come to love the people to whom they had been assigned by their calling. It would soon develop into a leading review attracting articles and book reviews, from both amateurs and professionals, on the theory, methodology, and experience of anthropology.

Contributions to the Methodology and Theory of Anthropology

The great age of missionary anthropology was built on tribal monographs taking a holistic approach to aboriginal communities. These works generally aimed to capture a picture of primitive society before it was transformed by capitalism and colonialism. Primitivism had many faces for these missionary anthropologists for, while it constituted the major obstacle to conversion, it also embodied the creative originality of a society that had not been corrupted by cold logic and dry materialism. These primitive communities displayed a respect for community, family, and hierarchy that Europe had forgotten. For a few missionaries, as for Marlow in Joseph Conrad's *Heart of Darkness*, the hollow nature of European 'civilization' was most evident in the African bush or on a Melanesian island. However, natives also practised customs that missionaries found repugnant and sought to suppress, such as infanticide, abortion, slavery, human sacrifice, and, in India, widow-burning, child marriages, and hook-swinging (a festival ritual in which a devotee is suspended by hooks piercing his flesh from a pillar in front of the temple and swings to and fro). Missionaries debated the morality of customs that some thought could be adapted to conform to their definitions of Christianity. The polygamous condition of men joining the Church was acceptable to Bishop John Colenso in Natal in the 1860s, for instance, because he wanted to avoid the pain caused by the dissolution of their marriages. But he refused to allow Christians to take new wives and he banned polygamists from holding office in the Church. Most missionary societies, on the other hand, allowed polygamists to join the Church as on-trial members but would not baptize them, or bring them into the congregation of communicants, until they had suppressed their polygamous marriages. In most cases, although a polygamist's wives could receive baptism, a Christian man could neither inherit wives nor secure his marriage through the payment of bride price. Some missions even obliged their Christian converts to terminate their polygamous marriages entirely by recalling the bride prices, paid for their wives, that held their in-laws' marriages in place.

The point is that missionary anthropologists were unable to observe aboriginal life without suggesting ways it could be improved. Indeed, they could hardly develop a purely scientific, objective gaze when their vocation required them to propagate a fundamental reformation of the lives of the people to whom they brought the gospel. Many missionary anthropologists were fully aware that, just as they documented aboriginal cultures, they were undermining and destroying those same cultures. Henri-Alexandre Junod tried to overcome this problem by appending to his 'scientific' monograph various appendices suggesting how missionaries and administrators might ameliorate the conditions of the tribe during a time of rapid change. However, few of Junod's readers made this distinction and, instead, tended to treat his monograph as a scientific work containing various proposals on how to 'improve' the lives of the people he studied.[11] The missionaries' attempts to 'salvage' or 'reconstitute' a picture of primitive society, even as they colluded in its destruction, met with no more success. The image of a pure, pre-contact indigenous society uncontaminated by colonialism or capitalism would eventually undermine the tribal monograph. This genre of writing made distant peoples far more visible to Europeans; but it was based on situations and suppositions that would rapidly be overtaken by events.

Meanwhile, many missionary anthropologists remained content to serve as local agents for metropolitan figures. James Frazer's set of questions encouraged several missionaries to adopt an evolutionary perspective and to concentrate on topics such as kinship and taboo. This led to some startling discoveries. Through comparative work engaged in an evolutionist register, missionary anthropologists working in very different parts of the world discerned a hierarchy of cultures that seemed to explain the successes and failures of different societies.[12] Aspects of missionary work also reflected some of the darker ideas of the age. Dudley Kidd noted that Africans suffered from a form of arrested mental development at puberty and, in a highly influential work, turned to eugenics to solve this problem. Even Henri-Alexandre Junod, whom Adrian Hastings portrays as the most eminent

[11] Edwin Smith, review of *Life of a South African Tribe*, IRM XIV (1928), pp. 381–3.
[12] Stocking, *After Tylor*, p. 45; H.-A. Junod, *Life of a South African Tribe*, 2 vols. (London, 1927), II, pp. 449–59.

missionary intellectual of his age, tentatively accepted the notion that Africans could be intellectually precocious as children and then experience an arrested development in mid-adolescence. He certainly believed that Africans had yet to evolve from childlike ignorance to the enlightenment of adulthood and exaggerated the weight of tribal traditions and customs. From his perspective, aboriginal intelligence was a collective act concerned with the well-being and reproduction of the tribe. Individuals performed specific functions, lived and died, were replaced and renewed, as if driven by instinct and habit rather than by will or reason; and only on very few occasions did they exercise the power of thought or the ability to act in innovative ways. Both Junod and Kidd opposed the extension of the Cape's qualified franchise when, in 1909–10, the British colonies and old Boer republics were incorporated into a new Union of South Africa.[13]

The professionalization of anthropology initially created vocational openings for some missionaries at colonial universities. But within a short time they found themselves excluded from the network of interests that developed along with the new discipline. The first salvo in the conflict between missionary and secular anthropology took place at the University of Cape Town, where, in 1918, South African lobbyists ensured the election of a missionary linguist to the first professorship of Bantu languages. Three years later an English advisory committee offered the Chair in Anthropology, the first in the British Empire, to a Cambridge graduate, A. R. Brown. The future Radcliffe-Brown set about defining the professional frontiers of his discipline on the basis of anthropological theories that left little place for amateur practitioners. Rather than focus his criticism on the evolutionist ideas of his patrons at home, Radcliffe-Brown turned on the missionary rivals with whom, in the colonial context, he competed for funding and posts. These included his hapless colleague Professor Norton, as well as some of the major figures in the field. In a seminal article published in the mouthpiece of the South African Association for the Advancement of Science he developed a functionalist critique of the evolutionist hypothesis used by Junod to explain the relationship between a Thonga man and his mother's brother.[14] In another, equally seminal article, he relegated all studies of culture and society that used an evolutionist approach to the category of 'ethnology'. This he

---

[13] Junod, *Life*, I, pp. 99, 545; D. Kidd, *Kaffir Socialism and the Dawn of Individualism* (London, 1908), pp. 114–16.

[14] 'The Mother's Brother in South Africa', *South African Journal of Science*, XXI (1924), pp. 542–55.

distinguished from 'social anthropology', which was concerned with 'the application of certain logical methods' and 'certain general laws'.[15] In this way, Radcliffe-Brown placed the tribal monographs written by missionaries somewhere between the travel literature of the nineteenth century and the social anthropology practised by the university graduates. In practice, he was unable to implement a clear distinction between the work of amateurs and professionals, partly because he had to rely on missionary monographs for teaching purposes and partly because, in the process of establishing the utility of anthropology, he ran diploma courses for missionaries and civil servants. These courses attracted a remarkable number and range of scholars working within the ambit of missionary anthropology. However, as anthropology grew stronger and more self-confident, this working alliance with missionaries would break down. In the meantime, the crack in the discipline would work its way from the periphery to the centre of Empire.

In Britain anthropology remained firmly in the hands of the friends of the missionaries. In 1920 W. H. R. Rivers continued to alert missionaries to the benefits of an understanding of native customs, particularly through means of intensive participant observation.[16] When Bronislaw Malinowski returned to London from Melanesia two years later, he brought an acquired antipathy towards missionaries, who, he considered, interfered unnecessarily in the lives of native peoples (though he limited any public expression of this opinion to a short caricature in the introduction to *Argonauts of the Western Pacific*).[17] In 1923, the year after the publication of his monograph, he employed the missionary as one of a series of shadowy straw men in his Frazer lecture. In outlining the methodological basis of his new approach to the discipline, Malinowski famously called on the anthropologist to relinquish the comfort of the long chair on the verandah of the missionary compound. At the same time he heaped public praise on the work of missionary anthropologists and developed a strategic relationship with their chief representative, J. H. Oldham.[18]

Oldham had initially seen anthropology as a rather impractical science devoted to theoretical issues; but Malinowski's stress on fieldwork convinced

---

[15] 'Methods of Ethnology and Social Anthropology', *South African Journal of Science*, XX (1923), pp. 124–47.

[16] W. Rivers, 'Anthropology and the Missionary', *Church Missionary Review*, LXXI (1920), pp. 208–15.

[17] B. Malinowski, *A Diary in the Strict Sense of the Term* (London, 1967), pp. 31, 42.

[18] Hortense Powdermaker, *Stranger and Friend* (London, 1966), p. 43.

him of the discipline's utility to the missionary movement. Missionaries played a key role in colonial education, and Oldham, as Secretary of both the Church Missionary Society and the International Missionary Council, sat on an important committee advising the Colonial Office in this domain. In 1924–5 he and his colleagues organized a series of conferences that resulted in the formation of the Institute of African Languages and Cultures. Through his contacts with evangelical movements in America, Oldham was able to link scholars at the African Institute with philanthropists in America, particularly the Phelps-Stokes Fund, Carnegie Corporation, and Rockefeller Foundation. (See p. 272.) By 1928 this alliance of missionaries, professors, and administrators, supported by American funders, had placed the southwest Pacific in Radcliffe-Brown's hands and was about to deliver Africa to Malinowski and Oldham.[19]

The American philanthropists valued the settler colonies in Africa as spaces in which to experiment with educational theories. In colonies of settlement, as in America, 'industrial' or 'adapted' education was aimed at reducing competition and conflict between the races. In colonies governed through indirect rule or limited self-government, members of the International African Institute saw this form of education as a means of encouraging and perpetuating the contribution to humanity of Africans as a group. This educational policy required a thorough, dispassionate understanding of all African cultural practices. Unlike the missionaries, who sought to amend, even suppress, cultural practices that contradicted their sense of morality, functionalist anthropologists insisted on the value of all African institutions, customs, and beliefs. In the lexicon of functionalist anthropology, even the most irrational or immoral practices served a purpose. For the new anthropologists, the institutions, customs, and beliefs of primitive societies were organically related in such a way as to maximize the smooth functioning of the whole. 'In all groups except the Nguni', Schapera wrote with icy detachment in 1937, 'it is not only justifiable but also customary to kill one or both of twins, or children born feet first, or cutting their upper teeth first, or presenting some other abnormality. Such children are regarded as evil omens who must be put out of the way as soon as possible lest they bring disease to their families.'[20] It was difficult for missionaries,

---

[19] Henrika Kuklick, *The Savage Within: The Social History of British Anthropology* (Cambridge, 1991), pp. 205–9; Stocking, *After Tylor*, pp. 397–406; Jack Goody, *The Expansive Moment: Anthropology in Britain and Africa 1918–1970* (Cambridge, 1995), pp. 13–25.

[20] Isaac Schapera, *The Bantu-Speaking Tribes of South Africa* (Cape Town, 1937), p. 210.

with their moralistic approach and interventionist tradition, to objectify their research in this way.

The effect of a rapidly changing world on primitive societies concerned the functionalist anthropologists even more than missionaries. From their perspective, the destruction of one element in the overall structure could lead to a social imbalance and the general decline of the group. The destruction of native cultures transformed aboriginal peoples into dangerous proletarians no longer subjected to the social and political controls of their communities. Alternatively, through the creation of 'black Englishmen' or 'copies of Europeans', missionaries and others obliterated the genius of African peoples and reduced their novel contribution to the growth and development of humanity.[21] This perspective underlay the new emphasis on education adapted to local aptitudes and conditions, and it called for new strategies of conversion concentrating on the organic community rather than the individual. It also deterred nationalist critics from denouncing the mission as a tool of cultural imperialism. In Asia the cultural arrogance of the early missionary movement had fired nationalist criticisms of colonialism; in Africa the situation could still be saved by a more sensitive approach to cultural differences.[22]

A growing number of missionaries believed that, through the 'retention and sublimation' of indigenous cultural practices, they could construct a form of Christianity adapted to the needs of local peoples. Initiation was a central cause of concern for it combined explicit references to sex, and deeply painful forms of excision, with educational practices that could be harnessed by the missionary.[23] An earlier generation had equated the transfer of bride wealth with the purchase of a wife but, on closer inspection, it became possible to see *lobola* as a source of dignity for the woman and as a guarantee of fair treatment by her in-laws. Sharp differences of opinion arose on these issues. Henri-Alexandre Junod was by this stage a retired, but still leading, missionary anthropologist. He stressed the continuing importance of 'salvage' or 'reconstructive' anthropology, for the 'conflict of cultures' could only be understood once missionaries had a good grasp of the meaning

---

[21] Diedrich Westermann, 'The Value of the African's Past', *IRM* XV (1926), p. 429.

[22] J. W. Cell, *By Kenya Possessed: The Correspondence of Norman Leys and J. H. Oldham* (London, 1976), p. 57.

[23] Dora Earthy, 'The Customs of Gazaland Women in Relation to the African Church', *IRM* XV (1926), pp. 662–74; W. Vincent Lucas, 'The Educational Value of Initiatory Rites', and J. Raum, 'Christianity and African Puberty Rites', *IRM* XVI (1927), pp. 192–8, 581–91; W. C. Willoughby, 'Building the African Church', *IRM* XV (1926), pp. 450–6.

of original, primitive practices. He was convinced that detailed ethnographic accounts were more valuable in recording cultural practices than functionalist theories or works concentrating on their disintegration. Ancestor worship, Junod thought, 'guaranteed social morality, respect for hierarchy, the maintenance of order and authority in the tribe'. He questioned the need to sublimate or temporarily allow practices such as bride price exchange that created bonds of indebtedness and mistrust between families.[24] Despite reservations of Junod and others, missionaries who attempted to naturalize Christianity in the field were drawn to the opinions of the proponents of indirect rule and the functionalist anthropologists.[25] Rather than destroy the finely balanced texture of primitive societies, they sought to build Christianity on the basis of indigenous beliefs and practices and in this way respond to the needs of local society. For the missionary committed to the construction of an indigenous Christianity, social anthropology was a key tool.

In the 1920s missionaries and professional anthropologists became alarmed at the large-scale movement of native peoples to the cities. As women moved to the cities in greater numbers, it became clear that the African family had rooted itself in the urban areas and that missionaries would have to familiarize themselves with its structure and problems. If the process of urbanization in the Empire was monitored and controlled, the work of scholars and social activists could serve to reduce the social disruption and class conflict caused by industrialization. With the centre of the 'native problem' moving from the rural areas to the settler-dominated cities, the spectre of racial competition and conflict became a growing reality; articles on economic conditions and social problems in the cities started to fill missionary journals and publications. In 1925 the General Missionary Conference of South Africa published a handbook filled with these topics, several written by black political leaders sympathetic to the missionary movement.[26] From the vantage point of the university, professional anthropologists were required to maintain more distance from the objects of their study. Nevertheless, the two approaches to urbanization frequently overlapped.

The policies adopted by the coalition of interests grouped around Malinowski and Oldham appealed to a human rights culture in Britain

[24] H.-A. Junod, review of E. W. Smith, *The Golden Stool*, IRM XV (1926), pp. 607–9, and id., 'Moral Sense among the Bantu', IRM XVI (1927).

[25] R. Sutherland Rattray, 'Anthropology and Christian Missions', *Africa*, I (1928), pp. 94–106.

[26] J. Dexter Taylor, ed., *Christianity and the Natives of South Africa: A Yearbook of South African Missions* (Johannesburg, 1925).

and Africa, but in racially divided colonies of settlement their ideas tended to support segregation. In South Africa this led to a growing divide within the anthropological fraternity. Isaac Schapera was one of the first to turn a critical eye on the homespun methodologies of the missionaries, as well as their notions of social change.[27] In 1928 Schapera fired a cannon across the bows of the missionary movement when he expanded the anthropologist's unit of study to include missionaries in the field. To understand the 'native problem', claimed Schapera, fresh from one of Radcliffe-Brown's classes at the University of Cape Town, anthropologists had to turn their gaze from the stable African tribe and focus on transitional figures like migrant labourers, as well as the dislocating forces of 'culture contact' and change. As segregation was clearly impossible within a common economy, anthropologists should include in their studies of African populations figures like the missionary, the native commissioner, and the labour recruiter.[28]

This perspective transformed the missionary from an empathetic observer committed to solving 'the native problem' into a major source of the upheaval that caused the problem in the first place. It was perhaps this concern with the compromised position of the missionary that led Schapera to exclude works by missionary anthropologists from his edited collection of essays *The Bantu-Speaking Tribes of South Africa* (1937). It might reasonably be suspected that Schapera's portrayal of the missionary as a compromised observer was dominated by his concern to undermine the position of a competitor in the workplace.[29] A more important criticism of missionary anthropology came from the ex-missionary educator and liberal politician Edgar Brookes, who, in 1934, declared that 'the older anthropological school' dominated by missionaries had 'supplied the segregationists with a badly-needed philosophy'. By regarding 'tribal natives' as the only phenomenon of study, it had created the impression that Africans formed a homogenous category and that they belonged in the rural reserves where they continued to live under chiefs 'on their own lines'. Through this native policy the development of the African population was held back and the contribution to the country of Africans in the city was ignored.[30]

---

[27] I. Schapera, 'The Present State and Future Development of Ethnographic Research in South Africa', *Bantu Studies*, VIII (1934), p. 244.

[28] I. Schapera, 'Economic Changes in South African Native Life', *Africa*, I (1928), pp. 170–88.

[29] Schapera advised anthropologists to emphasize kinship, 'where it would be easy for us to show our superior understanding' (Lyn Schumaker, *Africanizing Anthropology: Fieldwork, Networks, and the Making of Cultural Knowledge in Central Africa* (London, 2001), p. 241).

[30] Edgar Brookes, *The Colour Problems of South Africa* (London, 1934), p. 145.

W. M. Macmillan, Professor of History at the University of the Witwatersrand, also berated the 'scientists' who, by protesting against Europe's 'perverting influence' on 'pure African culture', were responsible for 'the break away from the ideal of common citizenship'. By contrasting 'a highly idealized African rusticity' with 'diabolical slums', anthropologists represented the rural reserves as the natural environment of the African population. 'The facts of Africa as we begin to know them', he continued, 'make nonsense of the dream that tribal life is a state of idyllic peace and contentment marred only when civilization interferes.' These rural societies were dominated by hunger and disease, witchcraft and superstition, and they lacked freedom and democracy. Macmillan found shards of the old anthropology in the work of the new generation. He criticized the patchwork approach taken by Schapera in his collection of essays on the tribes of South Africa because it racialized the tribe as the classic unit of study for Africans and represented the African population not as a national force, but as what Margery Perham would go on to call a 'multi-cellular tissue of tribalism'.[31] By stressing the importance of 'decaying native customs', Schapera's collection exaggerated the importance of ethnic and racial differences in the country. Only one isolated chapter was devoted to a history of the forces that united the members of the different tribes. Macmillan also criticized the anthropologists' concern with 'data collection' and 'social change' as this approach ignored the root causes of poverty in South Africa and obscured the need for a political solution. In sum, anthropological work was politically divisive and reformist in nature; and it offered, as a solution to 'the native problem', only an ameliorative form of social work.[32] More seriously, functionalist anthropology viewed social change as an unsolicited source of disruption to life in the timeless tribal village. From this perspective, change was a source of trouble and confusion rather than innovation and progress. It merely highlighted the Africans' inability to adjust and adapt to new conditions and served to legitimize the protective aspects of segregation.

Macmillan certainly overstated his position, for anthropologists like Schapera had shown how African laws and customs grew and adapted to suit the conditions of a changing society. But in general, the 'new anthropologists',

---

[31] M. Perham, 'The British Problem in Africa', *Foreign Affairs*, XXIX (1951), p. 638.
[32] C. C. Saunders, *The Making of the South African Past* (Cape Town, 1988), p. 56; W. Macmillan, *Africa Emergent* (Harmondsworth, 1938; new edn. 1949), p. 12.

particularly those working in the cities, portrayed Africans as victims of change. This outlook fuelled the popular opinion that the Africans' natural home lay in the rural reserves where they could be protected from the dislocating forces of change and undergo a period of tutelage. The opinion that the 'new anthropology' had not shaken off the segregationist bias of the previous generation was compounded by the prefaces written by the South African prime minister Jan Smuts to important monographs by Monica Hunter (Wilson) and Eileen Krige.[33]

A Gulf Opens between Missionaries and Professional Anthropologists

Professional anthropologists continued to distance themselves from missionaries during the early 1930s. Winifred Hoernlé had expressed privately the same reservations about missionaries as Malinowski when, in 1912, she undertook fieldwork in Namaqualand.[34] As the influential Head of Anthropology at the University of the Witwatersrand (1923–37), and one of the leaders of the 'social work' approach of which Macmillan was so critical, she often invited professional anthropologists to address welfare circles in Johannesburg. On one occasion, in July 1934, Malinowski, Hoernlé, W. M. Eiselen, Monica Hunter, and Isaac Schapera all addressed a New Education Fellowship Conference in Johannesburg.

The missionary anthropologist Henri-Philippe Junod attended the symposium, from which he departed with the feeling that missionaries and their anthropology, perhaps particularly that of his father, had been unfairly criticized by these 'scientists' for failing to accept native customs or protect them from the destructive forces of modernity. In a combative article in the *International Review of Missions*, the younger Junod defended the right of missionaries to protect the interests of their communicants by prohibiting or amending unacceptable cultural practices. The payment of bride wealth for a wife was acceptable, he essayed, but not the rights of possession that went with the *lobola* and that condemned a wife to be inherited by one of her deceased husband's male relatives. He rejected what he considered obscene aspects of initiation but praised their educative elements, and he stressed the importance of Wayfarers' and Pathfinders' associations in educating young

---

[33] M. Hunter, *Reaction to Conquest* (London, 1936); E. Krige, *The Realm of a Rain-Queen* (London, 1943).

[34] Deborah Gaitskell, *Religion Embracing Science? Female Missionary Ventures in Southern African Anthropology*, Basel Afrika Bibliographien, Working Paper 5 (1998), p. 5.

people. He also drew attention to the importance of religion and spirituality in the missionary anthropologists' work, which combated the sterile materialism that, he considered, was the real cause of the destruction of native customs. In a final outburst, Henri-Philippe Junod decried the detachment of professional anthropologists from their object of study and their tendency 'to preserve native custom as a curio for some African museum'.[35]

This form of confrontation was rare, at least partly because of the missionaries' silence on the issue. Instead, missionary anthropologists increasingly wrote textbooks for practitioners in the field or, like E. W. Smith, adopted a functionalist approach.[36] They also threw themselves into the study of social change in urban areas, where their work tended to be strongly empirical and concerned with the practicalities of welfare during a period when Malinowski continued to publish articles in the *International Review of Missions*. Professional anthropology in South Africa gradually divided into two wings. Anthropology in the English-speaking universities came to centre on social change, racial discrimination, and the applied anthropology that could ameliorate the deteriorating conditions under which Africans lived. At these institutions the children of Jewish immigrants, themselves the victims of local bigotry, came to replace Haddon's Cambridge imports in the mid-1930s.[37] Cultural relativism flourished at the Afrikaans universities and in the Ethnology Section of the Native Affairs Department. The old anthropology fed into the view of the tribe, defined by language and culture, as the primary social institution on which rested the stability of the black population. The children of German missionaries played a particularly important role in establishing a form of anthropology that called for Africans to develop along their own lines and in their own communities.[38] But other missionary children also supported this perspective, either through their work in the Native Affairs Department, or through an anthropology that continued to focus on rural communities and cultural difference.

[35] H.-P. Junod, 'Anthropology and Missionary Education', *IRM* XXIV(1935), pp. 213–28.

[36] T. Cullen Young, *Contemporary Ancestors: A Beginner's Anthropology for District Officers and Missionaries in Africa* (London, 1940); J. M. Graham and R. Piddington, *Anthropology and the Future of Missions* (London, 1940).

[37] Isaac Schapera replaced one of Haddon's students as professor at Cape Town, and Hilda Kuper replaced Winifrid Hoernlé as head of department at the University of the Witwatersrand.

[38] Notably, W. Eiselen, Professor of Ethnology at Stellenbosch, N. J. van Warmelo, who headed the Ethnological Section of the Native Affairs Department, G. B. A. Gerdener, Professor of Missiology at Stellenbosch University, and E. Westphal, Head of Bantu Languages at the University of Cape Town.

The decline of missionary anthropology in the 1930s was accompanied, even aided, by the Trojan horse role played by the functionalist paradigm. Many metropolitan Christians were confused by compromises with far-off cultural practices that seemed to contradict the essence of their religion. Others were disconcerted by the self-critical approach of missionaries who blamed themselves and their religion for destabilizing or destroying African societies. G. T. Basden's critical picture of the effects of Christianity and colonialism on Ibo society, following his thirty years as a missionary in south-east Nigeria, did little to encourage the support of the faithful at home. Nor did Bengt Sundkler's *Bantu Prophets in South Africa* (1948) inspire confidence in the supporters of mission work who read of converts' tendencies in the region to slide from the mission church to Ethiopianism, Zionism, and then back into the arms of animism.[39] Many metropolitan Christians failed to see a link between the advance of the gospel and the exposure, by missionary anthropologists, of poor conditions on the copper mines of Northern Rhodesia.[40] Perhaps as a sign of this faltering commitment, the *International Review of Missions* gradually stopped publishing anthropological articles in the late 1940s.

If the link between functionalist anthropology and the advance of the gospel was only vaguely perceived by Christians at the heart of Empire, it was more visible to their co-religionists in Africa. In Kenya a heated debate over female circumcision and schooling brought several missions into conflict with the growing nationalist movement. This encouraged Jomo Kenyatta, one of Malinowski's students in London, to write a monograph on the Kikuyu as an organic community. For Kenyatta, the missionaries had 'shattered' Kikuyu institutions and 'condemned customs they did not understand'.[41] In Nyasaland, Hastings Banda also rejected missionary criticisms of African 'traditions', while at the same time working closely with the missionary anthropologist T. Cullen Young to 'reconstitute' Cewa customs and to build democracy and Christianity on these indigenous practices.[42] In South Africa the rhetoric of African nationalism shifted from the 'grievances' expressed by D. D. T. Jabavu to the illegitimacy of minority rule. In 1949 Robert Sobukwe criticized missionaries for 'maintaining an unbroken and

---

[39] B. Sundkler, *Bantu Prophets in South Africa* (London, 1948), p. 297.
[40] R. J. B. Moore, *These African Copper Miners* (London, 1948).
[41] J. Kenyatta, *Facing Mount Kenya* (London, 1938), pp. 165, 271–2.
[42] Peter G. Forster, *T. Cullen Young: Missionary and Anthropologist* (Hull, 1989), pp. 62–3, 155–9.

monastic silence' during the years of the Smuts government and for 'bamboozling' the people; and a Cape Town Trotskyist, Dora Taylor (writing under the pen name Nosipho Majeke), produced an entire book on the missionaries' contribution to the conquest of African societies.[43] By this time, the missionaries' opposition to 'the old ways' in Kenya had grown into a bitter struggle against the cultural 'revival' associated with the Mau Mau insurrection.[44]

Conclusion

In the post-war climate of national self-determination and human rights, social anthropologists distanced themselves further from missionaries. They undertook fieldwork off the verandah, concerned themselves with theory, and practised a detached, secular, even scientific approach. Professional anthropologists documented rather than intervened in society; they were listeners rather than preachers and they built a network of social and intellectual capital that frequently excluded missionaries. In the late 1940s academic reviews like *Bantu Studies* (renamed *African Studies*) and *Africa* stopped carrying articles by missionaries. Many missionaries turned away from the politically sensitive discipline of anthropology to invest more time in the study of African languages. Yet the differences between missionary and academic anthropology were often more imagined than real and were often concerned with marking out territory rather than defining exclusive approaches. Many missionaries were trained in anthropology and several professional anthropologists had grown up in missionary homes, or supported the missionary cause. Professional anthropologists often intervened directly in the lives of the peoples they studied. Winifred Hoernlé left the University of the Witwatersrand in 1937 to concentrate on welfare work. She and Schapera served as consultants to the King of Swaziland, who, in an attempt to infuse young people with discipline and respect, wanted to revive initiation ceremonies and induct a new regiment. Although missionaries opposed the (re)introduction of these ceremonies, the South African anthropologists, with the support of Malinowski, viewed them as a valuable

---

[43] T. Karis and G. Carter, eds., *From Protest to Challenge*, II (Stanford, Calif., 1973), p. 335; Nosipho Majeke, *The Role of the Missionaries in Conquest* (Johannesburg, 1953).

[44] Bruce Berman and John Lonsdale, *Unhappy Valley: Conflict in Kenya and Africa*, 2 vols. (Oxford, 1997), II, pp. 441–7.

reassertion of traditional values in the face of Westernization.[45] Godfrey Wilson, as Director of the Rhodes–Livingstone Institute in Northern Rhodesia (Zambia) and husband of anthropologist Monica Hunter (the daughter of a missionary), preached an applied anthropology that, through controlled cultural change, aimed to improve the conditions of African mineworkers.[46] Some anthropologists entered government service and some missionaries taught anthropology.

As Empire gave way to Commonwealth and missionary societies transformed into African churches, missionaries at last became an object of study for anthropologists.[47] For some, this critical attention served to deepen the gulf separating the conflicting interests and approaches of academic and missionary anthropologists. For others, it merely drew attention to the shared values and common traditions of two streams in the field of anthropology.[48] During these years some missionary anthropologists developed a notion of Christianity that was far more accepting of African beliefs and practices. Under the influence of cultural relativism, others came to see African forms of spirituality as religions in their own right. However, by this time formerly colonized peoples were taking charge of their own world and missionary anthropology was quietly slipping into the domain of history.

Select Bibliography

JEAN COMAROFF and JOHN L. COMAROFF, *Of Revelation and Revolution*, 2 vols. (Chicago, 1991, 1997).

JACK GOODY, *The Expansive Moment: Anthropology in Britain and Africa 1918–1970* (Cambridge, 1995).

HENRIKA KUKLICK, *The Savage Within: The Social History of British Anthropology* (Cambridge, 1991).

LUCY MAIR, 'Anthropologists and Colonial Policy', *African Affairs*, LXXIV (1975), pp. 191–5.

---

[45] Adam Kuper, 'South African Anthropology: An Inside Job', *Paideuma*, XLV (1999), pp. 90–1; B. Malinowski, 'Native Education and Culture Contact', *IRM* XXV (1936), p. 512 n. 2.

[46] Godfrey Wilson, 'Anthropology as a Public Service', *Africa*, XIII (1940), pp. 43–61.

[47] T. O. Beidelman, 'Social Theory and the Study of Christian Missions in Africa', *Africa*, XLIV (1974), pp. 235–49.

[48] P. Hiebert, 'Missions and Anthropology: A Love–Hate Relationship', *Missiology*, VI (1978), pp. 165–80.

E. S. MILLER, 'Great Was the Company of the Preachers: The Word of Missionaries and the Word of Anthropologists', *Anthropology Quarterly*, LIV (1981), pp. 125–33.

CLAUDE E. STIPE, 'Anthropologists versus Missionaries: The Influence of Presuppositions', *Current Anthropology*, XXI (1980), pp. 165–79.

GEORGE STOCKING, *After Tylor: British Social Anthropology, 1888–1951* (London, 1996).

BENGT SUNDKLER, *Bantu Prophets in South Africa*, 1st edn. (London, 1948); 2nd rev. edn. (London, 1961).

—— *Zulu Zion and Some Swazi Zionists* (London, 1976).

SUSAN THORNE, *Congregational Missions and the Making of an Imperial Culture in Nineteenth-Century England* (Stanford, Calif., 1999).

SJAAK VAN DER GEEST, 'Anthropologists and Missionaries: Brothers under the Skin', *Man*, XXV (1990), pp. 588–601.

—— and J. P. KIRBY, 'The Absence of Missionaries in African Ethnography, 1930–65', *African Studies Review*, XXXV (1992), pp. 59–103.

PATRICK WOLFE, *Settler Colonialism and the Transformation of Anthropology* (London, 1999).

W. JOHN YOUNG, *The Quiet Wise Spirit: Edwin W. Smith 1876–1957 and Africa* (Peterborough, 2002).

13

Education and Medicine

NORMAN ETHERINGTON

After a brief period of pioneering work by European missionaries, local people took over the main work of preaching the gospel and making converts. However, two subsidiary branches of mission work, education and medicine, remained largely under the direction of overseas missionaries right up to the era of decolonization. It is easy to forget just how remarkable they were. When European states had barely begun to assume responsibility for public education, missionaries provided free schooling to people who had yet to grasp the benefits of literacy. Not only did they not charge the fees common in British private schools, they held out inducements for parents who would allow their children to be taught. Missions sought girls as pupils as well as boys and in many places introduced the first co-educational schooling. Missions were also among the first in the world to offer the services of medical practitioners free of charge. In some cases, advances made in missionary education and medicine were exported back to the mother countries. Missions figure prominently as pioneers of modern welfare states and international philanthropy. The first two-thirds of this chapter explore some aspects of mission education, while the more neglected topic of medical missions is taken up in the last section.

Education

Few missionaries treated education as an end in itself; schooling was ancillary to the primary object of Christian evangelism. Some missions neglected education altogether, believing that itinerant preachers going about in small groups could fulfil the biblical injunction to carry the gospel to the ends of the earth. (See p. 55.) The great majority of Protestant missionaries, however, understood Bible-reading to be an essential tenet of their faith. This had driven the remarkable spread of basic literacy through England, Scotland, and Wales and caused even the poorly educated missionaries first sent out by the London Missionary Society to make schooling, along with translating and printing Bibles, the first business of their missions to the South Pacific islands and southern Africa. Catholic missions had different but equally compelling reasons to spread schools. Servicing the Irish diaspora after the great famine of the 1840s absorbed most of the attention of the Irish Catholics, who dispatched thousands of priests, nuns, and lay staff to teach in schools like those established by the Christian Brothers in Canada, New Zealand, Australia, and South Africa.[1] Ireland alone could never have supplied all the needs of Catholic parishes abroad, so seminaries and convents sprang up in the new colonies to train male and female agents. Until well into the twentieth century the Vatican took the position that 'Christians' outside the Western Catholic Church had lost touch with God and were therefore worthy objects of missionary attention. Schools for new colonies of settlement were also essential if Catholic children were to escape induction into 'heretical sects'. The Jesuit Reductions of seventeenth-century Paraguay, where South American Indians had gathered together in pious Christian agricultural villages isolated from their former culture and defended against the greed of European settlers, provided an inspiration for many Catholic missions to the 'heathen'.[2]

The impact of Christian missionary education varied enormously with local circumstances. In most of sub-Saharan Africa the European concept of schooling was a novelty of unproved value. When people did not come running to their schools, missionaries were puzzled. In nineteenth-century Europe most people expected to pay for schooling, but in Africa early missions needed material inducements to attract students. American and Anglican missionaries in Natal and Zululand offered clothing and wages to children who attended their schools.[3] In order to reap these rewards without running the risk of conversion, parents often sent one of their children for a period of months and then replaced them with another. An added problem was that in the first instance most African societies refused to allow girls to be taught. Sometimes this reflected a general patriarchal anxiety about control

---

[1] Edmund M. Hogan, *The Irish Missionary Movement: A Historical Survey, 1830–1980* (Dublin, 1990), pp. 15, 17.

[2] John Webster Grant, *Moon of Wintertime: Missionaries and the Indians of Canada in Encounter since 1534* (Toronto, 1984), p. 126; Brendan Carmody, 'Catholic Schools in Zambia: 1891–1924, *History of Education*, XXVIII (1999), p. 78.

[3] Norman Etherington, *Preachers, Peasants and Politics in Southeast Africa* (London, 1978), pp. 65–6.

of women, which proved to be well grounded. Mission stations, like cities, offered unprecedented opportunities for African women to escape social control. Few, if any, missionaries were inclined to turn away women fleeing from an angry father or violent husband, unless compelled to do so by colonial officials. Chiefs and husbands complained that they had lost control of women and that mission stations made whores of their daughters.[4] Missionaries complicated their own attempts to attract women to school by opposing key cultural institutions, especially polygamy and bride wealth. Although rare individuals like the Anglican Bishop of Natal, John Colenso, countenanced conversion without insisting that existing wives cut loose from their husbands, neither he nor any other mainstream missionary would allow men to acquire new wives after their conversion to Christianity.[5] According to the custom of *lobola*, which pervaded Bantu-speaking Africa from Cameroon to South Africa, a man presented cattle or other gifts to the father of his bride as an acknowledgement and guarantee of the sanctity of his marriage. Most early missions misinterpreted this as bride purchase or even 'female slavery'. By prohibiting it in their congregations they interfered with the entire social system for the transfer and distribution of wealth. As knowledge of missionary attitudes on such intimate and central institutions of society spread, people were inclined to keep their children away from schools. Ironically, some missions reacted to this problem by making payments of cattle to acquire girls for their schools. Another indirect method of coercion was to require school attendance from children whose parents resided on mission-owned land. Decades passed before the changes wrought by economic development and colonial rule demonstrated the virtues of schools in Africa.

Such problems were practically unknown in the southern Pacific, where Christianity spread so quickly that schooling faced little resistance from traditionalist parents worried about the corrosive impact of missionary teaching. In Australia and Canada, however, missions faced obstacles of a different order. It was nearly impossible to provide conventional schooling for indigenous societies based on economic exploitation of sparse resources spread over vast distances and subject to seasonal variations. People moved

---

[4] *Evidence Taken before the Natal Native Commission, 1881* (Pietermaritzburg, 1882), pp. 256, 304, and 'Evidence of the Umvoti Subcommission', p. 15; Ben Carton, *Blood from your Children: The Colonial Origins of Generational Conflict in South Africa* (London, 2000), p. 72.

[5] Jeff Guy, *The Heretic: A Study of the Life of John William Colenso, 1814–1883* (Pietermaritzburg, 1983), pp. 73–4.

with the buffalo, the reindeer, or the rains. In these conditions missions turned to strategies designed to encourage settlement. This seemed a natural and obvious thing to do, because nineteenth-century missionary theory accorded a special place to self-sufficient agriculture and village life, perversely idealizing a way of life that was already disappearing in Europe. In an Anglican version of the Reductions of Paraguay, the South Australian archdeacon Matthew Hale tried a bold experiment in 1850.[6] He proposed to wrench Aboriginal people out of their 'nomadic' existence and protect them from abuse from white settlers by establishing a self-supporting agricultural community in an isolated location. When his first choice, a desert island, proved inhospitable, he settled his little community at Poonindie, near the village of Port Lincoln. At the centre of the settlement stood a stone church that doubled as a schoolhouse. Similar ideas of agricultural settlement, protection, and isolation motivated missions throughout Canada and Australia. When the missionaries could not persuade people to settle down, they asked that they allow their children to be taught in boarding schools. The impact of residential schools varied with the circumstances of the society around them.[7] In most parts of Africa, South Asia, and the Pacific the boarding school seldom stood apart from the local culture; parents, friends, and relatives were close by even if they took no interest in Christianity. Only elite institutions like Lovedale and Zonnebloem Colleges in South Africa aimed to be total institutions, controlling every aspect of student life.[8] In Canada and Australia, on the other hand, boarding schools aimed deliberately to cut students off from their cultural roots and to inculcate in them the norms of the dominant white settler society. The Canadian schools hoped that their students would return to their own people as adults and act as emissaries of 'Christian civilization'. Australian schools had a more sinister character. State policy made them a dumping ground for Aboriginal children of mixed descent, whose descendants, it was hoped, would eventually lose all visible traces of 'coloured' ancestry. Most of those children—the so-called 'stolen generations'—never saw their mothers again.[9]

[6] Peggy Brock, *Outback Ghettos: A History of Aboriginal Institutionalisation and Survival* (Cambridge, 1993), pp. 24–6.

[7] Grant, *Moon of Wintertime*, pp. 86, 94, 178, 200, 204, 225.

[8] Graham A. Duncan, ' "Coercive Agency": James Henderson's Lovedale, 1906–1930', DD diss. (University of South Africa, 2000), p. vi.

[9] Anna Haebich, *Broken Circles: Fragmenting Indigenous Families 1800–2000* (Fremantle, 2000). Contrast with Canadian experience in James R. Miller, *Shingwauk's Vision: A History of Native Residential Schools* (Toronto, 1997).

Mission schools in British India ran on very different lines. They had no need to hold out inducements to students where schooling with obvious material benefits had already struck deep roots in local cultures. 'Every larger Hindu village had its school on some *pial* (verandah) and every mosque its teachers.'[10] When boarding schools sprang up, they acquired some of the characteristics of elite public schools in the British Isles. The extent of organized education prior to the advent of missions was remarkable. A government survey of education in Madras in 1823–5 counted 12,498 schools teaching 188,000 pupils out of a total population of nearly 13 million, at a time when organized Christian missionary work was minuscule.[11] Not all of this schooling was traditional in language or culture. An appetite for Western education had been growing since the early eighteenth century, encouraged in the 1820s and 1830s by important government initiatives such as Governor-General Bentinck's 1835 Resolution directing that state funding should favour English-language schools. Thomas Munro, Governor of Madras in 1826, had proposed a sweeping plan of government-funded education ranging from outdoor village schools to universities. These initiatives arose less from abstract ideals than from the practical need for Indians to staff the lower levels of the public service. The government of India, no less than the army, relied principally on local talent. As opportunities for employment increased, so did demand for education in English. When sweeping schemes for government education—schemes that would have astonished the world—failed for lack of funding, missions helped fill the gaps. Their schools filled as fast as they could build them, despite obstacles caused by unwillingness to compromise on key issues of religious content, class, and gender. They instructed all pupils in basic precepts of Christianity, regardless of protests from Hindus and Muslims. They also insisted on opening the schoolhouse doors to people of all social castes and classes. In the early days some concessions to local sensibilities occurred. For example, the indigenous St Thomas (Syrian) Christians, whose Indian roots date back to the first centuries of the Christian era, ranked as equals to the higher castes.[12] Many Catholic and Protestant services in the nineteenth century

---

[10] Hugald Grafe, *History of Christianity in India*, IV/2, *Tamil Nadu in the Nineteenth and Twentieth Centuries* (Bangalore, 1990), p. 188.

[11] Robert E. Frykenberg, 'Modern Education in South India, 1784–1854', *American Historical Review*, XCI (1986), pp. 44–8.

[12] Dick Kooiman, *Conversion and Social Equality in India: The London Missionary Society in South Travancore in the Nineteenth Century* (New Delhi, 1989), p. 149.

catered to caste prejudices within their congregations.[13] (See p. 000.) However, over time it became apparent that most converts to Christianity came from the lower castes, pariahs and Harijans (Untouchables). Under these circumstances it seemed unscriptural and impractical to make caste distinctions in schools. Schooling for girls by its very nature carried revolutionary implications. As early as 1820 in the city of Madras girls constituted a third of all pupils and nearly half by 1838. The Medical College in Madras opened its doors to women in the mid-1870s, ahead of most institutions in Europe and North America.[14] Throughout the colonial period Christian women were disproportionately represented in Indian schools and universities.

The character and content of mission education reflected the incredible variety of societies and ideologies at work throughout the Empire. It would be a mistake to imagine that all or even most of them displayed the ordered character of Robert Moffat's Kuruman in South Africa or Matthew Hale's Poonindie in South Australia. In many places Christian schools resembled the Muslim Qur'ānic schools that may still be seen in many parts of Africa and the Middle East where children gather on the street with their slates and memorize verses. School might be a group gathered on the porch of a missionary's house or an unruly crowd stifling in the heat of a corrugated-iron shack. As an African priest in Northern Rhodesia remembered the Jesuit school he attended in the 1920s, 'we used rags for writing and we came together in a cowshed. Some time later we were given slates.'[15] Whatever the physical surroundings, the first task of all elementary education was to teach reading, even in Catholic schools, which disdained the Protestant emphasis on individual interpretation of Scripture. Ferocious arguments raged over the language of instruction. While nineteenth-century governments recommended English, most missions favoured elementary education in local languages as the fastest way to spread their religion. Although the initial work of translation was slow, once texts and concepts had been expressed in the vernacular, they could spread by word of mouth far beyond the reach of mission stations. It is safe to say that the translation of hundreds of languages into written formats would never have happened but for the missionaries' educational programme.

Secondary education progressed much more slowly than elementary schooling and aimed primarily to create an indigenous Christian pastorate.

---

[13] Grafe, *History of Christianity in India*, IV/2, *Tamil Nadu*, pp. 106–19.
[14] Ibid., pp. 203–5.   [15] Carmody, 'Catholic Schools in Zambia', p. 80.

Young men received instruction in European and ancient languages as well as basic science, history, and geography so that they could properly interpret the Bible and proclaim Christianity from the pulpit. Young women received the secondary education thought appropriate for pastors' wives and teachers. Almost all mission-sponsored university education grew out of theological seminaries such as Fort Hare in South Africa and Fourah Bay in Sierra Leone. Only in the twentieth century did some high-minded missionaries influenced by anthropology and cultural relativism begin to argue that non-European pastors needed both secular and theological education adapted to their own milieu. Following the work of theorists such as Edwin Smith, Henri-Alexandre Junod, Placide Tempels, and Charles F. Andrews, some mission education took an 'adaptationist' turn, grounded in local understandings of learning, ethics, and spirituality. (See pp. 255–56.)

Missionary aims were one thing and results another. Literacy could not be confined to the narrow, pious channels envisioned by mission societies in Europe and North America.[16] Some young men trained to read the Bible discovered messages and meanings that white missionaries had never preached to them. They read that Old Testament patriarchs had married numerous wives and kept concubines. They discovered biblical precedents for levirate marriage and the execution of witches. They read how Pharaoh's army perished trying to stop Hebrew slaves from escaping. Prophecies that 'Babylon the great' would perish in the Apocalypse brought some people a welcome sense that imperial rule might soon come to a spectacular end. John Chilembwe of Malawi believed that the battle of the nations in the First World War heralded the end of Satan's reign on earth and called his compatriots to rise against their oppressors.[17] If missions could not prohibit subversive readings of Scripture, they stood no chance of keeping inappropriate secular literature out of the hands of their converts. As colonial systems of migrant labour expanded across the globe, newly literate Christians gained access to a feast of literature: newspapers, cheap novels, and political tracts. In India and West Africa the imperial need for the low-level bureaucrat gave an added impetus to education in English, which ironically opened the door to unauthorized reading. Even when readers had only acquired literacy in

---

[16] Patrick Harries, 'Missionaries, Marxists and Magic', *Journal of Southern African Studies*, XXVII (2001), pp. 405–27.

[17] George Shepperson and Thomas Price, *Independent African: John Chilembwe and the Origins, Setting and Significance of the Nyasaland Native Rising of 1915*, 5th edn. (Edinburgh, 1987).

their native tongues, the output of mission presses brought them more than just religious tracts. Mission newspapers conveyed commercial and political information as well as morally uplifting stories. The Yoruba newspaper *Iwe Irohin*—the first ever published in an African language—originated as a fortnightly production of a mission press at Abeokuta in 1859. Many others followed this initiative, some of which became important conduits for the expression of political opinion, including John Dube's *Ilanga Lase Natal*, founded in 1904.[18]

Outsiders, settlers, and officials suspected literacy almost from the moment missions began to spread it. The South African high commissioner George Grey in the 1850s recommended that most African education should be practical, with literary instruction only allowed to a tiny elite.[19] A Canadian government commission in 1879 recommended that Indian education should be primarily 'industrial'.[20] By the turn of the twentieth century criticism of missionary education acquired a nasty edge. Cecil Rhodes sneered that mission schools in southern Africa 'seemed destined to produce a nation of preachers and editors'.[21] Mary Kingsley's influential *Travels in West Africa* (1897) argued that the utility of African workers was inversely proportional to the amount of missionary education they had received. The 'Kruman' with no education was 'as fine a ship-and-beach-man as you could reasonably wish for, but no good for plantation works'. The 'Accra' trained by Basel missions for practical work was 'a very fair artisan, cook, or clerk, but also no good for plantation work, except as an overseer'. And the Christian Sierra Leonean was 'a poor artisan, an excellent clerk, or subordinate official, but so unreliable in the matter of honesty as to be nearly reliable to swindle any employer'.[22] Kingsley had no doubt that the problem with missionary teaching was its failure to take account of racial difference:

The bad effects that have arisen from their teaching have come primarily from the failure of the missionary to recognise the difference between the African and themselves as being a difference not of degree but of kind. . . . the mental difference between the two races is very similar to that between men and women among ourselves.

---

[18] Bengt Sundkler and Christopher Steed, *A History of the Church in Africa* (Cambridge, 2000), p. 743; Les and Donna Switzer, *The Black Press in South Africa and Lesotho* (Boston, 1979).

[19] Duncan, 'Coercive Agency', p. 100.

[20] Grant, *Moon of Wintertime*, p. 158.

[21] Lord Hailey, *An African Survey*, revised 1956 (Oxford, 1957), p. 1143.

[22] Mary Kingsley, *Travels in West Africa* (London, 1897; repr. 1965), pp. 645, 657.

The novelist Joseph Conrad took up Mary Kingsley's critique in 'An Outpost of Progress', a short story that served as a dress rehearsal for his celebrated *Heart of Darkness*. The mission-trained Sierra Leonean Henry Price 'spoke English and French with a warbling accent, wrote a beautiful hand, understood bookkeeping, and cherished in his innermost heart the worship of evil spirits'.[23] Denunciations of mission education contained an obvious internal contradiction. On one hand, they complained that Africans, Canadian Indians, Australian Aborigines, and other peoples were incapable of understanding or making use of 'literary education' and should therefore be given manual training suited to their limited intellects. On the other hand, they argued that mission education at the higher levels would be only too well understood by converts, who might imbibe doctrines of equality, demand equal rights, and foment insurrections.

In most parts of the Empire the ability of the missions to withstand the onslaught of racist criticism was tempered by their need for financial assistance. With cash-strapped boards at home continually demanding that the missions be self-supporting, they grasped at government funding though they knew very well that it came with strings attached. A settler-dominated government in Natal began insisting as early as the 1860s that a certain portion of educational grants to missions be devoted to 'industrial education'. In the late 1870s the same demand surfaced in Canada. By the opening decades of the twentieth century the crass objective of confining colonized people through inferior education had been dressed up with 'scientific' justifications and permeated almost every corner of the Empire apart from South Asia. Alarmed by John Chilembwe's revolt in Southern Rhodesia, the government of Northern Rhodesia in 1918 tried to gain control of mission education by withholding registration from any school which spread teaching of a 'seditious nature'.[24] When the missions complained against this regulation of schools that had not received a penny in state support, the government responded by creating a system of tied grants for industrial education. The Graham Commission in Southern Rhodesia (1910) recommended that anyone in control of the native population be 'authorized and requested to preach the doctrine of labour as a civilizing factor'.[25] On the

---

[23] 'An Outpost of Progress', in Joseph Conrad, *'Heart of Darkness' and Other Tales*, ed. C. Watts (Oxford, 1990), p. 11.

[24] Carmody, 'Catholic Schools', p. 77.

[25] Dickson A. Mungazi, 'A Struggle for Power: Commissions of Inquiry into Education and Government Control in Colonial Zimbabwe', *International Journal of African Historical Studies*, XXII (1989), p. 273.

'mission farms' of Southern Rhodesia government grants were tied to demands for schools that would educate African boys to be manual labourers and girls to be servants.[26] It should not be imagined that such demands reflected the colonial State's requirement for labour on white farms, plantations, or mines.[27] Testimony at successive commissions on education reveals that almost any education was regarded as too much. As the Revd. R. Bathe of Southern Rhodesia remarked in 1902, 'I am sorry that on the part of the whites there is a reluctance to encourage education among the Natives under the pretext that they will not be useful as servants when they can read and write.'[28] A white woman solemnly testified to a later Rhodesian commission that after trying two 'mission girls', she much preferred to have 'a raw girl' doing her housework.[29]

Given the crudity of the assault it may appear surprising that many missionaries and some indigenous Christian educators took up the cause of industrial and agricultural education. Eighteenth- and early nineteenth-century missions cherished the hope of creating genuinely self-sufficient Christian farming communities. Moravian missions turned away from aggressive evangelization in favour of small, tightly regulated villages sealed against the evil influences of the outside world.[30] A museum version of Moravian village life can be seen today in Genadendal, South Africa. A somewhat similar educational village model developed by a Presbyterian missionary to the Cherokees in 1804 was regulated by a 'schedule that allotted equal time to study and to work in the fields, shops, or kitchen of the institution'.[31] Some Canadian Indians welcomed the experiment as a possible independent alternative to a life on the move in a land increasingly filled with white settlers. Similar visions motivated William Duncan and his followers at Metlakatla in British Columbia and Matthew Hale at Poonindie, South Australia. In the long run these versions foundered, partly on economic

---

[26] Steven D. Edgington, 'Economic and Social Dimensions of Mission Farms on the Mashonaland High Veld, 1890s–1930s', Ph.D. diss. (Los Angeles, 1996), pp. 139–43, 191–3.

[27] S. Sivonen, *White Collar or Hoe Handle? African Education under British Colonial Policy 1920–45* (Helsinki, 1995).

[28] Ibid., p. 271.

[29] Carol Summers, ' "If you Can Educate the Native Woman...": Debates over the Schooling and Education of Girls and Women in Southern Rhodesia, 1900–1934', *History of Education Quarterly*, XXXVI (1996), p. 469.

[30] G. Scriba and G. Lislerud, 'Lutheran Missionaries and Churches in South Africa', in R. Elphick and R. Davenport, eds., *Christianity in South Africa* (Oxford, 1997), pp. 174–5.

[31] Grant, *Moon of Wintertime*, p. 86.

grounds but mainly because of white settler resistance to any educational programme that might spawn competitors. Poonindie fell victim to its own success. When local farmers saw Aboriginal farmers making a good living, they pronounced the land too good for 'Natives' and pressured the colonial government into releasing the land for sale—a strategy that closed out Aborigines who lacked the ability to raise loans to buy their own farms.[32]

In other parts of the Empire, Christian converts proved equally adept at competing with white farmers but were too numerous to be easily pushed aside. Educational strategies designed to direct them into unthreatening channels owed much to theories and practices originating in the southern United States. As the courts opened the way to segregation of public facilities through the *Plessy* v. *Fergusson* decision, black Americans looked for ways to provide a first-rate training for people forced out of white schools. Booker T. Washington accepted the premiss of 'separate but equal' education as a necessary evil and aimed, through his Tuskegee Institute (1881), to train efficient farmers, mechanics, and tradesmen. Embarrassingly he found himself feted by white segregationists at home and abroad. Tuskegee spawned a clutch of imitators. Black men and women known colloquially as Jeanes teachers were employed as travelling vocational demonstrators of agricultural methods for men and 'home economics' for women. All pretence of equal education soon fell away as subject matter diverged sharply from state-funded programmes for whites.[33] As segregation spread through British colonies in southern and eastern Africa, so did variations on Tuskegee and the Jeanes system.[34] People unfamiliar with the circumstances that made industrial education popular in the United States often welcomed the practical emphasis. Lewanika, paramount chief of the Barotse kingdom, told the French Protestant missionary François Coillard why he had welcomed black industrial missionaries from the American Methodist Episcopal Church: 'What do we want with that rubbish heap of fables that you call the Bible?...What I want is missionaries...who build big workshops and

---

[32] Peggy Brock and Doreen Kartinyeri, *Poonindie: The Rise and Destruction of an Aboriginal Community* (Adelaide, 1989), pp. 66–71.

[33] Spencer J. Maxcy, 'Progressivism and Rural Education in the Deep South, 1900–1950', in R. K. Goodenow and A. O. White, eds., *Education and the Rise of the New South* (Boston, 1981), pp. 47–71.

[34] Paul Rich, 'The Appeal of Tuskegee: James Henderson, Lovedale, and the Fortunes of South African Liberalism, 1906–1930', *International Journal of African Historical Studies*, XX (1987), pp. 271–92; Sundkler and Steed, *A History of the Church in Africa*, pp. 638–9.

teach us all the trades of the white man... That's what I want, industrial missionaries; that is what all the chiefs want. We laugh at the rest'.[35]

John L. Dube, a Zulu Christian from Natal, returned from university studies in the United States and founded his own version of Tuskegee, Ohlange Institute. However, the dominant strain in the promotion of industrial education in white settler colonies was better represented by Natal's Chief Inspector of Schools, Charles T. Loram. After studying at Teachers' College, Columbia University, he used his influence to push fashionable American theories of separate education 'adapted to inferior intellects of African pupils'.[36] Distrusting mission schools in general, Loram ignored the dissenting voices of missionaries and African elites, and touted the role of the secular white expert. He acquired an unparalleled opportunity to influence education throughout British-ruled Africa when he joined the Phelps-Stokes Commission on African education in the 1920s. While it made praiseworthy efforts to raise government expenditure on primary education, the philosophical bent of the Commission was to push schools to adopt vocational curricula adapted to African needs. For example, the Commission commended the Church of Scotland mission schools in Kenya, whose philosophy was that 'only through working with the hands could the vices of idleness and ignorance be overcome'.[37] In line with Phelps-Stokes theories, Uganda in the 1930s made a determined effort to drag the Church Missionary Society away from literary subjects in the middle school syllabus while allocating 'periods to agriculture, carpentry, and instruction in the keeping of native court records, and the collection of poll tax'.[38] Only the African elites of West Africa and some institutions in Central Africa managed to hold the line at efforts to debase high educational standards. The durability of Mary Kingsley's thinking is reflected in Lord Hailey's amusement that 'a large mission school in the Gold Coast could in 1938 appeal for assistance in England on the ground that it performed a Greek play every year and "rendered the odes in the original Greek"'.[39] However, the whole drive to implant industrial

[35] James T. Campbell, 'Models and Metaphors: Industrial Education in the United States and South Africa', in Ran Greenstein, ed., *Comparative Perspectives on South Africa* (London, 1998), p. 115.

[36] Sue Krige, ' "Trustees and Agents of the State"? Missions and the Formation of Policy towards African Education, 1910–1920', *South African Historical Journal*, XL (1999), p. 80.

[37] David Githii, 'The Introduction and Development of Western Education in Kenya by the Presbyterians', Doctor of Missiology thesis (Fuller Theological Seminary, 1993), pp. 1–2, 106.

[38] Hailey, *African Survey*, pp. 1244–5.

[39] Ibid.

education suffered from no less ridiculous assumptions about the future of Africa. Too often, as James Campbell observes, it 'offered preparation for a life which never existed', reassuring settlers that African education was compatible with white supremacy by its inculcation of attributes 'such as docility and industriousness'.[40]

Mission schools in India also felt occasional pressure from the colonial State to emphasize vocational training.[41] However, the absence of white settlers protected them against the dramatic interventions seen in Australia, Canada, and Africa. (Maoris in New Zealand suffered similar regimes of practical education in the government school system.[42]) The presence of so many parents willing and able to pay fees freed many missions from government control. India's educational needs so outran the willingness of government to provide funds that in the end the State concentrated attention on the elite end of the scale, leaving the lower levels in private and missionary hands through the grant-in-aid system. An additional factor working against philosophies of manual and vocational training was the competition the South Asian missions faced from other faiths, particularly Hindus, who did their best to counter the challenge of Christianity by raising the volume and quality of their own schools. However, the persistence of patriarchal institutions left female education mostly in the hands of the missions. The heavily evangelized southern states of Tamil Nadu and Kerala attained female literacy estimated at 31 per cent in 1971, more than in any other Indian state. At Madras University in 1933, 56 per cent of the Bachelor of Science degrees were awarded to Christian Indian women.[43]

It is impossible to imagine what education under the British Empire might have been without the presence of Christian missions. They so dominated the provision of educational services for indigenous populations that in many lands the term 'native elite' was synonymous with 'Christian-educated'. Lord Hailey estimated in 1938 that as much as nine-tenths of education in Africa was in the hands of missionary bodies.[44] Only a tiny fraction of what they did

[40] James T. Campbell, 'Our Fathers, Our Children: The African Methodist Episcopal Church in the United States and South Africa', Ph.D. diss. (Stanford, Calif., 1989), pp. 335, 348.

[41] Vijaya Kumar, 'Ecumenical Cooperation of the Missions in Karnataka (India), 1834–1989: A Historical Analysis of the Evangelistic Strategy of the Missions', DD diss. (Lutheran School of Theology at Chicago, 1996), pp. 82–4.

[42] Donald Denoon and Philippa Mein-Smith, *A History of Australia, New Zealand and the Pacific* (Oxford, 2000), pp. 331–2.

[43] Grafe, *History of Christianity in India*, IV/2, *Tamil Nadu*, pp. 194, 202.

[44] Hailey, *African Survey*, pp. 1208–9.

was subject to direct government control or supervision, the most dramatic instances of which occurred when German-speaking missionaries were interned during the world wars and pupils were forbidden to learn German in many parts of the Empire. Missions bent to government directives on industrial training partly because some mission educators bought the Booker T. Washington line, but more often because they wanted to maintain control of their schools and keep Christianity on the curriculum. Students often expressed resentment at the controls implemented in mission schools—especially in Australia and Canada, where many schools forbade students to speak in their native tongues. Yet when the roll is called of leaders who agitated for freedom or led their new nations to independence, the products of mission education outnumber all others. Among the boys and girls dressed in white robes at a Presbyterian Easter service in Kenya 1912, was Jomo Kenyatta, who little imagined that his planned apprenticeship in carpentry would be sidelined by a political career that led him, via a colonial gaol, to the presidency of his country in 1963. Kwame Nkrumah sits in the middle row at the left in his 1927 class photo from Prince of Wales College (later Achimota College), unaware that his career would develop from his first job as a village schoolteacher, through study for a Bachelor of Theology degree from Lincoln Theological Seminary in the United States, to Prime Minister of the Gold Coast. Julius Nyerere's path to the presidency of Tankanyika included six years as a teacher in Roman Catholic schools. Another Catholic politician who led his country was Robert Mugabe, who obtained the first of his university degrees at a Protestant mission college, Fort Hare in South Africa. Nelson Mandela was merely one among many South African leaders who passed through Fort Hare; his 'long walk to freedom' began in a one-room Methodist school. As an Australian Aborigine removed from his family to St Francis Boys' Home, Charlie Perkins could not have realistically dreamed of becoming Prime Minister of his country, but he led 'Freedom Rides' to bust segregated facilities and went on to become head of the Australian Department of Aboriginal Affairs. When Colonel Rabuka seized power in a *coup d'état*, he remarked (provocatively) that being Methodist was part of what it meant to be Fijian, a statement that might have been echoed on many other Pacific Islands. The list could be almost indefinitely extended with names of influential men and women who passed through mission schools. Their influence appears likely to outlast the Empire by many centuries, just as the influence of Roman Catholicism lingered long after the last Roman citizen had passed away.

Medicine and Healing

When Rudyard Kipling advised the United States in 1899 to 'take up the White Man's burden... Fill full the mouth of Famine and bid the sickness cease', his appraisal of the imperial contribution to health was more than a little optimistic. Many historians would reverse Kipling, pointing to the myriad ways in which the expansion of Empire endangered and damaged the health of colonized people through introduced diseases, unbalanced diets, and epidemics that struck down both man and beast. Advances in public health, antisepsis, and antibiotics lagged far behind the new pathways for infectious disease that advanced across land cleared for cash cropping, along new railway lines, and down the paths of labour migration. The first priority of imperial medicine prior to the First World War was to keep soldiers and officials functioning in unhealthy environments.[45] Medical services for non-Europeans concentrated on mines and plantations. Others relied, as they always had, on traditional healers and remedies. Thanks to David Livingstone and Albert Schweitzer, Christian missions acquired an outsize reputation as conveyors of European medical science. Furthermore, it was certainly true that 'throughout most of the colonial period and throughout most of Africa, Christian missions of one sort or another provided vastly more medical care for African communities than did colonial states'.[46] That, however, is more a judgement on imperial neglect of medical services than on the achievements of missionary medicine. Nonetheless, in many parts of the Empire the only contact colonized people had with European medicine was through mission facilities.

As with education, evangelical rather than philanthropic imperatives guided mission medicine. Unlike literacy—a secular skill promoted as a guide to biblical truth—healing carried a heavy load of supernatural baggage. All churches regarded healing as an imitation of Christ, who had cast out devils, made lepers whole, enabled the lame to throw away their crutches, and raised Lazarus from the dead. 'God had only one son,' David Livingstone observed, 'and He gave Him to be a medical missionary.'[47] Even scientifically trained mission doctors acknowledged the role of prayer and miraculous

---

[45] Deepak Kumar, ed., *Science and Empire: Essays in Indian Context (1700–1947)* (Delhi, 1991), p. 17.

[46] Megan Vaughan, *Curing their Ills: Colonial Power and African Illness* (Stanford, Calif., 1991), p. 56.

[47] Quoted in H. O. Dwight, H. A. Tupper, and E. M. Bliss, eds., *Encyclopedia of Missions* (London, 1904), p. 447.

cures in healing. In sharp contrast to trends in the medical profession since the Enlightenment, missions refused to decouple disease from sin and morality. God's judgement on sinners could be delivered as in days of old through plagues, droughts, and visitations by locusts. John Williams, a nineteenth-century missionary to the Cook Islands, interpreted a local epidemic as 'a timely interposition of an all-wise and overruling Providence'.[48] The wages of sin was death, and mankind could not expect the conquest of disease before the Judgement Day. Mission congregations boomed out Isaac Watts's Hymn 55 with fearful hearts.

> The year rolls round, and steals away
>   The breath that first it gave;
> Whate'er we do, where'er we be,
>   We're trav'lling to the grave.
>
> Dangers stand thick through all the ground
>   To push us to the tomb,
> And fierce diseases wait around,
>   To hurry mortals home.

On more than one tragic occasion missions caused or exacerbated outbreaks of disease they could not cure. The first London Missionary Society agents scoffed at Tahitians' belief that 'that all their mortal diseases are from the ships' that followed Captain Cook to the southern Pacific.[49] Within a few years all missionaries in that region watched helplessly as measles, smallpox, syphilis, yaws, and a host of other introduced diseases decimated their congregations. John Geddie of the Presbyterian mission to Vanuatu at first exulted as measles literally put the fear of God into island communities. People who saw 'in this devastation all the wrath of God for their past wickedness' fled their old homes and concentrated themselves around the missionary's house—thus causing more outbreaks of disease until more than a third of the population of the island of Anumej had perished. Matthew Hale did not bring European diseases to the Aborigines of South Australia, but when he concentrated a large group at Poonindie Mission in the 1850s, death cut a fearful swath through the community. Unable to heal, the missionary went frantically about performing baptisms so that the immortal

---

[48] Raeburn Lange, 'European Medicine in the Cook Islands', in R. MacLeod and M. Lewis, eds., *Disease, Medicine and Empire* (London, 1988), p. 62.

[49] Norma McArthur, 'And, Behold, the Plague Was Begun among the People', in N. Gunson, ed., *The Changing Pacific* (Oxford, 1978), pp. 273–82.

souls of the dying might find eternal life. Similar catastrophes were re-enacted in twentieth-century Australia when rural whites, frightened of 'Aboriginal' diseases, successfully agitated for state action to close the 'blacks' camps' on the outskirts of their towns. When police round-ups dumped the hapless people on missions, once again the concentration of pathogens spread illness and death.[50]

While standard histories of medicine focus on the triumph of scientific models of disease in the nineteenth and twentieth centuries—and neglect medical missions—that same period witnessed the emergence of sects and churches specifically concerned with divine healing in Europe and North America. Christian Science and the Jehovah's Witnesses set their face deliberately against modern surgical procedures. Seventh-Day Adventists promoted a Providentially sanctioned path to health and wholeness through diet, most famously identified with the breakfast cereals developed by their devout follower Dr John Harvey Kellogg of Battle Creek, Michigan. Early Mormons and twentieth-century Pentecostals used 'healing handkerchiefs' to cure diseases, citing the precedent of Acts: 19: 11–12: 'And God wrought special miracles by the hands of Paul, so that from his body were brought unto the sick handkerchiefs or aprons, and the diseases departed from them, and the evil spirits went out of them.' Because the theory and practice of mission medicine diverged so sharply from mainstream scientific models, it tends to be neglected by general histories of medicine and even in books devoted specifically to imperial medicine.[51]

For all their stoic talk about God's mysterious ways, missions acknowledged that 'humanly speaking', doctors had roles to play in alleviating human suffering, opening the way for evangelists and attracting hearers to missionary preaching. The idea of enlisting medical aid seemed particularly attractive in dangerous climes. In the early years a 'call' to tropical Africa or South Asia could be a death sentence. Out of eighty-nine missionaries sent to Sierra Leone between 1804 and 1825, fifty-four died and fourteen returned home in broken health. Sixty-two of 225 missionaries sent by the Wesleyan

---

[50] Gordon Briscoe, *Counting, Health and Identity: A History of Aboriginal Health and Demography in Western Australia and Queensland, 1900–1940* (Canberra, 2003), pp. 228–30.

[51] Poonam Bala, *Imperialism and Medicine in Bengal: A Socio-historical Perspective* (London, 1991) does not mention medical missions. Mark Harrison, *Public Health in British India: Anglo-Indian Preventive Medicine 1859–1914* (Cambridge, 1994) allocates one paragraph to missionary medical work (p. 91). The large bibliography in Macleod and Lewis, eds., *Disease, Medicine and Empire*, pp. 317–32, contains only three citations to missionary medicine.

Methodist Missionary Society between 1835 and 1907 left their bones on West African soil.[52] One way around the problem was to send ex-slaves born in Africa as missionaries to these deadly climates. Another was to send European doctors as medical missionaries with the double charge of ministering to sick missionaries and attracting converts. Strictly speaking a medical missionary was a missionary trained in Western medicine. The first medical missionaries had what, from a modern perspective, appears to have been very rudimentary training, as illustrated by the world's most famous missionary doctor, David Livingstone. He studied medicine at Glasgow from 1836 to 1840 in a course with little clinical training. The stethoscope had only recently been invented and there was as yet no device to measure blood pressure. At the time two main theories of disease dominated the profession. One held that illness was caused by disorders in the blood, the other that disturbances in the gastro-intestinal tract were to blame. Like most other doctors, Livingstone gave some credence to both theories. Throughout his career he bled patients by applying leeches to their heads and abdomens. He also emphasized the importance of 'healthy excretions' and prescribed emetics and purgatives to rid the body of morbid substances. Although Livingstone's training in anatomy with the use of cadavers made him a far better surgeon than the traditional African doctors he encountered on his travels, he had a limited knowledge of pharmacology. That is why he did not hesitate to take medicines recommended by Africans with local knowledge when he fell ill. Nor did Livingstone present himself as an emissary of European well-being to African misery. He believed that the people he encountered in Central Africa enjoyed generally better health than the urban masses he had known in Britain.[53]

Medical missions grew very slowly; in 1849 it was estimated that only forty medical missionaries were at work throughout the entire world; Livingstone was one of twelve from Great Britain.[54] According to Brian Stanley, the foundation of the Medical Missionary Auxiliary in 1902 marked a belated acceptance by the Baptist Missionary Society that 'alleviation of physical suffering was in some sense an integral part of the overseas missionary commission of the Church'.[55] Even so, by the 1870s doctors were beginning

---

[52] E. E. Sabben-Clare, D. J. Bradley, and K. Kirkwood, eds., *Health in Tropical Africa during the Colonial Period* (Oxford, 1980), p. 46.

[53] Norman Etherington, 'Missionary Doctors and African Healers in Mid-Victorian South Africa', *South African Historical Journal*, XIX (1987), p. 78.

[54] Dwight *et al.*, eds., *Encyclopedia of Missions*, p. 445.

[55] Brian Stanley, *History of the Baptist Missionary Society 1792–1992* (Edinburgh, 1992), p. 239.

to emerge from among evangelized populations, undertaking their medical training in Europe and the United States.[56] For example, in 1888 Dr John Nembula, who had studied medicine in Chicago, was back home in Natal working part-time at Adams College for Zulu boys, 'prescribing for pupils who are ill' and 'teaching physiology, hygiene and penmanship'.[57] 'By the time of the World Missionary Conference in Edinburgh in 1910, medical missionaries were sufficiently numerous to form an annexe to the main gathering. In 1925 Protestant missions from Europe and North America employed 1,157 doctors and 1,007 nurses in overseas clinics and hospitals— even then, not a large number to be spread across the globe.[58] Catholic medical missionaries were slower to emerge, being inhibited from clinical practice until the 1930s by canon law, which forbade clergy to practise medicine or surgery (based partly on a fear of priests being tempted by contact with female patients).[59] With doctors supplying such a small part of mission needs, ordinary missionaries in isolated postings had to attend to their own health. Cook Islands missions in the nineteenth century had no doctors and only two personnel with rudimentary medical training. The rest of the missionaries relied on books and the experience gained through trial and error to treat themselves and other people.[60] During an epidemic of 1827 the missionary Charles Pitman simply opened his medicine box and indiscriminately fed laxatives and emetics to the whole island population until the supply ran out. Livingstone believed he had devised a pill that worked as a general prophylactic against all tropical fevers, until a group of Central African Anglican missionaries who had been relying on the pills fell ill and died. By the turn of the twentieth century some mission boards were insisting that a doctor reside at every mission station. Others introduced short courses in medicine and surgery for missionary candidates at institutions such as Livingstone College.[61]

---

[56] John Iliffe, *East African Doctors* (Cambridge, 1998), pp. 12–16.

[57] Annual Letter of the American Zulu Mission, 27 June 1888, Harvard University, Houghton Library, Archives of The American Board of Commissioners for Foreign Missions, vol. IX, fo. 15.4.

[58] S. Neill, G. H. Anderson, and J. Goodwin, eds., *Concise Dictionary of the Christian World Mission* (New York, 1971), p. 376.

[59] Hogan, *Irish Missionary Movement*, p. 106.

[60] Lange, 'European Medicine in the Cook Islands', p. 63.

[61] W. John Young, *The Quiet Wise Spirit: Edwin W. Smith, 1876–1957 and Africa* (Peterborough, 2002), p. 15; Frederick S. Downs, *History of Christianity in India*, V/5, *Northeast India in the Nineteenth and Twentieth Centuries* (Bangalore, 1992), p. 177.

Because there were never enough medical missionaries to meet demand, many, if not all, European missionaries kept their own medical kits and handed out medical advice. Paul Landau cites the case of W. C. Willoughby, a southern African missionary with no medical training who nonetheless kept a medicinal clinic open two hours each morning in 1893.[62] Such practices continued well into the twentieth century, not because missionaries wished to impersonate doctors but because people responded to what they did. The encounter between missionary healing and practices embedded in local cultures deserves more scholarly attention than it has thus far received. People who greeted Christian evangelism with indifference or hostility often proved avid consumers of missionary medical services ranging from prayers to pills. After an early relationship with American Congregationalists turned sour, the Zulu king Mpande issued a blanket prohibition against all missionaries. The Norwegian bishop Hans Schreuder opened the way for his Lutheran mission by responding to the king's call for medicine in 1850. Whatever it was—laxative or emetic—Mpande believed it had worked, enabling the Norwegians to plant stations in Zululand.[63] People from diverse cultural backgrounds all over the Empire demonstrated that medicine was not part of a take-it-or-leave-it Western cultural package. Like present-day Europeans and North Americans, Pacific Islanders, Africans, and Asians could mix 'scientific' medicine with alternative therapies, faith-healing, charms, and snake oil. Many traditional curatives remain a first-line defence against illness in parts of the former Empire. Until the development of antibiotics, European pharmacology had little to offer the regions where most missions operated. Missionary medicine had some of its clearest victories in elementary dentistry and surgery. Missionaries were in demand as pullers of teeth in South Africa. Hyman Wilder of Natal reported in 1860 that 'the missionaries who know how to do it have abundant practice in drawing teeth, and no accomplishment of theirs is more appreciated by the natives'.[64] Simple surgical procedures that removed cataracts and tumours also delivered impressive cures.[65] Other intrusions into the physical body that caused rural people to seek out missionaries were vaccination and

---

[62] Paul Landau, 'Explaining Surgical Evangelism in Colonial Southern Africa: Teeth, Pain and Faith', *Journal of African History*, XXXVII (1996), p. 267.

[63] Etherington, *Preachers, Peasants and Politics*, pp. 75–6.

[64] Wilder, Journal, 8 Apr. 1860, Harvard University, Houghton Library, Archives of the American Board of Commissioners for Foreign Missions, vol. VII, fo. 15.4.

[65] Vaughan, *Curing their Ills*, p. 59.

injection. Southern African people accepted vaccination against smallpox with surprisingly little fuss in the mid-nineteenth century. The chance discovery that the external symptoms of the disfiguring tropical disease yaws could be quickly removed though injections of bismuth sodium tartrate set off mass pilgrimages in East Africa. Thousands walked long distances in search of *sidano* (the needle).[66] Missionaries soon learned that such phenomena were a mixed blessing. Not understanding the pathology of the disease, people assumed that when their symptoms disappeared they could stop their treatment. If the disease recurred, many cast aside their faith in mission medicine.

From the missionary point of view, cures were never assured. Visitations of disease and miraculous recoveries both counted as manifestations of God's Providence. The mission clinic and hospital were instruments for saving sinners, not demonstrations of European superiority or disinterested philanthropy. Just as missionaries proffered inducements to parents who would send their children to boarding schools, some hospitals and clinics deliberately kept people under medical surveillance after treatment had finished, so the work of religious conversion could be finished. While all medical missionaries were healers, not all healers were doctors. Christian missionaries of all denominations acknowledged that God might work cures and miracles though their untrained hands. Or he might not. It all depended on his unknowable plan. Firmly believing that they worked under Divine guidance, missionaries could never be sure whether they should pray to end an epidemic or simply ask that God's will be done. Competing with traditional practitioners was a gamble that missionaries found hard to resist. Sometimes the pay-off exceeded all expectations, as when Taufa'ahau (later King George) of Tonga decided to use his own illness as a contest between the old Tongan gods and the missionaries' power. After the Rev John Thomas administered one of the usual emetics, the king began vomiting and feared for his life; fortunately he woke the next day feeling much better and became a champion of the new faith.[67] Healing in these circumstances could hardly be differentiated from other timely interventions by unseen forces. Faced with a fire that threatened to destroy their mission to the Aborigines,

[66] T. O. Ranger, 'Godly Medicine: The Ambiguities of Medical Mission in Southeastern Tanzania, 1900–1945', in S. Feierman and J. M. Janzen, eds., *The Social Basis of Health and Healing in Africa* (Berkeley, 1992), p. 267.

[67] Dorothy Shineberg, ' "He Can but Die...", Missionary Medicine in Pre-Christian Tonga', in Gunson, ed., *The Changing Pacific*, p. 289.

Benedictines at New Norcia in Western Australia advanced on the flames, holding aloft an image of the Blessed Virgin—and vowed to build a chapel in her honour after the winds changed. In 1932 another Catholic mission in northern Ghana conducted public prayers for rain after an extended drought. When the heavens opened, so did the hearts of the people, producing unprecedented mass conversions—at least so the local legend goes. A recent examination of the records suggests that during the same period large numbers of people were being treated at the mission dispensary for yaws and dysentery, so disease may have been the crucial factor.[68] The distinction between the two possible motives for conversion—supernatural intervention or medical assistance—which is of great interest to the anthropologist or historian of medicine, held no particular importance for the Catholic missionaries, who simply noted the power of prayer. Nor did it matter greatly to the LoDagaa people of the region, who disregarded twentieth-century European distinctions between religion, magic, and medicine. It was relatively easy for them to assimilate their ideas about the intervention of ancestors in daily life to Catholic ideas about access to saints and angels.

The reluctance of missions to admit similarities between their own ideas of healing and those held by the people among whom they worked puzzles historians. It might be supposed that a more tolerant approach would have provided more pathways to conversion. Terence Ranger wonders why, in a period that saw a recrudescence of 'spiritual healing' among Church of England congregations in Britain, Anglican missions in East Africa 'completely failed to respond to the African demand on them for spiritual healing... Despite all their reservations by this time about the position of the doctors, the clergy was nevertheless left offering only the hospital and the clinic as the contemporary fulfilment of the healing mission of Christ.'[69] There is no ready answer to Ranger's conundrum. One possibility is that by the early twentieth century most missions and their supporters were too committed to viewing their work as a battleground between the diametrically opposed forces of Christian truth and 'heathen superstition'. Whereas Dr Henry Callaway (later Bishop Callaway) in the 1860s had sought collaboration with African healers in South Africa, the immensely popular 'Jungle

---

[68] Sean Hawkins, 'To Pray or Not to Pray: Politics, Medicine, and Conversion among the LoDagaa of Northern Ghana, 1929–1939', *Canadian Journal of African Studies*, XXXI (1997), pp. 50–85.

[69] Ranger, 'Godly Medicine', p. 276.

Doctor' books of the mid-twentieth century revolved around set-piece confrontations in which the missionary doctor (black or white) defeats 'the witchdoctor'.[70] Whether that genre will survive remains to be seen. Post-Second World War mission theorists rediscovered nineteenth-century fulfilment theology, which emphasized the points of similarity between Christianity and other religions, including so-called 'primal religion'. The medical model of disease faces challenges not only from old faiths but also from Pentecostals, who have breathed new life into the old idea that illness has a moral dimension which faith alone can address.

The importance of missionary medicine to the Empire lay not so much in its quantity, which was always small, but in its bias towards rural communities with little or no access to any other European methods of healing. In many places missionaries were commonly called 'doctor' as well as pastor.[71] They faced diseases that most Western medicine neglected in situations where colonial development was continually eroding general health. In the 1970s Anthony Barker looked back with mixed feelings on a South African missionary career that began in an English medical school thirty years before:

Mission hospitals were not likely to be the places where the sophisticated biochemical understandings were worked out... but theirs was the job of observation and of the working out of treatment by informed experience. In our crude ways, this is what we did. Our contribution, in those early[!] days, was to find out things about the disease. We noticed, and acted upon, the patient's loss of temperature regulation... We checked the stools for lurking Giardia and unsplit fat.... It was possible, too, without using too rosy a tinted pair of spectacles, to see a dent in childhood tuberculosis following years of patient BCG inoculation.

Yet every small triumph was clouded by the knowledge that 'the unjust society' in which he worked wrought more damage every day than his hospital could repair:

Our children were stunted in growth and easy prey to infectious fevers. They lost out at school because they went hungry to school: they lost out in health because they were largely unprotected from avoidable disease: nobody had given them their shots, or taught their mothers how to shield them from wasteful illness or premature death.... Yet I believe in our hospitals still, for the marvellous contribution they made to the relief of human suffering. They seem to have still

---

[70] Vaughan, *Curing their Ills*, pp. 155–78.
[71] Sundkler and Steed, *A History of the Church in Africa*, p. 307.

upon them the stamp of a true obedience to the vision of a God-run, God-saved world. We ought not, because we cannot do everything, fail to do what we can.[72]

Select Bibliography

GORDON BRISCOE, *Counting, Health and Identity: A History of Aboriginal Health and Demography in Western Australia and Queensland, 1900–1940* (Canberra, 2003).

PEGGY BROCK and DOREEN KARTINYERI, *Poonindie: The Rise and Destruction of an Aboriginal Community* (Adelaide, 1989).

JAMES T. CAMPBELL, 'Models and Metaphors: Industrial Education in the United States and South Africa', in Ran Greenstein, ed., *Comparative Perspectives on South Africa* (London, 1998).

ROBERT E. FRYKENBERG, 'Modern Education in South India, 1784–1854', *American Historical Review*, XCI (1986), pp. 44–8.

HUGALD GRAFE, *History of Christianity in India*, IV/2, *Tamil Nadu in the Nineteenth and Twentieth Centuries* (Bangalore, 1990).

JOHN WEBSTER GRANT, *Moon of Wintertime: Missionaries and the Indians of Canada in Encounter since 1534* (Toronto, 1984).

ANNA HAEBICH, *Broken Circles: Fragmenting Indigenous Families 1800–2000* (Fremantle, 2000).

LORD HAILEY, *An African Survey*, revised 1956 (Oxford, 1957).

JOHN ILIFFE, *East African Doctors* (Cambridge, 1998).

R. MACLEOD and M. LEWIS, eds., *Disease, Medicine and Empire* (London, 1988).

JAMES R. MILLER, *Shingwauk's Vision: A History of Native Residential Schools* (Toronto, 1997).

T. O. RANGER, 'Godly Medicine: The Ambiguities of Medical Mission in Southeastern Tanzania, 1900–1945', in S. Feierman and J. M. Janzen, eds., *The Social Basis of Health and Healing in Africa* (Berkeley, 1992).

E. E. SABBEN-CLARE, D. J. BRADLEY, and K. KIRKWOOD, eds., *Health in Tropical Africa during the Colonial Period* (Oxford, 1980).

DOROTHY SHINEBERG, ' "He Can but Die...": Missionary Medicine in Pre-Christian Tonga', in N. Gunson, ed., *The Changing Pacific* (Oxford, 1978).

S. SIVONEN, *White Collar or Hoe Handle? African Education under British Colonial Policy 1920–45* (Helsinki, 1995).

MEGAN VAUGHAN, *Curing their Ills: Colonial Power and African Illness* (Stanford, Calif., 1991).

---

[72] A. Barker, 'A Zulu Contribution', *Symposium: The Contribution of Medical Missionaries to Tropical Medicine, Transactions of the Royal Society of Tropical Medicine and Hygiene*, LXXIII (1975), pp. 364–5.

14

Decolonization

DAVID MAXWELL

Global prospects for mission Christianity looked bleak by the mid-1950s. In China and India anti-colonial nationalist movements appeared to have ended all hope of creating self-sustaining national churches. Mission Christianity in China seemed to have been dealt a near-fatal blow, swept away by Communist victory in 1949. The newly independent Indian nation came to be ever more closely defined in Hindu terms. Religious pluralism guaranteed the survival of the Christian minority, but Prime Minister Nehru aimed to reduce the numbers of foreign missionaries. In Africa, where missionary personnel were most numerous, the situation appeared dicey. Missionaries had looked on with horror at events in Asia, wondering what might take place in their own mission fields.

The large majority of white missionaries... accepted... the legitimacy of a movement towards self-government but greatly hoped it would not come too fast; they welcomed the increased subsidies most governments were now offering the missions for schools and hospitals. In practice they deeply distrusted the rise of political parties and were inclined to see 'communism'—a vague and abusive word—under every bed. Existing government was good enough and should not be challenged, at least in public.[1]

Along with their aversion to communism, missionaries worried that African cultural nationalism might revive paganism. The blood-curdling oaths sworn by Kenya's Mau Mau freedom fighters and attacks on church leaders provoked fears of similar outbreaks elsewhere. While most missionaries were at best ambivalent towards decolonization, African clergy in the 1950s, with some notable exceptions, were too few and too badly trained to be heard. The most audible African Christians were the nationalist elites. Educated in mission schools, these men understood the potency of Christian symbols and ideas. But Christianity was only one of the ideologies they used to

---

[1] Adrian Hastings, *A History of African Christianity, 1950–1975* (Cambridge, 1979), p. 97.

capture the popular imagination. Ambivalent towards the missions that had nurtured them, they embraced nationalist and socialist ideologies. More often than not they ignored the mobilizing potential of the churches, preferring to work with other institutions within civil society. If Africa had a Christian future it seemed to lie with the so-called African Independent Churches.

Yet Christianity's African future turned out to be far from bleak. After independence Christian adherence experienced phenomenal growth, from approximately 75 million in 1965 to 351 million in 2000, with much of the growth occurring within the former mission churches.[2] Whereas church leaders played a small part in the anti-colonial struggle, they took a leading role in the 'second democratic' revolution against 'one-partyism' at the end of the 1980s and in the popular struggle against 'presidential third-termism' in the 1990s. China and India also experienced remarkable growth in Christian adherence in the latter part of the twentieth century.

Empire assisted the spread of Christianity, but the faith outlasted its framework of transmission. 'The irony of world Christianity from the Second World War through the 1970s was that even as scholars were writing books implicating Christianity in European imperialism, the number of believers began growing rapidly throughout Asia, Africa, and Latin America.'[3] Clearly the grass-roots adherents ignored the criticisms of the intellectual elites. Indeed, Christianity's severance from colonialism pre-dated independence. It began with movements of mass conversion—in parts of India at the end of the eighteenth century, Africa in the late nineteenth century, and China in the early twentieth century—in which missionaries played little or no part.[4] The Great Depression of 1929 proved a crucial turning point in Africa when mission Christianity went into quiet decline and African Christians seized the initiative. Henceforth, African laity—peasants, workers, and professional elites—drew increasingly upon biblical idioms both to critique and undermine colonial rule and to respond to the

---

[2] Bengt Sundkler and Christopher Steed, *A History of the Church in Africa* (Cambridge, 2000), p. 906.

[3] Dana Robert, 'Shifting Southward: Global Christianity since 1945', *International Bulletin of Missionary Research*, XXIV (2000), p. 53.

[4] Robert Frykenberg, 'India', in Adrian Hastings, ed., *A World History of Christianity* (London, 1999), p. 187; Daniel Bays, 'The Growth of Independent Christianity in China, 1900–1937' in Bays, ed., *Christianity in China: From the Eighteenth Century to the Present* (Stanford, Calif., 1996), pp. 307–16; Adrian Hastings, *The Church in Africa 1450–1950* (Oxford, 1994), pp. 437–53.

exigencies it created. The mass of African laity sought a liberation beyond anything that could be achieved within the narrow parameters of formal politics. While nationalist elites toyed with socialism and Marxism–Leninism, popular Christianity gathered pace, succeeding even where financial or security restrictions forced the withdrawal of formal Christian workers. The primary concerns expressed by African Christians were their relationship with God and the search for healing and personal security. Thus the role of Christianity in the era of anti-colonial struggle revolved around ordinary folk coping with rapid social change powered as much by black nationalism as by imperialism and colonialism.

Missionaries and Colonialism

While the nationalist charge that missionaries were simply the handmaids of colonialism still persists in some quarters, notably among African clerics and in religious studies departments, most historians see a more complex relationship. As Andrew Porter remarks, 'religion and empire frequently mingled, but were as likely to undermine each other as they were to provide mutual support'.[5] The sheer diversity of mission organizations divided by denomination, theology, nationality, class, and historical context meant that relations between Church and State were never straightforward. 'A fusing of the two presupposes a degree of unity upon the ecclesiastical side' that was seldom present.[6]

At certain times, especially in colonies with significant white settler populations, there seemed to be little distinction between missionaries and Europeans. In Southern Rhodesia, Anglicans and aristocratic English Jesuits acted as chaplains and padres to soldiers and schoolchildren; they were regular guests at settler clubs and dinner tables. Some of them came to accept the colour bar. Here too Anglicans attempted to make themselves into the quasi-establishment Church. But the sheer diversity of Empire and the plurality of missions thwarted such schemes. 'The British government, having long ruled a multicultural and multireligious Empire, whose most important territory was Hindu and Muslim India but which also included Catholic countries like Malta and Quebec, let alone Ireland, had every incentive for maintaining its

[5] Andrew Porter, 'Religion, Missionary Enthusiasm and Empire', in Porter, ed., *OHBE* III, *The Nineteenth Century* (Oxford, 1999), p. 245.

[6] Adrian Hastings, 'The Churches and Democracy: Reviewing a Relationship', in Paul Gifford, ed., *The Christian Churches and the Democratisation of Africa* (Leiden, 1995), p. 40.

distance overseas from the Protestantism of Britain.'[7] The British Empire never forged as close a link with the established Church of England as the Portuguese and Belgians maintained with particular denominations. Moreover, many missionaries, particularly Nonconformists and Pentecostals, remained apart from settler society, disapproving of its moral failings and excesses. Catholic priests with no family and thus no 'domestic colonialism' often preferred to take their 'emotional refreshment' from Africans whose lifestyles posed less of a threat to their vows.[8] Having chosen celibacy, Catholic and Anglo-Catholic priests could 'live in' African societies in a way that was difficult for married missionaries with families. Class or social background excluded others from settler societies. In Kenya an Italian Consolata Father might be left standing outside a settler back door rather like an African visitor. In Southern Rhodesia, German Trappists were interned during the First World War. In other British colonies German missionaries were expelled or forced to flee.[9] Throughout the twentieth century there was a steady increase in the number of American Protestant missionaries whose religious heritage left them with a deep-seated mistrust of the British colonial establishment. Unfettered by a colonial nexus, American and Scandinavian missionaries could uphold an international humanitarian tradition. Cutting across settler and non-settler colonies was a rural–urban divide. Missionaries with black congregations in the bush had more room to manoeuvre than those in town, who had to guard against upsetting white congregations.

Many missionaries envisaged an Empire radically different from the designs of secular colonial officials. While the incarnationalist aspects of Catholic teaching could stimulate nationalism, particularly within Europe, its universalist tradition asserted, for example, by *propaganda fide* looked to a global communion transcending such particularities. Moreover, its clericalism made it less vulnerable to local pressures than many other churches. None of these tendencies, universalism, incarnationalism, or clericalism, bolstered the notion of formal colonial rule. A similar internationalism underpinned the work of Protestant organizations such as the International

---

[7] Adrian Hastings, 'The Churches and Democracy: Reviewing a Relationship', in Paul Gifford, ed., *The Christian Churches and the Democratisation of Africa* (Leiden, 1995), p. 40.

[8] John Lonsdale, 'Mission Christianity and Settler Colonialism in Eastern Africa', in Holger Bernt Hansen and Michael Twaddle, eds., *Christian Missionaries and the State in the Third World* (Oxford, 2002), p. 195.

[9] Hartmut Lehmann, 'Missionaries without Empire: German Protestant Missionary Efforts in the Interwar Period (1919–1939)', in Brian Stanley, ed., *Missions, Nationalism and the End of Empire* (Cambridge, 2003), p. 36.

Missionary Council and the World Council of Churches. On a more mundane level mission organizations often worked in a landscape bearing little relation to the colonial State. Pioneering missionaries located their mission stations on highways or natural frontiers with little concern for the region's eventual political landscape. The pioneers of the Universities' Mission to Central Africa station had this in mind when they built a station on Likoma Island, Lake Malawi.

The clergy of mission churches showed an increasing openness to democracy. The connection was becoming clear in the late nineteenth century in Anglo-Saxon and Free Church Protestantism. The Catholic Church moved more slowly but was energized in the 1920s by the threat of communism and loss of monarchical allies. After 1945 it supported democracy in politics but not within its own church structures. A similar situation pertained within the Anglo-Catholic movement, which stressed the authority of episcopacy. By the 1930s the leadership of the main Anglo-Saxon missionary churches 'felt committed, gently but fairly explicitly, to a democratic future for Africa towards which they had a duty to work'. In the meantime they reasoned that British colonialism was increasingly benign, and saw themselves as having a 'watching brief of a basically political sort to safeguard African interests until Africans could do so for themselves within a Western-style political arena'. A decade earlier they had shifted their attentions from the pastoral needs of the countryside to the formation of a new elite through secondary schooling, whose leading institutions were modelled on British public schools and universities. All were 'almost self-consciously cradles of democracy, even if run a little autocratically'.[10]

It was precisely in this modernizing project of education (and healthcare) that mission and colonialism came closest together. In a post-Versailles age, epitomized by Lugard's Dual Mandate (1922) and the Phelps-Stokes Commissions on African education, missionaries helped provide a crucial legitimizing ideology of development to the colonial State, receiving in return much-needed subsidies. Thus, despite their increasing democratic sensibilities, missionaries became a pillar of colonial rule. There were critics of missionary strategy such as Arthur Shearly Cripps in Southern Rhodesia. Though Cripps was a lone figure, remote from ecclesiastical establishments, his misgivings about the growing identification of missions with the temporal authority in the field of education proved prophetic. Cripps not only

[10] Hastings, 'The Churches and Democracy', p. 42.

perceived the danger of becoming an appendage of the State in the domain of education, but also comprehended the strength of the African response to the Christian message, arguing that proselytization and pastoral care should be missionary priorities.

Missions and Decolonization

Missions do not feature in explanatory models of African decolonization, whether viewed as metropolitan or peripheral–nationalist forces of change. Their absence stems in part from the paucity of research on missions in this period, but it is evident that most missionaries remained aloof from formal politics, quietly grateful for the subsidies they received from the colonial State. Indeed, for post-war British governments promoting colonial economic and social development, missions were key players. Missions knew the terrain and had a modicum of the necessary personnel. As they drew ever closer to colonial governments in the provision of social services, they were less well placed to evangelize or offer a perspective on independence movements.

Many missionaries harboured suspicions about anti-colonial movements that were to some extent well founded. They had seen the effects of communist nationalism in China and narrowly defined cultural nationalism in South Asia. The varieties of African cultural nationalism were more vaguely defined than in the Indian case, as much imagined as real. But the nationalist emphasis on traditional religious values and idioms as the essence of the people appeared a grave danger to mission work. Moreover, as one African nationalist victory followed another, missionaries were unnerved by the rise of authoritarianism, whether of the one-party or of military state, even if they felt powerless to respond.

Although few missionaries connected with the rising momentum of African nationalism in the 1950s and 1960s, there were exceptional individuals. In Nyasaland missionaries attached to the Church of Central Africa Presbyterian successfully mobilized the socially conservative Church of Scotland against the federation imposed by the British government. And just as there had been a spirited group of Anglican clerics sympathetic to Indian nationalism in the last decade of the Raj, similar men appeared in Africa: Trevor Huddleston, John V. Taylor, and Michael Scott. There were other whites exemplified by Geoffrey Clayton, Archbishop of Cape Town, who represented the liberal voice of the English-speaking

Church. Benign but paternalist, such men never met seriously with African leaders but rather spoke to other whites about 'natives'. But the loudest white voices were heard trumpeting the virtues of a racist 'Christian nationalism'. In Southern Rhodesia, Ian Smith billed his Unilateral Declaration of Independence in 1965 a 'blow for the preservation of justice, civilization and Christianity'.[11] In Zambia it seemed to the radical Methodist missionary Colin Morris that mission churches were so slow in coming to terms with African nationalism that it only happened 'an hour after midnight'.[12] The same was true elsewhere across the continent.

The muted missionary response to African nationalism in the 1950s and 1960s did not spring just from self-interest. Most Protestant missionaries lacked a theology of the State to help them engage with politics, apart from a simplistic recognition of the secular authority of the State grounded on Romans 13. Less theologically impoverished Catholics of non-British nationality were acutely aware of their foreign status and hesitated to express a political view. Moreover, since the 1930s an increasingly significant body of evangelical American Protestant missionaries treated politics as a distraction from the main business of preparing for the imminent return of Christ. Evangelicalism had also been steadily growing among British Protestants since the turn of the century. While some Anglicans continued to advocate Christian socialism, it was a 'guilty socialism, driven to transform relationships rather than reform structures'.[13]

There were, of course, black clergy, but they were few and far between in the 1950s, especially in the upper echelons of the Church. Within the Anglican Communion in Africa there was not a single black diocesan bishop in 1950. In the Catholic Church there was only one—the Ugandan Joseph Kiwanuka. In the lower ranks of the Protestant churches the clergy were at a distinct disadvantage when compared to the laity. Theological institutions lagged far behind the mission schools that trained the clerks, teachers, lawyers, and eventually the politicians of the late colonial period. The situation was compounded by the low salaries paid to ministers of religion relative to those received by schoolteachers. Catholic priests had the benefit of a long and rigorous seminary education but one intended to screen them from contact with the outside world. Moreover, the very clericalism of the

---

[11] Cited in Hastings, *World History of Christianity*, p. 138.
[12] Colin Morris, *The Hour after Midnight* (London, 1961).
[13] John Lonsdale, 'Mission Christianity', p. 202.

Catholic Church and its strong universalism imbued black priests with loyalties that conflicted with their growing sense of nationhood. A formal African theology that addressed the material and intellectual challenges of independence was slow to develop, and often simply mirrored cultural nationalism when it did emerge.

Some exceptional African clerics deserve a mention. The Methodist Thompson Samkange was a key figure in the development of a Zimbabwean nationalism. James Calata, Anglican priest and Secretary-General of the African National Congress (1936–49), moved from a liberal to a more militant leftist mould within South African politics. Another outstanding priest from the Church of the Province of South Africa was Fr. Theophilus Hamutumpangela, whose statue stands outside Parliament in Windhoek, alongside other heroes of the Namibian independence struggle. Desmond Tutu would emerge from the same remarkable southern African Anglican tradition. John Lester Membe of the African Methodist Episcopal Church (AME) was perhaps 'the most distinguished Zambian of his generation'. Although never particularly interested in politics, he led protest against federation out of a general desire to improve the human well-being of his fellow Africans. When Congress called two days of national prayer in April 1953, Membe preached to a large meeting in Lusaka on the text 'Let no man despise thee or thy youth', a reference to European disregard of African opinion.[14] There was also a collection of distinguished black Christian academics, Professors Z. K. Matthews and D. D. T. Jabavu in South Africa along with J. B. Danquah, K. Busia, and C. G. Baeta in the Gold Coast. Such men represented a bridge between Church and more secular politics, which the next generation of politicians chose not to traverse.

As African independence dawned, so too did the Africanization of ecclesiastical hierarchies, often only marginally in advance of the political changes. The Catholic Church led the way, making twenty African bishops between 1951 and 1958. Such appointments were possible due to a new network of seminaries in East Africa and an increase in the number of African priests studying in Rome. These developments in turn drew a good deal of impetus from the deliberations and proclamations of the Second Vatican Council, which so neatly coincided with African independence. By the 1970s a critical mass of black clerics, and a number of radical leftist missionaries open to

---

[14] A. Hastings, 'John Lester Membe', in T. Ranger and J. Weller, eds., *Themes in the Christian History of Central Africa* (London, 1975).

liberation theology, were in place to engage with the second wave of nationalist movements against white settler regimes in South Africa and Southern Rhodesia. By this stage the stakes were far higher as African nationalists drew inspiration from Marxism–Leninism or Maoism in their violent struggles against intransigent white nationalism.

But the general picture for 1950 'at the level of high leadership the... churches looked overwhelmingly white and missionary... as dependent as ever upon earnest committees in London or New York' for direction and resources, while 'at the level of much of the membership, at least in the larger and older churches, the missionary and his concerns were already receding into the distance. The village with its own narrow tangled hopes and fears, its grass-roofed chapel, its poorly trained catechist, its occasional visits from a native minister on his bicycle, was the place where the church had now to stand or fall.'[15] As the elites became disengaged from normal church life, the African poor came to the forefront of church leadership: the catechist, evangelist, pastor, and perhaps most importantly the Bible women organized into their Anglican Mothers, Unions, Wesleyan *manyano*, East African Revival sororities, and a host of other fellowship groups. These were the footsoldiers of the African Church, who held it together at its rural and urban township roots.

The Making of the African Church

The shift from mission to church pre-dated movements of decolonization. The first wave of African mass conversions followed the imposition of colonial rule, which provided their crucial backdrop. From the 1880s the exploitative and rapid social and economic change that accompanied mining, plantations, and white settlement created intense social, intellectual, and religious disturbance. Africans sought a measure of conceptual control over these global forces by turning to world religion, Christianity or Islam. Converts also gained access to new ideas and tools that helped them relate to the colonial economy. The first major conversion movement happened in Catholic Buganda, East Africa, in the last fifteen years of the nineteenth century. Similar movements soon traversed other parts of the continent. In the Ivory Coast they were led by the dynamic Liberian Grebo, the Prophet, William Wade Harris. Among the Bakongo of Belgian Congo a chief agent of

---

[15] Hastings, *History of African Christianity*, p. 54.

conversion was the former Baptist catechist Simon Kimbangu. In southern Africa a host of prophetic leaders founded Christian movements informed by Pentecostalism and Methodist revivalism. But whether led by independent church prophets or mission catechists and evangelists, these movements formed a rich spectrum of popular Christianity. All of them were self-consciously modernizing, displaying an aggressive rejection of traditional religious objects and practices and a strong desire to acquire bush schools and literacy. Hymn-singing and the public reading of the Scriptures became the most prominent feature of this new mass Christianity.

The Bible inspired both ordinary and educated minds, albeit in different ways. Richard Gray points out that the majority of African Christians consistently saw their faith as immensely relevant to 'the sufferings associated with disease, poverty, and death and also the misfortunes inherent in human experience', while 'an educated few saw the Kingdom of Heaven in terms of overcoming the evils of racial discrimination and political oppression, and this particular appropriation of Christianity powerfully fostered many elements in African nationalisms'.[16] It was among this latter group of African clerks, pastors, and schoolteachers that the Ethiopian movement emerged at the end of the nineteenth century. In South Africa a black Christian intelligentsia inspired by the biblical image of the ancient autonomous Christian kingdom of Ethiopia broke away from mission churches in frustration at missionary racism and hypocrisy. The Lutheran Bapedi Church and the Zulu Congregational Church resembled former mission churches, though they took a more liberal attitude towards polygamy. The major difference from the European missions was their shortage of resources for health and education. It was this desire for a modernizing gospel, along with misplaced notions of America as a place of black emancipation, which led some breakaways to join forces with Afro-American missionaries from the AME. Although AME leaders such as Bishop Henry Turner proved to be as intensely conservative in the treatment of their African flocks as their white missionary counterparts, the aspirations of the movement's African leaders and laity gave it a political dimension. At one end of the spectrum it provided a seedbed from which a good number of the founder members of the African National Congress emerged. Even more significantly, AME ministers, dependent on their flocks for the subsistence, were drawn into a range of local struggles over health and housing, transport and education.

[16] Richard Gray, *Black Christians and White Missionaries* (New Haven, 1990), pp. 69–70.

It was this broad urban populism of the AME leadership that moved James Campbell to argue that African Methodism was far more radical than early elite-driven South African nationalism.[17]

In Nyasaland, Ethiopian ideas found fertile ground among Africans educated in the Scottish Presbyterian tradition. Here too a biblically informed idea of racial oppression as a manifestation of evil was common among the key dissenting figures. The former Presbyterian Charles Domingo, who founded his own church between 1907 and 1910, proclaimed, 'The gainers of Money and Missionaries are very poor to try and conquer the wiles of Satan... [They] do form the same rule to look upon the native with mockery eyes.'[18] Some of Domingo's insights appear in the words of John Chilembwe in conversations he had with members of the Blantyre mission in the lead-up to the 1915 Rising. Chilembwe accused the Blantyre missionaries of hypocrisy in preaching the Ten Commandments from the pulpit while condoning the colonial government's action in stealing African-owned land.

Movements such as the AME were never able to compete with missionaries on the same ground. In South Africa and Zimbabwe the drive for state recognition and the perennial shortage of resources tempered their initial political fervour. While they helped train the first generation of African political elites, the ambitious African tended to remain in the better-funded mission churches. The major exception came in Northern Rhodesia, where the mission churches proved so sluggish in coming to terms with nationalism that political elites turned back to the AME, making it 'the established church of the Congress Party'. Increasingly, though, AME members placed their hopes in economic rather political liberation, a gospel of thrift, sobriety, industry, and respectability.

The fortunes of mission Christianity changed drastically in the period 1929–45, which coincided with the crisis of Western capitalism during the Great Depression followed by the Second World War. As the pace of development slowed and agricultural production yielded diminishing returns, so colonial administrations grew increasingly conservative, blocking the advance of educated elites and consolidating alliances with traditional leaders. Given that the colonial State was in good part a religious construct, legitimized by both the ideologies of modernizing mission Christianity and customary law, it is hardly surprising that disillusionment was expressed in

[17] James Campbell, *Songs of Zion* (Oxford, 1995), pp. 151–2, 248.
[18] Gray, *Black Christians*, pp. 99–100.

religious terms. Christian Africans seized the initiative, founding new independent churches and energizing those already in existence. Given their fiery critique of worldly missionaries and demon-possessed customary rulers, two key pillars of the colonial order, it is hardly surprising that such movements so unsettled imperial officials.

Mission Christianity did not die, however, but was saved by the revivalist activities of women and youth. This was often the pattern throughout East Africa, where the Revival, or Balokole, movement spread from Rwanda in 1939, touching numerous Protestant churches. Revivalists preached against the institutionalization of mission churches, emphasizing confession of personal sin and drawing heavily on the biblical language of renewal. The increasing availability of the Scriptures in the vernacular fired both independency and revival, acting as 'a consistent force in transferring authority from the culture of the European missionary translator to that of mother tongue speakers'.[19]

By 1949, whether by means of revival or independency, a shift in the balance of power between black and white Christians had occurred. As African Christians seized the religious initiative, formal connections between Christianity and Empire diminished. With Christianity more profoundly indigenized than ever before, there was no contradiction between a sharp increase in Christian adherence and the growth of anti-colonial sentiment.[20] But African Christians had done more than seize the religious initiative; they had learned that religious idioms could both legitimize and condemn political systems. By 1950 'everyone claimed... the sanction of religion in some form', and this profoundly shaped the decolonization process.[21]

The African Church and Decolonization

On the eve of African decolonization the future of the African Church lay squarely on the shoulders of the laity. Even here its prospects did not initially appear particularly rosy. The mission-educated leadership of nationalist movements was distinctively lukewarm towards the Church. In South Africa

---

[19] Lamin Sanneh, 'Translatability in Islam and Christianity in Africa: A Thematic Approach', in Thomas D. Blakely, Walter E. A. van Beek, and Dennis L. Thomson, eds., *Religion in Africa: Experience and Expression* (London, 1994), p. 44.

[20] According to Sundkler and Steed, *History of the Church in Africa*, p. 906, Christian adherence increased from 4 million in 1900 to 34 million in 1950.

[21] Hastings, *World History of Christianity*, p. 17.

the new men, Nelson Mandela, Walter Sisulu, and Oliver Tambo, remained Christians, but their religion was increasingly peripheral to their public voice. This scenario was common elsewhere across the continent. Missions had been central to the creation of nationalist elites but their legacy was ambivalent. The often quoted observation of Shepperson and Price that Livingstonia was the seedbed of the Nyasaland African Congress could be generalized to missions in many other British colonies.[22] E. A. Ayandele's path-breaking work on the missions in Nigeria remains one of the most comprehensive explanations of the missionary contribution to African nationalism. He showed how African converts had acquired European political and economic aspirations as they had embraced modernization. Secondly he demonstrated how religious journals and newspapers had familiarized black Christians with new powerful modes of political expression and communication. Thirdly, he noted that Africans gained vital skills in leadership and organization through Christian service, which readily transferred into secular leadership of political parties. Finally, Ayandele observed that missionaries preached an intoxicating message of Christian equality and fraternity, which inspired converts to seek the privileges of whites. Because missionaries did not practise what they preached, Christian elites felt ambivalent towards their Christian heritage.[23] Although grateful for education, many felt betrayed by churches whose missionary leaders did so little to advance equality and social justice. While schools and colleges inculcated virtues of democracy, they functioned in an authoritarian manner. Indeed, several educational institutions had become sites of mini-nationalist struggles. Although Christian missionaries propagated the revolutionary idea that all Africans were one people, regardless of tribal origin, that did not necessarily translate into nationalism, contributing just as readily to new ethnic and pan-African solidarities. Nationalist elites who moved in sophisticated secular international circles demystified their former missionary mentors and turned to voluntary associations, trade unions, and political parties to advance their interests.

Despite growing disillusionment with mission churches, most nationalist politicians retained Christian affiliations. Cultural nationalism appeared antagonistic towards Christianity, but in a number of instances it was

---

[22] G. Shepperson and T. Price, *Independent African: John Chilembwe and the Origins, Setting and Sign of the Nyasaland Native Rising of 1915* (Edinburgh, 1958), p. 414.

[23] E. A. Ayandele, *The Missionary Impact on Modern Nigeria, 1842–1914* (London, 1966).

paper-thin, its intellectual content elaborated, post hoc, after independence. In Zaire, Mobutism ignored traditional insights in favour of synthesized models of African religion elaborated by Christian theologians. In former Lusophone Africa, Marxist cadres sought to identify traditional belief in order to transcend it. Anti-colonialism did not necessarily engender opposition to the ideals and principles of Western institutions, including Christianity. Indeed a great deal of anti-colonialism was based on the acceptance of these ideals and principles, accompanied by an insistence that conformity with them indicated a level of progress that qualified the African elites the right to govern their own nation-states. Nationalism, like Christianity, was essentially modernizing.

It was hardly surprising that African nationalism drew upon evangelical language. In Northern Rhodesia in March 1953 Harry Nkumbula, an ex-mission teacher, now AME member, publicly burned seven pages of the White Paper outlining plans for federation in the presence of a number of chiefs and a large crowd after singing 'O God our Help in Ages Past'. Six years later, in Nyasaland, Hastings Banda told jubilant crowds, 'To hell with federation' and 'Let us fill their prisons with our thousands shouting Hallelujah.' By using simple biblical models and parallels Bachama Christians in Nigeria's Middle Belt were able to sanctify colonial politics and justify their activism. They were to be like 'the Salt of the earth' (Matthew 5: 13) or Christ cleansing the Temple (Mark 11: 15–17). Biblical characters became models for political action. King David was taken to be at once 'a man of God and a man of the world', while Moses was the prototypical political leader who took his people out of captivity. Christian hymns were used in political mobilization stressing unity in the face of a common Muslim Fulani enemy. Finally, because Nigerian cultural nationalism had deep historical roots, Bachama Christians began to identify points of congruence with their faith to build a new ethnic culture shared by Christians and traditionalists alike.[24]

Scripture had a significant ideological input into the 'discursive arena' of 'moral ethnicity' through which Kikuyu of Kenya understood themselves. They read the Bible as 'an allegory of their own history—a story of servitude and salvation, exile and return'. In the early stages of their struggle to forge an ethnic nationalist consciousness, on the eve of the Mau Mau emergency, they embraced the Exodus story, likening themselves to the Children of Israel and the British to Pharaoh's Egyptians. The force of such a comparison was

---

[24] Niels Kastfelt, *Religion and Politics in Nigeria* (London, 1994), pp. 125–52.

grounded in the publication of the Kikuyu Old Testament in 1951.[25] While Christianity was central to the creation of tribes in Nigeria and Kenya and elsewhere, as Hastings has argued, it also provided through the Bible the original model of the nation, suggesting at the same time that it was the God-given unit of political action.[26]

Although revisionist historiography of African nationalism stresses the divergent class interests that divided leaders from the rank and file, there were points of connection between them. Often they lived in close proximity in the segregated suburbs of colonial cities. As recycled elites, nationalist leaders rubbed shoulders with industrial workers and domestic servants in sporting and cultural associations, as well as in churches. Both retained a foothold in the rural areas. Teachers trained in mission schools and colleges mediated between town and countryside. These nationalist footsoldiers carried the message 'from party headquarters to the villages and translating it into attractive and concrete terms'.[27] Given that teaching rather than Christian ministry continued to attract the most able, it was hardly surprising that schools rather than churches were often the local sites for nationalist organization.

Peasants and workers who participated in rallies could be enchanted by the millennial promises of nationalism, but they were never completely captured. Some turned away from politics. Popular participation never equalled popular empowerment. While those in the large political gatherings sympathized with the humanitarian and evangelical sentiments advanced by the demagogues who addressed them, they had other concerns and drew a different sort of inspiration from the Christian faith. Some sought personal security, health, and healing through prayer. Others looked to the Church for more explicit clues on how to enter modernity through becoming respectable and economically solvent. In sociological terms their dominant concern was not politics but social reproduction. Many within this broad swath of popular Christianity remained within the historic mission churches, but there were new areas of growth, movements whose concerns ran against African nationalism as much as they ran with it.

---

[25] John Lonsdale, 'Kikuyu Christianities: A History of Intimate Diversity', in David Maxwell with Ingrid Lawrie, eds., *Christianity and the African Imagination: Essays in Honour of Adrian Hastings* (Leiden, 2002), pp. 158, 180.

[26] Adrian Hastings, *The Construction of Nationhood: Ethnicity, Religion and Nationalism* (Cambridge, 1997), p. 4.

[27] Sundkler and Steed, *History of the Church*, p. 902.

The first growth area was Christian independency. By the 1950s the founding prophets of the independent churches had passed away and the larger churches had grown, with the help of complex bureaucracies, into sprawling transnational movements. Some, like the Apostles of Maranke and Masowe, whose networks stretched from southern to eastern Africa, were vigorously modernizing, financed by chains of village stores, bus companies, and illegal currency exchange. But for every large movement there were myriads of smaller local ones, often highly schismatic, with little knowledge of their antecedents. Next to these came a more consciously modernizing cluster of churches, Pentecostals, Evangelicals, and Charismatics, the forerunners of the contemporary born-again movement. These derived for the most part from North American missionary activity, reflecting denominational shifts in American Christianity. In the era of decolonization the movement was most visible in the crusading activities of Billy Graham and Oral Roberts but was also linked to older Pentecostal movements such as the American and British Assemblies of God. Alongside independency and the fledgling born-again movement stood Watch Tower, more usually known as the Jehovah's Witnesses. By the 1950s the movement had shed much of its subversive millennial character. Bureaucracies in Kitwe and Salisbury oversaw many of its disparate village groupings, promoting the virtues of respectability and a puritan work ethic. Jehovah's Witnesses stood aloof from nationalist politics in a similar manner to which they had shunned the colonial State. They also avoided voluntary organizations and welfare societies. The same was true for the great raft of independency and newer born-agains, all of which, at this stage, were highly sectarian. Their adherents cared for their own sick and buried their own dead. Self-help and not politics was the answer. For its rejection of formal politics this growing body of Christians was often rewarded with violence from the nationalist youth, who also extended their punishment to mission communities that remained aloof.

If these sectarian movements had a voice in the 1950s, it was that of the Zulu evangelist Nicholas Bhengu. A one-time member of the Industrial and Commercial Workers' Union and South African Communist Party, Bhengu turned his back on formal politics when he converted. Eschewing nationalism as well as communism, he argued that the 'new nation' would be 'born from above with the likeness of God'.[28] He believed that political equality

---

[28] T. Balcomb, 'From Apartheid to the New Dispensation: Evangelicals and the Democratisation of South Africa', in Terence Ranger, ed., *Evangelical Christianity and Democracy in Africa* (Oxford, 2005).

with whites invited them to define the content of African aspirations. Narrow Western definitions of liberation left him unimpressed. His message of spiritual renewal, elaborated in his Back to God campaigns of the 1950s and 1960s, had a number of strands. He emphasized autonomy, dignity, Africa's rich Judaeo-Christian heritage, and its place in the Scriptures. While he worked in association with missionaries from the Assemblies of God, he argued that Africans should be free to define their faith in their own terms. The new believer was to be honest, respectful, and self-sufficient. Bhengu also encouraged church members to engage in handicrafts and penny capitalism, and to tithe in order that the Church become self-supporting and free from missionary control. Piles of surrendered weapons and stolen goods often accompanied his preaching. Finally, Bhengu envisioned a continent 'Christian from Cape to Cairo'. Although he was branded a sell-out by Manilal Gandhi, the son of Mahatma Gandhi and President of the Natal Indian Congress, Bhengu's movement and others like it evolved into some of the most vital manifestations of Christianity in post-colonial Africa.

The well-documented case of Southern Rhodesia exemplifies the complexity of missionary and African responses to decolonization. Christian responses to the hegemony of an entrenched white settler community took a long time to work themselves out. While the Anglican Church assumed a quasi-establishment character symbolized by the location of its cathedral adjacent to the parliament building, the larger Roman Catholic Church was also part of the establishment. Catholic missionaries had accompanied the 'pioneer column' of settlers across the Limpopo, and, along with American Methodists, they had been rewarded with large mission farms. English Jesuit priests in the Salisbury Club rubbed shoulders with tobacco barons, civil servants, and the Anglican bishop. Bishop Ashton Chichester aptly summed up the Catholic Church's position in his consecration speech when he spoke of 'the fine relationship between Church and civil authorities both striving for the welfare of the same people'.[29] Chichester 'ruled' the Church from 1931 to the mid-1950s, sorting out difficulties with the State by means of a private and personal word with the appropriate minister or secretary. But this upper-class English Jesuit hegemony was gradually undermined as Chichester was forced to recruit Swiss Bethlehem missionaries, Irish Carmelites, and Spanish Burgos Fathers to help manage the Church's expansion.

---

[29] Ian Linden, *The Catholic Church and the Struggle for Zimbabwe* (London, 1980), p. 29.

When Zimbabwean and white settler nationalism first clashed in 1956, neither the Anglicans nor the Catholics were well placed to mediate. To begin with, the prophetic voice came from Bishop Ralph Dodge, leader of the United Methodist Church and head of the Christian Council of Rhodesia. Dodge was deported soon after the Rhodesian Unilateral Declaration of Independence in 1965, of which he had been an outspoken critic. Bishop Abel Muzorewa subsequently replaced him. Between 1965 and 1970 a consensus emerged among the church leadership in Rhodesia. The rebellion of Ian Smith against Queen and country outraged Anglicans and freed non-British missionaries to speak out. Mission churches criticized individual injustices, and all roundly condemned the proposed segregationist constitution of 1969 as contrary to the teachings of the New Testament. However, as Zimbabwean nationalism, in the face of white intransigence, was forced from a reformist to a revolutionary path, so church hierarchies and laity fractured. The Anglican hierarchy took an increasingly pro-white line. After the Anglican Bishop of Matabeleland, Kenneth Skelton, resigned in 1970, declaring 'Justice is more important than Law and Order,' Bishop Paul Burroughs and Father Arthur Lewis spoke up for white Rhodesians. Burroughs, a regular correspondent in *The Times* (of London) concerning the dangers of Marxism, had actively campaigned for the racist constitution of 1970. Lewis, a Rhodesia Front senator, extolled the virtues of Ian Smith as the champion of Christian civilization in a booklet entitled *Rhodesia Undefeated* (1976).

After initial confrontations with the Rhodesian State, the Catholic hierarchy proved unwilling to condemn the guerrillas or their cause. The bishops' focus slowly changed from an ecclesiocentric desire to defend their primary schools from the Rhodesie Front's Community Development policy to a broader commitment to issues of African rights and social justice, exemplified by the pastoral of 1969 *A Call to Christians*. Nevertheless, their pronouncements remained couched in the language of individual rights. Even the most outspoken of them, Donal Lamont, found difficulty coming to terms with nationalism and communism. Eventually his implicit support for the guerrillas in his Manicaland Diocese gained him the respect of rural people—and deportation from Rhodesia after a long trial, which captured the world's attention. With Lamont's demise the initiative within the Catholic Church shifted from the bishops to more radical institutions run by liberal whites and the first generation of black priests. These representatives of what Ian Linden calls 'listening Church' were the School of Social Work, Silveria House, the radical monthly *Moto*, and most importantly the

Commission for Justice and Peace.[30] There were also Catholics who lived in solidarity with the guerrillas in their camps in Mozambique. Spanish Burgos Fathers drew on their experience of working in Latin America and the Frelimo-controlled areas of Mozambique to develop a liberation theology of their own. But the most explicit Christian support for the liberation movement came from the nationalist leaders. Despite his image in the Rhodesian and British press as a gun-toting guerrilla, Muzorewa's demands for African emancipation were always couched in biblical language. It is clear from his autobiography, *Rise Up and Walk*, that Scripture provided personal legitimization as well as a model of liberation, spiritual and material.[31] For Ndabiningi Sithole, a Wesleyan preacher, the Bible was a source of liberating modernization, redeeming Africans from 'the power of superstition, individuality-crushing tradition, witchcraft and other forces which do not make for progress'. 'When Europeans took our country,' he recalled, 'we fought them with our spears, but they defeated us because they had better weapons... But lo! The missionary came in time and laid explosives under colonialism. The Bible is now doing what we could not do with our spears'. As Lonsdale points out, for Sithole the well-known aphorism 'In the past the Europeans had the Bible and we had the land; now they have our land and we have the Bible' was more ambiguous than it may have at first appeared.[32]

Despite the Christian credentials of the nationalist leadership, connecting with the rural and urban poor was both a slow and a partial process. Although early nationalist meetings in urban Salisbury began with prayers and hymn-singing, when nationalist youth attacked churches and evangelistic meetings some Christians withdrew from nationalist politics. Others never made connection at all. On the eve of the era of open mass nationalism on 12 October 1955 Southern Rhodesia's capital, Salisbury, witnessed its largest gathering to date. A crowd of 30,000 Jehovah's Witnesses assembled to hear not an African nationalist, but a white New Yorker, Mr G. Hershel, talk about religion. In 1960 multiracial audiences of a similar size gathered in Salisbury and Bulawayo to hear the globe-trotting evangelist Billy Graham, notwithstanding his insistence that 'only spiritual revival can improve the social, political and economic life of the Federation'.[33] No movements of

[30] Ian Linden, *The Catholic Church and the Struggle for Zimbabwe* (London, 1980), p. 194.
[31] Abel Muzorewa, *Rise Up and Walk* (London, 1979), pp. 55–9, 124–31.
[32] Cited in Lonsdale, 'Mission Christianity', p. 195.
[33] *African Weekly*, 20 Apr. 1960, 12 Oct. 1955, 17 and 24 Feb. 1960; *Rhodesia Herald*, 22 and 24 Feb. 1960.

popular Christianity in eastern Zimbabwe expressed enthusiasm for mass nationalism in the late 1950s. But most of them—folk Catholicism, folk Anglicanism; even African-run Elim Pentecostalism and younger members of independency, as well as traditional religion as expressed through the spirit mediums—joined with the guerrillas during the war. This came about because the liberation war was fought in alliance with much of the peasantry and came to reflect many of their aspirations. The holy men of popular Christianity—black pastors and priests and white missionaries—provided guerrillas with symbolic and ritual power. And guerrillas in turn respected Christian ceremonials and rituals, and came to use Christian idiom and song in their attempts to mobilize the peasantry. Nevertheless, some movements such as the Assemblies of God, African, which had antecedents in Bhengu's Back to Africa campaign in Salisbury in 1960, remained aloof from formal politics. Following a parallel but different trajectory, which focused adherents' energies on transforming themselves and their communities through cultural reformation and economic advance, it spread from township to township and across borders into Zambia and Mozambique, carried by zealous labour migrants. After independence in 1980 this movement would be one of Zimbabwe's fastest-growing churches.

Christian idioms and practices figured more highly in Zimbabwe's liberation war than in Kenya's Mau Mau movement, probably because Zimbabwe was more Christian than Kenya in the 1950s. Forty per cent of Zimbabweans in the 1970s were estimated to be Christian, while missionaries had reckoned Kikuyu Christians at only 10 per cent in 1952. In the South African liberation struggle of the 1980s and 1990s, recourse to Christianity was even more pronounced. South African politicians had long mined the Bible to enhance their calls for liberation, and the tendency to do so increased as apartheid neared its end. David Chidester notes that virtually all major parties, including the 'secular' African National Congress, claimed the message and authority of the gospel in their election campaigns in 1994.[34] Moreover, while Christians in earlier nationalist struggles had read the Scriptures in a somewhat literal manner as a source of hope, action, and endurance, South African Christians elaborated more formal political theologies. The most influential was the Kairos Document, signed in 1985 by more than 150 South African theologians, black and white. Alert to issues of context and power, they offered a powerful critique of state and church theology before

[34] D. Chidester, *Christianity in South Africa: An Annotated Bibliography* (London, 1997), p. 1.

advocating a preferential option for the poor. The Kairos Document prompted a response from 132 concerned evangelicals the following year. Setting out to critique Kairos theology, they soon felt compelled instead to put their own house in order, repenting of their dualistic theology and their narrow concern with personal moral failings at the expense of ignoring the sinful structures of apartheid. Both of these theological statements came at the height of the State of Emergency, when townships were caught in a spiral of violence and repression. In this context, even members of independent churches issued formal theological statements. In 1994 Archbishop Ngada and other members of the African Spiritual Churches Association published *Speaking for Ourselves*. While the document shows Ngada and his colleagues cautiously exploring the political implications of their faith, its real significance lies its recognition of Christian independency's constituency: 'the members of our Churches are the poorest of the poor, the people with the lowest jobs or no jobs at all. When people become highly educated and begin to earn big salaries they usually leave our churches.' What mattered to those who remained was healing: 'in these churches we have been able to experience the healing and salvation of the Spirit now and not in the afterlife'.[35] These South African documents epitomize the spectrum of African Christians' responses to political change during decolonization. The Kairos theologians stood at the end of the Christian humanitarian tradition, including Ethiopians like Domingo, missionaries such as Cripps, and nationalist leaders such as Muzorewa. The African Spiritual Churches Association reasserted the centrality of personal security, a dominant theme of popular Christianity. Between them lay evangelicals and Pentecostals, asserting a faith at once aggressively modernizing and intensely personal. But across the entire spectrum of African Christianity prayer rather than politics remained the primary focus.

Select Bibliography

JAMES CAMPBELL, *Songs of Zion: The African Methodist Episcopal Church in the United States and South Africa* (Oxford, 1995).

FREDERICK COOPER, 'Conflict and Connection: Rethinking Colonial African History', *American Historical Review*, CLXXXIX (1994), pp. 1516–45.

---

[35] *The Kairos Document* (London, 1985); *Evangelical Witness in South Africa* (Oxford, 1986); N. H. Ngada, *Speaking for Ourselves* (Braamfontein, 1985).

NORMAN ETHERINGTON, 'Missionaries and the Intellectual History of Africa: A Historical Survey', *Itinerario*, VII/2 (1983), pp. 116–43.

—— *Preachers, Peasants and Politics in Southeast Africa 1835–1880* (London, 1978).

—— 'Recent Trends in the Historiography of Christianity in Southern Africa', *Journal of Southern African Studies* XXII (1996), pp. 201–19.

EDWARD FASHOLE LUKE, RICHARD GRAY, ADRIAN HASTINGS, and GODWIN TASIE, eds., *Christianity in Independent Africa* (London, 1978).

KAREN FIELDS, *Revival and Rebellion in Colonial Central Africa* (Princeton, 1985).

PAUL GIFFORD, *African Christianity: Its Public Role* (London, 1998).

—— ed., *The Christian Churches and the Democratisation of Africa* (Leiden, 1995).

ADRIAN HASTINGS, 'From the End of Colonialism to the "Young Churches"', *Christianesimo Nella Storia*, XXII (2001), pp. 747–74.

—— ed., *A World History of Christianity* (London, 1999)

ELIZABETH ISICHEI, *A History of Christianity in Africa: From Antiquity to the Present* (London, 1994).

PHILIP JENKINS, *The Next Christendom: The Coming of Global Christianity* (Oxford, 2002).

JOHN McCRACKEN, 'Church and State in Malawi: The Role of Scottish Presbyterian Missions 1875–1965', in Holger Bernt Hansen and Michael Twaddle, eds., *Christian Missionaries and the State in the Third World* (Oxford, 2002).

DAVID MAXWELL, *African Gifts of the Spirit: Pentecostalism and the Rise of a Zimbabwean Transnational Religious Movement* (Oxford, forthcoming).

—— *Christians and Chiefs in Zimbabwe: A Social History of the Hwesa People c.1870s–1990s* (Edinburgh, 1999).

TERENCE RANGER, *Are We Not Also Men? The Samkange Family and African Politics in Zimbabwe 1920–64* (London, 1995).

—— 'Taking on the Missionary's Task: African Spirituality and the Mission Churches in the 1930s', in David Maxwell with Ingrid Lawrie, eds., *Christianity and the African Imagination: Essays in Honour of Adrian Hastings* (Leiden, 2002).

BRIAN STANLEY, ed., *Missions, Nationalism and the End of Empire* (Cambridge, 2003).

INDEX

Aaron, Tamil teacher 126
ABCFM *see* American Board of Commissioners for Foreign Missions
Abeokuta 53, 268
Aberdeen, Scotland 37
abolitionists *see* slavery
Aborigines
  Australian 72–6, 78, 105, 242, 264, 274
Aborigines Protection Society 61, 71, 74, 81, 83–4, 241
Achimota College *see* Prince of Wales College
Adams College 279
Adams, W. J. 56
Aden, William 212
adivāsi' (Aboriginal/Tribal) communities 107, 115, 117
Advisory Committee on Education in the Colonies (1925) 12
Africa 1–2, 4, 7, 11, 16, 33, 35, 37–8, 50, 52–61, 65, 81, 86–8, 90–2, 94–5, 97, 100, 104–5, 132, 135, 138, 154–5, 158–9, 163, 166–7, 169, 170, 177, 181, 188–9, 190, 195, 197, 201, 203, 211, 213, 216–17, 221–2, 224–5, 227, 230–1, 239, 241, 245, 250–1, 253–4, 257–8, 262–4, 266–8, 271–3, 275, 277–8, 281–2, 285–6, 289, 290–4, 296, 298, 300–5
  East 92, 155–7, 159, 231, 293
  religious systems 33, 35
  Southern 92, 230
  West 155, 268, 272
African Americans 33–6

African Apostolic Church (Vapostoris) 223–4
African Civilization Society 52
African Independent Pentecostal Church, Kenya 219
African Inland Mission (AIM) 197–8, 218
African Methodist Episcopal Church (AME) 217–18, 292, 294–5
African National Congress (ANC) 292, 294, 304
African nationalism 285
African Orthodox Church of South Africa (AOC) 219
African Tidings (originally *Children's Tidings*) 158
Afrikaner people of southern Africa 222, 227
Agbebi, Mojola *see* Vincent, David Brown
agricultural education *see* education, agricultural
agriculture, idealization of 264
Akan peoples of Ghana 33, 155
Akinsowon, Christiana Abiodum 222
Aladura churches, West Africa 221
Alaska 144
Albrecht, F. W. 136
Alexander Duff's College 126
Alexander, Daniel William, Archbishop (AOC) 219
Alice Foxley ('A.F') 165
Alice Springs, Australia 149–50
Allahabad 56, 127
Allegheny River 21

INDEX

alphabets 194
Amatonga language 195
Ambimoya, Patrice 160–3
American Board of Commissioners for Foreign Missions 37, 49
American Indians 20–4, 33, 42–3, 262
American Methodist Episcopal Church 271
   American missionaries 3, 20, 127, 154, 294
American missionary societies, origins of 37
American Revolution 6, 29–30, 32, 36, 47
   effects on religious organizations 36–7
Ames, Nathaniel 25
An Account of the Writings, Religion, and Manners of the Hindoos 204
Anderson, Rufus, ABCFM Secretary 53
Anderson, William 207–8
Andrews, Charles F. 267
Anglican *see* Church of England
Anglo-Catholic Christianity
   mission theory 58 *see* Church of England
anthropology 4, 10–11, 149, 175–7, 238–9, 241–2, 245–67
Antigua 33–5
Anti-Idolatry Connexion League 111
Antilles Islands 27
Antioch, Catholics and patriarchs of 122
Anti-Slavery Society 61, 84
Anumej Island 276
apartheid 195, 304–05
Apia 101
Apostle Thomas 122
Apostolic Faith Mission (AFM) 222–4
Apostolic Sabbath Church of God 224
Arabic language 195

arathi 233
Archbishop Laud, Archbishop of Canterbury 20
Armenian Christianity 110
Arnold, Matthew 81
Arrernte language and people of Australia 136, 147–50
Asbury, Francis 45
Ashanti War (1869–70) 169
Asia 7, 285 *see* India, China
Assam 112, 116–17, 204
athomi 197
Atuaniu (Maori term for God) 220
Australasia 38 *see* Australia, New Zealand
Australia 12, 16, 38, 44, 66, 71–3, 75–6, 78, 82–3, 88, 90, 101, 103, 118, 136–7, 147, 150–1, 174, 177, 188, 190–1, 242, 262–4, 266, 269–70, 273–4, 276–7, 282
āvarna caste 115
Awabakal people of Australia 74
Ayandele, E. A. 297
Azariah, V. S., Bishop of Dornakal 115
Azusa Street revival meetings 222

babalawo, Yoruba religious specialist 196
Babalola, Joseph ('Baba Aladura') 222
Babylon, Patriarchs of 122
Bachofen, Johan 241
Backhouse, James 66, 71
Bacon, Thomas 34
Badagry 53
Baeta, C. G. 292
Bagamoya 159, 162, 166
Baker, Shirley 91, 103
Bakongo people 294
Balokole movement 296
Banda, Hastings, president of Malawi 257, 298

Bangalore Conference of, 1879 118
Bank Islands 141
Bantu language studies 248
Bantu Prophets 257
Bantu Studies (later *African Studies*) 258
Bantu-Speaking Tribes of South Africa 253
baptism
   Bengali translation of 203
Baptist Church and Baptists 30, 31–7, 44, 46–8, 53, 60, 65, 108–9, 115–16, 185, 202, 216, 224, 231, 278, 294
Baptist Missionary Society (BMS) 46, 202, 278
   Serampore Trio 108, 203–5
   split on racial lines 36
Barbados 23, 34, 36, 44, 66, 69
Barker, Anthony 283
Barker, John 8, 200
Barotse kingdom 271 see Lozi
Barotseland (Zambia) 218
Basden, G. T. 257
Basel 48, 241
Basle see Basel
Basotho see Lesotho
Basotho people of southern Africa 240
'Basters' of southern Africa 208
Basu, Ram 205
Basuto see Basotho
Basutoland see Lesotho
Bathe, R. 270
Bay of Islands, New Zealand 101, 180
Bayly, Susan 10
Beagle Bay mission 191
Bechuanaland see Botswana
Beecham, John, Secretary of WMMS 72
Belgian Congo 293
Belgian empire 288
Belgium 158
Belknap, Jeremy 21

Bemba people and region of Zambia 235
Benedictines 282
Bengal 47, 56, 58, 61, 108–9, 118, 182, 191, 194–5, 202–4, 206, 212
Benjamin Franklin 32
Bentinck, Lord William, Governor-General of India 110, 265
Bentinck, William, Governor-General of India 49
Berhampur 182
Berlin 48
Berlin Missionary Society 48
Beschi, Constantius Giuseppe 108
Beschi, Giuseppe 124
Bible 2, 9–11, 14, 16, 23, 27, 47, 49, 51, 53, 55–6, 66, 96–7, 135, 139, 143, 151, 153, 168, 187, 190, 194, 196–9, 203–4, 211, 227, 235, 271, 293–4, 298–9, 302–5
   New Testament 97
   Old Testament 10, 32, 220, 226, 229, 233, 240, 267, 299
   translation 9, 10
Biddulph, T. J. 67
Bishop of London 29, 42, 46
Bishops College, Calcutta 57, 126
bismuth sodium tartrate 281
Blake, Sophia Jex 186
Bloemfontein 229
Bombay (Mumbai) 108, 124, 126–7
Bonnand, Clément, Bishop of Pondicherry 125
Bonomi, Patricia 23
Book of Common Prayer 121
Booth, Joseph 231
Boston, Massachusetts 25, 37, 146
Botswana 91, 104, 229
Bourke, Richard, colonial governor 67, 75
Brahmans 107, 108, 113–15, 122, 124, 128, 190, 203, 205

Brahmo Sahba organization 205
Brahmo Samaj (Transcendent Deity Society) 205–6
Brandt, Joseph 21
Brazil 196
Bright, John 82
British and Foreign Bible Society 49
British Columbia 100, 136, 146–7, 270
British East India Company 2, 15, 49, 66, 107, 194, 202
British Empire, Church-State relations 41–4
British Kaffraria, South Africa 83
British Navy 157
British Raj in South Asia 8, 107–30
Broadbent, Samuel 209–11
Brock, Peggy 8, 155
Brooke, G. W. 55
Brookes, Edgar 253
Brotherhood of the Epiphany 57
Broughton, William Grant, Archdeacon of New South Wales and Bishop of Australia 72–5
Brouwer, Ruth C. 178, 188
Brown, David 46
Brown, John, American abolitionist 232
Brown, Lydia 183
Bruhmhu (Bramah) 206
Brumhu (Bramha) 204–5
Bryan, William Jennings 18
bubonic plague 222
Buchanan, Claudius 49
Buchler, Johannes 222
Buddhists and Buddhism 8, 15
Buganda Kingdom of Uganda 293
Bullah, Peter 149
Bullhoek massacre 230, 232
Bulu, Joel, Tongan missionary 139
Burma 8, 115, 117
Burns, Minnie 183

Busby, James 77
Busia, K. 292
Buxton, Priscilla 66, 70
Buxton, Sarah Maria 66
Buxton, Thomas Fowell 64–72, 74–5, 77, 80–1, 84

Cakobau I of Fiji 89–91
Calabar 53, 60, 187
Calata, James 292
Calcutta 44, 49, 57, 108–10, 118–19, 121, 124, 126–7, 183, 203, 212
Caldwell, Robert 119
Caledon River 222
Caliban 10
Callaway, Henry, Bishop of St John's 282
Calvinists and Calvinism 15, 24
Cambridge Mission to Delhi 57, 58
Cameroon 263
Campbell, James 273, 295, 305
Campbell, John, LMS secretary 207–8
Canaan 194
Canada 37, 43–4, 82, 133, 136, 143, 146, 174, 178, 183, 186, 188, 238, 262–4, 268–70, 273–4
 Maritime provinces of 37, 42
Canada Act (1791) 44
Caner, Henry 29
Cape Colony 44, 50–1, 64, 67–8, 70–1, 75, 83, 207, 217
Cape Province, South Africa 229
Cape Town 57, 67, 231, 248, 253, 258, 290
capitalism 4
Cappellari, Cardinal see Gregory IV, Pope
Capuchin order 124
Carey, William 100, 109, 126, 202–4
Caribbean 34–5, 42, 49–50, 80
Carlyle, Thomas 81–2
Carmichael, Amy 187

Carnegie Corporation 250
Carnegie Hall 17
Casalis, Eugène 240
Casely Hayford, J. E. 154
Catholic Church and Catholicism *see* Roman Catholic Church
Catholic Emancipation Act of 1829, 125
celibacy 288
Central Africa (UMCA journal) 158
Central Africa, the journal of the Universities' Mission to Central Africa 157
Cewa people and customs 257
Ceylon 8, 113, 119, 124, 209
Chalmers, James 104
Chambers, George, Bishop of Tanganyika 188
Champness, Thomas 59
Charles VI, Holy Roman Emperor 25
Charlevoix, François-Xavier de 238
Charter Renewal Act of 1813, British East India Company 109
Chase, J. C. 67
Chennai, India *see* Madras
Cherokee people 270
Chesapeake Bay region 27, 33
Chewa people of Zambia 212
Chewa secret society (*dini*) 212
Chicago 222, 279
Chidester, David 240, 304
children
    mission literature for 158
    sexual abuse 164
Chilembwe, John 231–2, 267, 269, 295
Chin people 115
China 1, 5, 8, 53, 55, 61, 117, 159, 184, 188, 286, 290
    Communist Revolution 285
China Inland Mission (CIM) 55, 59, 184
Chinook lingua franca 146

Choo, Christine 191
Christ, Jesus *see* Jesus Christ
Christian Apostolic Church 222
Christian socialism 291
Christianity, historical expansion of 1–3, 5–8, 14, 40
Church membership
    North American Colonies 32
Church Missionary Intelligencer 56
Church Missionary Society 3, 46, 86, 133, 144, 184, 188, 216, 272
Church Missionary Society (CMS) 46–9, 50, 53, 55–6, 59, 60, 72–3, 76–8, 113–15, 118, 122–3, 144, 183, 185, 216, 227, 250
Church of Central Africa Presbyterian 290
Church of England 14–15, 19, 20–4, 26, 27–32, 34–7, 40–7, 49, 57, 59, 66, 107, 112, 115, 117–19, 121–4, 128–30, 136, 147, 159, 163, 166, 185, 188, 190, 199–201, 212, 216–17, 219, 221–2, 240, 243, 262–4, 279, 282, 287–8, 290–2, 301–2
    consitutional position of 14
    high church theory of missions 57
    Mothers Union 293
    policy on bishops 52
Church of Ireland 14
Church of Scotland 14–15, 27, 218, 272, 290
Church of Scotland Mission (CSM) 218
Church of Scotland Mission CSM 218
Church of the Lord, South Africa 225
Church of the Seven Rules of Jehovah, New Zealand 219
CIM *see* China Inland Mission
circumcision, female *see* women: circumcision controversy

circumcision, male 218
Civil War (US) 23
Civilising Subjects: Metropole and Colony in the English Imagination 1830–1867 178
Clah, Arthur Wellington 136, 143–7, 149–51
Clapham Sect 50, 65, 69, 109, 113
Clarke, George 78–9, 83
Clarkson, Thomas 65
Clayton, Geoffrey, Archbishop of Cape Town 290
Clive, Robert 203
CMS House 56
Coates, Dandeson, Secretary of CMS 72–3, 77
Cochin 124, 125
Code of Gentoo Laws 203
Codrington, Robert 201, 243
Cohen, Charles 38
Coke, Thomas 45
Colenso, John W., Bishop of Natal 81, 240, 246, 263
Colenso, William 199
College of New Jersey (after 1896, Princeton University) 29, 31
Colonial Bishoprics Fund 52, 57
Colonial Office, Great Britain 69, 71, 80, 107, 250
colonialism 3, 55, 70, 84, 119, 129, 132, 141, 143, 150, 178, 187, 189, 192, 226, 233, 246–7, 251, 257, 286, 287–9, 298, 303
Columbia University 272
Comaroff, Jean 225
Comaroff, Jean and John 4
communism 3, 285, 300, 302
Concordat of 1940, 11
Concordat of 1860, 125
Confucians and Confucian religion 15
Congo Balolo Mission 55

Congo Reform Association 61
Congregational Church 21, 24, 27
Congregational Churches and Congregationalists 28–9, 32, 44, 90, 280
Connecticut 29
Conrad, Joseph 246
  Heart of Darkness 246, 269
  'An Outpost of Progress' 269
Constantine, Emperor of Rome 89
conversion
  role of local agents in 7–8, 132–3
convict transportation 72, 77, 88
Cook Islands 94, 96, 136, 138, 140, 276, 279
Cook, Captain James 198, 202, 276
Copenhagen 118
Copperbelt, Zambia 218, 235
Corbett, Miss of Darjeeling 188
Cornwall 24
Coromandel Coast, India 124–5
Corrie, Daniel, Bishop of Madras 111
Côte d'Ivoire *see* Ivory Coast
Courmont, Mgr. de (Spiritan) 160
Crais, Clifton 4
Cranganore 124–5
Cripps, Arthur Shearly 289
Crocombe, Marjorie 135
Crowther, Samuel Ajayi, Nigerian bishop 53, 59, 168, 196, 216–17
Cuba 196
cultures 9–10, 14, 16, 59, 97, 99–100, 104, 108, 132–3, 151, 153–4, 158, 162, 175–6, 181, 191, 213, 241, 245–7, 251, 265, 280
Cutler, Timothy 27, 28

'*Dalit*' ('Untouchable') communities 107
Danish colonies and missionaries in India 109, 112, 118, 202–3

Danquah, J. B. 155, 171, 292
Dartmouth College 21
Darwin, Charles 82
Daughters of our Lady, Queen of the Apostles 191
Davenport, James 29
Davies, John 88
Davies, Samuel 25, 31
Deaconess House, Sydney 188
Debhikr 122
decolonization 2, 4, 12, 155, 261, 285, 290, 293, 296, 300–1, 305
Demarara slave rebellion 50
dentistry 280
devadasis 111
Dickens, Charles 81–2
Dig-Darshan 205
Dimock, Joseph 37
Diophysites 122
disease 8, 117, 145, 178, 220, 250, 254, 275–9, 281–3, 294
Dissenting Churches and Dissenters 14, 20, 28–30, 44–5, 119, 128
Dithakong 207, 209
Dodge, Ralph, Methodist bishop 302
Domett, Alfred 79
Domingo, Charles 295
Dominica 174
Dowie, John Alexander 222
Dube, John L. 268, 272
Duncan, William 144, 147, 183, 270
Dundee 187
D'Urban, Benjamin, colonial governor 69
Durham Report 82
Durham, New Hampshire 31
Dutch empire *see* Netherlands
Dutch Reformed Church 29
Dutch Reformed Church (DRC) 224
Dwane, James Mata 217

East Africa 57, 60, 154–5, 231
Edict of Nantes 25
Edinburgh 18, 46, 60, 187, 245, 279
Edinburgh Missionary Society (after 1818 the Scottish Missionary Society) 46
education 9–12, 15, 21, 44, 50, 76, 87, 92–5, 102, 117, 126–7, 135–6, 138, 159, 174, 179, 180, 183–5, 188–92, 194–5, 204, 217–18, 231, 245, 250–51, 257, 261–75, 289–91, 294, 297
  adaptationist 267
  agricultural 270–1
  ancient languages 272
  boarding schools 12, 93, 182, 264–5, 281
  elite schools in India 126
  industrial 269, 270, 272–3
  language of instruction 266
  Macaulay's Minute on Education, India 127
  secondary 266–7
  vocational *see* education, industrial
  women 126–7, 204, 261, 263, 266–7, 273
Edward VII, King 234
Edwards, Jonathan 30
Efik people of Nigeria 187
Egypt 194
EIC *see* British East India Company
Eiselen, W. M. 255
Ekuphakameni 224–5, 228
Elekana, Rarotongan missionary 139
Ellis, William, LMS Secretary 70, 72
Emgwali mission 137
England 24
'Enquiry into the Obligations of Christians to Use Means for the Conversion of Heathens' (1792) 109

Episcopal Church (US) 37
Erlank, Natasha 7
eshu, Nigerian concept of 196, 213
Estado da India 124
Etherington, Norman 11, 20
Ethiopia 2, 294
Ethiopian Church, South Africa 217
Ethiopianism 218, 257, 294
Ethnological Society of London 241
European imperialism 104–5, 158
Evangelical Alliance 38
Evangelical Review 47
Ewe people of Nigeria 169
Exeter Hall, figurative headquarters of missionary and humanitarian action 13
Eyre, Edward J., colonial governor 82

Facing Mount Kenya 198
Fairbairn, John 68
Fairweather, Marion 186
faith missions 54–7, 59, 60, 118, 129
Faith Tabernacle, Nigeria 221
Family and Gender in the Pacific 177
farangi (Indian word for Europeans) 108
Federation of Central Africa 290
female circumcision controversy, Kenya *see* women:circumcision controversy
female genital mutilation *see* women:circumcision controversy
Fernando Po 53
Fields, Karen 231
Fiji 89, 91, 97, 101, 138–9, 141, 143, 183, 242, 274
Firth, Raymond 201
Fison, Lorimer 242–3
Fitzroy, Robert, colonial governor 79
Flinders Island 72

folklore 240, 242–4
Foreign Missions of the United Presbyterian Church 135
Foreign Missions Society of Paris 124
Forman Christian College 126
Forman, Charles 138
Fort Hare College and University 84, 267, 274
Fort William College 109
Foster, H. P. 203
Fourah Bay College 267
Fourth Decennial Indian Missionary Conference 118
Foxley, Alice ('A.F') 163–5
France 11, 20, 158
  empire 53
Francke, August Herrmann 28
Frankfurt 48
Frazer, J. G. 213, 241, 247
Free Church of Scotland 118, 231
'Freedom Rides' (Australia) 274
Freetown, Sierra Leone 50, 60
French and Indian War *see* Seven Years War
French Revolution 15, 17, 47, 124
French, T. V., Bishop of Lahore 57
Fry, Elizabeth 66, 72
Frykenberg, Robert 8
fulfilment theology 16, 283

Gandhi, M. K. 129, 301
Ganges River 200
Garo people 115–16
Gavin, Anthony 33
Geddie, John 276
Genadendal 270
Gender and Empire 173
General Conference of Bengal Protestant Missionaries 118
General Magazine (Philadelphia) 32

General Missionary Conference of
    South Africa 252
genocide 76
    Australian Aborigines 73
George V, King of England 18
Georgetown, Madras 110
Georgia Orphan House 31
German immigrants in Pennsylvania 26
German immigrants to British North
    American colonies 28, 43
German missionaries interned 274, 288
German Palatinate 25
Germans in missions 26, 119
Germany 28, 158
Ghana 33, 212, 282
Gikuyu see Kikuyu
Gilbert and Ellice Islands *see* Tuvalu
Gilman, Nicholas 31
Gipps, George, colonial governor 74–6
Gisborne 234
Giustiniani, Louis 75
Glasgow 31, 46, 68, 278
Glasgow Missionary Society 46, 68
Glasgow Weekly History 31
Glenelg *see* Grant, Charles, Lord Glenelg
globalization 4
Goa 122, 125
Godhula 116
Godlonton, Robert 68
Gold Coast 155, 171, 245, 272, 274, 292 *see*
    Ghana
Gordon, General Sir Charles 56
Goschgoschuenk 21
Gould, Eliga 6
Graf, Simon 25
Graham Commission, Southern
    Rhodesia 269
Graham, Billy 300, 303
Graham's Town Journal 68, 75
Grant, Charles 49, 66, 69, 109

Grant, Charles, Lord Glenelg, Colonial
    Secretary 69–71, 75, 77, 80
Great Awakening 27
'Great Commission', Christ's missionary
    charge to his disciples 13
Great Depression (1929) 286, 295
Greek Septuagint 204
Gregory IV, Pope 125
Grey, George, colonial governor 83,
    268
Griffiths, Gareth 8
Grimshaw, Patricia 9, 177
Griqua *see* Khoe
Griqua Independent Church 229
Griqua people of southern
    Africa 207–9, 228–9
Griqualand East 228–9
Guardians of the Great Commission 176
Guinness, Mr. and Mrs. H. G. 55
Gujarat 117
Gunn, Mrs., missionary teacher in New
    Hebrides 190
Gurney, Anna 66, 69–71
Guy, Jeff 240
Gwydir River valley, New South
    Wales 74

Haddon, Alfred Cort 256
Hailey, William Malcolm, Baron 11,
    272–3
Hakluyt, Richard 20
Hale, Matthew, Bishop of Perth 264,
    266, 270, 276
Half-Way Covenant 24
Halhed, Nathanial B. 203
Hall, Catherine 80, 178
Halle 112, 116, 118
Halley's comet 229
Hamutumpangela, Theophilus 292
Hancock, W. K. 6

Hanover County, Virginia 25
Hanover, Germany 16
Hanover, Virginia 31
Harijans see Untouchable castes
Harms, Louis [Ludwig] 16
Harries, Patrick 10
Harris, William Wade 293
Hart, Anne 35
Hart, Elizabeth 35
Hastings, Adrian 97, 247, 299
Hastings, Warren 108, 203
Hausa people of Nigeria 56, 196
Hawai'i 90–4, 96, 98–9, 101, 103–5
Haweis, Thomas 38, 48
Hay, George, eighth marquess of Tweeddale 111
Hayward, Charles 174–5
Hazelton mission station 183
Heart of Darkness 246, 269
Heber, Reginald, Bishop of Calcutta 16, 119, 123
hell
  concepts of 142
Henbury station, Australia 149
Hendricks, Jan 208
Herbert, George Robert Charles, Earl of Pembroke 103
Hermannsburg Missionary Society 136, 149
Hermannsburg, Australia 148
Hermannsburg, Germany 16
Herrnhut 116
Hey, Mary Ann 181
Hey, Nicholas 181
high god
  African concept of 213
Hill, Mary 182
Hill, Micaiah 182
Hill, Patricia 176
Himalayas 188

Hindus and Hinduism 8, 11, 15, 107–12, 114, 116, 119–24, 126–8, 130, 186, 190, 194, 202–6, 265, 285, 287
'Histoire d'Angelina' 159
Histoire d'un voyage en terre du Brésil 238
History of Melanesian Society 201
History of the Yorubas 196
Hobson, John A. 1
Hobson, William 77–8
Hodgkin, Thomas 71
Hodgson, T. L. 210
Hoernlé, Winifred 255, 258
Holland *see* Netherlands
Holy Ghost Mission (Te Hahi o te Wairua Tapu) 220
Holy Sacrament 219
Holy Trinity 221
Home missions 15
Hong Kong 188
Honolulu 101–2
Horton, Robin 213
Houailou language 212
Hough, James 113
Howe, K. R. 91
Howitt, A. W. 242
Huddleston, Trevor 290
Hudson's Bay Company 136, 144
Hugli region of India 109
hula dance 99
humanitarianism 13, 34, 50, 61, 64–5, 68–71, 74–5, 78, 80, 82–4, 178, 241, 288, 299, 305
Hunter, Jane 176
Hunter, Monica 255, 259

Ibaden 196
Ibo people of Nigeria 257
Ifa verses 196
Ilanga Lase Natal 268

Imperialism, European 60, 86–7
Inanda Reserve 224
India 56, 62, 63, 107–130, 192, 200, 214, 284. *See* South Asia, British East India Company
Indian 'Mutiny' 82
Indian Empire, British. See British Raj in South Asia.
Indian Female Normal School and Instruction Society 183
Indian Rebellion of 1857. *See* Indian Mutiny
Indians, American *see* American Indians.
indigo workers of Bengal 61
Indirect Rule 250, 252
Indonesia 48
Indore 186
influenza 220–23, 229, 232
Inglis, Charles, Bishop of Nova Scotia 37
Institute of African Languages and Cultures 250
International African Institute 250
international missionary conference of 1900, 17
International Missionary Council 250
International Review of Missions (later *International Review of Mission*) 245, 255–7
Io, Maori concept of 202
Ireland 14, 24, 47, 262, 287
Irish immigrants to North American colonies 28
Irish emigration 125
irua (clitoridectomy) 198
Islam 2, 33, 56–8, 61, 108–9, 111, 117, 124, 126–7, 130, 161, 194, 196–7, 213, 266, 287, 293, 298 *see* Muslims

Israelites
  of New Zealand 234
  South Africa 229, 230
itinerant preaching as an issue in in British North American colonies 29–30
ituika 197
Ivory Coast 293
Iwe Irohin 268

Jabavu, D. D. T. 257, 292
Jakoba
  Jacobite Christians of India 122
  Jacobite movement 28, 122, 128
Jamaica 33, 35–6, 44, 50, 65, 81, 82
James I, King of England 20
Japan 8, 60
Java 48
Jay Creek ration depot 149
Jeanes Teachers 271
Jehovah's Witnesses (Watchtower Bible and Tract Society) 14, 212, 230–2, 277, 300, 303
Jesuit
  missions 20–1, 26, 41, 124–5, 203, 238, 266, 287, 301
  Reductions of Paraguay 262, 264
Jesus Christ 10, 12–13, 16, 17, 22, 25, 48, 53, 55, 57–8, 98, 125, 142, 145, 147, 160, 194, 196, 198, 204–5, 213, 220, 224, 227, 230, 235, 275, 282, 291, 298
Jews 15, 32, 47, 56
John Anderson Christian College 126
John the Baptist 203, 223–4
John Wilson College 126
Johnson, Edward Ralph, Bishop of Calcutta 57
Johnson, James 196
Johnson, William 43
Johnston, Mrs. George 174

Jolly, Margaret 177
Jones, Hugh 23
Jones, William 203
Joyful News Evangelists 59
'Jungle Doctor' series 282–3
Junod, Henri. See Junod, Henri-Alexandre
Junod, Henri-Alexandre 247, 248, 251–2, 255, 267
Junod, Henri-Philippe 255–6
jāti
 concept of 120, 128

Ka'ahumanu 93
Kachin people 115
Kaffraria *see* British Kaffraria, South Africa
Kakkerlak, Cupido 208
Kamwana, Elliott Kenan 231–2
Kanya Kumari 117, 126
Kapwepwe, Simon 235
Karachi 126
Karen people 115
Karnataka region of India 115
Kasomo 235
Kat River 67
Kat River settlement 67
kattanārs 122–3
Kaunda, Kenneth 235
kava plants 139
Kayastha caste 108
Keesing, Roger 201
Kellogg, John Harvey 277
Kendall, Thomas 199, 212
Kennett, White 22
Kenya 191, 195, 197–8, 218–19, 225, 233, 257–8, 272, 285, 288, 298–9, 304
Kenyatta, Jomo, President of Kenya 155, 170–1, 198, 257, 274
Kerala 273

Kereopa, New Zealand cult 202
Keswick Conferences 59–60
Khama the Great of Botswana 91
Khartoum 56
Khasi people 115–16
Khoe people and language of southern Africa 206, 208 *see* Khoisan
Khoisan peoples of South Africa 67
Kidd, Dudley 247–8
Kikuyu Central Association 233
Kikuyu Independent School Association 219
Kikuyu language and people of Kenya 155, 191, 195, 197–8, 205, 218–19, 233, 257, 298, 304
Kikuyu people of Kenya 195, 206
Kilnerton Institution 217
Kilwa 161
Kimbangu, Simon 294
Kingsley, George H. 103
Kingsley, Mary 268–9, 272
Kinnaird College 127
Kipling, Rudyard 275
Kiribati 138
Kiwanuka, Joseph, Bishop, Uganda 291
Knibb, William 35, 65, 81
Knox, William 42
Kock, Leon de 4
Kohima 126
Kok, Adam II 207–8
Kongo 212
Konaṭṭu 123
Koonen Kurisu (Koonen Cross), India 122
Kora (Korana) groups in southern Africa 206–7, 209
Koran 161
KoTeKawenataHou 199–200
Kottayam 122–3
Kranshoek 229

Krige, Eileen 255
Krishna 205
Krumen of West Africa 268
Kuruman 266

labour
  recruiting 102
  migrant 195, 253
Ladies' Society of Calcutta 183
Lafitau, Jean-Marie 238
Lagos 56, 59–60, 216, 221–2
Lahore 57, 126–7
Lake Macquarie 73
Lake Malawi 160, 289
Lake Nyasa *see* Lake Malawi
Landau, Paul 9, 280
Lang, J. D. 72–3, 75
lang'o spirit possession cult 225
Langmore, Diane 177
language and languages 10, 194–213
Latukefu, Sione 142
Lazarus 275
Le Fleur, A. A. S. 228
Le Roux, P. L. 222
Le Roy, Reverend Pere (Spiritan) 160
Lebanon, Connecticut 21
Leenhardt, Maurice 212
Leeward Islands 35
Lefroy, George Alfred 58
Lekganyane, Ignatius 228
Lenshina, Alice 235
Leopold II, King of Belgium 84
Léry, Jean de 238
Les Bassoutos 240
Lesotho 195, 222–3
Lester, Alan 6
Lévi-Strauss, Claude 238
Lewanika, King 218, 271
liberation theology 293, 303

Life of Aaron Kuku of Eweland 169–70
Life of Chief Wangombe wa Ihora 170
Likoma Island 289
Lincoln Theological Seminary 274
linguistics
  missionary work on 244
Lion, Edward. *See* Tau, Edward
literacy 9–11, 113, 123, 126, 139, 153, 179, 194–6, 211, 261, 267–8, 273, 275, 294, 296
Little Books For Africa 166
Livingstone College 279

Livingstone Inland Mission 55
Livingstone, David 5, 7, 53–5, 84, 100, 275, 278
Livingstonia 100, 297
LMS. *See* London Missionary Society
lobola (bride wealth) 251, 255, 263
LoDagaa people of West Africa 282
London 67, 110
London Missionary Society (LMS) 4, 7, 15–16, 37–8, 46–8, 50, 52, 66–8, 70–5, 88–90, 92, 94–7, 103–4, 114, 139, 179, 181–2, 184, 199, 207–10, 262, 276
London School of Medicine for Women 186
Long, James 61
Lonsdale, John 197–8
Loram, Charles T. 272
Lord's Prayer 199, 209
Louis XIV, King of France 25
Lovedale College 152, 264
Loyalty Islands 140, 200
Lozi people of Zambia 218
Lugard, Frederick J. D., Baron 289
Lumpa Church 235
Lusaka 292
Lushai people 116

Lutheran Churches and Lutherans 26, 28–9, 47, 115, 118, 121, 136, 148–9, 280, 294

Ma' Nku 224
Macaulay, Colin 122
Macaulay, Zachary 65
Macdonnell, Chief Justice of Northern Rhodesia 232
Macintyre, Martha 177
Mackenzie, Charles, Bishop to Tribes dwelling in the neighbourhood of Lake Nyasa and the River Shire 57
Mackenzie. John, missionary in Botswana 104
Macmillan, W. M. 254
Madagascar 5
Madras (Chennai) 108, 110–12, 114–15, 119, 121, 124–7, 202, 265–6, 273
Madras, Bishop of 111
Madurai 124–5, 127
Maharashtra 117
Mahon, Edgar 222
Mahutu, wife of Mothibi 207
Maine, U. S. A. 37
Maitland, Peregrine, Brish general and colonial governor 111
Majeke, Nosipho, *nom de plume see* Taylor, Dora
Malabar 125
Malankara 122–3
  Nazaranis of 122
Malawi 2, 61, 157, 160, 231, 235, 257, 267, 289–90, 295, 297–8
Malayālam 122–3
Malietoa, Samoan high chief 96
Malinowski, Bronislaw 249–50, 252, 255–8
Malpān, Philipose, Mar Dionysius IV *see* Mar Dionysius IV

Malta 287
Malua Institute (Samoa) 95
mana, Polynesian concept of 90, 95–7, 103, 201, 212–13, 243
Mandela, Nelson, President of South Africa 274, 297
Mangaia Island 140
Manihiki Island 140, 142–3
Manu'a Island 141
Maori people of New Zealand 76–9, 83, 88, 180–1, 198–9, 202, 205, 212, 219, 220–1, 226–7, 234
Mar Dionysius II 122
Mar Dionysius III 123
Mar Dionysius IV 123
Mar Thoma Evangelistic Association 123
marae (Polynesian religious grounds) 143
Maramanu 123
Maranke Reserve 224
Maranke, Johane 223–4, 300
Marathas 112
Marau, Clement 141, 143
Mare Island 140
Maretu, Rarotongan missionary 135–6, 138–40, 142–3
Maroon War, Jamaica (1665–1739) 33
Marsden, Samuel 50, 66, 74, 199–200
Marshman, Joshua 202, 205
Marxism-Leninism 287, 293
Masai language and people of East Africa 170, 197
Masowe movement 224, 300
Masowe, John 223–4
Massachusetts 9, 32
Matthews, Z. K. 292
Mau Mau insurgency (Kenya) 198, 258, 285, 298, 304

Maui 95
Maulvi 'Imad ud-din 128
Maungapohatu 234
Maxwell, David 12
Mbweni girl's training institution (UMCA) 159, 163, 165
McCullough, William 61
McKinley, William, President of the United State 18
measles 220, 276
Medical Missionary Auxiliary (Baptist) 278
medicine 11, 93, 180, 186, 192, 194, 204, 220–1, 223, 235, 261, 275, 277–83
  British Empire and medical services 12
  medical missions 12, 61, 261, 277
Meghalaya 116
Melanesia 53, 91, 94, 99, 102, 200–1, 243, 246, 249
Melpakkathar movement 119
Membe, John Lester 292
Menezes, Alexius de, Archbishop of Goa 122
Methodist Church and Methodists 11, 14, 24, 28, 30, 32, 34, 35–7, 45–8, 50, 52–3, 56, 58–9, 60, 65–6, 69, 73, 89, 91, 96–7, 103, 115, 144, 146–7, 174, 199, 209, 216–17, 224, 226, 242, 271, 274, 277–8, 291–5, 301–3
  Wesleyan Methodist Missionary Society (WMMS) 14, 69, 72, 278
Metlakatla, British Columbia 100, 270
Mgijima, Enoch 229
Mi'kmaq Indians 21
Middle East 2, 61, 266
Middle Passage (trans-Atlantic slave trade) 33
migrant labour 195, 253

Mildmay Institution 59
Mill, John Stuart 82
millenarianism. See millennial expectations and millennialism
millennial expectations and millennialism 16–17, 36, 47–8, 54–6, 96, 216, 229, 230–2, 234, 299–300
Miller, William 127
Mishmi people 116
Mission Secretaries Association 56
Missionary Seminary (Hawai'i) 95
Mizo people 115
Mizoram 116
Mlanjeni, Xhosa visionary 227
modimo, Tswana word for ancestor or God 206–12
Moffat, Mrs. Robert 211
Moffat, Robert 209–11, 266
Mohawk Indians 21–2, 43
Moi, Toril 211
Mokalapa, Willie 218
Mokone, Mangena 217
Monophysites 122
Moor's Charity School for Indians 21
Morant Bay Revolt, Jamaica (1865) 82
Moravian Church 21, 25, 28, 32, 34, 45–6, 113, 180–1, 270
Morgan, Lewis Henry 241–2
Morgan, Philip 35
Moriah, northern Transvaal 228
Morija, Lesotho 195
Mormon Church and missions 14, 277
Morris, Colin 291
Moses Tjalkabota 136, 147, 149, 151
Moshoeshoe (Moshweshwe), king of Lesotho 195
'Mother Hubbard' dresses 99
Mothers Union, Church of England 190, 293

Mothibi, Tswana chief 207–9
'Motu', creole language 200
Motu dictionary 201
Motu Island 200
Mount Holyoke College 9
Mount of Olives 13
Moyo, Shoniwa 224
Mpande, Zulu king 280
Mugabe, Robert, President of Zimbabwe 274
Muhammad 204
Muhlenberg, Henry 26
Mukasa, Ham 154
Mukkavar fisherfolk of India 124
Muller, Carol 225
Müller, Max 242
Multa Præclare, papal decree 125
Mumbai, India. *See* Bombay
Munro, John 122–3
Munro, Thomas, Governor of Madras 49, 109, 265
Muscat 161–2
music 96
Muslims 8, 15, 56, 58, 127, 130–1, 196, 265 *see* Islam
Muthirugu protest song 219
Muttusami Pillai 120
Muzorewa, Abel, Methodist bishop, Southern Rhodesia 302
Mwari cult, Zimbabwe 223
myalism 81
Myall Creek massacre (1838) 76
Myanmar. *See* Burma
Mylapore 124–5
Mylaudy 114
Mysore 49
Māvālikkara Assembly (1836) 123

Nadars of India 113–15, 128
Naga people 115–16

Ao Nagas 116
Nagaland 116
Nagari 203–4
Nagarkoil 114
Namaqualand 255
Namibia 292
Napoleonic Wars 124
Narayan Vaman Tilak 128
Natal 81, 246, 262–3, 268–9, 272, 279–80, 301
nationalism 17–18, 107, 197, 212, 257, 285, 287–8, 290–93, 295, 297–304
 African 297
 Indian 107
Native Affairs Department, South Africa 256
Native Agency in Pacific islands missions 94–5
Native Baptist Church, Lagos 216
Natives Land Act (1913), South Africa 227, 229
Nayars 114, 122
Nazareth Baptist Church 224
Ndlambe Xhosa chiefdom 68
Nehru, Jawaharlal, Prime Miinister of India 285
Nelson Examiner 78–80
Nelson, New Zealand 79
Nembula, John 279
Nestorian Christians 122, 128
Netherlands 48
 conquest of Cochin in India 122
Netherlands Missionary Society 48
New Brunswick 21, 37
New Caledonia 5, 136, 139–41, 212
'New Christian' evangelists, definition of 132–3
New Education Fellowship Conference 255

New England 20, 22, 24–5, 27–8, 30–2, 36–7, 43
New Guinea (island of) 104, 218 *see* Papua
New Hampshire 21, 27, 31
New Hebrides 87, 138, 141, 190, 276
New Jersey 21, 32
New Norcia monastery 282
New South Wales 44, 64, 66, 72–5, 80, 186
New South Wales Presbyterian Women's Missionary Association 186
New York City 22, 29
New York State 32, 37
New Zealand 2, 38, 50, 52–3, 64, 70, 76–80, 82–3, 88, 90–1, 93, 97, 143, 180, 188, 199, 201, 212, 216, 219–21, 226, 229, 234, 262, 273
New Zealand Company 77, 79
Newburyport, Massachusetts 32
Newfoundland 27
Newport, Rhode Island 25
newspapers, mission 268
Neylan, Susan 133
Ng'anga, Joseph 233
Ngai (Kikuyu word for God) 197–8, 233
Ngidi, William 240
Nguni language and cultural group 211, 250
Niger Delta 216
Niger Expedition (1841–42) 52–3, 81, 168
Nigeria 2, 60, 168, 187, 195, 216, 221, 257, 297–99
  Niger Mission (CMS) 59
Nisga'a people of Canada and Alaska 133, 143
Nkrumah, Kwame, President of Ghana 274
Nkumbula, Harry 298
Nkwenkwe, Nontetha 232–3

Nobili, Roberto de 108, 124
Nonconformists, British 45, 288
Norfolk Island 200
Norkopping 48
North America 2, 5, 6, 14, 21, 28, 32–3, 35, 37, 41–4, 129, 188–9, 266–7, 277, 279
North American missionary expansion in late twentieth century 300
North Carolina 34
North Pacific Mission (CMS) 144
North West Provinces of British India 56
Northern Rhodesia 218, 232, 235, 257, 259, 266, 269, 295, 298 *see* Zambia
Norton, Alfred, professor of Bantu languages 248
Norwegian missions 280
Norwich 71
Nott, Henry 89
Nova Scotia 21, 35, 37, 43
Ntabelanga 229
Ntsikana, Xhosa teacher and prophet 227
Nukulaelae Island 139
nursing 184
Nxele, Xhosa prophet 227
Nyasaland *see* Malawi
Nyasaland African Congress 297
Nyassa. *See* Malawi
Nyerere, Julius, President of Tanzania 274

O'Brien, Susan 30
obeah religious groups and practices 33, 81
occultism 25–6, 32
Occum, Sampson 21
Odunlami, Sophia 221
Ogilvie, John 43
Ohlange Institute 272

Old Side Presbyterians 28–9, 32
Oldham, J. H. 245, 249, 252
olorun, Nigerian concept of 196, 213
Oneida Indians 21
Orange Free State 222
Orange River 206
Order of Ethiopia, South Africa 217
Ordinance 50 (Cape Colony) 67, 75
orisa rites, Nigeria 196, 221
Orishatukeh Faduma (William Davis) 196
Orissa 117
Oriya translation of the Bible 204
Oro religious cult of Tahiti 88–9
Oshitela, Joseph 222
Ottawa 183
Owen, Nicholas 1
Oxford History of the British Empire (*OHBE*) 1, 3, 11, 173
Oxford Mission to Calcutta 57
Oyo, Nigeria 196

Pacific islanders 1, 7, 10, 15, 37, 50, 53, 66, 86–8, 92–6, 99, 101–4, 133, 136, 138–9, 141–5, 147, 177, 187, 189–90, 194, 198–203, 209, 249–50, 264, 274, 280
Pacific Islands 1, 7, 8, 15, 47, 52, 70, 86–8, 92–3, 96, 98, 103, 133, 139–40, 143, 190, 262–3, 274, 276. *See* Polynesia, Melanesia
Pacific islands and Pacific islanders 101–2, 139, 147, 280
padroado 14, 17
Paihia mission, New Zealand 180
Paihia, NZ 78
pakeha (Maori term for Europeans) 220, 226, 234
Palestine 2, 9

palmyra trees 110
Pan-Africanism 297
pandarams 114
pandits (Indian scholars) 108, 203–4
'Panya' 163–5
Papua 138–9, 141, 177, 199
Papua New Guinea 138–9
Paraguay 262, 264
Paraiyar Christians 120
Paravar fisherfolk, India 124
Pariahs see Untouchable castes
Paris 48, 124, 218
Paris Evangelical Mission Society (PEMS) 218
Parvati-Rani 122
Patcheapah's Institution 112
Paths of Duty: American Missionary Women in Nineteenth Century Hawaii 177
Patterson, E. Palmer 133
Patteson, John Coleridge 7
Paulinus, Father, Sancto Bartholomeo 203
Pedi people of South Africa 211
Peel, J. D. Y. 106, 133–4, 196
Pennsylvania 21, 25–6, 28–30, 32, 42–3
Pentecostal churches and missions 13–14, 18, 115, 118, 198, 219, 221–4, 228, 277, 283, 288, 294, 300, 304–06
Pères de Saint Esprit (Spiritans) 159
Perham, Margery 254
Perkins, Charlie 274
pharmacology 278, 280
Phelps-Stokes Commission 13, 245, 272, 303
Phelps-Stokes Fund 250, 272, 289
Philadelphia 26, 29, 36

Philip, John, LMS Superintendent 50, 52, 66–70, 75
photography 239
Piedmont region of Virginia 24
Pietersburg 228
Pietists and Pietism 28, 109, 112, 121
Pilgrim's Progress 211
Pillai, Muttusami 120
'Pious Clause' in British East India Company Charter 109
Pirouet, Louise 133
Pitman, Charles 139–40
Pius IX, Pope 125
Plessy v. Fergusson 271
Plettenberg Bay 229
Plymouth Brethren 115, 118
Polokwane, South Africa 228
Polygamy *see* polygyny
polygyny 98, 185, 187, 216, 222, 228, 235, 246–7, 263, 294
Polynesia and Polynesians 88, 91–9, 101, 104, 142. See Pacific islands, Pacific Islanders
Pomare I of Tahiti 88
Pomare II of Tahiti 88–90, 93
Pondicherry 124–5
Pontiac, Chief of Ottawa Indians 43
Pontiac's War (1763–4) 43
Poonindie 264, 266, 270–1, 276
Pope, George Uglow 121
Port Lincoln 264
Porter, Andrew 1, 6, 19, 84, 96, 287
Portugal 3, 11, 18, 61, 124
Portuguese Empire 11, 14, 61, 122, 124, 288, 298
  Estado da India 122
postcolonialism 173, 177–8
post-millennialism 16 *see* millennial expectations and millennialism
Pottinger, Henry, colonial governor 67

Precious Water prayer group, Nigeria 221
pre-millennialism 16, 60 *see* millennial expectations and millennialism
Presbyterian Church and Presbyterians 25, 27–30, 32, 34, 40, 44, 47, 53, 56, 60, 72, 116, 135, 178, 181, 186–8, 198, 235, 270, 274, 276, 290, 295
  New Side 29
  Old Side 28–9, 32
Pretoria 217, 232
Price, Thomas 297
Prince of Wales College, (later Achimota College) 274
Princeton University (formerly College of New Jersey) 29
printing presses, mission 8, 102, 116, 126, 154–5, 166, 194–5, 268
propaganda fide of the Roman Catholic Church 17
Prospero 10
protectors of Aborigines 78, 82
  New Zealand 78–80, 83
Protestants and Protestantism 3, 9, 13, 14, 19, 20–3, 25–8, 31–3, 35–8, 40, 43–5, 48, 54, 93, 118, 121, 125, 129, 136, 147, 159, 177, 188, 200, 203, 240, 261, 265–6, 271, 274, 279, 288–9, 291, 296
  African-American distinctiveness 35
Providence Industrial Mission 231
'Province of Freedom', Sierra Leone 50
Punjab 58, 127, 204
Puritans and Puritanism 24

Quaker Church and Quakers 26, 28, 31, 42, 66, 71–2
Quatre ans chez les Achanties 239
Quebec 32, 42–4, 287

Queen Adelaide Province 69, 71, 78, 83
Queensland 102, 104–5

Rabuka, Sitiveni 274
racism 12, 60, 82, 100, 181, 194, 216, 239, 248, 256, 264, 268–9, 291, 294, 302
Radcliffe-Brown, A. R. 248–50, 253
Raj *see* British Raj in South Asia, India
Rajanayakam 126
Rakahanga Island 140
Ramabai, Pandita 128, 190
Rama Varma, Rajah 122
Ramanandi sect 206
Ramnad 112
Ramseyer, Fritz 239
Ranger, Terence 282, 306
Rarotonga Island 140
Rarotongan people 136, 139
Ratana Church 221
Ratana Pa 221
Ratana, Tahupotiki Wiremu 220–1
Rath Yatras 111
Read, James 75, 207–8, 212
Reformation, Protestant 9
religious revivals and revivalism 29–32, 35, 37, 58–60, 81, 100, 294, 296
Researches in South Africa 67
revivals, religious. *See* religious revivals and revivalism
Rhenius, Karl 113, 118–19
    'Rhenius Affair' 118
Rhodes, Cecil 268
Rhodes-Livingstone Institute 259
Ridley, Jane 183
Ridley, William, Bishop 183
Rikiriki, Mere 220
Ringeltaube, William Tobias 114
Rivers, William H. R. 201, 249
Robert, Dana 176

Roberts, Oral 300
Rockefeller Foundation 250
Roe, Bryan 59
Roho churches, Kenya 225, 233
Roman Catholics and Catholicism 3, 9, 11, 14, 17–18, 20–1, 25–6, 32, 40, 43–4, 47, 53, 104, 109, 113, 115, 118, 122, 124–5, 128–9, 159, 177, 189, 191, 200, 235, 262, 265–6, 274, 279, 282, 287–9, 291–3, 301–4
    Benedictines 282
    Jesuit missions 20–1, 26, 41, 124–5, 203, 238, 266, 287, 301
    Second Vatican Council 292
    Trappists 288
Rotterdam 48
Rountree, Kathryn 180
Roy, Ram Mohun 205, 212
Royal Anthropological Institute 11
Royal Anthropological Society 11
Rua Kenana, Maori prophet 234
Russell, Charles Taze 230
Rutherdale, Myra 178
Rwanda 296

Said, Edward 178
Salem, Massachusetts witch trials 25
Salvation Army 59, 118, 129, 147
Samachan Darpan 205
Samkange, Thompson 292
Samoa 91, 93–7, 99, 101, 104–5, 138, 140–1, 200
Samuelite movement 229
San (Bushmen) people of southern Africa 207
Sanneh, Lamin 9
Sanscrit *see* Sanskrit
Sanskrit language and scholarship 124, 128, 195, 199, 203–4

Saraswati Mahal Library 113
Sastri, Vedanayakam 107, 120–1
sati (widow burning) 110, 185, 204
Saunders, John 71
Savai'i Island, Samoa 91
Schapera, Isaac 211, 250, 253–5, 258
Schaw, Janet 34
Schön, J. F. 168
Schreuder, Hans, Norwegian Lutheran bishop 280
Schwartz, C. F. 118–19, 121
Schweitzer, Albert 275
Scotland 14–15, 26, 30–1, 37–8, 48, 135–6, 261
Scott, Michael 290
Scottish immigrants to North American colonies 28
Scottish Missionary Society *see* Edinburgh Missionary Society
'Scramble for Africa' 104–5
Sechuana language 211
Secker, Thomas, Archbishop of Canterbury 42
segregation, racial 253
Select Committee on Aborigines 1835–7, Parliament of Great Britain 52, 64, 70–8, 80, 82
Seleka Rolong community, South Africa 229
Selwyn, George Augustus, Bishop of New Zealand 52–3, 199, 201
Semitic orthography 194
Serampore 108–9, 126, 195, 202–3, 206
Serampore Trio 108, 202–5
Seraphim healing church, Nigeria 222
Seven Years War 43
Seventh-Day Adventists 14, 277
Seychelles islands 231
Seymour, William 222
Shadore, Joseph 221

Shakespeare, William 10
Shanar. *See* Nadars
Shangaan migrant labourers 195
Shangani Point reception house (UMCA) 159
Sharkey, Heather 185
Sharpe, Granville 65
Shaw, William, WMMS Superintendent 52
Sheldon Press (SPCK) 166–9
Shembe, Isaiah 224–5, 228
Shepperson, George 297
Sherlock, Peter 9
Shiva 205
Shivaganga 112
Shona people of Zimbabwe 223–4
Shrewsbury, William 66, 69
Sierra Leone 47, 49–50, 56, 267–9, 277
Sierra Leone Company 50
Singh, Sadhu' Sundar 128
Sinwano, Hanoc 231
Siovili 96
Sisulu, Walter 297
Sixth Frontier War (South Africa) 68
slave trade, trans-Atlantic
religious consequences of 33
slavery and slaves 33–6, 41–2, 45, 50, 52–3, 61, 64–7, 80–2, 88, 92, 102, 105, 109, 114, 119, 154, 156–64, 166–8, 174, 187, 207, 239, 241, 246, 263, 267, 278
abolition 7, 32, 115, 146
abolitionists 36
Arab traders 160, 163, 165
emancipation 36, 64, 68, 78, 80
in Africa 84
Middle Passage (trans-Atlantic slave trade) 33
release narratives 158–9, 161–2, 164, 167, 169

Slessor, Mary 187, 190
smallpox 220, 276, 281
Smith, Edwin 11, 238, 256, 267
Smith, Ian, Prime Minister of Southern Rhodesia 291, 302
Smith, J. Z. 202
Smith, William 26
Smuts, Jan, prime minister of South Africa 255, 258
Sobel, Mechal 35
Sobukwe, Robert 257
Society for Promoting Christian Knowledge (SPCK) 14, 19, 21, 23, 26–8, 31, 41, 46, 110, 118, 166
Society for Promoting Female Education in the East 183
Society for the Propagation of the Gospel in Foreign Parts (SPG) 14, 19, 20, 22–3, 27–8, 30, 33–4, 36, 41–6, 52, 57, 118–19, 121
Society of Friends *see* Quaker Church and Quakers
Society of Jesus *see* Jesuit
Soeurs de Sacré Coeur de Marie 159
Soga *see* Tiyo Soga
Soga II, Solomon Islands chief 200
Soga, Solomon Islands chief 200
Solomon Islands 102, 138, 200
Solomon, King 10
Sotho language group and people of southern Africa 195, 211
South Africa 2, 6, 18, 44, 47, 49, 67, 70, 77, 135, 137, 185–6, 195, 209–11, 217–19, 222, 227, 229, 232, 234, 240, 245, 248, 252–8, 262–4, 266–8, 270, 274, 280, 282–3, 292–6, 300, 304–5
South African Association for the Advancement of Science 245, 248
South African Commercial Advertiser 67–8

South Asia 5, 8, 56, 58, 117, 127, 185, 190, 200, 204–5, 264, 269, 277, 285, 290 *see* India
South Australia 83
South Carolina 30, 33–4
South India Missionary Conference (1858) 118
South Pacific 5, 11, 200, 262
Southern Rhodesia 223 *see* Zimbabwe
Spain 3, 18
Spanish Empire 14, 101
spirit churches 216, 222, 224–5
Spiritans *see* Pères de Saint Esprit
St. Stephen's College 57
St. John's Apostolic Church 224
St. Paul 13, 277
St. Thomas Christians. *See* Thomas Christians
Stanley, Brian 172, 278, 306
Stephen, James 65, 69
Stewart, Captain of the *Elizabeth* 77
Stiles, Ezra 25
Stock, Eugene, CMS Secretary 54
'stolen children' 12
Stories of Old Times: Being the Autobiographies of Two Women of East Africa. Grandmother Narwimba and Chisi-Ndurisiye-Sichayunga 167
Stubbs, Thomas 67
Student Volunteer Missionary Union (UK) 60
Student Volunteer Movement (USA) 60
Sudan 2, 55, 185
sugar plantations 24, 102
Sundaranandam, David 113
Sundkler, Bengt 257
Supreme Being
    search for concept of 240
Surat 49

Swahili language 157–8, 163, 197
Swan River 75
Swan River Colony 75
Swaziland 258
Switzerland 48
Sydney 189
Sydney Morning Herald 74, 75
Synod of Māvālikkara (1818) 123
Synod of Udayamperur (Diamper) in 1599, 122
syphilis 276
Syrian rite of Christianity 122–3, 128, 265
systematic colonization 77

Ta'unga, Rarotongan missionary 136, 138–43
taboos, Polynesian concepts of 90, 220
Tahiti 5, 53, 88–92, 94, 96, 103–5, 202
Tahitian 94, 96, 140, 143
Tambo, Oliver 297
Tamil Nadu 273
Tamils 110, 112–3, 118–19, 121, 126, 273
Tanganyika *see* Tanzania
Tanzania 167, 188, 246
tapu, Polynesian concept of 213, 220, 234 *see* taboos
Taranaki 202
Tasmania 72
Tau, Edward (Edward Lion) 222
Tāufa'āhau (King George) of Tonga 281
Taylor, Dora 258
Taylor, Hudson 184
Taylor, J. Hudson 55
Taylor, John V. 290
Te Hara, Maori healer 220
Te Ranghaeata, Maori chief 79
Te Rauparaha, Maori chief 79
Telugu 115
Tempels, Placide 267
Ten Commandments 90, 295

Tennent, Gilbert 29, 31–2
Test Acts, repeal of (1828) 125
Thaba 'Nchu 229
Thailand 117
Thanjāvur 107, 112–14, 120–1, 126
tharavad houses 122
The Southern Cross 201
The Story of Dorugu 168
The Times (London) 80, 82
The World Their Household 176
Thomas Christians of India (Syrian) 114, 121–3, 203, 265
Thomas, John 281
Thomason, Thomas 49
Thornton, Henry 46
Thornton, John 33
Threlkeld, Lancelot 73–6
Thuo, Moses 233
Tikopia 201
Tiruchirāpalli 112
Tirunelvāli 112–16, 118–19, 126
Tiruvanthapuram *see* Travancore
Tiyo Soga 135–8, 149, 150
Tjalkabota, Moses 136, 147–50
Tlhaping (BaTlhaping) of South Africa 207–08
tobacco 222, 226, 235, 301
Tohunga Suppression Act 234
Tonga 89–91, 94–7, 99, 103–4, 138–9, 281
  constitution and laws 90–1
Touws River 229
Tranquebar 28, 109, 112, 126, 203
translation
  of Christian texts 97, 116, 121
  of religious concepts 9
  of religious texts 266
  of texts 11
Transvaal 217, 228
Trappists 288

Travancore (Tiruvanthapuram) 7, 112, 114–15, 121–3
Travels in West Africa 268
Treaty of Waitangi 77–9, 221, 226
Trevelyan, Sir Charles, Governor of Madras 115
tribe, concept of 194
Tsimshian people of Canada and Alaska 133, 136, 143–4, 146–7, 151, 183
Tsonga people of Mozambique 195
Tswana 4, 55, 206–9, 211
Tswana people of southern Africa 206
Tuauru language 136
Tucker, Ruth 176
Tunisia 2
Tupou College (Tonga) 95
Turkey 56
Turner, Henry McNeil, Bishop (AME) 217, 294
Tuskegee Institute 271–2
Tutu, Desmond 292
Tuvalu 95, 138–9, 200
Tweeddale, Lord *see* Hay, George
Tylor, Edward 241, 243
Tāufa'āhau 89–90, 93, 103

Uganda 61, 105, 133, 164, 190, 272
Ulawa Island 141, 143
UMCA. *See* Universities' Mission to Central Africa
Unilateral Declaration of Independence (UDI), Southern Rhodesia 302
Unitarianism 205
United Concert of Prayer 30
United National Independence Party, Zambia 235
United Native African Church, Nigeria 217

United States 3, 6, 11, 18–19, 22, 32, 36–8, 42–3, 65, 135, 174, 176, 184, 217, 241, 271–2, 274–5, 279. *See* American
Universities' Mission to Central Africa (UMCA) 56–8, 157–9, 163, 165, 289
University of Cape Town 248, 253
University of Halle 28
University of the Witwatersrand 254
Untouchable castes of South Asia 200, 266
Upolu Island, Samoa 91
Upper Canada 43
Urdu language 204
Urewera Reserve, New Zealand 234

vaccination 280–1
vamsha, concept of 120
Vancouver Island 144
Vanuatu 141. *See* New Hebrides
Vedamanickam 114
Vedanayakam Sastri 112–13
Vedic religious texts 206
Vellalar Christians 112, 120
Venn, Henry, CMS Secretary 53, 59, 86
Venn, John 69
Vepery 120
Vibuthi Sangam (Ashes Society) 114
Victoria, British Columbia 136, 144
Victoria, Queen 79, 146
Victorian Presbyterian Women's Missionary Union 181
Vidyalankar 205
Vincent, David Brown 216
Virgin Mary 199
Virginia 23, 24, 31, 33–5, 231
Virginia Company 20
Vishnu 205
Viswanathan, Gauri 154–5, 169

Wahi Tapu ('sacred places')
  movement 220
Wairau 'Affray' (1843) 79–80
Waitangi, Treaty of. *See* Treaty of
  Waitangi
Wakefield, Arthur 79
Wales 24, 27, 261
Walker, George 71
Walls, Andrew 2
Wangombe wa Ihora 170, 171
Wantage, England 190
Ward, James 181
Ward, Matilda 181
Washington, Booker T. 231, 271, 274
Watch Tower movement. *See* Jehovah's
  Witnesses
Waterston, Jane 186
Watson, W., CMS missionary 73
Watts, Isaac 276
Wentworth, John 27
Wesley, Charles 28
Wesley, Samuel 28
Wesleyan Methodist Missionary Society
  (WMMS) 14, 69, 72, 278
Wesleyans. *See* Methodist Church and
  Methodists
West Africa 9, 33, 50, 53, 58, 278
West Indies 122, 6, 23–4, 27, 32–4, 36–7,
  47, 54, 64–5, 67, 80–3, 174, 178, 208
Westcott, Brooke Foss, Professor of
  Divinity at Cambridge
  University 58
Western Australia Missionary
  Society 75
Weymouth 66
whaling and whalers 77
Wheelock, Eleazar 21
'White Man's burden' 275
white settlers and missions 6, 9, 12, 27,
  52, 199, 217, 234, 264, 270, 273

Whitefield, George 19, 20, 26, 30–2,
  34, 38
Whitehead, Henry 57
Wilberforce College 217
Wilberforce, William 65–7, 217
William Ward 108, 202, 204
Williams, Edward 78
Williams, Henry 77–8, 180
Williams, John 52, 94, 96, 104, 276
Williams, Marianne 180
Williams, Roger 24
Williams, William 202
Willoughby, W. C. 238, 280
Wilson, Daniel, Bishop of Calcutta 49,
  118, 120–1, 123, 183
Wilson, Godfrey 259
Wilson, Monica. *See* Hunter, Monica
Windhoek 292
Winks, Robin 173
Winthrop, John 20
witchcraft
  beliefs and practices 25, 98, 102, 138,
    222, 224, 231, 233, 235, 254, 303
  trials 25
Witwatersrand 246, 254–5, 258
WMMS. *See* Wesleyan Methodist
  Missionary Society
women
  'missionary heroines' 187
  and healing churches 220–2, 224
  and humanitarian agitation 66,
    69–70, 72
  as authors of mission texts 158, 165
  as supporters of missions 61
  church membership in American
    Congregational Churches 24
  circumcision controversy in
    Kenya 191, 197–8, 218, 257
  clothing as an issue 99
  drawn to spirit churches 224

women (*cont'd*)
  education 126–7, 204, 261, 263, 266–7, 273
  feminist scholarship 173, 175–6
  in Roman Catholic missionary orders 189
  indigenous, as missionaries 189–90
  indigenous, role in religious change 207
  isigodlo Zulu enclosure for 228
  married women's roles in missions 159
  medical missionaries 186
  missionaries in South Asia 127
  'missionary heroines' 179
  missionary roles of 8, 9
  missionary wives 179–83
  missions as an escape for 263
  ordination 188
  outnumbered men in imperial missions 174, 184
  role in the exercise of colonial power 178–81
  St. Stephen's Community of Anglican 57
  single female missionaries 184
  submission in patriarchal churches 225
  trends in historical writing about 175–6
  urbanization of Africa 252
  writings underrepresented in mission archives 175
  See *zenana* missions
Women and the White Man's God 178
Women's Christian College, Madras 127
Women's Association for Mission (Scottish Presbyterian) 188

Woodmason, Charles 30
World Council of Churches 18, 289
World Missionary Conference, Edinburgh (1910) 18, 60, 187, 245, 279
World War II 12, 116

Xaba, Jacobus 217
Xhosa people of South Africa 68, 69, 71, 83, 135, 136, 137, 138, 147, 227, 232

Yale College 27
yaws 276, 281–2
Yorkshire 24
Yoruba Heathenism 196
Yoruba people of Nigeria 133, 195–7, 205–6, 216, 221–2, 268
Young Men's Christian Association (YMCA) 37
Young, Florence 187
Young, T. Cullen 257

Zambia 212, 218, 257, 259, 295 see Northern Rhodesia
zamindars 114
Zanzibar 158, 160, 163, 165–6
zenana missions 57, 185
Ziegenbalg, Bartholomaeus 108, 126
Zimbabwe 22–4, 295, 304, 306
Zinzendorf, Nicholas von 21
Zion Christian Church, South Africa 228
Zion City 222–3
Zionist churches and Zionists 222–5, 228
Zonnebloem College 264
Zulu people of South Africa 10, 81, 84, 228, 240, 272, 279–80, 294, 300
Zululand 262, 280